BACKWOODS CONSUMERS AND HOMESPUN CAPITALISTS

The Rise of a Market Culture in Eastern Canada

In the late eighteenth and early nineteenth centuries, a local economy made up of settlers, loggers, and business people from Lower Canada, New Brunswick, and New England developed on the banks of the Upper Saint John River in an area known as the Madawaska Territory. This emergent economy was ostensibly part of the Atlantic capitalist system but differed from it in several major ways.

In *Backwoods Consumers and Homespun Capitalists*, Béatrice Craig analyses this economy from its origins in the Native fur trade, the growth of exportable wheat, and the selling of food to new settlers and ton timber to Britain. Craig vividly portrays the role of wives who sold homespun fabric and clothing to farmers, loggers, and river drivers, helping to bolster the local economy. The construction of saw, grist, and carding mills, and the establishment of stores, boarding houses, and taverns are all viewed as steps in the development of what the author calls 'homespun capitalists.' The territory also participated in the Atlantic economy as a consumer of Canadian, British, European, west and east Indian, and American goods. This case study offers a unique examination of the emergence of capitalism and of a consumer society in a small, relatively remote community in the backwoods of New Brunswick.

BÉATRICE CRAIG is a professor in the Department of History at the University of Ottawa.

BÉATRICE CRAIG

Backwoods Consumers and Homespun Capitalists

The Rise of a Market Culture in Eastern Canada

UNIVERSITY OF TORONTO PRESS
Toronto Buffalo London

© University of Toronto Press 2009
Toronto Buffalo London
www.utppublishing.com

Reprinted in paperback 2016

ISBN 978-0-8020-9317-2 (cloth)   ISBN 978-1-4875-2148-6 (paper)

Library and Archives Canada Cataloguing in Publication

Craig, Béatrice
Backwoods consumers and homespun capitalists : the rise of a market culture
in eastern Canada / Béatrice Craig.

Includes index and bibliographical references.
ISBN 978-0-8020-9317-2 (bound).   ISBN 978-1-4875-2148-6 (paperback)

1. Madawaska (N.B. : County) – Economic conditions – 19th century. 2. Rural
development – New Brunswick – Madawaska (County) – History – 19th
century. 3. Capitalism – New Brunswick – History – 19th century. 4. New
Brunswick – Rural conditions – History – 19th century. I. Title.

HC117.M243C73 2009   330.9715'5402   C2007-907462-6

This book has been published with the help of a grant from the Canadian
Federation for the Humanities and Social Sciences, through the Aid to
Scholarly Publications Program, using funds provided by the Social
Sciences and Humanities Research Council of Canada.

University of Toronto Press acknowledges the financial assistance to its
publishing program of the Canada Council for the Arts and the Ontario Arts
Council, an agency of the Government of Ontario.

Canada Council   Conseil des Arts
for the Arts   du Canada

ONTARIO ARTS COUNCIL
CONSEIL DES ARTS DE L'ONTARIO
an Ontario government agency
un organisme du gouvernement de l'Ontario

Funded by the   Financé par le
Government   gouvernement
of Canada   du Canada

Canadä

Contents

Illustrations follow page 150

List of Figures, Maps, and Tables

Figures

Maps

Tables

Acknowledgments

I have had a long love affair with the history of Madawaska – longer than I care to admit – and I have picked up a few debts in the long process that led to this book. The Faculty of Arts of the University of Ottawa and the university research fund have provided me with travel money, and the book has received a grant from the Aid to Scholarly Publications program of the Social Sciences and Humanities Research Council. The France-Québec research group provided a good venue to test some of my hypothesis, as did various conferences where I presented some of my conclusions (Institut d'histoire de l'Amérique française, Canadian Historical Association, Atlantic Canada workshop, and European Social Science History conference). Those venues provided me with much precious feedback, for which I am grateful. The comments from the readers at the ASPP were also invaluable, and I want to thank Len Husband, editor at the University of Toronto Press, for his able assistance with improving the manuscript. It is customary to thank the assistance of numerous archivists; however, I was fortunate enough to work in archives so well organized that only perfunctory assistance was needed from people at the desk. The Provincial Archives of New Brunswick fit my idea of the ideal place to work (if it were not for the hills on the UNB campus). However, I do want to thank Lisa Ornstein from the Acadian Archives at Fort Kent, who kept an eye out for any material that may have been of use to me, and drew my attention, among other sources, to the holdings of the Archives du Collège Ste Anne de la Pocatière.

BACKWOODS CONSUMERS AND HOMESPUN CAPITALISTS:
THE RISE OF A MARKET CULTURE IN EASTERN CANADA

Introduction. From 'Market' to Markets: New Trends in Rural Economic and Social History

In the late eighteenth and early nineteenth centuries, settlers, lumberers, and business people from Lower Canada, New Brunswick, and New England converged on the banks of the Upper Saint John River in an area known as the Madawaska Territory. In doing so, they created a local economy that was visibly part of the Atlantic capitalist economy. Upper Saint John Valley capitalism, however, was more than an import that the lumberers brought with them in their haversacks: it also grew from within. And the region's market activities went beyond producing staples for Liverpool. Market involvements predated the beginning of the forest industry by almost half a century, and by the middle of the nineteenth century they were no longer limited to production.

The Upper Saint John Valley is a good locale in which to investigate the relationship between rural people and their markets in the nineteenth century. More particularly, analysis of this settlement can shed some light on aspects of this relationship that are increasingly attracting the attention of historians. Export-led models have long dominated the economic history of eighteenth- and nineteenth-century North America and have strongly affected our understanding of agriculture and rural life in the same period. On the one hand, exports are easier to measure than other forms of production. On the other, long-distance trade is often seen as closer to the abstraction economists call 'the market': it was impersonal, uncontrollable by either sellers or buyers, and thus more genuinely competitive than local trade, which was often contaminated by personal relationships. Although export-led models met with some criticism, they remained the dominant historiographic framework until recently. But in the past fifteen years, some historians have shed a new light on changes in the rural econ-

omy and rural life in late-eighteenth- and early-nineteenth-century
British North America and northeastern United States. Instead of
focusing on a reified market, they investigate concrete exchange networks, and participants' agency and choices. This shift in perspective
on rural life has had several consequences: a new emphasis on regional
and local markets as engines of growth and development in their own
right; and a move away from the equating of 'rural' with 'farming' and
of 'market participant' with 'men' or 'producers.' Occupational pluralism is no longer viewed as symptomatic of a stagnant agriculture,
women now matter, and consumption, the flip side of production,
should be included among market activities. Some American historians have gone further, discussing not only the 'rise of a market
culture,' but also challenging the very notion of an abstract market.
'The market' is not a timeless concept: the ability to conceptualize
exchange activities in abstract terms, to think about a reified and timeless market, was part of this new market culture.

In Canada, the model used to explain rural economic evolution was
the long-standing 'staple thesis.' It accounted for Ontario's dynamism,
Quebec's lag, and Maritime underdevelopment. It suggested that
some staples were more propitious to development than others. Wheat
made Ontario rich, timber provided New Brunswick with a very
modest competency, and cod kept Newfoundlanders poor.[1] But timber
was also detrimental to agriculture. Quebec historians developed the
notion of the 'agro-forestry' system, which they initially described as
promoting a stagnant agriculture unable to support farmers.[2] Maritime historians promoted a 'two world view': rural society was made
of part-time subsistence farmers who were also part-time lumberers or
(and sometimes and) fishermen. Farming was outside the market
economy; lumbering and fishing were very much controlled by capitalists.[3] Although American economic historians do not use the label
'staple thesis,' they think along the same lines just the same. Colonial
economic history has presented the foreign sector as the driving force
and the antebellum South was of course a quintessential staple
economy. But even the economic history of the antebellum North and
northeast has privileged the role of long distance and export trade.[4] As
Atack and Bateman pointed out: 'Even excluding raw cotton exports,
the export value of agricultural commodities exceeded that of semi-
manufactured and finished goods until the 20th century.'[5] The key to
explaining north and northwestern economic growth and development was therefore to be found on the farm – and in the farmers'

ability or willingness to commercialize production and enter into long distance trading networks.

This understanding of the nature and role of commercial production has cast a long shadow.[6] It underlies the protracted and still inconclusive American debate over the 'transition to capitalism' in the countryside. U.S. economic historians have presented us with the notion of farmers willingly, if not eagerly, embracing opportunities to sell their goods on national and international markets. This pursuit led farmers to discard home manufacturing and replace those items with store bought and usually factory made ones, and to specialize in a limited range of commodities. Commercialization and specialization inevitably went hand in hand.[7] Many social historians, however, have been very critical of this interpretation, and depict farmers' bitter resistance to 'market' or 'capitalist' encroachments on community-based exchange networks. Those farmers would have entered commercial networks only to trade their leftovers ('surpluses') for the few necessities their community could not produce.[8]

Attempts at bridging the gap between the two interpretations usually result in farmers not only being defined as 'transitional types' between 'self-sufficient' and 'commercial' farmers, but as Allan Kulikoff stated, 'living in a capitalist world, but not of it.'[9] The transition is not the farmers' choice; Kulikoff's explanation for the transformation of rural society lay outside its boundaries: 'capitalists' built canals and railroads, opened banks and built factories, and created the new conditions to which farming families had to adapt.[10] In Canada, Gérard Bouchard's 'co-intégration' model is a similar attempt at trying to handle the two-world universe in which farmers were supposed to operate.[11] But even historians who dislike the concept of 'transition' types do not fully manage to free themselves from the dualistic typology they reject. Richard Bushman, for instance, argues that 'transitions are teleological, deriving significance from changes many decades in the future. The term implies that a farm was not what it was, but the embryo of something it was going to be.'[12] Nonetheless, Bushman's 'composite farm' ended up being a hybrid creature too.

Canadian historians for their part first had to clear out the staple thesis before being able to propose genuinely alternative models. In Canada, the most damaging blows to the staple thesis have been delivered by Marvin McInnis, Doug McCalla, Frank Lewis, and M. C. Urquhart. They showed conclusively that the economy of Upper

Canada grew and diversified before wheat exports became significant, and also that wheat represented a rather small proportion of provincial and farm income. McCalla further emphasized the economic importance of local and regional exchanges of a wide range of agricultural commodities. McInnis showed that even the farms with the largest surpluses remained unspecialized and continued to devote significant acreages to commodities with only local and regional markets.[13]

The challenge to the staple thesis has been less systematic among Quebec historians. Their preoccupation was rather to explain why Quebec lagged behind Ontario, and then to demonstrate that the province's economy developed along the same lines as other North American rural regions. In the process, some of them were nonetheless able to show that local and regional exchanges were key factors in the economic history of the province, and that its successes or failures could not be explained merely with reference to participation in a staple trade.[14]

Maritime historians have also come to question the staple thesis, but initially this challenge did not involve the study of farming, but of the manufacturing sector. The revision of the traditional image of Maritimes agriculture was the cumulative result of several studies that undermined some of the assumptions underpinning export-led models. For example, the absence of agricultural export from a province did not mean its farm sector was stagnant or limited to subsistence, but simply that it was too small to support the province's population. This fact also implied that farm produce was sold on local and regional markets, and that those were necessarily the ones critical to farmers' prosperity. Maritime historians have also questioned the notion that prosperous farmers must specialize in farming. Combining the production of agricultural and other commodities, doing farm work and wage work was not necessarily a consequence of poverty, but could be an intelligent use of available opportunities and a way to secure a competency. Access to wage work, local and regional markets for farm and natural products, services, and locally made goods would then be key elements in the economic development of the Maritimes, as they were in the development of Upper Canada.[15]

American historians, too, are now paying closer attention to local and regional markets and to their articulation with each other and with long distance trading network. As in British North America, com-

mercial exchanges in the northeastern United States underwent significant qualitative and quantitative changes in the early nineteenth
century, which initially should have been favourable to local producers. Local and regional exchanges intensified considerably during this
period. Lower value or perishable farm commodities and North American manufactured products entered those exchange networks in ever
greater quantities.[16] This intensification was the result of increased
population density, new technologies, a developing infrastructure,
and growing regional, especially urban, demand for North American
commodities.

Market expansion was also accompanied by the rise of a market
culture. The growth of market exchanges could include the development of new business methods and new labour relations and be supported by statutory and sometimes constitutional changes. Market
growth was paralleled by changes in consumption patterns and those
markets soon became the dominant form of exchange. They marginalized local barter governed by use value as new forms of neighbourhood exchange reflecting deeper market embeddedness developed as
alternatives to back fence barter. Labour began to be priced to reflect
value added, local prices fluctuated with metropolitan ones, and cash
played a growing role in local store transactions. The old mercantile
networks that had controlled transatlantic trade faded away, their
members dying off, going bankrupt, or moving into new types of ventures. Many of the latter led to corporate capitalism. Whether the
growth of regional and sectional markets signalled the arrival of capitalism as an economic system should be considered as a separate question, as markets, and even the presence of capitalists, are not necessarily evidence of a capitalist economy.

The geographic coverage of those studies, however, remains
uneven. Regions where agriculture was commercialized early attract
more attention (Upper Canada, the St Lawrence and Richelieu valleys,
Massachusetts, the Connecticut and Hudson valleys, and the Philadelphia hinterland for instance).[17] Historians are less interested in remote
districts not located within easy reach of a burgeoning urban centre or
of a major port. Yet most nineteenth-century rural areas were not well
located. Important distances separated them from markets, the local
roads were poor, the rivers not always navigable, and the railroads
took forever to reach them. The work that does exist suggests that
rural areas were not averse to commercial exchanges, but these did not
necessarily involve agricultural commodities or the commodities for

which there was an expanding market.[18] Hal Barron's study of
Chelsea, Vermont, for instance, describes a township involved in commodity production from the days of its founding. When the price of
wool declined and the price of dairy products increased, farmers did
not switch production but increased the size of their flocks. Barron
presents the farmers' decision as economically rational: farmers fac-
tored their time into their calculations and they earned more per time
spent raising sheep than producing dairy products.[19] But even the
inability to trade in farm products did not mean farmers were shut out
of market activities. Wynn, Lewis and Urquhart, Little, and Bouchard
argue that the forest industry allowed farmers in remote areas to
survive until their farms could support them or until they could
connect with extra local markets, and it provided them with alternate
sources of income when local conditions were really not propitious to
agriculture.[20]

Local markets then mattered – and they mattered a lot. However, the
growing understanding of their role has not led to the elaboration of
a new conceptual framework to replace the staple thesis. As Ruth
Sandwell has noted, placing local markets at the heart of a new model
would not solve all problems but would merely replace one form of
economic determinism by another and would not account for the com-
plexities of rural growth and development.[21] And, one can add, there
is the real risk of letting the pendulum swing too far in the other direction, and paying inadequate attention to the role staples played in the
economy.

There are also deeper problems. One must challenge some pre-
conceptions about what belongs to the economic sphere or more
accurately, about what is supposed to lay outside of it in some parallel, non-economic universe. The economy is still too easily understood as the sum of the activities of rational producers operating in
the public sphere whose decisions were unaffected by personal or
family relationships. Those producers are also implicitly, or even
explicitly, depicted in terms that apply only to (male) heads of
households, but what is happening within those households is
ignored. This view generates a number of binary oppositions that
are too easily taken for granted: subsistence versus commercial;
employer/capital versus wage earners/labour; production versus
consumption; family versus economy. Consequently, according to
Ruth Sandwell, 'Given the confused thinking about the family as an
economic unit, the theoretical invisibility of subsistence agriculture,

and rigid notions about the nature of capitalist enterprises, it is not surprising that historians of Canada are having difficulties coming to terms with the distinctive rural society and economy emerging from the recent literature.'[22]

Clearly, more than the dominant role of exports in growth and development must be jettisoned before alternative models can be developed. The boundary between the 'economic sphere' and 'non-economic' activities must be shifted as well; the household should be recognized as a site of genuine market activities; market activities should not be limited to production; and decisions that fail to adhere to a narrowly defined 'economic rationality' should not be dismissed as irrelevant.

Most models are one-directional: they involve only producers. Consumers are oddly absent from the narrative.[23] It is perhaps revealing that in his introduction to a special issue of the *William and Mary Quarterly* on the economy of British North America, John MacCusker refers to consumption as the flip side of production, but the articles themselves do not directly address this issue, with the exception of Lewis and Urquhart's on Upper Canada.[24] T.H. Breen, in discussing the 'transition to capitalism,' noticed the phenomenon, which he argued rested on 'a fundamental misunderstanding of the relationship between consumption and production. It privileges the work place as the ultimate source of values, of social attitudes and of interests and passions.' Consumption, he claims to the contrary, was also used to create meaning and thus connected market involvement to political ideology.[25] Producers may have been economic, social, and political agents but so were consumers, and producers were consumers too.

And those consumers included women. Elizabeth Manke claimed that women consumed to produce;[26] European historian Jan DeVries claimed they produced to consume. He placed women at the heart of an 'industrious revolution' that would have preceded the better known industrial one in England and continental Europe. Rural women, he argues, shifted their efforts from the production of goods and services for the household to the production of goods and services for the market. At the same time, households replaced the goods women used to produce with purchased ones, spurring the demand for manufactured goods. De Vries claims his model applies to the colonial United States;[27] work by U.S. historians such as Joan Jensen, Nancy Grey Osterud, Lee Craig, and Thomas Weiss seems to suggest De Vries's model could also apply to the nineteenth century. In the northeastern United States farm production increased because outputs of commodities traditionally produced by women increased. The growth of markets was also shaped by decisions taken by women.[28]

Farmers, then, were not exclusively adult male heads of households. Few farms would have survived for long without the work of women and children. Women's activities were different from men's and subject to different constraints. Yet most of the literature (women's historians, Allan Kulikoff, and very recent titles are the most notable exceptions), even when recognizing the specificity of women's work, is written as if the sex of the producer was irrelevant. Women are often assumed to have been denied economic agency by patriarchy, to be confined by a separate sphere ideology to strictly non-commercial activities, or to have responded to market stimuli exactly like men. Sally McMurry, however, has shown the fallacy of these assumptions. Not all women viewed the market as a source of opportunities. In New York's Oneida Valley, women quickly decided that increased market involvement meant more work for them and bailed out.[29]

The term farmer included women and children but it did not specifically refer to those who specialized in agricultural commodity production. The line between farmers and non-farmers, between the production of agricultural commodities and engaging in other activities, was porous. Farmers, it turns out, did not specialize in farming until the late nineteenth century. However, the persistence of activities other than crop growing, stock raising, and dairy and poultry production should not be taken as evidence agriculture was stagnating, could not feed its practitioners, and forced them to look for supplementary sources of income. Instead, it was part of an income diversification strategy. Depending on the assets at their disposal and local opportunities, farm household members engaged in craft, trade, manufacturing, or worked for wages.[30]

The boundary between farmers and local entrepreneurs was similarly blurred.[31] It was the entrepreneurs who engineered the development of local and regional markets and often provided the necessary links with long-distance trading networks. Small-scale merchants, millers, brewers and distillers, potash makers and the like tend to be neglected by historians of farmers, or viewed in instrumental terms. Conversely, historians of rural business tend to turn farmers into a one-dimensional supporting cast. Adepts of the household economy model, for instance, usually see rural entrepreneurs, especially merchants, as agents of capitalist penetration of the countryside. Merchants and other local entrepreneurs were instrumental in bringing to rural communities not only outside goods, but also the rhythms, vagaries, and uncertainties of long-distance trade.[32] This may be true, but rural entrepreneurs were more than mere intermediaries between local and surrounding economies, or agents of Liverpool. They also ensured the circulation of goods and credit within local communities. Self-sufficiency would not have been possible without a good deal of local exchange, much of which appears to have been orchestrated by merchants and country storekeepers.[33] But more importantly, rural entrepreneurs pursued their own goals, used their own comparative advantages, and faced their own constraints.[34] They probably did not care whether or not they were rural capitalism's midwives. Their goals and aspirations did not necessarily coincide with those of their clients or suppliers, nor were they necessarily approved by the authorities. Rural entrepreneurs must be studied as agents in their own right, whose actions contributed to shaping local markets as well as mediating the relationship between local people and the outside world. The growing importance of local and regional markets consequently shifts some of the initiative behind market transformations back to rural people, who can no longer be cast in purely reactive terms. Rural people did not embrace or resist reified market forces coming from the outside. They built up multi-layered markets through their own efforts and for a multitude of reasons, greed included.

Discussing the spread of markets or the rise of a market culture however does not solve every problem. What exactly is a market? To a large extent, the continuous debate in the United States stems from the term's semantic elasticity: it is used for anything from face to face exchanges to capitalism. To clarify the matter, it may be useful to go back to Fernand Braudel. Braudel distinguished between three types of exchanges. Local barter, governed by use value, was part of material rather than economic life. Transactions in the middle layer, which he labels 'the market,' were governed by exchange value. The Braudelian market was competitive, transparent in the sense that buyers and sellers knew the prevailing conditions, and predictable in the sense that all participants knew how the others would behave under a given set of circumstances. The market was not necessarily geographically circumscribed; it could cover large areas as long as information flowed reasonably freely. For Braudel, price synchronicity, which he could detect even in fairly remote places by the eighteenth century, signalled market exchanges.[35] In contrast, the world of international trade did not display those characteristics before the end of the eighteenth century. Only the intermediaries knew the situation at both ends of the chain of exchanges. Defective information flow made transactions opaque, uncompetitive, and easily manipulated by the merchants, who consequently stood to make lots of money from the process. This is the layer Braudel called 'capitalism.'[36] One may or may not agree with his denial that barter was a market activity, with his choice of labels, or with his timing.[37] Mancke, Carter, and Wallace-Casey's work has shown that in eighteenth- and nineteenth-century Nova Scotia and New Brunswick at least, barter was no longer part of 'material culture.'[38] Braudel himself confessed to using the term capitalism because it existed, and seemed better than possible alternatives.[39] However, Braudel's distinction between competitive exchanges detached from social obligations and open enough for prices to fluctuate according to supply and demand on the one hand, and trading activities controlled or easily manipulated by oligarchies on the other, should be kept in mind. Not all commercial exchanges generated genuine markets, and not everyone who engaged in commercial exchanges wanted to play by market rules. It is precisely this lack of distinction between the different types of commercial exchanges that led U.S. market and social historians to speak past each other. A producer's lack of interest in producing for the most visible forms of exchange does not necessarily make him (or her) market adverse. A farmer's indifference to unpredictable export trade merely means he is economically prudent. And a farmer's willingness to produce commodities for a regional market does not mean he would be equally eager to produce for distant markets about which he can get no reliable or timely information.

But even our own use of terms such as market, capitalist, and capitalism should give us pause. The apparent usefulness of those concepts for historians lies in their fixity: markets and capitalists share the same fundamental characteristics, wherever and whenever they are found, and historians ask whether the organization of production or trade they are describing fits this pre-existing definition. This framework obscures the fact that the agents whose actions are described did not experience the realities behind the concepts as fixed ones. Martin Bruegel noted that nineteenth-century American definitions of capital and capitalists were not static and eighteenth-century colonists did not even use those terms. At the beginning of the nineteenth century, capital referred to merchants' assets and capitalists were people with money to invest. Only in the mid-nineteenth century did capital become an abstraction and a metonymy for capitalists. The term Market underwent a similar transformation, from a place where goods changed hands, to a set of transactions between human beings, to an abstraction used to conceptualize all forms of impersonal, competitive, and monetarized exchanges. The rise of a market economy, argues Bruegel, entailed a conceptual shift 'from an understanding of the world rooted in concrete and particular experience to general abstractions.'[40]

Joyce Appleby had noted the same kind of transformation among English thinkers in the seventeenth century, and argued the same point for the United States in the post-revolutionary period. Margaret Newell shows how extensive debates over economic policies gave birth to a new understanding of economic activities and to new economic values in eighteenth-century New England.[41] Only when market activities and the use of capital became both routine and varied did the need arise to develop concepts that set those congeries of experiences apart. Complex market activities, however, were neither forced on people, nor hard-wired in their brains. People stumbled towards modern capitalism trying to solve the concrete, mundane problems of everyday life, from putting a roof over their head and food in their plate, to raising their children, improving the quality of their life, supporting their pastor, or ensuring the security of their old age. Capitalism was neither the inevitable end of history, as economists tend to present it, nor a predefined external force that imposed itself on the North American countryside, as some American social historians describe it. Historians such as Clark, Vickers, Newell, and Bruegel reject the notion that capitalism was either a natural outcome of human nature, or the result of outside coercion. Farmers, merchants, millers, and other local agents produced capitalism, most likely unintentionally. It developed as the result of myriad individual decisions taken by local people, decisions that could just as easily have been different. Rural people would thus have been active agents in this process, not merely reacting to changes they neither initiated nor defined.[42] This is also a point made by Doug McCalla, who argues the story historians should tell is the one that stresses human agency, not natural resources, and that 'orients us to real processes rather than the at-time imaginary tales Canadians have spun around staples.'[43] Early economic and social developments at Madawaska were similarly the product of human agency on the ground, rather than the consequences of abstract forces unleashed by the staple trade or by a reified capitalism. Human agency could even successfully counteract the impact of adverse external factors, such as boundary disputes, killing frosts, or commodity market crashes.

The Madawaska Territory was opened to white settlement in 1785, when a group of Acadians and French Canadian families, some from southern New Brunswick, others from the St Lawrence Valley, came to take land above Grand Falls, which breaks the course of the river as it veers due south towards the Bay of Fundy. Immigration from the St Lawrence Valley (especially from Kamouraska and Rivière Ouelle) continued until the twentieth century. The first Madawaska settlers received grants of land from the New Brunswick provincial government. But by the 1790s, the American and British governments were disagreeing on the exact location of the eastern boundary between their territories. The Upper Saint John Valley was in the middle of the disputed territory and the provincial government ceased to issue land grants there. This did not stop French-Canadian immigration, and by 1840, the population exceeded 3,500. The boundary dispute was settled in 1842 by the Webster Ashburton treaty, when London and Washington chose the river as the boundary, splitting the settlement in half. Local people ignored the boundary and went about their business as usual and the terms of the treaty, which guaranteed free navigation of forest and agricultural products on the Saint John River, were designed to minimally disrupt the local economy. French-Canadian immigrants were equally oblivious to the division and kept coming. By 1870, the Canadian and American Madawaska combined population numbered about 15,000 people, spread over an area approximately seventy miles long and three to five miles wide.

    The name Madawaska, which initially referred to a local tributary of the Saint John, was adopted in the 1780s by the New Brunswick authorities to describe the area inhabited by the French-speaking settlers: as the population grew, so did the area called Madawaska. The boundary dispute retarded the incorporation of the new settlement into a civil parish, the basic unit of local administration in the British territories at the time.[44] The Madawaska settlement simply became an unincorporated territory in the civil parish of Kent. The Catholic Church organized the settlement into an ecclesiastical parish in 1792.

Like the Madawaska Territory, the Catholic parish of St Basile had no precise geographic boundary and included all Saint John Valley Catholics above Fredericton. St Basile was first split in 1838, when the governor of New Brunswick paid a priest to minister to the Saint John Valley Native people. The priest's home base was the church of St Bruno in the eastern part of the Madawaska Territory. The ecclesiastical parish of Ste Luce was erected in 1842 to serve the rapidly growing population of the western section of the territory; like St Basile and St Bruno, it served both sides of the river. The priests were initially appointed by the bishop of Quebec, and even after the territory was included in the newly constituted bishopric of Charlottetown, Quebec continued to supply it with priests. The civil and ecclesiastical Madawaska were therefore elastic geographic units.[45] Nowadays, besides referring to a county in New Brunswick and a town on the U.S. side of the river, Madawaska is still loosely used to refer to the part of the Saint John Valley inhabited by French speakers, the area between the mouth of the St Francis River and Grand Falls. The forest still marks the southern and northern boundaries of the region.

The territory has always been geographically well circumscribed, being separated from other populated areas by wide belts of timberland and barely populated townships. If one looks at a current map of the region, one gets a feeling for the remoteness and isolation of the Upper Saint John Valley. From an American point of view, it is literally the end of the road: U.S. Route #1 begins here. On a Canadian map, the valley looks squashed between Quebec and Maine. The situation was quite different in the past, when it was a way station on a major communication artery and a magnet for various interests. Until the 1870s, the Madawaska Territory was connected with the outside world by the Saint John River and the Temiscouata Grand Portage. The Saint John River is navigable by flat-bottomed craft from the French settlement to its mouth in the Bay of Fundy, but its course is interrupted by an impressive cataract, the Grand Falls just below the Madawaska Territory. Timber rafts were sent through the whirling waters; other goods had to be portaged about a mile. The Madawaska settlement was also connected to the St Lawrence River by two portages: the lesser used Rivière Ouelle portage, and the more travelled Temiscouata or Grand Portage. The latter route connected Rivière du Loup to the Saint John Valley through Lake Temiscouata and the Madawaska River. The Saint John River–Temiscouata portage route had been used by Amerindians and French during the colonial period, and was the only all-British winter route between Halifax and Quebec until the building of the rail-roads. As such, it was of critical strategic importance, and explained why Britain clung so tenaciously to those few acres of timberland. Although the Madawaska Territory was not isolated by lack of com-munication, it was nonetheless very distant from many potential markets. Only the arrival of the railroads, which reached the valley in 1876, altered this situation.[46]

Until the 1820s, the local economy was based almost exclusively on agriculture and fur. Lumbering began officially during the 1823–4 season. The boundary dispute soon put an end to legal lumbering operations but the industry continued unabated all the same. Both the U.S. and British governments had agreed on a moratorium on the issuance of timber licences. The Americans were in no position to enforce the ban, and the New Brunswick government preferred to fine illegal loggers rather than to stop them from working. The signing of the treaty merely made possible the entry of large scale operators into the industry. Agriculture faced its own challenges during the period, the most serious being a dangerously short growing season and the repeated destruction of the wheat crops by pests and diseases between the 1840s and the 1870s. Farmers coped by finding alternate markets for substitute crops. Lumbering and its spin-off, pulp and paper pro-duction, and agriculture have remained the mainstays of the valley's economy to this day. For most of the nineteenth century, staple pro-duction was important in this region, manufacturing non-existent, urban markets distant and limited in size. In this context, what did market activities mean?

Its location, the nature of its resources, and its uncertain political status for most of the period under consideration resulted in the Madawaska Territory being part of three overlapping regions: the 'Timber Colony' of New Brunswick, New England, and Lower Canada. The valley residents took part in the timber trade directly as producers and indirectly as suppliers and labourers. Lumberers, mer-chants, and millers orchestrated the flow of goods in and out of the region and competition between U.S. and British lumbermen led to a large influx of currency into the region. The Madawaska settlers' will-ingness to produce for markets and their participation in the Atlantic economy may have predated the arrival of the timber trade: following pre-settlement and even pre-Conquest precedents, they participated in the fur trade at the end of the eighteenth century. In addition, from that

time on a growing proportion of local farmers displayed a strong inclination to step up production to respond to the demands of whatever
market was accessible and profitable. First they grew wheat, which
was shipped downriver; then shanty supplies; and finally, after the
railroads came, American Madawaska switched to potatoes, some of
which were shipped as far as Texas, and the rest turned into starch for
the cotton mills of southern New England. Canadian Madawaska, like
the rest of northwestern New Brunswick, continued producing fodder,
which was exported as far away as South Africa.

However, the settlers' actions were not solely responses to external
stimuli. They also grew a wide range of surplus foodstuffs for the local
market and tapped lesser markets, including one for handwoven textiles. The latter was not part of a putting out system, as it had been in
New England in the early years of the nineteenth century. Local textile
production flies in the face of most of the existing Canadian literature on the question, which presents nineteenth-century rural handweaving as a cost avoidance strategy by impoverished households.[47]
Madawaska textile production does not fit this pattern at all. The
Madawaska farmers were also unmistakeably commercially minded:
their exchanges clearly went beyond the swapping of leftover and incidental surpluses with neighbours and storekeepers. They even settled
most of their store accounts with commodities grown for the purpose,
or with currency. The region's producers were always integrated into
regional markets, just as they were always trading in one staple or
another. But their markets changed over time and expanded sufficiently to sustain population growth.

Market changes also affected the consumption habits of the valley's
inhabitants. A surprising volume of currency seems to have circulated
in the region by mid-century, aided and abetted by a well developed
network of British North American banks. The transportation revolution also significantly affected the valley's consumption patterns. At
mid-century, a valley resident could eat bread made from Upper
Canadian flour (itself perhaps ground from American wheat) with
Canadian mess pork or Newfoundland cod, drink East Indian tea
sweetened with West Indian sugar in English earthenware, use U.S.-
manufactured screws alongside New Brunswick-made nails in construction, wear shirts or aprons made of American cotton, New
Brunswick-mass produced shoes, or Native-made moccasins, but don
clothes made of local homespun to plough the fields or milk the cows.

The Madawaska consumer, like the Madawaska producer, was at a crossroads between local and regional as well as continental and transatlantic exchanges.

Since the beginnings of white settlement, the valley has remained overwhelmingly French-speaking, even on the American side of the border. French culture had very little visible impact on the economic decisions taken by the Madawaska people. Religion played a role in local economic life: it prevented intermarriages between the local French and local Anglo-Protestant elite, or between the local French elite and the Provincial one, thus impeding the creation of kin networks. But there was no hint of the existence of a Catholic economic culture distinct from a Protestant one. Protestants and Catholics seem to have pursued the same broad goals, but being members of different social and kin networks, they had to draw on a different social capital to reach them.

Were the Madawaska farmers capitalists? I will argue the great majority were not, their fondness for trade notwithstanding. A Marxist definition of capitalism as a system in which some individuals (the capitalists) exploit a waged labour force to extract plus-value that is in turn reinvested (as capital) in additional exploitive endeavours will not do here. Such a definition assumes a clear distinction between employers and labour that makes little sense in early nineteenth-century northeastern rural economies. Most small producers relied on family labour, seasonally or sporadically supplemented by hired workers, or they found working partners. The labour these households were most likely to exploit was their own.

There is a tendency in the literature to equate 'commercial exchanges' with capitalism and capitalism with a certain set of values including individualism and a single-minded search for financial profit or profit-maximization. This equation has blurred the picture rather than clarified it. First, profit-maximizing behaviour is not a good criterion by which to determine whether an individual was capitalist or not. Naomi Lamoreaux makes the often overlooked point that firms are profit maximizers and human beings utility maximizers. Humans seek economic as well as non-economic goals: a good reputation, prestige, power, security, salvation, leisure time. Their object is to try to reach whatever is, for them, the optimal combination of outcomes. Nineteenth-century entrepreneurs were no different; they adopted the very behaviours historians identify among farmers as hallmarks of 'non-capitalist *mentalité*.' Like most small producers, farmers included, merchants and manufacturers relied on cooperation and mutuality, placed a high value on honesty, reliability, and trustfulness, put family needs and obligations first, loaned money and goods without interest, and did not understand accounting. The latter characteristic made estimating profits difficult. Yet one cannot deny that nineteenth-century seaboard merchants and manufacturers were full participants in a commercial and even capitalist economy.[48]

Second, there is often no way to really know what motivated farmers to act in a particular way. Their motivations end up being deduced from behaviour, but their behaviour is sometimes given meaning by reference to their alleged motivations or *mentalités*.[49] The connection between market involvement and capitalism can lead and has led to circular reasoning. I am proposing here that we revert to a nineteenth-century definition of capitalist that does not require second guessing people's values: a capitalist was an individual who used capital to make money and tried to increase his (and sometimes her) income by multiplying investments. People who engaged in market activities, whether controlled by distant merchants or not, without making any significant investments were merely commercially minded.[50] This definition is much less ambiguous than one based on an individual's value, and therefore much more operational. The objection may be that it too attempts to divine what went on in people's minds. There is, however, a significant difference between observable patterns of behaviour that are responses to identifiable constraints and opportunities, and long-term strategies shaped by a person's values. When someone invests money in a venture that can be reasonably expected to generate a profit, it is reasonable to assume that person is trying to make a profit. Saying that someone tried to profit through investments is neither the same as guessing what that person thought of the ethics of investments nor the same as guessing the reasons the person wanted to make money in the first place, which could include greed, search for prestige or security, desire to provide for the children, or Puritan anxieties about salvation. My suggestion is that historians cease to infer moral or cultural values solely on the basis of behaviours that have left traces in the historical record.[51]

As for capitalism, I take my cue from Michael Merril: 'Capitalism is a market economy ruled by, or in the interests of capitalists.'[52] The existence of capitalists or even capitalist trading networks like the timber trade was a necessary but not sufficient condition to make an economy capitalist.

Few Madawaska farmers could be construed as being capitalists under this definition. Farmers appear to have invested little in their farm besides the initial purchase price, but they occasionally invested in other ventures. Farmers who did not invest did not necessarily use their profits to establish their children, which is what non-capitalist farmers throughout North America are supposed to have done. Their land transmission practices were similar to those that prevailed in areas engaged in commercial agriculture but not to those found in regions poorly articulated to markets. Farmers' preoccupation with their children's economic fate and active measures to provide for them do not seem to have lasted beyond the first generation of settlers. Life chances at Madawaska did not depend heavily upon inheriting land. Markets for land, labour, agricultural and natural commodities, and, one suspects, credit, made it possible for children to successfully raise the necessary funds to acquire a holding with limited or no assistance from their parents. Instead of deploying lifelong strategies to establish their children, farmers seem to have been more interested in raising their standard of living, purchasing consumer goods, and providing for security in their old age. Most farmers turned out to have been utility maximizers and the utility they maximized was the one that benefited themselves and their wives.

Some farmers did invest, but in rural infrastructure: stores, mills, smithies, ferries. Aspiring capitalists ceased to be full-time farmers when they were successful, but stayed clear of direct involvements in foreign trade. They preferred to provide their neighbours with services and therefore contributed to the development of local and regional markets. Local capitalists were local in terms of residence and in terms of the geographic scope of their ventures. They usually did well, but their success cannot be solely attributed to their willingness to take risks or to their business acumen. Kinship ties were the common thread that linked most locally born businessmen. Among second and third generations the best predictors of an individual's business involvement were the activities of his father, uncles, or other close kin. Personal networks mattered. Only in the 1860s did kinship cease to structure local business life.

Farmers-turned-entrepreneurs kept their distance from the timber trade, and with good reason. Lumbering appears to have been as good a road to riches as riverboat gambling. Lumberers, big or small, and the men most dependent on them for their fortunes, like saw millers and the local merchants who supplied them, usually went bankrupt unless they had the good sense to shift occupations before the next economic downturn or, as in the case of one storekeeper, die just in time. Lumbering created few linkages in the valley, as impermanent as the industry that gave them birth. However, it did play a major role in monetizing the local economy. The benefits of lumbering were circuitous and accrued largely to those who took advantage of the temporary fortunes of others.

Capitalism, then, operated at two distinct levels in the valley. First, the trade in staples ensured that the valley was always part of a capitalist economy, albeit a mercantile one. It brought money and credit into the region and kept its mental horizons wide open. Second, the expansion of local and regional markets by midcentury allowed the emergence of a limited group of small-scale but genuine neighbourhood capitalists, men who invested in infrastructure but also played political roles and, at the end of the period, detached themselves from family clans. Markets bred indigenous capitalism, and this may explain why the process appears to have generated little anxiety among the local population.

The economic, political, and social life of the settlement followed parallel courses that obeyed their own logic. Agriculture and the forest industry, the two mainstays of the valley's economy from the 1820s onwards, did not evolve in lockstep either, and for the first twenty years, the market was not the place where they met. A periodization that clarifies the history of the one muddles the history of the other. Politics similarly had a life of its own, which may or may not have had a hand in determining the course of social and economic local life. Consequently, I have organized the chapters of this study thematically rather than chronologically. The first focuses on the settlers: who they were; where they came from; why they migrated to Madawaska and when; and what type of society they eventually produced. Some aspects of their previous experience made them receptive to, or looking for, commercial opportunities. The second chapter focuses on early leading men, individuals who tried to rise in the local social hierarchy but did not necessarily turn to the market to do so. The third describes the origins and subsequent development of the forest industry and the activities of the men who bet their fortune on the timber trade. The next two are devoted to local entrepreneurs, individuals who sometimes acted as links with the outside world and always created commercial relations. Many of them can be viewed as representative of their socio-economic category, if not of their social class. The spotlight then shifts to the farmers. What did it mean to be a farmer on the New Brunswick frontier? How commercial was Madawaska farming? Were all farmers equally commercial? What strategies did they use to meet their goals? Did Madawaska witness a De Vries-style industrious revolution? And finally, why did farmers seek markets? Was it to perpetuate a 'peasant society,' unchanged from one generation to the next, or to join the market as consumers?

1 People on the Move: Migrations and Networks

We have not been in any hurry to write to you since our return to Quebec, as we often had the opportunity to send you some news about ourselves, or receive some about you from people from your place who we had the pleasure of meeting in Quebec

Charlotte, Marie, and Elizabeth Audibert to their brother Joseph
at Ste Luce du Madawaska, 1854[1]

The Acadian French, who are settled in numbers in the upper part of this valley, are described as fine industrious men; but the Lower Canadians who came across from the shores of the St. Lawrence, are represented by the English settlers as a 'miserable set.' This probably arises from the fact that, as the Irish do with us, the poor Lower Canadians come into and through the country as beggars in great numbers.

J.F.W. Johnston 1851[2]

The Audibert sisters were working-class women who lived with their husbands in St Roch, Quebec City's shipbuilding district, in the 1840s and 1850s. The sisters had no difficulty communicating with their brother, a carpenter at Madawaska, either by letter or by word of mouth, both conveyed by what appears to have been a significant number of people travelling back and forth between the two locales. They also made a visit to their brother in 1854.

This thumbnail sketch does not jibe with conventional images of the Madawaska Territory and its habitants. The territory, so the story goes, would have been founded by Acadians who had escaped the Deportation of 1755 and, after many tribulations, resettled in southern New

Brunswick, only to be displaced, if not evicted, by the Loyalists in 1783. They would then have taken refuge upriver and kept their distance from their persecutors.[3] This vision of Acadians keeping to themselves in isolated areas dovetails neatly with an enduring image of pioneer settlements as self-sufficient and equalitarian communities: if self-sufficiency was not a choice stemming from the pioneers' desire for independence, it was a necessity imposed on them by constraints such as small population size, insufficient infrastructure, distance, and poor communications. Whether a by-product of eighteenth-century wars or one of the many islands of white settlement springing up in the interior, Madawaska in the first half of the nineteenth century would have been 'un ilot relativement clos, presque un isolat social,' as P.L. Martin describes it.[4] The Audibert letter suggests a different reality. There was frequent population movement between the St Lawrence and Upper Saint John valleys. Although contemporaries did not believe that Madawaska was an isolate, they did feel that those movements had turned it into a two-tier society. They may have seen the Audibert women as part of the 'beggary set' described by J.F.W. Johnston, instead of pleasure travellers.

   The fictions of Evangeline and Crusoe-like hardy pioneers cast a long shadow over the early history of the Madawaska Territory, but those images mask a less heroic and more positive reality. The Acadians were neither helpless victims nor the only early Madawaska white settlers. The Acadians started a settlement on the banks of the Upper Saint John, but were immediately joined by Lower St Lawrence French Canadians. After the War of 1812, the forest industry attracted large numbers of people into the region, more French Canadians, but also Yankees, Provincials, and even a sprinkling of Irish Catholics.

   Emigration from the region began right away, and circular migration was not unheard of.[5] Outside economic opportunities such as lumbering and farmland availability in the Old Northwest, and industrialization in New England were responsible for most outmigration, as well as for the through-migration of former Lower St Lawrence inhabitants to southern destinations. After 1820 Madawaska became a destination, a point of departure, and a way station for people on the move. The constant movements of population had two consequences. They brought the local population in contact with outsiders and provided them with links to the larger world and, at a very practical level, with conduits for information, as was the case with the Audibert family. Immigrants also affected the composition of the Madawaska

population, which became simultaneously more fragmented and stratified. A stable core of 'Acadians' coexisted with insular groups of
Anglo-Protestants, and all were surrounded by a footloose population
of mostly French-Canadian ancestry – the 'miserable set' that Johnston
described, as opposed to the 'fine industrious' Acadians.

Migrations

Acadian Resettlements

In 1768 two cousins, Jean Baptiste Thibodeau and Jean Baptiste
Cormier, sold their sawmill at St Thomas de Montmagny on the Lower
St Lawrence.[6] They and a score of other families relocated above St
Ann's Point (now Fredericton), near the Native village of Ekoupag (or
Aupac or Aukpoc; the spelling varies from source to source) in 1767
and 1768.[7] Their nearest Euro-American neighbours were a colony of
New Englanders who had been established across the river in the
township of Maugerville since 1763.[8] Thibodeau, Cormier, and their
companions were no ordinary habitants. They were Acadians, originally from the Beaubassin–Chepody area, who had had escaped the
Deportation of 1755 and taken refuge in the St Lawrence valley.[9] After
the signing of the Treaty of Paris in 1763, the refugees began to trickle
back towards Nova Scotia. By 1783, sixty-one families, numbering 368
people, lived above and below Ekoupag. Other Acadian families – an
unknown number of people – were strung along the Saint John below
St Ann's Point, and another, smaller Acadian settlement was situated
further below, on the Kennebecassis River (see map 1).[10]

The Acadians were squatters who had moved onto already granted
land. A section of the Lower Saint John had been divided into large
townships granted to absentee landlords in 1765. Ekoupag, around
which the bulk of the Acadians lived, became part of Sunbury Township. The great proprietors were supposed to bring in Protestant settlers who would be their tenants but very few made any efforts to
fulfill the terms of their grants, and none succeeded.[11] During the
American Revolution, the Acadians sided with the British, and served
as scouts and pilots.[12] They pointedly refused to join Jonathan Eddy
and his band of rebels, despite the latter being headquartered at
Ekoupag.

Natives, Acadians, and New Englanders residing on the Lower Saint
John engaged in what appears to have been a thriving commercial

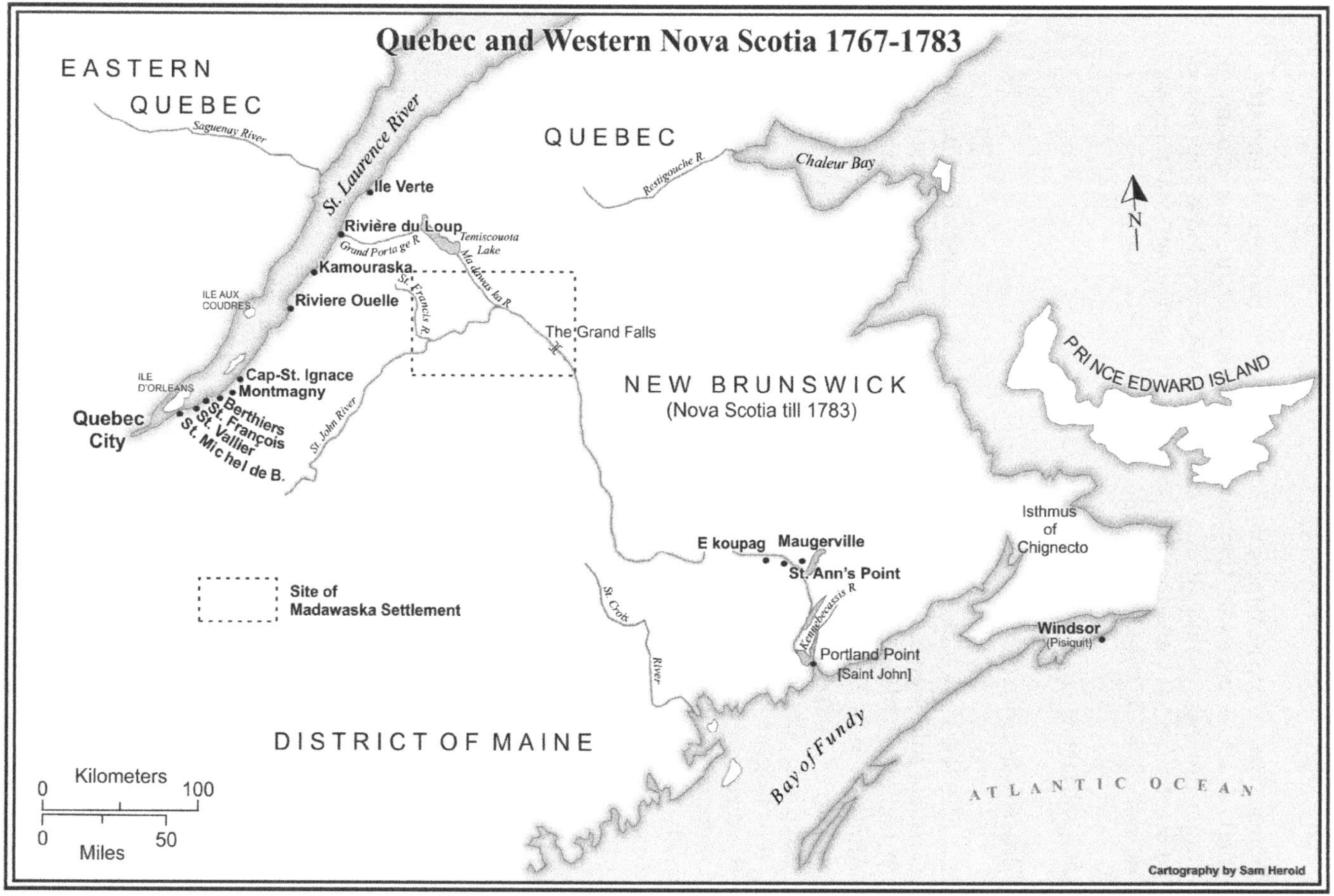

Quebec and Western Nova Scotia 1767-1783

EASTERN QUEBEC

QUEBEC

Saguenay River

St. Lawrence River

Ile Verte

Rivière du Loup

Grand Portage R.

Temiscouata Lake

Kamouraska

Ma dawas ka R.

Riviere Ouelle

St. John River

Francis R.

Cap-St. Ignace

Montmagny

Berthiers

St. François

St. Vallier

St. Mic hel de B.

ILE AUX COUDRES

ILE D'ORLEANS

Quebec City

The Grand Falls

Restigouche R.

Chaleur Bay

NEW BRUNSWICK
(Nova Scotia till 1783)

E koupag

Maugerville

St. Ann's Point

Kennebeccasis R.

Portland Point
[Saint John]

St. Croix River

River

Bay of Fundy

Isthmus of Chignecto

Windsor
[Pisiquit]

PRINCE EDWARD ISLAND

ATLANTIC OCEAN

N

Cartography by Sam Herold

Site of
Madawaska Settlement

DISTRICT OF MAINE

Kilometers
0   100
Miles
0   50

Map 1

micro-economy. In 1763 a trio of Newburryport, Massachusetts, merchants, Simonds, Hazen, and White, had opened a trading post at the mouth of the river in a place they called Portland Point, which soon grew into a small colony of about 150 persons. The partners later opened another post at Oromocto, near Maugerville. They traded in fur, feathers, and fish, burned lime, and made barrel staves. The Lower Saint John Native people and settlers were drawn into their activities as suppliers of trade goods and foodstuff, as labourers, and as customers. Simonds, Hazen, and White provided them with imported textiles, metal and metalware, and West Indian goods.

Five Acadians appear in a 78-page account book covering the years 1775 to 1779[13]: 'John' and 'Francis' Robichaud (Jean and François), Augustin 'White' (Leblanc), 'Oliver Thebedo' (Olivier Thibodeau) junior, and 'Francis Violet' (François Violette). The men settled their accounts mostly with cash. Violette bought 12s.6d. worth of cooking utensils and a bushel of salt in July 1776, and proffered 10 shillings towards payment. Olivier Thibodeau bought two sashes with glass panes worth 15 shillings in April 1775. The purchases were charged to another person's account. In the fall of 1778, Thibodeau bought some pins and two blankets worth £1 11s.6d. He settled his account in cash the following July. François Robichaud paid cash for tobacco and rum in March 1778. Jean Robichaud's account began in October 1777 with purchases of iron, molasses, powder and shot, pins, a hat, and a scythe handle. In November and December, he bought two blankets and some fabric. He received a credit for 10 shillings which brought his balance down to 7s.3d. In January and February he bought more fabric (onasbruck and red camlet), some rum, and a pewter dish. Two of those items (pewter and camlet) were luxury goods. He brought farm products the next winter for credit: 7.5 bushels of meal and 2 bushels of beans. He then purchased more rum, some molasses, a coffee pot, and a scythe. The account was settled in January 1779, but the book does not say how. Augustin Leblanc worked for the merchants. In August 1778 they paid him £1 6s.6d. for cutting their hay. He earned 3 shillings a day, plus his board and a ration of rum, but seems to have taken additional money instead of food and drink. The account book records the Acadians' familiarity with trade, money, and fancy goods through their connection with the Massachusetts merchants.

The relationship between the merchants and the settlers was reinforced in 1779 when Simonds, Hazen, and two other men in successive partnership, secured a masting contract with the British navy. The merchants hired the settlers to cut timber and masts and purchased corn (wheat or maize) from them. Wages apparently rose, not only because Simonds and Hazen's demand for labourers had increased, but because the partners had competition.[14] Another merchant with a masting contract had relocated from the Miramichi to Maugerville to escape privateers, and Beamsley Glazier, a veteran officer of the French and Indian wars, had built an enormous sawmill at Marysville, next to Maugerville and almost across from Ekoupag.[15] Native people and settlers were selling their labour where they could get the best deal. Some fancy goods also appear to have become objects of common consumption. In February 1783, Peabody informed his partners Simonds and Hazen that his masting crew were 'murmuring' because he was only able to serve them spruce tea. He wanted the partners to send him something more suitable: chocolate![16] The world of goods and the culture of trade were thus not alien to the Lower Saint John inhabitants, Native or European, Acadians or New Englanders. The above-mentioned account book is also evidence that, for a while at least, the economy was monetized.[17]

Participating in a commercial economy was nothing new for the Acadians. The pre-deportation Acadians had traded actively with both the French and British, and Quebec merchants traded at Beaubassin on the eve of the Seven Years War. One of them, Jean Baptiste Grandmaison, married the sister of Jean Baptiste Thibodeau mentioned above; he had relocated in Kamouraska by 1757, where he was a merchant trader.[18] After the Treaty of Paris, Côte-du-Sud and Lower St Lawrence merchants and their Quebec City patrons sought to redirect the Saint John Valley fur trade towards their stores and warehouses, and they relied on people experienced with trading in the region, like the Acadian Pierre Robichaud. Robichaud's son Régis and his nephews Michel and Anselme succeeded him after 1774. The Native people were not very happy about the situation. The rights to the Saint John Valley hunting and trapping grounds had been reserved for them in 1765, yet in 1768 they were complaining that Canadians from Kamouraska and Acadians were trespassing on their hunting grounds.[19] The fur trade was only one of many activities carried out by the residents of the Lower St Lawrence. The Côte-du-Sud inhabitants made a living from commercialized agriculture as early as the mid-eighteenth century, supplemented by various other commercial, but casual or seasonal, activities: in-shore fisheries; the hunting of sea mammals for their oil; the production of cordwood for the Quebec market; and the building of *goelettes,* the small craft that were ubiquitous in the gulf. In the seventeenth century, Intendant Talon had tried to promote tar-making; it was never a successful industry, but limped along till the Conquest and provided its producers with an additional source of income.[20] Like the Lower Saint John settlers, the Lower St Lawrence French Canadians were familiar with trade, and entered into local, regional, and extra-regional commercial networks. Despite being refugees, some of the Acadians took part in this commercial economy: ten years after being chased away from their home at the head of the Bay of Fundy, Cormier and Thibodeau were business owners. The British had devastated the Côte-du-Sud in 1759, burning farm houses and outbuildings as far down as Kamouraska. There was a crying need for building material, and it appears that the two men took advantage of this opportunity. They were not the only Acadians who surface in the sources as more than labourers. Jacques Cyr, also from Beaubassin and living in St Thomas, was a *navigateur* (pilot) in 1765.[21]

Loyalist Arrival

The aftermath of the revolution dramatically changed the course of life on the Lower Saint John. Between March and December 1783, more than 10,000 people, mostly New Yorkers and disbanded soldiers and officers from Loyalist volunteer regiments, were put ashore at the mouth of the Saint John River. They were supposed to receive grants of land to compensate them for their losses or as reward for their services, but nothing was ready for them, and many over-wintered in tents.[22] The situation soon became chaotic: exasperated Loyalists commissioned private surveys and settled on the land on their own, and land sharks preyed upon pre-Loyalist settlers.[23] The Loyalists decided that matters should be taken into their own hands and pressed for secession from Nova Scotia. In 1784 the British government created the separate province of New Brunswick. Sir Thomas Carleton, brother to Sir Guy Carleton, governor-in-chief of British North America since 1783, was appointed first governor.[24] Under his direction, the executive council spent most of its first year allocating land to all those who were eligible. These included Anglo-Protestant pre-loyalists and the Acadians.[25] The Acadians understood the proper procedures: Augustin 'White' Leblanc presented his petition to the governor three days after the latter had landed in New Brunswick in November 1784, and others soon followed suit.[26]

The Acadians were either granted their own blocks of land, or were included in block grants to newcomers. As no complete list of Acadians nor complete list of grants exists, it is not possible to know what proportion of Acadians, if any, were not quieted in their possession. There is no clear evidence of discrimination against them but there was no lack of wrinkles to iron out. The province operated with a skeleton staff, and consequently some grants were slow in coming: the governor-in-council was still issuing block grants in 1787. Surveys were contested and boundary disputes between neighbours, which were sent to the surveyor-general or to the governor-in-council for arbitration, were not always dealt with expeditiously, or in a manner deemed satisfactory by the petitioner.[27] Two of Jean Baptiste Cormier's sons, François and Amand, had to go to court to challenge a writ of eviction brought against them (they won, but the 'gentleman' kept harassing them until they asked the governor of New Brunswick to intervene). Courier Louis Mercure and his neighbours at the Madamkeswick had to appeal to Governor Parr in 1784 to correct a survey granting their improvements to disbanded soldiers. Mercure's co-petitioners waited until 1797 for a grant from New Brunswick; Mercure's lot was reserved for him but never granted, perhaps because he left the area.[28]

Despite receiving their grants, the Acadians almost all left the area within months, if not weeks, of being granted title to their land. Louis Mercure had been one of the first to sell: he held a Nova Scotia grant for an island in the Saint John, which he sold to a merchant in September 1785 for £150.[29] Jean Baptiste Cormier sold a 1784 grant in 1790 to a Loyalist for £68. Ten of the eighteen Acadians included in the grant to Augustin 'White' (Leblanc) in January 1786 had sold their holdings within six months for an average sum of £36 10s. currency (about $145).[30] The departing Acadians applied and received new grants in other parts of the province. Their reasons for removing their applications included anxiety over delays in receiving titles, the desire for better access to priests, and the need for additional land for their numerous offspring.[31] Most Acadians probably had no desire to live in a predominantly Anglo-Protestant environment. Most, but not all: within ten years some returning Acadians had settled a new French Village at Kingsclear, not far from Ekoupag and several of them were included in a block grant in the township in 1799.[32] The French Village lasted for several generations before its members were assimilated into the surrounding English-speaking population. The Acadians who left permanently, however, thoroughly resented the fact that they had had to move, and nursed their grievance for a long time.[33]

Why Madawaska?

The Acadians who permanently left the Lower Saint John did not all head to the same destination. Some left for the Chepody area; others for the northeast coast of New Brunswick.[34] One group led by former courier Louis Mercure pushed north and relocated above Grand Falls, which interrupts the course of the Saint John before it veers south towards the Bay of Fundy. Destination was determined by a variety of reasons: place of origin, family ties, and, in the case of the Madawaska settlers, official encouragement. The Saint John River was a vital component of the British North American communication system. Ice blocked the St Lawrence estuary for several months in winter, shutting down maritime communication between Halifax and Quebec City. After 1783 sending government dispatches by an American overland route was out of the question, and Governor Haldimand brought back into use an old French route between the St Lawrence and the Bay of Fundy, which followed the Grand Portage, Temiscouata Lake, the Madawaska, and the Saint John River. Royal couriers began using the route on a scheduled basis that winter.[35] No settlements except for Native villages existed between the St Lawrence and the tiny French villages above St Ann's Point, leaving the couriers vulnerable to accidents and attacks during the two-week trip. A seasoned courier and his companion were murdered in the summer of 1784, and Mercure himself was the target of an assassination attempt the same year.[36]

In the fall of 1783 Mercure had proposed a solution to Governor Haldimand. He claimed that the Acadians were planning to re-emigrate to Quebec in order to have access to priests and suggested they would just as soon resettle on the Upper Saint John given the proper incentive. Haldimand enthusiastically endorsed the idea. So did his successor, Dorchester, and Dorchester's younger brother, who happened to be Governor Carleton of New Brunswick. Carleton offered grants to all those who were desirous of settling above Grand Falls. This cost him politically in the late 1790s, when the settling of the Upper Saint John was challenged by the opposition as a costly and useless scheme.[37]

Promises of grants were not enough to motivate all Acadians to relocate above Grand Falls. Movement out of the Lower Saint John was a typical chain migration under family auspices. A foreguard left to reconnoitre an area and begin clearing, and was later joined by members of the extended family. For almost ten years many Madawaska families kept their connections with the Lower Saint John: either the family was split between the two locations, or the Madawaska pioneers delayed selling their property.[38] Additional family factors could come into play. Many members of the Chepody group returned to their grandparents' birth place.[39] Madawaska-bound 'Acadians' almost all had a relative on the St Lawrence, and the group included a few Acadian-Canadian or entirely Canadian couples. The Acadians who moved to other parts of New Brunswick, on the other hand, did not have French-Canadian relatives.[40]

Family ties played the same role channelling French-Canadian migration towards the Upper Saint John.[41] The migrants originally resided in the parishes that dotted the south shore of the river between L'Islet and Kamouraska. Rivière Ouelle and Kamouraska, near the portage routes linking the St Lawrence and Saint John River valleys, sent the greatest number of people to the Upper Saint John Valley, part of an eastward population movement that had begun around 1680.[42] Kinship played an important role in the movements of population into and within the region, as it later did in the migration towards the Upper Saint John Valley. Early settlers in a new parish were normally clusters of related families; single male migrants were more likely to stay permanently in the Côte-du-Sud if they married locally than if they married another migrant.[43] By the end of the eighteenth century, the Côte-du-Sud began to run out of farmland. Outmigration now affected the entire region, and migrants followed one of four directions: towards the Beauce region; towards the Gaspé Peninsula and the Chaleur Bay; across the St Lawrence and up the Saguenay River; and finally south. French-Canadian migrations to the Upper Saint John Valley following the old Rivière Ouelle portage, or the Grand Portage through Rivière du Loup and Temiscouata Lake, began in the 1780s (see fig 1).[44]

Until the mid-1820s, most French Canadians who migrated to Madawaska joined a relative already established there.[45] In the 1780s and 1790s, Canadian relatives of Acadians provided the bulk of the migrants. By 1800, three quarters of the Madawaska male and female heads of households had relatives at Madawaska even before moving

there; more significantly, three quarters of the heads of family established at Madawaska in 1800 had an Acadian *and* a Canadian relative
in the community.[46] Early migrants to Madawaska were consequently
a self-selected group, and family ties were the criteria of selection. The
founding of the Madawaska settlement was like a big family reunion.
Further intermarriages quickly reinforced the relationship between the
two groups.

Between 1800 and the beginnings of the forest industry, Madawaska continued to attract small numbers of immigrant couples and
individuals. There were no obstacles to their occupying the land. The
New Brunswick government had issued a grant to a 16,000 acre block
containing seventy-four lots in 1790. Most of those lots were immediately claimed (see map 2).[47] The same year, Britain ordered the
North American provincial governments to cease land grants,
pending new guidelines. They were not issued until 1807, at which
time the boundary dispute between Britain and the United States had
surfaced.[48] The provincial government did not grant land in the disputed territory until after the boundary settlement 1842, with the
exception of twenty-four scattered lots in 1794 (possibly to people
whose application pre-dated 1790).[49] Although the New Brunswick
government was no longer issuing grants in the Upper Saint John
Valley, it did nothing to discourage the extension of settlement. Saint
John Valley settlers petitioned the provincial government for land
until the 1820s, and the provincial surveyor laid out lots and issued
location tickets at Madawaska until the end of the same decade.[150]
No one asked the Natives whose village was located at the confluence of the Saint John and Madawaska rivers their opinion; when
they applied for a grant for the land where the village stood in 1792,
they were turned down.

With rare exceptions, immigrants all came from the Rivière Ouelle-
Kamouraska area. Slightly more than half the couples joined relatives
already established on the Upper Saint John. The others did not last
very long; two thirds of them were gone within five years (as opposed
to 10 per cent of the related migrants). Intermarriage between the children of newcomers or single migrants and charter family members
were the norm.[51] There were two consequences to this process. First,
immigration did not significantly alter the composition of the settlement, which continued to be made of tightly woven clusters of interrelated families.[52] Second, it kept the links between the Madawaska
settlement and the Lower St Lawrence alive.

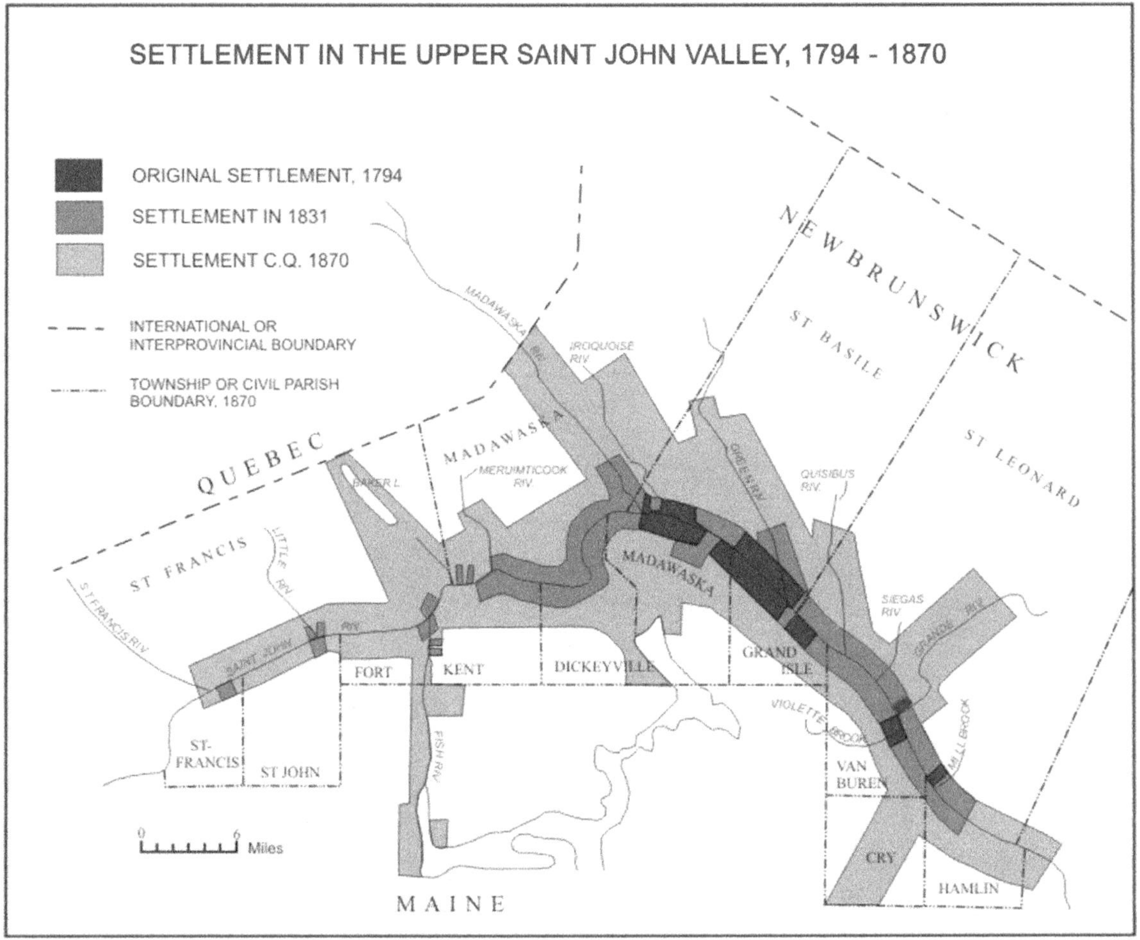

SETTLEMENT IN THE UPPER SAINT JOHN VALLEY, 1794 - 1870

ORIGINAL SETTLEMENT, 1794

SETTLEMENT IN 1831

SETTLEMENT C.Q. 1870

INTERNATIONAL OR INTERPROVINCIAL BOUNDARY

TOWNSHIP OR CIVIL PARISH BOUNDARY, 1870

NEW BRUNSWICK

QUEBEC

MAINE

ST LEONARD

ST BASILE

GRAND

MADAWASKA

DICKEYVILLE

KENT

FORT

ST JOHN

ST-FRANCIS

ST FRANCIS

VAN BUREN

CRY

HAMLIN

MADAWASKA

GREEN RIV

IROQUOISE RIV

MERUMTICOOK RIV

BAKER L

LITTLE RIV

ST.FRANCIS RIV

FISH RIV

VIOLETTE BROOK

QUISIBUS RIV

SIEGAS RIV

GRAND RIV

MILL BROOK

MADAWASKA RIV

0   6
Miles

Map 2

After 1825, this trend changed (see fig. 1). The 1820s and 1830s witnessed the arrival of two large waves of immigrants sandwiching a
short period when the level of outmigration caused the settlement's
population to drop. These brutal fluctuations were a new phenomenon. Until 1825 immigration to the valley had been slow but steady.
But after 1825 additional economic opportunities were available to
newcomers. Not only could they claim a piece of farmland, but they
could work in the lumber camps for wages, or even log on their own
to survive until their farm could support them. Newcomers were no
longer dependent on the good will of the neighbours to tide them over
the difficulties they might encounter in the first years of settlement.

Migrants were more numerous but also much more vulnerable to
economic fluctuations that could affect population growth and movement. The first wave of immigrants followed closely the opening of
lumber camps on the Upper Saint John in the winter of 1824; the
second coincided with the frantic illegal cutting of the late 1830s,
which angered the government of Maine to the point that it sent the
state militia to the valley to put an end to it. The decline of the late
1820s coincided with two, or perhaps three, successive failures of the
wheat crop in 1828, 1829, and possibly 1827.[53] The decline continued
until the disastrous crop failure of 1833. That year immigration
reached its lowest point since 1819, and emigration its highest.[54] In the
1840s the crops failed again,[55] New Brunswick managed to put a halt
to almost all lumbering activities in the disputed territory, and again
immigration declined and emigration increased. Immigrants who
arrived after the 1842 treaty were confronted with an additional
problem: the increasing difficulty in securing good farmland. There
was less to be had and after 1842 it had to be purchased from either the
state or the province.[56] In 1848 the timber market crashed, non-farm
employment in the logging camps became very scarce, and emigration
again exceeded immigration. The slow decline in the population
growth rate and the increased outmigration in the 1850s and 1860s
were very likely the result of the shortage of good farmland. By the
mid-1850s most Maine public land had been purchased by timber
interests, and the remainder was given away to the European and
North American railroad in 1868. Would-be settlers faced two choices:
purchase land from an established farmer, or squat on proprietors'
land. Many squatted. In 1873, 393 families were settled on proprietors
land at the rear of the U.S. treaty lots. Eighty-four of the lots thus occu-

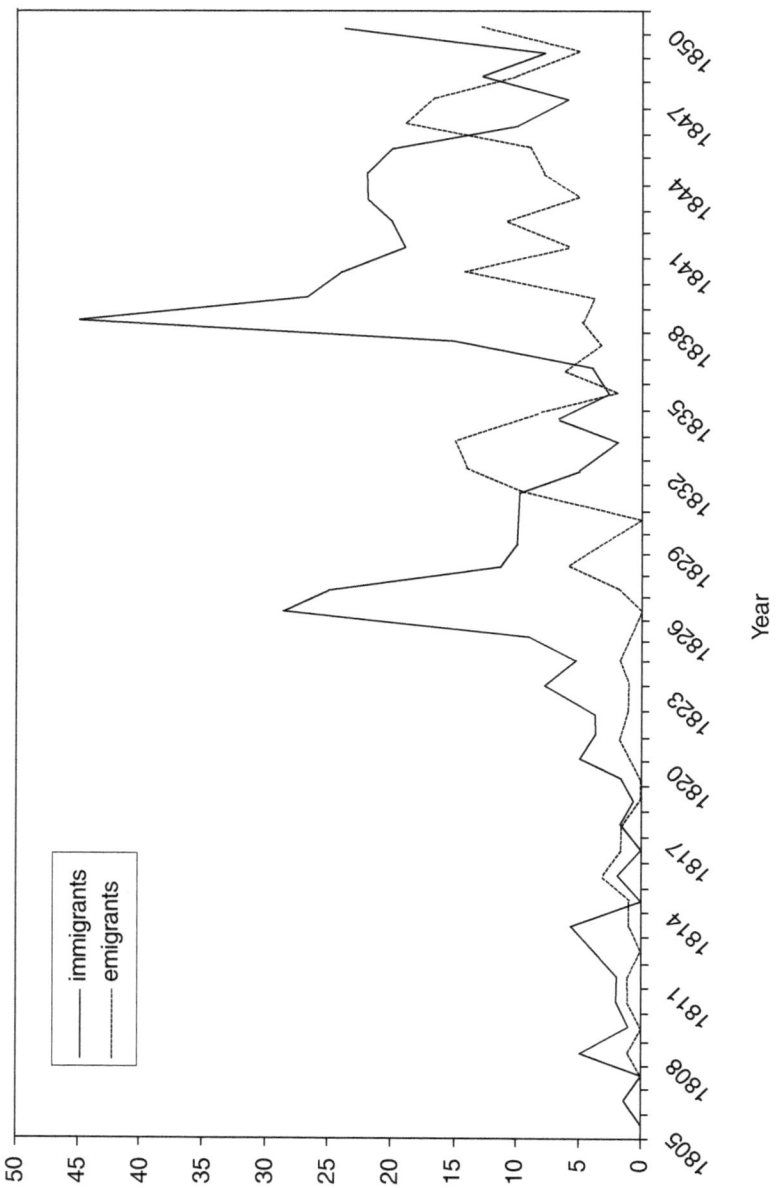

Figure 1. Immigrant and emigrant couples, 1806–50

pied had been taken in the 1840s, 227 in the 1850s and 117 in the 1860s. The extent of the squatting problem highlights the difficulties families met when seeking inexpensive land to farm. But despite the difficulties, the territory's population continued to grow at a respectable rate: it more than doubled between 1830 and 1850, and again between 1850 and 1870. At the end of the period, there were about 14,000 people living in the Saint John Valley.

Despite the coincidence between peaks in the lumber industry and immigration, immigrants were not primarily looking for wage work. If this had been the case, they would have gone back to their parish of origin at the end of the season and left no traces in the record. The local priest, commenting on the large-scale migration of the late 1830s, did not see the newcomers as lumberers, but as people in search of farmland. In 1841 he informed the bishop of Quebec that 'there is still lots of available land along the Saint John River in this parish [Ste Luce], and the first one to take a claim is welcome; he need account for his actions to nobody, so that the population, which numbered 500 souls two years ago, has now reached 850' (my translation).[57] The immigrants whose movements can be documented are couples who stayed long enough to have a baby and be recorded in the parish registers. Almost all of the immigrant families are listed as farmers in the registers, and are found in the various land agent records of the 1830s and 1840s.[58] Contemporaries also noted the connection between local economic conditions, and more particularly the situation in agriculture, and immigration. In 1857, the secretary to the Maine board of agriculture commented that 'the injury which ensued from the early and late frosts from 1842 to 1847 was in many cases of a serious character and had a very discouraging effect upon immigration.'[59]

Communication Networks

Migrations continued to weave connections between the valley and the outside world. The experience of a few individuals who have escaped obscurity show how this worked or how the people in question took advantage of the communication networks thus created. The first example shows that Madawaska people had a good knowledge of geography.

Firmin Cyr was an Acadian from Beaubassin, who moved to Madawaska with his six brothers in the 1780s. He soon married and received a land grant in 1790. One of his daughters, Judith, married at Madawaska in 1813, the last time Firmin, his wife, and their children, Judith excepted, were ever mentioned in local sources.[60] Neither landowner- ship nor family ties could keep Firmin at Madawaska. According to land agents Deane and Kavanagh, Firmin Cyr left the Saint John Valley for Montreal around 1816, after selling his farm to a neighbour.[61] He was between 50 and 60 years of age at the time.[62] Firmin resurfaced ten years later not in Montreal, but in Lacadie, where his son and name- sake married in 1822. In 1825 Firmin was listed in the census of the seigneurie De Lery as living with his son. Some of his other children married at Napierville. Lacadie and Napierville were both parts of the seigneurie De Lery in the Richelieu Valley, and had been partly settled by Acadian deportees returning from Pennsylvania and New York, including some Beaubassin families.[63] This raises an intriguing ques- tion: How did Firmin and his family know about this distant Acadian community where a fair number of their Beaubassin cousins had rebuilt their lives? The information had obviously travelled over long distance. There is evidence Madawaska residents were in contact with the wider world at an even early date. In January 1809 the Madawaska parish priest missed the courier and had two of his parishioners going to Niagara drop his letter at the bishop's house in Quebec on their way.[64] Madawaska settlers knew about Upper Canada, and thus must have known about other places in between. Individuals could connect distant settlements.

A better understanding of the mechanisms through which infor- mation travelled over long distances can be had thanks to the corre- spondence between the various members of the Audibert family, and the circular migrations of their neighbour Jacques Hamel. Charlotte, Marie, and Elizabeth Audibert were the daughters of a downwardly mobile farmer from Ile d'Orléans who died a day labourer in Quebec City. The sisters lived in St Roch in the 1840s and married respec- tively a carpenter (Joseph Levêque), a shoemaker (Charles Beaupré), and a day labourer (Jean Baptiste Blouin). Their brother Joseph, also a carpenter, established himself at Madawaska in 1847, where he married Marguerite, the daughter of Thomas (Chrysostome) Martin and Marie Luce Cyr, both of Acadian ancestry. He died ten years later, of unknown causes. Joseph was well-educated and bilingual. He wrote a beautiful hand, spelled perfectly in French and almost perfectly in English, and knew the rules of French grammar. The sisters' letters and the one by Charles Beaupré display the same characteristics.[65]

Although the sisters were of very modest means, they took a vacation in 1854 to visit their brother at Madawaska. Clearly travelling and visiting was not limited to the middle and upper class. As the quote at the beginning of the chapter shows, the sisters knew enough people travelling back and forth that they did not to have to correspond to exchange news. Correspondence was not limited to family news either. Charles Beaupré's one and only letter, written to Joseph Audibert and dated 29 October 1854 shortly after the sisters' return home, was all business (my translation):

Dear Sir, please inform M. Martin senior that flour currently sells for 9 a quart; one is under the impression the price will go down in a few days. Please let me know whether M. Nadeau [husband to one of Marguerite Audibert sisters, an inn- and storekeeper] is satisfied with the goods I sent him per your order. I would like to know whether the stuff [fabric] was of adequate width for the use he has of it.

The lath M. Blouin mentioned to you is ready, and we are waiting for the first suitable opportunity to ship it to Rivière du Loup, and as soon as it will be loaded to go down, I will let you know. I will send it care of Mr. George Pelletier, Merchant [at Rivière du Loup]

I remain your devoted servant.

Charles Beaupré.

This short letter provides a lot of information. First, if Beaupré wrote it himself, he was extremely well educated, like his brother-in-law. Second, it reads like a merchant's letter, but Beaupré was no merchant. The letter shows that shoemakers, men plying a poor man's trade, could gather mercantile information and engage in business transactions on behalf of less well-located relatives, or even relatives of relatives. Day labourers knew how to send cargo and where. Nadeau, an innkeeper in a very remote place used a brother-in-law who knew a brother-in-law to acquire trade goods. Thomas Martin, a successful but illiterate farmer similarly used family connections to keep track of the price of agricultural commodities in an important marketplace. He presumably wanted to know how much he could expect to pay for his flour, and when was the best time to buy.

Individuals with relatives outside Madawaska could act as conduits for information between the settlement and the rest of the world. Jacques Hamel's life shows that contacts could be even more direct: he was a circular migrant. He was also the schoolteacher Thomas and

Marie Luce Martin turned to when they wanted to send letters to their son-in-law who was in Portland in the summer of 1852. Hamel did not always live at Madawaska, and was not always a white-collar worker. The previous January, a Lower Canada census taker had found him in St Roch, Quebec City's shipbuilding district. Hamel, listed as born in Quebec on 13 August 1806, was a carpenter. He lived in a wooden, two-storey, single family house with his wife Suzanne Long, born in Madawaska in December 1808, and their six children: Josephine, born in 1833 in Quebec City; Jacques, a cabinetmaker's apprentice born in 1836; Edmond (b. 1838); Hilaire (b. 1842); and Marie (b. 1845), all natives of Madawaska. Baby Eléonore, however, had been born in Quebec City in July 1850. The couple had also lost a child in 1851 in Rivière du Loup.[66]

Hamel, like Audibert and Beaupré, was a craftsman, and like Audibert he was splendidly literate. He was also very mobile, like his wife Suzanne. She had lost her parents, who lived at Madawaska, when still in her teens. Instead of moving in with one of her Madawaska older brothers, she found her way to Quebec City, her mother's hometown. There, she met and married Jacques Hamel in 1832. The couple then moved back and forth between Quebec City and Madawaska but they came back to the valley permanently after 1852 where they had two more children, in 1854 and 1856. Suzanne died in 1861 and Hamel in 1865, at age 54. Hamel apparently plied different trades in different places – schoolmaster in the country, carpenter in the city – and had his son learn a semi-luxury trade: cabinetmaking (*ébenisterie*).

Geographically mobile men like Jacques Hamel were probably not rare; what is rare is to find the proof of their existence. Similar links between Madawaska and other areas (Nova Scotia, southern Maine, Wisconsin, and other Great Lakes regions) occasionally surface in the parish registers, or in the register of the deeds when an individual who had moved elsewhere had given a third party power of attorney to sell his land. People moved away from Madawaska at a relatively early period and relocated at sometimes considerable distance. If we exclude migrations to industrial centres in southern Maine and New England, however, they seem to have ended up in areas very similar to what the Saint John Valley had been a generation or two previously: heavily forested frontiers, with plenty of land available for farmers. In one of the two letters he sent his son-in-law, Thomas Martin expresses his sorrow at some of his children's plans. They were suffering from 'Bourbonnais fever,' and planned to emigrate if they could sell their farm for a good price. Bourbonnais, in Illinois, was a magnet for French-Canadian migration and could still boast a population of identifiable French-Canadian origins between the two World Wars.[67] What the stories of the Audibert and Hamel families shows, is that lower class, literate, or not, people travelled, sometimes for no better reason than a visit, and that they corresponded with each other. Information could travel far, and was not limited to family news. Lower Canada and New Brunswick appear to have been overlaid by a gossamer web of communications, which left only tenuous traces in the historical sources. Kinship could knit distant regions together; it could also connect different spheres of activity. Firmin Cyr may merely have been an early example of the impact of such networks. One of the prerequisites to the emergence of competitive markets is a reasonably free flow of information. Cyr and the Audibert and Hamel families show that this flow existed and could penetrate remote regions.

Stratification and Segmentation

British agronomer J.F.W. Johnston, who criss-crossed the province in 1850 to evaluate its farming potential at the demand of the provincial government, noticed the distinction English-speaking provincials made between the 'fine Acadians' and the 'beggarly' French Canadians. His own opinion of the French Canadians was not much better: they were squatters and 'both needy and indifferent farmers'.[68] Johnston's and the provincials' distinction between Acadian and French-Canadian Madawaska residents was a recent but increasingly common phenomenon in midcentury. Earlier accounts of the settlement had not distinguished between the two groups, nor ranked them in terms of status.[69] The comments reflected a genuine change: the homogeneous, tightly knit community of the first generation had given way to a heterogeneous and stratified one. The forest industry was the main force behind this change: it allowed poor men without relatives in the settlement to move to the Upper Saint John, start a farm, and survive. Before 1825, slightly more than half the couples who migrated to Madawaska joined at least one already established relative.[70] By the late 1840s, barely a quarter were in that situation. Even so, unrelated migrants were much more likely to stay at Madawaska than their counterparts in the previous generation. Only one third of the post-1825 unrelated migrants left within five years, half the proportion of the first quarter of the century.

Persistence nonetheless did not translate into integration or equality. After 1830 newcomers and their descendents were generally worse off than members of the charter families. By midcentury most of them constituted a distinct and visibly poorer socio-economic stratum. A survey conducted in 1833 to ascertain the needs of the settlers in the midst of particularly disastrous crop failures highlights their poverty and vulnerability.[71] The document enumerates 403 families. All claimed land, except 27 tenants, only 2 of whom were locally born. Of the 32 male family heads listed as labourers, 85 per cent of them were immigrants. Male immigrants headed 168 families, half of them identified as destitute and in need of immediate assistance. Only a quarter of the families headed by a founder or one of his descendents were in that predicament. Immigrants had less stock, less crops, or no crops at all. Thirty years later, in 1860–1, non-charter family members were still poorer. The 1860 U.S. and 1861 New Brunswick censuses give the value of real estate owned by the people enumerated, the only time real estate values are given in a New Brunswick or Canadian census. Table 2 shows how farm values were distributed according to the status of the owners. Members of the charter families were still considerably better off than immigrants and their descendants.[72] Three-quarters of the non-charter families had farms worth less than $500; 55 per cent of the charter families' farms were worth at least this amount. (The wealth difference was not age linked; similar results occur if one controls for age.)

Charter families became more and more endogamous. Before 1825 two-thirds of the non-locally born individuals married at Madawaska had married into one of the charter families After 1825 most of them did not, and members of the charter families were three times less likely to marry an outsider than before. Their increased endogamy bordered on the incestuous. After 1825 half the marriages between charter family members were marriages of cousins. Before, the proportion had only been one in four. And this occurred despite strong resistance from the Church, and increased opportunities to marry outside the kin group.[73] By midcentury, some couples needed two, three, or even four Church dispensations to marry (meaning they were cousins in two, three, or four different ways). Members of the charter families stuck to their own. By the end of the period reduced immigration and increased emigration among locally born males again facilitated the blending of the two groups. The proportion of households headed by a male and a female who were both born in Canada dropped by half between 1850 and 1870. Only 7 per cent of the households listed in the 1870 U.S. census or the 1871 Canadian one, had children born in Canada, as opposed to one-quarter in 1831. 'Outsiders' were more and more likely to have grown up in the valley, and their pedigree was probably not the social handicap it once had been.

English-speaking migrants blended even less, separated by religion and occupation. The Anglo-Protestants who migrated to the Upper Saint John Valley from the late 1810s onward, did so for economic reasons like the French Canadians, but they migrated under professional, not family auspices. In the late 1810s and early 1820s, Anglo-Protestant immigrants to the valley sought lumber and acquired land incidentally. Between 1816 and the late 1820s, a dozen or so New Englanders, some with their families, settled west of the French, between the Meruimticook and the St Francis Rivers. The Bakers were among the first members of that group. Most Americans migrants were originally from southern Maine, like the Bakers, but some came from further afield: Charles McPherson was from Rhode Island; Jesse Wheelock from Northborough, Massachusetts. Some moved directly to the Upper Saint John; others followed a more circuitous route. John Baker first went to Chaleur Bay; Wheelock initially settled at Saint John, New Brunswick, and owned a share in a vessel. There he may have met Barnabas Hunnewell, another Kennebec man, who spent the early 1820s in the port city before moving to the Upper Saint John. McPherson came to the Saint John Valley via the Restigouche, another New Brunswick lumbering region.[74]

After the signing of the 1842 treaty, Anglo-Protestant immigrants were entrepreneurs or would-be entrepreneurs. Some moved closer to the operations they financed, like provincial John Glazier, Maine's Shepard Cary, or the Jewetts, from Bangor and Saint John. Some of those men lived in the Saint John Valley, but their stays were usually not permanent. Others came as employees, became partners, and finally set up shop on their own, like Mainer Samuel Stevens. Born in 1819, he came to Fort Kent in 1845 to work as a clerk in the Jewett and March hotel and bought the hotel and the store adjoining it in 1848. Stevens ran the hotel until his death, and let the store to rent. New Brunswicker George Seeley is another example of this type of migrant. He came to the Saint John Valley to work as a clerk, first for John Glazier, who ran a store ten miles above Fort Kent on the Canadian side, then for John Gilman of Fort Kent. By 1860 Seeley was operating a store on Stevens's property. In 1862 he went into lumbering as well, and in 1866 acquired a mill on the east side of the Fish River, as well as two townships' worth of timberland.[75]

These men were unexceptional in many respects. Their brief biographies in Wiggin's *History of Aroostook* resemble those of the first settlers in most Aroostook county communities included in this volume: they came from southern Maine, sometimes from Massachusetts, sometimes from New Hampshire or New Brunswick. They may have come directly from their place of origin to northern Maine, or they may have wandered around, but always in regions involved in the timber trade. They settled in areas with few or no permanent residents, built mills, brought in shingle and clapboard machines, opened stores and taverns, and provided the nucleus of the new settlements. They usually combined farming with their other activities. They may have gone into partnership with others, and their partners may have been provincial men. Most of those men came after the resolution of the boundary dispute; the Baker Brook New Englanders were only noteworthy for the precocity of their endeavours.[76]

The men who founded an establishment in the eastern part of the valley followed the same pattern. Abraham Close Hammond was the son of a Planter who received a grant in Kingsclear in 1799 and thus became neighbours with Acadians coming back from Madawaska.[77] Abraham first kept a store in Fredericton. When it burned in 1825, he moved to Andover, New Brunswick, where he and his brother had farmed and lumbered together. He moved from Andover to what would become Van Buren in the early 1840s and died at Van Buren in 1884. His brother Charles had moved to Grand Falls, the gate to the Madawaska settlement, where he ran a hotel and became a justice of the peace and a member of the provincial parliament. Abraham's only surviving son, Charles Frederick, went clerking for his uncle Charles when he was sixteen. Five years later, he was hired by W. Cunliffe of Fort Kent to work in his lumber store. He then moved back to Van Buren, where he worked for William Cook Hammond (a brother to his father's first wife), who made a living as a farmer, lumberer, lumber manufacturer, and merchant. In 1870, he went into business for himself, after marrying William Cook's daughter.[78]

Moves to the Saint John Valley could be deliberate, as in the case of the men mentioned above, but they could also be accidental. This was the case of I.H. Page, who followed his father, a member of the U.S. military stationed at Fort Kent, as a young lad, clerked for different local businessmen between 1856 and 1865, worked for Seeley (who had married his sister), and finally became his partner until his death in 1874.[79] Finally, some men moved because they were forced to. Major William Dickey first came to Fort Kent and bought a mill, because he suffered from lung problems and believed the northern air would cure him. In 1854 he moved to Massachusetts where he opened a sash and doors works. Unfortunately, the factory burned two years later and Dickey came back to Fort Kent to try to rebuild his fortune. He died at Madawaska, after becoming a successful local businessman and politician.[80] One local township was briefly named Dickeyville after him. Although some of the Anglo-Protestant merely passed through, many, like Page, Cunliffe, and Hammond, sunk permanent roots in the Saint John Valley. They and some of their descendants are buried either in the Van Buren protestant cemetery, or in the tiny graveyard which surrounds the Fort Kent Congregational Church. These men engaged in a mix of activities, which included farming, lumbering, lumber, shingle, and clapboard manufacturing, hotel and storekeeping. They met with varying degrees of success. Some became elected representatives or were appointed to official positions. Although partnerships developed between Provincials and Americans, the Americans seem to have preferred to join forces with other Americans. The same may have been true of marriage, although in the absence of records, it is necessary to fall back on graveyard inscriptions and genealogies to find out who was married to whom. Provincials appear to have preferred to marry Provincials and Yankees other Americans.[81] There is also no evidence that the Anglo-Protestants and the French went into business together. As for the occasional unions between Anglo-Protestant men and French women, they involved men who were farmers. Their children grew up Catholic and French, even if the couple had not married in the Catholic Church. Otherwise, the members of the Anglo-Protestant business community did not marry into the French population, and this reinforced their aloofness from the rest of the Madawaska population.

Conclusion

Although distant from other settled areas, Madawaska was neither isolated nor insulated from the outside world. It was not an island in the wilderness, but a way station on a major communication artery, the equivalent of a village at the foot of a ramp off highway 401. Its natural resources were known to all who had travelled the Saint John-Temiscouata route, but also to those who had contacts with those travellers.

Word of mouth brought to the Upper Saint John distinct categories of individuals who may have faced different 'pushes,' but all were pulled to a greater or lesser extent by the economic opportunities the region presented. Acadians and French Canadians were looking for land. Outside economic interests seeking to exploit the local forest resources soon intruded in their life. The forest industry triggered a boundary dispute whose resolution imposed on some of the settlers a nationality not of their own choosing; it disrupted earlier patterns of migration and social organization; and by midcentury the Madawaska population had become both segmented along linguistic and religious lines and stratified according to ancestry. But with the obvious exception of the Acadians, members of the various groups kept their connections with their communities of origin alive, and kept the region at the heart of continent-wide webs.

The Acadians were the first to come. They could easily be cast as hapless victims of imperial wars and revolutions. One should, however, be rid of the Evangeline syndrome once and for all. The Acadians were victimized, but refused to be victims, and they were rather good at this. The founding of the Madawaska settlement exemplifies the remarkable ability of a people caught in events beyond their power to keep some degree of control over their own fate: the Acadians were not knocked about like so many billiard balls. Like most eighteenth-century migrants, the Acadians wanted land for themselves and their sons (and occasionally daughters). More specifically, they wanted something that had eluded them since 1715: clear title to the land they occupied. Like most Catholics, they wanted their own resident priest. They also appear to have wanted to remain among themselves, possibly to preserve existing kin networks and a familiar way of life (another common motivation among migrants). This can explain their eagerness to sell their holdings interspersed among Loyalist land grants.

The Madawaska founders were strikingly similar to their contemporaries in western New York as described by Alan Taylor, or to the New Englanders who had moved to Nova Scotia or southern Maine a generation before. The migrations to Nova Scotia had been organized affairs like the Acadian migration to the Upper Saint John. The Planters, as they came to be known, sent agents to investigate prospective settlements, and commonly sent a vanguard to start the new establishment, the rest of the families following when shelters had been erected and enough land cleared to survive. Planter migration also received the encouragement and assistance of the government. Settlement of land hungry people by governments to establish juris- diction or for defence purposes was nothing new either; New England authorities had pursued this strategy since the seventeenth century. Migrations to southern Maine in the 1760s and to western New York a generation later may have been less organized and did not attract such a degree of government solicitude. The goals of the migrants – land for themselves and for their children, and reliance on kin networks for safety – were, however, features they shared with the Planters and the Madawaska founders.[82]

The Acadians easily integrated their Lower Canadian cousins into their community, but were much less welcoming to unrelated immi- grants. In the early years, the latter rarely lasted longer than a few years. The pioneer generation also relied extensively upon mutual help among close relatives to improve the land and survive the farm- building years. Neither social exclusiveness nor co-operation turned the territory into a parochial, inward-looking settlement. The Acadians and the French-Canadian cousins who joined them in the eighteenth century believed in family-based mutuality, but they were also very much aware of the potential offered by commercial exchanges through their own ventures, like Cormier and Thibodeau, or through their dealings with the likes of Simonds, Hazen, and White. Migrations created resilient networks of families that spread beyond the bound- aries of the valley or of any given locality. In return, those networks channelled further movements of population, as well as the circulation of information towards the valley.

The motivations of the Lower Canadians who followed the forest industry to the Saint John Valley were more narrowly economic than those of the Acadians. They sought wage work and land, and tolerated not having title to the land they occupied. They were also a fairly foot- loose population, who left as easily as they had come when economic conditions became unfavourable. The generation of charter family males who came of age at the time of the 1842 treaty resembled them. At a time when the 'Ohio fever' swept Maine, they were seized by the 'Bourbonnais fever.' Those were men and women who did not seek security in their social and family networks, but in freeholds on a fron- tier – any frontier. They had become individualistic. Those who stayed behind circled the wagons against the interlopers. By midcentury, an extremely close-knit core of charter families, usually labelled Acadians irrespective of their ancestry, had emerged as the 'better sort': long established, monopolizing old British grants, wealthier, they appeared far more respectable to visitors than the poorer late-comers. The lumber industry had made it easier for Lower Canadians to resettle at Madawaska, but did not facilitate their integration into the existing community.

The forest industry also weakened the valley's homogeneous French character. Like the French migrants, English-speaking settlers sought and found economic opportunities, but in trade rather than in farming. They did not integrate into the French community at all. Language, and more importantly religion, were insuperable barriers. The New Englanders and the Provincials appear to have lived side by side, despite a common language and a common Protestantism. By mid-century, the Madawaska population had become both segmented along linguistic and religious lines and stratified according to ancestry.

By the time of the 1842 treaty, a desire for economic advancement could be found among the members of all groups living at Mada-waska: charter families ('Acadians'), French Canadians, and English speakers, whether American citizens or British subjects. The fact that the valley continued to be a 'world without borders' after 1842 made it easier for these people to achieve their goals. Family networks in the case of the French and commercial ones in the case of the Anglophones doubled as communication networks between the valley, Lower Canada, New Brunswick, New England, and even points beyond. Information, a prerequisite to the free circulation of goods and people, could and did travel, through the mail and through word of mouth. The valley was also integrated into larger economic and political entities through the actions of ambitious individuals who acted as ties between their community and the world beyond.

2 Principal Men

I have made Mercure very happy by giving him the island he so much wished for; it gives me pleasure to have in my power to assist men of merit and those who behaved well during the late Rebellion, but particularly those recommended by your Excellency.

Governor Parr to Sir Frederick Haldimand, 14 January 1784[1]

Men of merit, especially when recommended by high-ranking government officials, deserved rewards and assistance. Rewards were not solely symbolic; Governor Parr was allocating economic assets to government favourites – and islands in the Saint John were coveted grazing grounds. Many members of the Loyalist elite shared a belief in the superiority of a hierarchical society characterized by deference and paternalism, and by control of the uneducated masses by men from the elite.[2] The notion that privileged men and their clients should have privileged access to economic resources and opportunities was not unique to British governors and Tories. The turn-of-the-century Maine Great Proprietors investigated by Alan Taylor readily agreed with this philosophy. They believed that their claims to the land and to the increase in value brought by clearing it were stronger than the claims of the men and women who had settled it. They also believed that the profits from trading rightfully belonged to them, or at least to men of their own choosing. Settlers who insisted on trading independently were interlopers, trespassing on their betters' economic preserves.[3]

Nonetheless the post-revolutionary frontier teemed with individuals determined not to stay in their place: petty speculators, small scale merchants, and local entrepreneurs – often one and the same people. These 'Principal Men' also acted, or tried to act, as agents of their community and as intermediaries between their neighbours, the outside world, and higher authorities. They were the men Taylor describes as able to 'take out the most strategic economic positions on the frontier, to emerge as the mediators between, on the one hand, their neighbours as small producers, on the other hand, external markets and suppliers of trade goods. Such a man could expect in time, a coveted appointment by the governor and council [...] He became a political mediator between his neighbours and the Commonwealth's rulers.'[4]

Individual ambitions and the elite's understanding of the natural ordering of society often clashed. Late eighteenth- and early nineteenth-century leading men have generated opposing reactions from historians and contemporaries. Historians may be inclined to view these men in positive terms as useful, if not necessary, agents of development. The men themselves probably thought of themselves in those terms. Contemporaries, especially members of the elite, were ambivalent. William Cooper of Cooperstown fame, an archetypal 'principal man,' elicited mixed feelings from the better sort of New Yorkers he hoped to join. Admired for his initial successes, despised for his lack of breeding and his rapid upward mobility, he was deserted at the first opportunity, probably with a sigh of relief, by his Federalist patrons.[5]

Men such as Timothy Dwight, a crusty Federalist and president of Yale, were uncompromisingly negative. 'Another evil [...] is found in the character and influence of many of those who are considered as principal men in every newly settled country. Among those, not a small number have arisen to importance merely by their wealth. Adventurous at an early period, and sagacious in discovering those means of acquiring properties which are always opened by circumstances in the progress of civilization. They bought lands cheap and sold them dear; and by dealing largely in this profitable commodity came suddenly in the possession of great estates.'[6]

Dwight's principal men were parasitical speculators whose undeserved wealth allowed them to assume equally undeserved social positions. They disrupted society's natural hierarchy, and if they could not be eliminated, they should at least be neutralized. Before its pine forests attracted the attention of entrepreneurs tied to the Atlantic economy, Madawaska could boast a few 'principal men' cast in this pre-industrial mode. This first generation of Madawaska's principal men more closely fit Dwight's description than Taylor's. Their role as economic intermediaries between their neighbours and the outside economy was not key to their success. The five groups of men discussed in this chapter strove to improve their material conditions, but often did so through speculation. They acquired wealth as a means to achieve social prominence and owed their success to the protection of powerful men with political connections. The first generation of Madawaska principal men were clients who tried to become local patrons, a fact that did not necessarily endear them to either their betters or their neighbours. They were not men who would deliberately promote free markets; they were more likely to view trade in the same way as the capitalists described by Fernand Braudel – an activity to be manipulated and reserved for the members of a clique. Yet despite the contempt they may have earned and their limited roles as economic intermediaries, they acted as important linchpins, familiarizing their community with the surrounding political and legal culture and helping it integrate into the larger body politic.

Frontier Hustler: Pierre Duperré

'Sir – after paying you my respects, I shall be very glad if our jurisdiction be enforced as usual in Madawaska,' wrote militia captain Pierre Duperré to New Brunswick Judge Bliss in September 1818. Duperré was reporting the arrival of American interlopers on territory claimed by the province. He concluded with an offer of services: 'I hope that your honour will be pleased to have me in your consideration relating this matter.'[7] If Duperré was hoping to be instructed to handle the problem, he was mistaken. He was asked rather curtly to submit a detailed report and once this was done, was ignored by the authorities.

In his letter Duperré clearly tried to curry favour with the Fredericton authorities. Some power to deal with the American problem could have enhanced his status in the community – at any rate it would have enhanced Duperré's opinion of himself. Duperré spent much of his adult life acting as the mouthpiece and deputy for his community, whether his neighbours wanted his services or not. Twenty years previously he had risen to the defence of New Brunswick interests against the encroachment of an outside power, in that case his native province of Lower Canada. Then, as in 1818, his motives were suspect.

Hold-up on the Saint John

Duperré's earlier incident is part of the historical record – the aggrieved party sued, brought numerous witnesses to the trial, and the trial transcripts have survived.[8] The protagonists were the Robichaud brothers and their hired hands on one side and Augustin Dubé, Pierre Duperré, and some of their men on the other. Anselme and Michel Robichaud were merchants at Rivière des Caps, situated just below the mouth of the Temiscouata portage on the St Lawrence River. Their family tree included three governors of Old Acadia. The family had a long history of trading with the Saint John River Natives, and we encountered Robichaud père trading with Hazen and White in chapter 1.[9] The brothers' suppliers in Quebec were Fraser and Young, a large merchant firm, who obtained several fur trading licences on their behalf in 1789.[10] One licence allowed them to take three canoes and three men to the Saint John River to trade merchandise including 30 gallons of rum or brandy, 20 gallons of wine, 12 guns, 200 pounds of gun powder, 6 hundredweight of shot, and other merchandise to a total of £200 and 15 shillings currency.[11]

Duperré's history was less illustrious. His first cousin, Jean Baptiste Duperré, was a leading man in Rivière Ouelle: merchant, major of the militia, and agent for the seigneuresse.[12] Pierre unfortunately came from the empty-pocketed side of the family. His father, who died when he was five, left him with very little.[13] Pierre Duperré managed to pick up a good education somewhere; his penmanship, grammar, and composition skills were excellent. Around 1779 Duperré became a partner to one of the Robichauds' competitors, the newly arrived Alexander McLennan. Although the partnership was officially terminated the same year, Duperré being in charge with collecting the debts from Natives and French clients from Temiscouta to the mouth of the Saint John River, the two men appear to have continued doing business together on an informal basis. Duperré was one of the first white residents of the Upper Saint John. Around 1783, with his thirteen-year-old half-brother, Pierre Lizotte, Duperré (who was 24 at the time) started a trading post on the Saint John River.[14] In 1784 the store generated £240 of profit. Duperré purchased a tract of land at the entrance to the grand portage in 1785. By 1789 McLennan was bankrupt and Duperré was challenging the Robichauds' right to trade on the Upper Saint John.[15]

In May 1789, Duperré and his next door neighbour and former McLennan employee, Augustin Dubé, intercepted a Robichaud canoe under false pretences and refused to release the goods, claiming that the Robichauds' licence was invalid. Duperré and his confederates (who included Louis Mercure) also managed to prevent the other Robichaud men from trading with the Natives. In July 1789 Louis Mercure, Duperré, and Costin, the justice of the peace appointed by Governor Carleton, petitioned the New Brunswick authorities for a judge and a militia captain at Madawaska as protection against shady deals by Canadian merchants who were retailing liquor to the Natives. Needless to say, the Robichauds were less and less amused. In August, they sued Duperré and Dubé for loss of trade. Duperré and Dubé argued that the Quebec Court of Common Pleas had no jurisdiction over the area, as it was part of New Brunswick. Rubbish, replied the judge, the licence proves jurisdiction. Duperré and Dubé were found guilty in September 1790 and damages were estimated by an arbitrator in January 1791. In November 1791 the *Quebec Gazette* carried notice of the sale by the sheriff of Duperré's land at Madawaska. Interestingly, that summer Thomas Costin had informed executive council member Edward Winslow that he had fined the Robichauds £5 for causing a disturbance and for selling liquor to the Natives.[16]

Local militia captains François and Jacques Cyr were charged with the duty of seizing and auctioning Duperré's property.[17] They had been appointed by Governor General Lord Dorchester. Duperré sued the Cyrs for unlawful seizure of his property, again arguing that the governor of Quebec had no jurisdiction over New Brunswick territory. Jacques Cyr (the former pilot) also seized goods belonging to Duperré's neighbour, François Albert, who had been successfully sued for debts by the Robichauds. Thomas Costin arrested Cyr and jailed him at the garrison at Grand Falls. Cyr had to compensate Albert to secure his release, and was subsequently reimbursed by the Quebec government.[18] Dorchester thought the best way to avoid such problems in the future was for him and the New Brunswick governor to appoint the same men as militia officers and magistrates. However, only Carleton signed Duperré's commission as captain of the militia. Duperré also became commissioner of the highways and overseer of the poor.

This episode is interesting for several reasons. First, it shows that the fur trade was not a marginal activity. The Robichauds were licensed to trade £200 of goods with the Saint John River Native people; they also received £800 worth of merchandise from their suppliers, Young and Fraser of Quebec City, and received an additional £900 the following year. The Lower Saint John Acadians had been accustomed to trade through their relationship with Simonds and Hazen; the Lower St Lawrence inhabitants may similarly have come in contact with the world of goods through partners of Fraser and Young, such as the Robichauds.

Second, the Native people were also familiar with this world of goods. They obtained guns and ammunition from the traders, which they used for hunting moose, and they exchanged the hides for consumer products. According to testimony, the Robichauds' intercepted canoes contained scarlet and green cloth, printed and paisley calico, silk kerchiefs, and silver jewellery called *argenterie sauvage*. One wonders what the Madawaska settlers themselves wore. Were they satisfied with homespun when the *'sauvages'* were parading around and attending their church clad in broadcloth and silk and adorned with silver? The fur trade and its impact on the Natives' appearance could have spurred on the Madawaska settlers to find something to trade in order not to appear more primitive than the 'primitives.' No one wanted to be upstaged in the fashion department by those deemed social inferiors – it was enough to send a person moose hunting.

Frontier Speculator

Duperré's eagerness to defend New Brunswick jurisdiction over the Madawaska territory appears to have been a justification after the fact. The Robichaud misadventures look very much like a turf war. It is unclear whether Duperré traded under licence, as the lists of licences for eastern Quebec and New Brunswick are extremely incomplete. His behaviour towards the Robichauds, however, raises some doubts. Ensuring that Lower Canada had no jurisdiction over the territory was a way for him to bypass the licencing problem. From that moment on, Duperré seized every opportunity to reassert New Brunswick jurisdiction over Madawaska. In 1795 he led a group of nineteen Acadian freeholders to the polling station. The men were told they would have to take oaths contrary to their Catholic faith in order for their votes to be counted. Duperré later said that he had secured a translation of the oaths and had concluded that they were acceptable to him and to the other Acadians. He then sent a petition on behalf of the entire group (but bearing only his signature) to the legislative assembly, requesting that their votes be counted as entered in the poll book. The province had not yet decided whether Catholics should be allowed to vote, and so took no action.[19] The Upper Saint John Valley settlers petitioned again after the 1803 elections, this time protesting that no poll had been erected within a reasonable distance of their settlement. The two petitions, witnessed by Duperré, contain exactly the same number of signature – twenty – suggesting that they were signed by Duperré's two militia companies.[20]

This incident took place against the backdrop of a mounting opposition to Carleton's policies by landowners and traders alike. Carleton, among his other sins, was accused of having planted a settlement and established a garrison above Grand Falls for no useful purpose, but at great cost to the provincial treasury.[21] The man who turned the Acadians away from the poll was no less than Stair Agnew, a leading member of the opposition to Carleton. One suspects that the Acadians did not vote for him; their vote would then have mattered. Their turning up at the poll also brought to the forefront the pesky issue of the Catholic vote.

Duperré was no frontier farmer. He pursued every possible opportunity to enrich himself and capitalize on his personal assets in order to rise in the social hierarchy. Duperré keeps appearing in the sources, in part because he was literate, and in part because he was a frontier hustler. Besides his lot 38 opposite the Madawaska River, he also claimed the landing site at The Grand Falls.[22] When it was taken away from him in 1790 to erect a military post (Fort Carleton), he was given his choice of land in compensation. In 1796 he selected five hundred acres six miles above the falls and far from the nearest settlement, close to or including Six-Mile Brook. The place may have been a millsite or important for the Indian trade. He sold it in 1802 for £15. Duperré benefited from the building of Fort Carleton in other ways, as the construction crews used his boat.[23] In 1800 Duperré filed a more than usually fawning petition, asking to be given a grant for 'Indian improvements' at the junction of the Madawaska and Saint John River. The piece of property was ideally situated for an inn or a trading post. Its proprietors 'hath proposed and offered freely of their own accord to sell and dispose to your petitioner' wrote Duperré, 'finding and seeing that the said improvements is of no benefit to their persons by reason that it is not in their power to secure the same from the destroying of the grain every year by the inhabitants' cattle.' How much truth there is in Duperré's statement is anybody's guess. Duperré thought he could improve his own claim by pointing out to the council that 'the said people are destitute of ability and incapable of acting in their own light.' Council took Duperré's story at face value – their summary reads 'ask for land sold to him by the Indians at Madawaska' – but did not give him the grant. It is doubtful the decision was to protect the Natives' interests.[24]

In 1808, Duperré sold a grist- and sawmill he had acquired from Mercure a few years previously for what must have looked like the astronomical sum of £610 9s. The buyers were both merchants, Peter Fraser in Fredericton and John Robinson in Saint John.[25] By his own account, Fraser had been acquainted with Duperré since 1784 and with the Madawaska settlement since 1791 or 1792. He made sure that the Madawaska settlers were given the right to vote and, in return, they voted for him.[26] Fraser, a member of the legislative assembly after 1809, was also a militia officer and a vice-president of the Bank of New Brunswick. As he was one of the major fur traders and fur exporters in the province, it would make sense that Duperré would have done business with him, especially if he had burned his bridges in Lower Canada. Fraser would have been a powerful patron because of his personal connections. He was in partnership with Provincial Treasurer John Robinson's between 1801 and 1806, and the two men continued to collaborate later.[27] The Madawaska mill may have been one of their joint ventures. Fraser provided supplies to the British and American teams who surveyed the boundary before 1820. He was also the major of the 4th battalion of the York militia, which included the Saint John Valley French of which Duperré was a captain.[28] Duperré, who could have retired after selling his mills, engaged in another speculative venture in 1814 as Fraser's confederate. He and sixteen other Madawaska residents applied for and received grants at the confluence of the Aroostook and Saint John Rivers. Fraser soon after purchased the lots of the grantees. Most received £10 for their claim; Duperré walked away with £100. In all, Fraser acquired 3,200 acres of prime timberland for £300.[29] Having upheld New Brunswick's rights over the Madawaska Territory in 1790 although for highly interested reasons, Duperré continued to defend his adopted province against outside encroachments. He reported the arrival of Americans in the western part of the valley as soon as they dropped their luggage. His offer of services, however, merely elicited a request for additional information.[30]

Duperré was a high-profile man in his community, not only because of his business and speculative ventures and his militia captaincy, but also because he was one of the few literate Madawaska residents. He penned petitions, witnessed formal acts, brought batches of deeds to be registered at the county registry office in Fredericton, and on occasion acted as estate administrator and will executor. His services were not always welcome. In 1803 Firmin Cyr's widow wrote to the surrogate judge to ask if Duperré had a right to take letters of administration for the estate of a man who had left a will. She thought the cost of recording and probating the will was excessive. She wanted to avoid charges on the estate in order to leave it intact for the children, and asked that she and her brother in law be named as executors.[31] She probably thought Duperré was a busybody, and an expensive one to boot. Duperré's services did not come cheap: the same year, he administered the estate of Joseph Thériault and charged £11 13s. 4d. for his services, half for his expenses and half for his time. Theriault's estate was only worth £94 6s. Duperré even felt powerful enough to oppose the parish priest. In 1812 the priest decided to lock the church doors at the beginning of the service, to dissuade parishioners from coming in and out of the church during Mass. Duperré charged him with illegally detaining the inhabitants and would have taken him to court had the priest not consented to paying a fine of £8 13s.3d. ($35), which Duperré collected.[32]

Duperré's wealth and prominence were not gained through farming, trading, and perhaps even not through milling, but through speculation and the full use of his educational and social capital. He used his literacy and his connections to the fullest and likely would not have succeeded without them. He acted as the settlement's self-appointed representative to higher authorities and its defender against outside aggressors. Lord Dorchester does not seem to have held him in high regard, but Sir Guy Carleton bestowed appointments on him. Duperré had succeeded in becoming a mediator between the Madawaska community and the provincial authorities but by 1818 the province was in no hurry to involve him in its dealings with American trespassers. For all his success, Duperré did not have the trust and respect of all his neighbours, and some likely resented what they perceived as his meddling and hustling. They would probably have concurred with Timothy Dwight's depiction of the evils of 'principal men,' and thought it fit Duperré rather well.

Rising from the Ranks: The Héberts and Thibodeaux

In October 1825, Messrs Irish and Coffin, land agents respectively for the states of Maine and Massachusetts, travelled through the Saint John Valley to investigate the claims of the settlers in the disputed territory. In order to do so they met with those they deemed the region's 'leading men.' Their account starts in the Grand Rivière settlement to the east, where they stayed with François Violette. On 2 October they canoed past St Basile's church and enquired after 'Simonet Bares [*sic*] Grand sachem of this French settlement.' Simonet *Hébert* must not have been available – the men camped out that night. The next day they continued westward to the American settlement, stopping en route at the home of militia captain Michaud, and then retraced their route. On 4 October they dined with Hébert and spent the night with another militia captain, Firmin Thibodeau.[33]

Simonet Hébert and Firmin Thibodeau were prominent – even notorious – residents. They had a lot in common, but the American land agents who followed in Irish and Coffin's footsteps viewed them in different lights.

'Favourites of the British': Simon Hébert and His Sons

Land agents Messrs Deane and Kavanagh were not dissatisfied with the progress of their enquiries in the fine days of July 1831. The Madawaska settlers answered their questions without apparent reticence until they reached Simonet Hébert's public house. The meeting did not start well. The Americans ordered supper but the food was substandard: the pork was rancid, the butter very poor, the bread and tea middling. Only the potatoes were palatable. The bill was nonetheless 'extravagant' and the men advised that visitors stay instead where the fare was 'half as dear.' Things went from bad to worse when the agents moved onto the real object of their visit: How had Simonet come into possession of his land? How much did he claim and where was it located? Simonet replied with his own queries: What right did the agents have to ask all those questions to begin with? Their commission did not impress him one whit. And why should he account for his claims? Didn't he have grants to his holdings from the British? Why should this not suffice to legitimize his claims? Hébert held his ground and refused to answer the Americans' questions. Deane and Kavanagh were visibly miffed and attributed Hébert's attitude to his being a 'favorite of the British.'[34]

Hébert's influence was felt in the vicinity; it was the only section of the south bank of the river where settlers refused to answer the agents' questions. Simonet's father Simon, who was visited by the Americans the next day, was equally uncooperative and challenging. So was Joseph Hébert, Simonet's brother. By then, Deane and Kavanagh had an explanation for the Héberts' obstinacy. Not only was Simon a 'favorite of the British,' but 'by their aid [had] dispossessed several settlers, and he and his family are now enjoying the fruit of their labor.' Whether motivated by the rancid pork, the Héberts' refusal to recognize American authority, or the sense of an injustice having been done, Deane and Kavanagh concluded that the Héberts should be shown no mercy. 'Whenever the settlers are quieted by the State, if ever, it is to be hoped, that such as have been unjustly dispossessed, will be restored, and that those persons, who are hostile, will not be prominently favored. Let them seek favor of the British of whom they would rather like better to receive it, than from us,' they advised.[35]

Were the Héberts really that bad? The rumour mill soon provided the Americans with accusations of malfeasance, and their report contains several examples that showed the Héberts responsible for dispossessing others. It is impossible to know if the accusations were true. Messrs Deane and Kavanagh cannot really be considered impartial witnesses and in any case the Héberts may not have been the only ones guilty of stealing their neighbours' land. Accusations to that effect against others were occasionally made to the authorities in Fredericton.[36] Guilty or not, the Héberts were successful at accumulating property. They almost always held appointments as civil parish officers, father and sons were commissioned in the militia, and Simon benefited from a degree of governmental favour. Deane and Kavanagh's report also shows that the family had enemies in the community who seized the opportunity not only to denounce them, but also to try to undercut the root of their power – their landownership.

Simon Hébert was born in 1764 and was married around 1785 to Marie Josephte, daughter of Joseph Daigle. He died in 1843, followed three years later by his wife. The couple had three children. Simon aka Simonet, was born in the late 1780s, married in 1810, and had fourteen children (eleven surviving). Suzanne was born in 1791 and married a Canadian, François Durepos, in 1815. She had no children. In 1816 she received a belated wedding present from her father. Simon Hébert, identified as a 'gentleman' in the registry of the deeds, sold his daughter a 103-acre lot with a house, barn, furniture, one horse, one yoke of oxen, four cows, four sheep, and three hogs for five shillings and love. Four years later, Durepos acquired another lot from his father-in-law but it was no gift. Hébert had paid £25 for it and sold it for £200 to his son-in-law. The last child, Joseph was born in 1795. He married in 1815 and had fifteen children of whom thirteen survived.[37]

Simon was an ambitious man. By 1803 he was one of the largest grain growers in the valley, producing far more than his family could consume (see chapter 7). In 1807 he acquired a mill site and water rights next to Duperré's old lot. He erected a grist- and sawmill that was still operating at the time of Deane and Kavanagh's visit. Besides milling and farming, Simon was very busy accumulating land. The York county registry records that he acquired six farm lots between 1799 and 1830 in addition to his British grant. Among these was Duperré's lot 38, which he purchased in 1815.[38] His sons followed his example. Deane and Kavanagh managed to identify seven lots, totalling about 1,400 acres, that belonged to the three men. They also met several other men who claimed land by right of purchase from the Héberts. The Héberts appear to have been in the business of marking lots, sometimes clearing a few acres on them, and then selling them to newcomers.[39] They continued accumulating property after Deane and Kavanagh's departure. Simonet was granted 1,013 acres in the United States and 192 in New Brunswick (the average size of a U.S. grant was 120 acres and in New Brunswick 160) under the terms of the treaty of 1842. These grants did not include any land in New Brunswick that may have been granted by the British, as the New Brunswick land commissioners did not re-issue titles for the original grants. Throughout his life, Simonet owned no fewer than eight farms (farm lots averaged 150 to 180 acres, as the older holdings were considerably larger than the later ones) and two mills. He sold most of them to his children in 1848. He also sold a mill to his cousin Hilarion Daigle for $400 in 1845, and his father's mill to his son-in-law Sylvain Daigle for $500 in 1848.[40] Joseph for his part also continued to buy and sell land. Deane and Kavanagh identified four farm lots as being his. Joseph Hébert received grants for 914 acres in the United States and 936 in New Brunswick and later acquired ten additional farms. One wonders whether the brothers' frenzy of accumulation was motivated by the need to establish their twenty-five children. The answer depends on how one defines 'establish.' The Héberts did not give land away, they sold it to their sons at market price. Between 1847 and 1865 Joseph sold his children sixteen pieces of land for a total of $ 6,300, divesting himself of his American holdings first. He traded a farm at the mouth of the Madawaska River to his son Vital in 1856 for maintenance in old age. Simonet sold all his American property between 1845 and 1848 for a total of $5,400. The land all went to seven children, except for the mill ($400) and a lot he sold to the Ste Luce priest ($200).

The Héberts' best real estate coup, though carefully planned, slipped through their fingers at the last moment. In January 1824 Armine Mountain, brother of the Anglican bishop of Quebec, stopped at Madawaska on his way back from a visit to Provincial Secretary William Odell. He spent a night at Firmin Thibodeau's and the next day stopped at Simon Hébert's in order to recruit a new team of guides. Hébert volunteered to accompany him halfway to Lake Temiscouata, at no cost. He took advantage of the opportunity to lay out his business plan to Mountain. He intended to build an inn at the junction of the Madawaska and Saint John Rivers on the same lot Duperré had coveted a quarter of a century earlier. He also claimed that he had purchased the lot from the Natives and was eager to obtain a provincial grant to secure his title. Mountain, very much impressed by Mr. Hébert's demeanour and helpfulness, accepted his story and acted on cue. 'I told him,' he wrote Odell, 'that I did not flatter myself with possessing much influence over you, but that I would certainly mention to you what his plans were. Old Simon is really something more than his neighbours in intellect and honest good will as well as in years.'[41] 'Old Simon' received a grant for 250 acres, signed by Odell, in 1825; in 1831 he got a twenty-one-year lease for an additional 130 acres.[42] He did not have to pay any rent, but he would not receive compensation for his improvements at the end of the lease, and the government could take the land back from him at any time.

In 1848 the land commissioners decided the lease did not entitle Simonet Hébert as heir to a grant under the terms of the treaty. Instead, the government reclaimed the land, laid down a town platt at the junction of the rivers, and divided the area into pasture and town lots, which it began to sell at £100 and more an acre. This action started a string of petitions from Hébert, who first tried the patriotic line. He claimed that he had moved to the British side in 1842, made considerable improvements on the lot, cleared 70 to 80 acres, and built a house, barn, outhouse, and blacksmith shop (no mention was made of an inn). The governor and council were initially sympathetic. They granted Hébert the land where his buildings stood, and set aside the proceeds from the sale of thirty-five town lots, (£1,000), which they later argued was 'ample remuneration for all improvements or any claim Mr. Hébert can possibly have upon this House or the government.' Hébert begged to differ and petitioned three more times. In his last petition, he complained that his compensation was 'disproportionate' to the profit made by the government.[43] 'His' windfall, stalked for a quarter of a century, had gone to the province. The government was rather indulgent towards him, considering that Hébert was entitled to nothing and was trying to profit from pure speculation. Fredericton tried to placate Hébert with a small share of the profits and continued to appoint him and members of his family to parish officers' positions. Despite his temper tantrum, Hébert remained, on a small scale, a favourite.

As sawmill owners and large grain-growers, the Héberts acted as intermediaries between the local and provincial economies. However, as landlords, blacksmiths, public-house keepers and gristmillers, they were not just intermediaries but important players in the local economy. They also derived a significant part of their wealth from land speculation. One member of the next generation continued the pattern laid down by father and grandfather. The first French-speaking member of the legislative assembly of New Brunswick for Victoria County was Vital Hébert, who was elected in 1866. He had been appointed county deputy treasurer the previous year owing to the patronage of James Tibbits, who was member of the legislative assembly at the time.[44] Vital unfortunately died the following year at age 59. Like his father and grandfather, he had accumulated a large amount of real estate but he died insolvent. His widow fortunately showed good business sense. She was entitled to dower rights in some of her husband's mortgaged properties, which she sold for $250, opening a boarding house in Edmundston.[45]

Firmin Thibodeau, Country Squire

Government favouritism was not a prerequisite to becoming a large landowner. At the time of Deane and Kavanagh's visit, Simon Hébert was not the valley's largest landowner. The title belonged to Firmin Thibodeau, locally known as the 'seigneur' (the squire) for his generosity.[46] The seigneur was a real estate magnate. Deane and Kavanagh list six lots totalling in excess of 1,200 acres under his name, many purchased from immediate relatives, and most previously granted by the British. Thibodeau also operated a grist- and sawmill on the south bank, opposite Grand Isle. He was one of the few local men who cut wood under British licence before the treaty and at some point had been a store owner. In 1825 he was running a licensed inn where Mountain, Coffin, and Irish had once spent the night. He also served as a militia captain. Coffin and Irish liked Thibodeau very much. He refused any payment from the two men and gave them the impression that he was pro-American. 'Mr. Thibodeau is very friendly to the Americans,' they reported, 'and desirous of having an organized government at Madawaska and to be represented in the General Court, to have parish officers and officers of their own choice in the militia. He observed he was now a captain of the militia, commissioned from the government of New Brunswick, but he would never call his men out under that commission.'[47] The Americans left Thibodeau with a proclamation to be posted at his inn, promising 100 acres for the cost of the survey to those who would apply to the state land agent in Houlton. Thibodeau instead immediately handed over the proclamation to his commanding officer, Peter Fraser.[48] Thibodeau later willingly answered agents Deane and Kavanagh's questions, and they duly noted some trespass on his lands. Thibodeau had not made a fuss in order 'to keep the peace,' but he wanted the record set straight.

By 1831, however, he had already divested himself of several lots through sales or gifts to his six children. The seigneur's domestic arrangements were unusual. A widower, he had remarried in 1821. Six years later, his youngest son, Vital, married his stepsister, and the two couples lived together. Shortly after Deane and Kavanagh's visit, Firmin and his wife gave Vital and his wife their largest lot (900 acres) in exchange for support in old age.[49] Thibodeau, a very large-scale farmer, miller, storekeeper and inn-keeper, fitted Taylor's description

of a mediator between economies. But he avoided political appointments – or the province avoided appointing him. He was a leading
man, but not a leader, and was perceived as a devoted father and good
neighbour. In 1845 the Americans granted him 1,100 acres. The U.S.
mill was granted to Vital, who also collected six lots totalling 1,175
acres in New Brunswick. His father's 900 acre lot was already covered
by eighteenth-century grants. Firmin sold most of his property in the
late 1840s and early 1850s. Father and son finished their days on
British soil. In the end, Firmin decided the British were tolerable
enough, but perhaps he never really had any wish to become American. Vital became a militia captain in 1842 and a justice of the peace in
1847. Firmin's children, as discussed in the next chapter, benefited
from their father's prominence.[50]

Downward Mobility: The Mercure Brothers

Upward mobility was not the lot of all frontier adventurers. Louis
Mercure and his brother Michel seem to have followed the opposite
path. Louis had a good head start in life. His father, Joseph, was a
captain in the Ile St Jean garrison who moved from Ile St Jean to
Quebec City, where he was wounded and discharged. He may have
been involved in trade in October 1750. The records show that 'Anne
Gautier wife of Joseph Mercure, reformed ensign from the Garrison at
Quebec' sold away a 45-ton *goelette*, a type of small craft commonly
used in the Gulf of St Lawrence for coastal trade. Anne Mercure was a
daughter to one of the wealthiest merchant families of Louisbourg, the
French fortress on Cape Breton Island.[51] During the Revolutionary
war, Louis served as lieutenant in the regiment of rangers that Robert
Rogers was raising in New Brunswick[52] and later became an official
courier between Halifax, Castine, and Quebec. Louis erected a mill on
a lot he claimed at the mouth of the Nashwack River, laid out for him
by the surveyor of Nova Scotia in 1783 and was granted an island in
the Lower Saint John River. His brother Michel was a courier as well.[53]
By the eve of the Loyalists' arrival, Mercure had joined the ranks of
Glazier, Simonds, and Hazen and had become a Lower Saint John frontier entrepreneur.

　　Louis acted as a spokesman for the Lower Saint John French and initiated the process through which they received grants at Madawaska.
He acted as colonization agent, but he was suspected of engrossing

land and never received an official appointment.[54] In the 1780s, he purchased a mill site at Madawaska, which he quickly sold to Duperré. He subsequently laid claim to an isolated location at the confluence of the Saint John River and River de Chute, which he sold in 1809 for £50 to a Woodstock man.[55] He died seven years later. His brother followed in his footsteps. Although he had been granted land at Madawaska, Michel received another grant at the mouth of the Salmon River, a tributary of the Saint John, five miles below Grand Falls. Five years later, in 1797, he requested two additional grants at the same location, one for himself, and the other one for his son, who was only seven at the time. Michel's plans for the site are unclear. In 1791 there was a village on the site, where the Natives planted fields of corn and harvested wild oats and wild wheat.[56] Both the River de Chute and the Salmon River sites were similar to the lot at the mouth of the Madawaska River that had attracted Duperré and Hébert. The sites would have been suitable for a sawmill, a fur trading post, a relay for government couriers and other travellers, or as an observation post against the Americans. All were activities for which the Mercures were well suited but by 1805 Michel and his family were at Madawaska, where he died in 1810.[57] Louis and Michel's children did not distinguish themselves in any particular way and seem to have fallen back into the ranks of the ordinary settlers, except for Michel junior, who was commissioner of highways and overseer of the poor from 1821–2.[58] The younger Mercures did not achieve any higher rank than ensign in the militia.

The Mercures staked strategic economic positions on the frontier but did not emerge as mediators. They started out as useful intermediaries and tried, in vain, to translate these initial advantages into economic ones. As Sheila Andrew concluded in her sketch of Louis Mercure's life: 'His leadership in the community depended on his literacy and on government favour. When the favour was withdrawn, leadership passed to others in the community.' The same may have been true of Michel Mercure. What the Mercures actually did to displease the authorities is not clear. For one, Louis Mercure was suspected of abusing his position as colonization agent.[59] Whether the charges were justified or not is irrelevant: a tainted reputation may have led the provincial authorities to think that despite his pedigree Louis Mercure was not respectable enough to deserve their favour. Governmental favours were not easily gained and could be easily lost. Without them, economic advancement was difficult, and in the case of the Mercures, impossible.

The Failure of Capitalism: Louis Bellefleur

On 1 December 1819, Rev Lagarde celebrated the marriage of Léon Gatté Bellefleur and Elizabeth Thibodeau, both from the parish of St Basile. Elizabeth was one of Firmin Thibodeau's cousins. Léon was son of Sieur Louis Gatté dit Bellefleur, *négociant*, and Dame Alexandrine Parent, also from St Basile.[60] No one in the parish records had yet deserved the titles of Sieur (esquire) and Dame (lady), not even the Mercures. What convinced the priest he was dealing with a gentleman? Perhaps it was an awareness of Louis's pedigree. Louis and his father and his sons exemplify the possibilities and the limits of upward mobility offered by the New World and by the frontier. Louis's father, also called Louis, was a Frenchman and a sergeant with the French colonial troops in Quebec when he married in 1756.[61] The end of the war threw him out of a job. He chose to stay in the New World, and at the baptism of his son Louis in 1764 in Quebec City, he declared his occupation as *commerçant* (tradesman or storekeeper). When his daughter Geneviève was baptised in 1768, he had upgraded his occupation to *marchand* (merchant). By the time his children married, he was a *négociant* (merchant-trader or wholesaler). Louis's steady economic progress enabled his surviving son and daughter to marry well.

Marie Josette (born 1760) married into the large Cherrier family in 1777. Her husband, Joseph Marie, was a son of François Pierre Cherrier, a merchant and government official (*notaire royal*). The British authorities renewed his commission as *notaire*; his business unfortunately suffered irremediably from the Conquest. However, his descendents bounced back: all his sons were professionals, two of them members of the provincial legislative assembly; one became a famous Montreal lawyer worthy of a street name; and his grandchildren included the first bishop of Montreal, Mgr Lartigue, and patriots Denis-Benjamin Viger and Louis Joseph Papineau.[62]

The Cherrier connection may have helped Louis junior obtain the hand of Alexandrine Parent in 1781. Louis was seventeen; the bride, twenty-one. Marguerite Louise Alexandrine Parent was the daughter of Charles Antoine, *négociant* in Quebec City, and Marguerite

Louise Fournel. The bride's maternal grandmother was the interesting character in the family. As a widow in her forties, Marie Anne Barbel had taken over the business of her husband, Louis Fournel or Fornel, one of the largest merchants in Quebec. The Seven Years War undid the house of Barbel-Fournel: She surrendered the leases on her fur-trading and sealing posts at Tadoussac and on the Labrador coast, which could not be protected from the enemy, and her warehouses were badly damaged during the bombardment of Quebec City. She nonetheless managed to rebuild, if not a fortune, at least a competency, and died in 1793 at the age of 89.[63] She was present at Alexandrine's wedding. Like the Cherriers, the Barbel/Fournel/Parent connection had seen their fortunes badly compromised by the war, but did not give up. Louis Gatté père was an upstart, but apparently a successful one. He offered the Cherrier and Parent children economic resources; they offered his children considerable social capital.

This, however, did not benefit the second Louis much in the end. Louis's first three children were born in Quebec City; he was listed as a merchant and then *négociant* in the baptismal records. Subsequent children were born after 1785 in St Vallier and Berthier, where Louis remained a merchant at least until 1799.[64] In 1807 Louis appeared in the records at Madawaska, as signatory of a petition and as a witness to a marriage.[65] Louis's son, also named Louis, a saddlemaker, married there in 1812. Alexandrine was absent, her residence reported as St Vallier. Daughter Marie Anne was the next to marry, in 1818. By that time, Alexandrine had joined the rest of the family at Madawaska.[66]

At Madawaska Bellefleur first became a merchant, and then acquired a mill. Deane and Kavanagh reported that he had purchased the Duperré mill from Peter Fraser, but they do not give a date for the acquisition, and it is not listed in the county land registry. Bellefleur either had capital or was able to secure it. According to Deane and Kavanagh, he paid $ 1,000 for the mill and invested a further $ 2,000 in it. In 1831 Bellefleur claimed a grist- and sawmill and three houses, as well as two other farm lots in the settlement. He also engaged in lumbering: he held a provincial licence in the mid-1820s. The move to Madawaska seems in character for Bellefleur: he was looking for trading opportunities. Bellefleur may also have tried to take advantage of the wheat trade that developed out of the valley sometime after the

War of 1812 (as discussed in chapters 6 and 7). He died at Madawaska, and his children married locally. His son Antoine owned a store, two houses, and two barns on the lot next to the main church in 1831. The Bellefleurs were literate and held positions as civil parish clerks and assessors between 1821 and 1832.[67]

Social standing, capital, and/or credit, however, were not enough to guarantee success. The wheat crop repeatedly failed in the 1830s, never to recover.[68] By 1836 Peter Fraser was dead and his executor, Beverley Robinson (son of John), sold 'a lot lately in possession of Louis Bellefleur' at Madawaska, 300 acres in size with a grist- and sawmill, to Firmin Thibodeau's son Francois. In 1845 the Americans issued a grant for the lot less the millsite to the heirs of Fraser and Robinson.[69] Thibodeau registered his deed to the property very shortly afterwards. Bellefleur no longer owned the mill when he died and perhaps had never owned it. He may have purchased the mill on credit, which would explain why the transaction was not registered, and why his $1,000 purchase price was less than Fraser and Robinson had paid Duperré for it (£610 Halifax currency or $2440). Perhaps Fraser, Robinson, and Bellefleur had been partners in a flour business, and the first two dumped the latter unceremoniously when the business ceased to be profitable on account of the crop failures of the mid-1830s. What is clear is that Bellefleur, who could have qualified as a capitalist on account of his willingness to invest in infrastructure, failed. His son Antoine may also have encountered a rough patch: he sold his store to the Dufour brothers in the 1840s.[70] The aspiring entrepreneur and his descendants were absorbed into the ranks of the well-to-do farmers.

Partial economic failure, however, was no obstacle to the ambition of becoming a principal man. The Bellefleurs continued to receive government favours. Antoine Bellefleur became a justice of the peace and a major in the militia. Brother Léon acted as procurement agent for the surveying parties that drew the boundary between the provinces of New Brunswick and Quebec in 1853, and was appointed justice of the peace the following year.[71] Like Duperré and probably Mercure, Antoine Bellefleur saw himself as one of the settlement's natural leaders. In 1849 a large number of Madawaska residents petitioned the bishop for the removal of their priest, Mgr Langevin, whom they accused of an impressive list of misdeeds. Bellefleur spearheaded a counter-petition stating that 'the people who initiated the petition are people we consider to be scum.' But he could only muster eight co-signers in opposition to the forty-four denouncers. His supporters were the usual suspects: Joseph Hébert, militia captain, François Thibodeau, justice of the peace, Vital Thibodeau, militia captain, Régis Thériault (who will appear in chapter 4), militia captain, Francis Rice, former justice of the peace and future member of the legislative assembly, and two 'respectable farmers.'[72] Bellefleur's image of himself was larger than his real influence. By 1850 the days when government favours were more important than economic success for acceptance by the community as a leading man were gone, but the province apparently had not yet noticed.

Conclusion

Undeserving parasites or community builders? Who were Madawaska's early principal men? The five groups we have just encountered more or less fit Taylor's description; they also more or less fit Dwight's. Duperré, the Mercures, and the Héberts were speculators: they bought land cheap, when they bought it at all, and sold it dear. The Thibodeaux and Bellefleurs did not refrain from accumulating real estate either. The Thibodeaux and Bellefleurs were, or tried to be, mediators between their 'small producer' neighbours and the 'external markets and suppliers of trade goods.' It is not clear to what extent the Héberts or the Mercures played this role; if Duperré did, it was as a fur trader.

But even when they were not intermediaries between two economies, all these men in their own ways contributed to the building of the settlement: they secured the initial grants of land; embedded the region into a political and administrative structure; and contributed to the development of its infrastructure. The Madawaska settlement in part owes its foundation in 1785 to the fact that one man, Louis Mercure, believed that by establishing Acadians on the Upper Saint John both the Acadians' and the British authorities' problems would be solved. Duperré incited his neighbours to become active citizens by accompanying them to the poll station and writing a petition protesting their disenfranchisement. The fact that it was Peter Fraser who introduced the bill to give the right to vote to Catholics was likely not coincidental. Whatever his personal motivations, Duperré led his neighbours to think of themselves as members of a community larger than their settlement; membership in the militia reinforced this sense of belonging to a larger, extralocal community. The latter had its own rules, which affected all concerned. Duperré's registering the deeds of his some of his neighbours or trying to administer their estates drove the point home. So did the appointment of many principal men as petty civil officers, and after the Catholic Emancipation Act of 1830, as justices of the peace.

Principal men also played a role in developing the local economy. They owned custom mills, which provided the local population with flour, meal, and building material. They operated stores where local goods could be exchanged for outside ones, and public houses where men could socialize among themselves and meet travellers – and the Saint John was a very well-travelled route. Stores, inns, and taverns served as the place where the local population gained its information about the outside world: Coffin and Irish left their notice to be posted at Thibodeau's inn, for example. The Bellefleurs and Héberts were rewarded with political appointments as civil parish officers; Duperré, the Bellefleurs, and Thibodeau with militia commissions. The Mercures, on the other hand, were demoted. In other words, leading men came in many shapes: some were nice neighbours and some were grasping individuals; some were upwardly mobile and some were on their way down.

Some of those men disrupted traditional hierarchies and others reinforced them. Duperré did not 'know his place.' Neither did the Héberts or Firmin Thibodeau. The latter, however, appears to have been better equipped to play the role of the benevolent and patriarchal country squire. Thibodeau understood the symbolic value of hospitality and appearances – to be treated like a gentleman, one had to act and look the part. The Héberts, or at least Joseph and Simonet, did not: they came across as too covetous. The Bellefleurs had a pedigree and seem to have known how to live up to it; they were gentlemen who were made officers. The Mercures had an even better pedigree and a war record, but this counted for naught when the authorities decided that these officers seemed too greedy to be gentlemen.

This diverse group of men also shed some light on the place of neighbourliness and individualism in early nineteenth-century frontier society. Only one earned the reputation of being a good neighbour and three were considered quite the opposite. Only two helped some of their children get a start in life: Hébert père and Thibodeau. Duperré did not bother with a family – he never married. With the exception of Thibodeau, the men come across as individualistic, if not selfish, and acquisitive to the point of antagonizing their neighbours in the process. Individualism and acquisitiveness were not enough to make them players in the dawning new economic era, however. Only Belle-fleur could qualify as a genuine capitalist: he invested money to make money but he eventually failed. Born into wholesale trade, he died a farmer. The other men followed ancien régime strategies: speculation, estate building, collecting of ground rents, and exploiting privileged connections with powerful men close to the government, or with the government itself. They do not appear to have had overarching business plans. Instead, they grabbed whatever opportunity came along, and rode it for as long as it was worth it. Allan Greer, investigating the activities of a late eighteenth-century Richelieu Valley merchant, noted that 'For Samuel Jacob, as for most eighteenth century merchants, business was not so much a continuous process as a series of discrete "adventures."'[73] Jacob diversified his activities as a form of insurance against failure, and dreamed of speculative windfall but ignored the 'routine attention to profit and loss' required to be a genuine capitalist entrepreneur.[74] Our men appear to have done the same. For them, the economy was a game of chance. Duperré, the Mercures, and the Héberts, probably shared that view. These men may have been individualistic and acquisitive, but they were a far cry from our images of the capitalist entrepreneur. Capital was the one tool they did not use to try to get ahead and market activities did not have their undivided attention either.

Market production and capitalism may have been the ways of the future. But at Madawaska in the first third of the nineteenth century, they were not the inevitable ways of the present. The ways of the past – speculations, patronage – were still effective, and perhaps perceived as more reliable than distant markets. It is probably no accident that among these men (Thibodeau may have been an exception) the ones who succeeded did so only as long as they benefited from the patronage of more powerful men. Their examples also suggest that government patronage offered better protection against economic downturns than that of men of business. The Belle-fleur/Fraser/Robinson partnership did not survive the crisis of the mid-1830s, but the government continued bestowing appointments and government contracts on Louis's sons. In contrast, the loss of political patronage relegated the Mercures to an honest economic mediocrity. In this context, was it worth risking one's time, efforts, and assets on trade and capitalism? The answer would seem to be no. The men discussed in the next chapter, who invested heavily in the staple trade, were additional proof that certain forms of capitalism were uncertain paths to riches; not following those paths was an economically rational choice.

3 A Connective Enterprise: Madawaska Lumbering

Mr. W. H. Cunliffe first came to Fort Kent in 1846, in the employ of Shepard Cary. He continued in Mr. Cary's employ in the lumber operation until 1857, when he went into the lumber business on his own account. He soon afterwards bought the Cary property at Fort Kent, where he established a permanent residence. In 1865, he formed a partnership with W.H. Cary, a brother of Hon. Shepard Cary, and the firm of Cary & Cunliffe carried on an extensive lumber business upon the upper St. John and its tributaries. In 1873 Mr. Cary withdrew from the firm and removed to the West and Mr. Cunliffe took as a partner Mr. S. Walter Stevens. The new firm of Cunliffe and Stevens continued the business on a still extensive scale, cutting one year as many as twenty two million feet of logs. Mr. Cunliffe was also at the same time a partner in the firm of B.W. Malett and Co., who carried on an extensive business in trading and buying shingles, having a large store on the New Brunswick side of the river opposite Fort Kent. In 1876 came the disastrous Jewett failure which carried both the above named firms down.

Edward Wiggin, *History of Aroostook*.[1]

I do not wish to be understood as condemning the lumbering business of the country. If I did so, facts and figures would be against me: Yet, it seems reasonable that if the farmer would sell his produce to the large operators, or, if at most, he would confine his winter operations to what he could manage within himself, it would be better for his own interest, and for that of the community generally.

Charles Lugrin, 1871[2]

William Cunliffe was typical of a new breed of entrepreneurs. Born in New Brunswick on 2 February 1820, he moved to the Upper Saint John Valley as a young single man.[3] He clerked for an American lumber operator and purchased the store when his employer went bankrupt. He went into the lumbering business in partnership with Americans Holman Cary and Samuel Stevens and traded shingles in partnership with Mallett, an American whose store was located in New Brunswick. In 1873, Cunliffe and Stevens had secured permits from Quebec to log in the former disputed territory, at the heads of the Saint John and Big Black rivers (Bellechasse and Islet counties).[4] Stevens, born in 1819, was a former clerk for Jewett & Co., a transnational concern, and had bought their store and hotel in 1848; he held their supply account. Mallett, from Penobscot County in Maine had clerked, milled, lumbered, farmed, and manufactured clapboard before going into storekeeping and shingle trading.

According to the staple thesis, export trade in raw or semi-processed commodities such as fish, fur, wheat, and timber/lumber spurred economic development by creating linkages (processing, transportation, banking, and insurance) that could also be used by the local economies for their own needs, as well as for capital accumulation. The Upper Saint John Valley forest industry had the protential to produce those results. Cunliffe moved to bigger and bigger ventures, Mallet and Stevens opened stores and hotels, and the industry provided farmers with a winter harvest of trees. But the Cunliffe and Mallet stories ended in bankruptcy and farmer-lumberers did not fare any better. The forest industry was not necessarily the road to riches. The market for wood products was volatile, and the industry vulnerable to business-cycle downturns. The effects of its precarious nature were worsened by a heavy reliance on credit. A downturn in the demand in Liverpool or Boston could start a cascade of bankruptcies that ultimately left the shanty men in possession of worthless promissory notes and credit for stores that had gone under. The consequences for a province like New Brunswick, whose economy was dependent on the wood trade, could be disastrous.[5] Locally, as this and the subsequent chapters will show, the forest industry had an uneven impact on the different groups of people involved.

The forest industry also produced a new kind of intermediary between local communities and the outside world: their functions were more narrowly economic than the ones of the previous generation's leading men. Cunliffe, Cary, Mallett, and their colleagues were part of a group of entrepreneurs who moved goods and credit up and down a provincial hierarchy composed of merchant-wholesalers based in ports and inland businessmen: contract or speculative lumberers, sawmillers, country storekeepers, brokers, and jobbers.[6] They acted as were intermediaries between the local economy and the larger one dominated by the timber trade, an activity that Graeme Wynn has labelled 'connective enterprise.' They traded in forest products, some, like shingles, lumber, and timber, either made by or purchased from local people, some produced by themselves with local labour. These men were not dependent on a hierarchy of patrons and clients, culminating with government officials. Instead, they relied heavily on a network of peers that ignored boundaries and nationalities, and on connections with large-scale mercantile firms in Saint John, Massachusetts, or even Britain. Outside connections allowed the lumberers to get the necessary credit and contracts to launch and sustain their business, but it also meant their fortunes were tied to the one of the trading houses with which they were affiliated. The failure of those houses inevitably brought the lumbermen down with them. These men were also less interested in politics or in assuming local leadership roles than the previous generation. Large lumber operators may have been elected to the provincial legislative assembly or the state House, but they could not be bothered with examining fences or drilling militiamen. They were willing to look after the industry's interests, but they were not particularly concerned with parish or municipal housekeeping. Smaller businessmen, on the other hand, were willing to retire from lumbering to become elected or appointed civil officials.

Although they were a different breed of intermediary, all these men still shared some similarities with the principal men described in the previous chapter. Most diversified their activities, and pursued series of discrete business ventures, grabbing opportunities as they arose. They also shifted much of the risk of their activities onto others. These men may have relied less on patronage than earlier leading men, but their actions were still influenced by that old ways of doing business – capitalism does not appear to have been a surer road to success in the 1860s than in the 1830s. The same is true of farmers who lumbered on the side. Lugrin's advice was not the typically condescending counsel of a gentleman who knew better to obdurate peasants who should have been wiser. The example of Madawaska farmer-lumberers shows that at that level, participating in the staple trade did not lead to economic success either.

The Beginnings of Lumbering and the Boundary Dispute

The colonial timber trade was a consequence of the Napoleonic Wars. Britain, cut off from its Baltic supplies by the continental blocade, turned to her colonies for a new supply of timber. The timber trade survived the fall of Napoleon and the end of the blockade. Between 1815 and 1846, preferential tariffs protected colonial timber from non-imperial competition on British markets. New Brunswick rapidly emerged as one of the leading supplier of ton timber.[7] As the best trees were culled from the coastal areas, logging parties pushed further and further inland, following the course of rivers that could be used to float the wood towards useable harbours (see map 3). The first timber licences for the Upper Saint John were issued in 1823. In 1825, however, the provincial government stopped issuing logging permits for the area as a result of the boundary dispute.[8]

The first loggers on the Upper Saint John were not Provincials but Americans.[9] As early as 1810, scattered bands of loggers were moving inland, and in 1816 some Kennebec men, Nathan Baker, his brother John, and John Harford senior and junior, reached the Upper Saint John. Nathan settled at the mouth of the Meruimticook, later renamed Baker Brook, cleared land, built a house, and erected a saw- and grist-mill. He was, however, a squatter. By the 1818–19 season, Nathan had become partner with Samuel Nevers, a Saint John merchant of pre-Loyalist stock. Nathan worked for him as a timber cruiser, and was joined by his brother in 1820. Nathan died soon thereafter, and John took over both the business and the family (he married his sister-in-law).[10]

The beginning of logging activities on the Upper Saint John, and Maine's accession to statehood in 1820 brought the boundary dispute to a head.[11] Neither Maine nor New Brunswick was willing to allow the other to strip the territory of its merchantable timber. New Brunswick stopped issuing timber licences for the Upper Saint John after Maine protested, and it appointed James Maclauchlan as warden for the disputed territory.[12] Maclauchlan, a veteran of the War of 1812, was deputy provincial surveyor. Along with the land agents from Maine, he was instructed to seize illegally cut wood, auction it off, and put the proceeds in a 'disputed territory trust fund.'[13] On the ground, however, loggers ignored all regulations designed to stop them, often with the complicity of local juries when they were brought to court.[14] The continuation of logging was facilitated by the difficulties in dis-

Lumbering Districts in Maine and New Brunswick

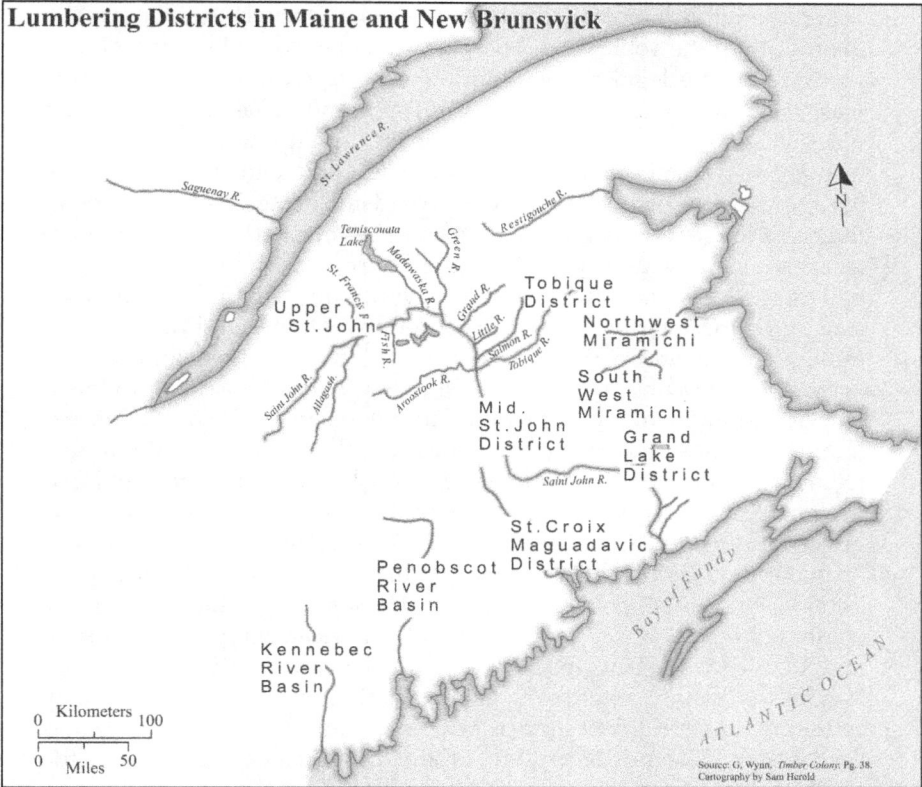

Map 3

tinguishing legal from contraband wood. In New Brunswick, grantees were allowed to cut all the wood they wanted on their grants and there were one hundred granted lots at Madawaska. Location ticket holders were allowed to cut up to one hundred tons of merchantable timber on their claim, and could sell it to whomever they wished.[15] Wood could also be legally cut around Temiscouata Lake, which was under the jurisdiction of Lower Canada. The only way to move the wood out of the area was along the Madawaska and Saint John Rivers. Trespassers usually claimed they had purchased their wood from the settlers or cut it around the lake. Settlers also passed off as their own wood they had cut on the public land at the back of their lots. Once the timber reached the mouth of the Tobique and Salmon Rivers, it could be conveniently mixed with the legal timber coming from upriver. Clearly, cheating was very easy, and it took place on a grand scale. By 1837–8 the wooded areas at the back of the settlements and up the Fish River were teeming with lumberers and their animals[16] and some of the trespassing crews were being supplied by Woodstock merchants.[17] Three of the eight loggers licensed during the 1823–4 and 1824–5 seasons were local Frenchmen Alexandre Bourguoin, Firmin Thibodeau, and Louis Bellefleur.[18] The last two owned sawmills at Madawaska. In 1838 several of the logging parties identified by Maine land agent Buckmore were led, and perhaps even outfitted, by local Frenchmen.

By the following year, illegal logging had almost led to open warfare. Maine sent the state militia to put an end to the depredations, and New Brunswick sent some British regulars to prevent the militia from occupying the disputed territory. Washington promptly replaced the militia with federal troops headed by General Winfred Scott. The governor of New Brunswick and the American general were old acquaintances, which made managing the crisis easier. Both sides built booms across the Saint John to intercept illegal logs, and by 1840 the combined efforts of the provincial and American officials had put an end to illegal logging in the territory but severely impaired legal logging as well.[19] Two years later, Washington and London finally settled the matter: the St Francis and Saint John Rivers were chosen as boundaries. The northern side of the rivers remained British, the southern one became American. Maine kept the Aroostook valley and received free navigation rights on the Saint John for her forest and agricultural products. This clause satisfied the lumberers' interests as free navigation rights were essential for the expansion of the lumber industry in the American Saint John River basin. Britain kept the Temiscouata route, the only thing that really mattered to her. Bona fide settlers with at least six years' residence were to receive titles to the land they occupied.[20] The settlers were never asked their opinion, and the ones living on the south bank were handed over to the Americans like trade goods.

The resolution of the boundary dispute had little immediate impact on the lives of the settlers, French or American. Ecclesiastical parish boundaries intersected the international one until the late 1860s. Better-off settlers who owned more than one piece of land sometimes owned property on both sides of the river; people of more modest means might sell a piece of property on one side to purchase one on the other shore.[21] In any case, settlers moved freely from one side of the river to the other. One family counted by the U.S. census marshal in 1850 had moved to New Brunswick in time to be enumerated in the 1851 provincial census. The U.S. census listed them as natives of Maine and the New Brunswick one as natives of New Brunswick. Deeds were issued to occupants under the treaty, irrespective of citizenship. Americans living on the north side of the river became New Brunswickers, John Baker among them, despite a gentlemen's agreement struck by Webster and Ashburton. Baker's land was to be appraised, and purchased by the British government. Instead, Baker received a title for his 887 acre claim, and died at Baker Brook in 1868, apparently a satisfied Canadian and subject of her Majesty Queen Victoria.[22] He has since been reburied in the United States by his patriotic American descendants.

In the absence of decent roads the river remained the settlement's main highway, and communications firmly tied the region to New Brunswick, to the point that a state official could declare in the late 1850s: 'Except in the matter of jurisdiction, this vast and fertile region is (almost, if not quite) as really annexed to New Brunswick, as if so stipulated in the treaty of 1842.'[23] He was referring to the entire northern section of the state, not merely to the Saint John Valley. When the reciprocity treaty ended, the U.S. federal government considered taxing as British imports wood products from the county shipped to the United States through the Saint John River. Aroostook residents lobbied hard to scuttle the plan and won. The Pike Act of 1866 allowed lumber manufactured in New Brunswick by American citizens from logs cut in Maine to enter the United States duty free.[24] But who was an American citizen was not self-evident. An investigation into illegal voting in 1858 revealed that all men who had reached the age of majority and were born in the disputed territory were allowed to cast a vote. When the enquiry asked where he had been born, François Thibodeau, who until 1849 had been a New Brunswick justice of the peace, answered: 'I was born here and have always resided here.' All depended on the definition of 'here.' The enquiry did not settle the matter. Twenty years later another commission investigated alleged electoral frauds. The commissioners, after noting that 'Questions of birth, parentage and residence, and of the character of the residence, whether temporary or permanent, on one side of the boundary line or the other' all had to be taken into account, concluded that it was inevitable that some people would vote who should not, but that such actions were not evidence of deliberate fraud.[25]

The Post-treaty Forest Industry

Maine and New Brunswick pursued different policies relative to timberland. Maine alienated the public land in the former disputed territory as soon as it was able to do so. It classified public land as either settling land or timberland. To prevent lumbermen from purchasing only the best forested land and leaving the rest in the hands of the state, timberland was auctioned off in quarter, half, and whole townships. By 1853 a large proportion of the townships north of the tenth range not allocated to settlers had been alienated. Timber holdings were quickly concentrated in a few hands: David Pingree of Salem, Massachusetts, owned 38 of the 138 townships north of the tenth range after 1853.[26] In 1868 Maine sold one million acres of timberland in the Saint John and Penobscot river basins for $1.00 to the European and North American Railroad.[27] To all practical purposes, this move alienated whatever was left of public land in northern Maine. New Brunswick, on the other hand, retained control of its timberland and used it as a source of revenue. Lumberers logged on public land under licence; until 1844 they had to pay a stumpage fee proportional to the amount cut. As this easily led to abuse, stumpage fees were replaced by a general export duty of 1 shilling per ton or per 1,000 board feet that applied to all timber and lumber exported through New Brunswick ports, regardless of origins. U.S. lumber and timber floated down the Saint John River and exported through the port of Saint John was therefore liable to this duty. The timberland in the New Brunswick section of the former disputed territory remained in the hands of the provincial Crown land office until the 1870s, when it was given to the New Brunswick Land and Railway Company.[28] Both Maine and New Brunswick thus subsidized the construction of railways on their territories through massive gifts of land, one million acres in the case of Maine, over two million in the case of New Brunswick.

The resolution of the boundary dispute did not usher in a trouble-free era for the lumberers. They immediately faced another difficulty: Britain's elimination of colonial preferences. The first measure was taken in 1842, when she reduced the duties on foreign timber from 55 to 25 shillings per load (from $11 to $5), and those on colonial timber from 10 to 1 shilling per load (from $2 to $.20). Duties were further reduced in 1851, and after 1860 foreign and colonial timbers were both charged 1 shilling per load. The impact of the measures was initially mitigated by the British railway boom. Exports from New Brunswick peaked in 1846 and then fell dramatically. In 1848 the bottom fell out of the market, and according to A.R.M. Lower, 1846–9 were 'the worst years the colonies had ever known.'[29] Recovery did occur and accelerated when the Crimean War broke out, but it did not last very long. The American Civil War caused a recession in Britain, which depressed demand until 1863. The timber trade subsequently enjoyed ten good years, until the panic of 1873. The repeal of colonial preference did not immediately reorient the trade, which continued to cater to the British market. As Britain gradually turned towards the Baltic market and as the prized white pine was getting scarce in New Brunswick, lumberers sought alternatives. They found it to the south. American cities needed construction lumber, which can be manufactured from trees too small for ton timber. The reciprocity treaty (1854–66) established free trade in natural products between British North America and the United States, facilitating this trade.

It is unclear exactly what impact the cycles in the timber trade and the product shift had upon the industry in the Upper Saint John River basin. The most systematic of the scanty available sources are the export figures from Saint John, but they include all the wood shipped from that port, not merely that cut on the upper reaches of the river. Licence lists are useful as well, but after 1844 lumberers were not licensed to cut a specified quantity of wood, but on a specified acreage of timberland.[30] Export statistics suggest a shift from square timber to sawn lumber at mid-century (see figures 2 and 3). Surprisingly, they also suggest steady growth, contrary to what the secondary literature has led us to believe.[31] Timber licence figures, on the other hand, provide an altogether different picture (see figure 4). If output was roughly proportional to acreage under licence, the industry went into free fall in 1848 and ground to a halt in 1849 and 1850. Subsequent fluctuations closely parallel the ones described by Smith: the mid-1850s and the late-1860s were good; the late-1850s and 1862 were poor. On the whole, the industry moved in fits and starts: a few adequate years alternated with several very bad ones. This pattern may explain why most licensees, who were often non-local men, seldom re-applied for licences over a long period. They logged for one, two, or three years, and then were gone, never to be seen again. The industry was unstable, and so was most of its personnel.

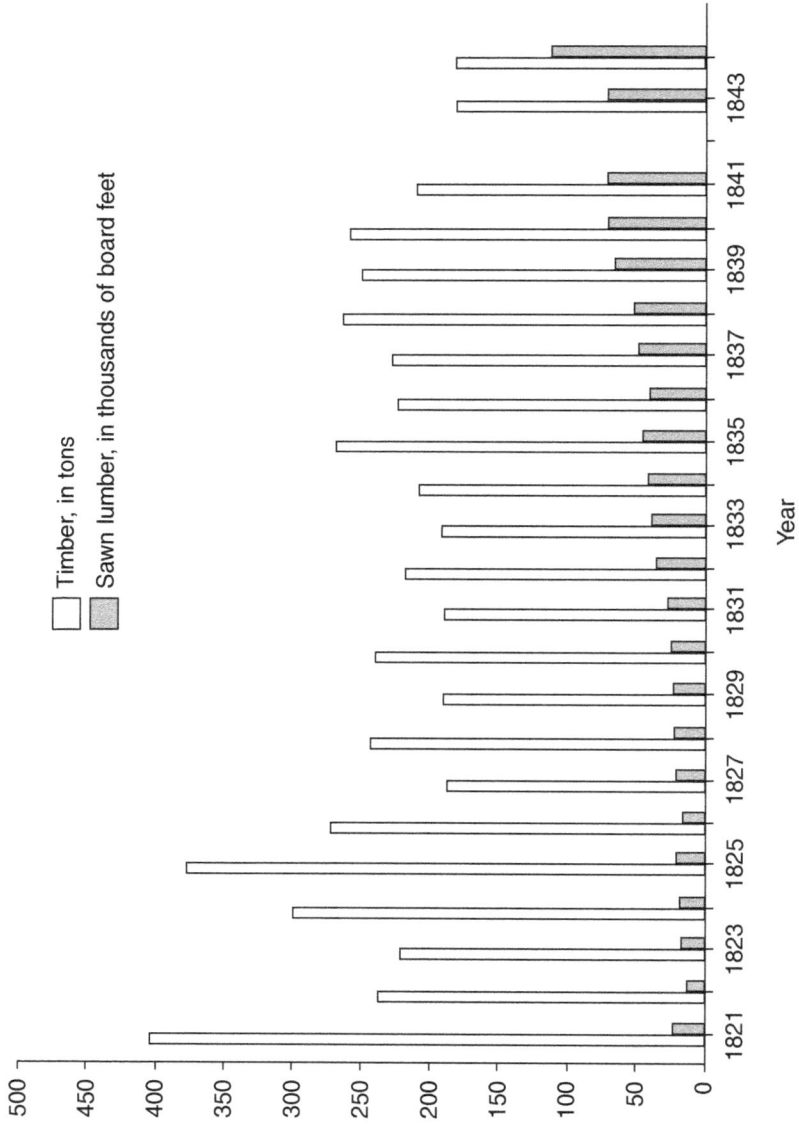

Figure 2. Quantities of timber and lumber exported from the port of Saint John, 1821–44

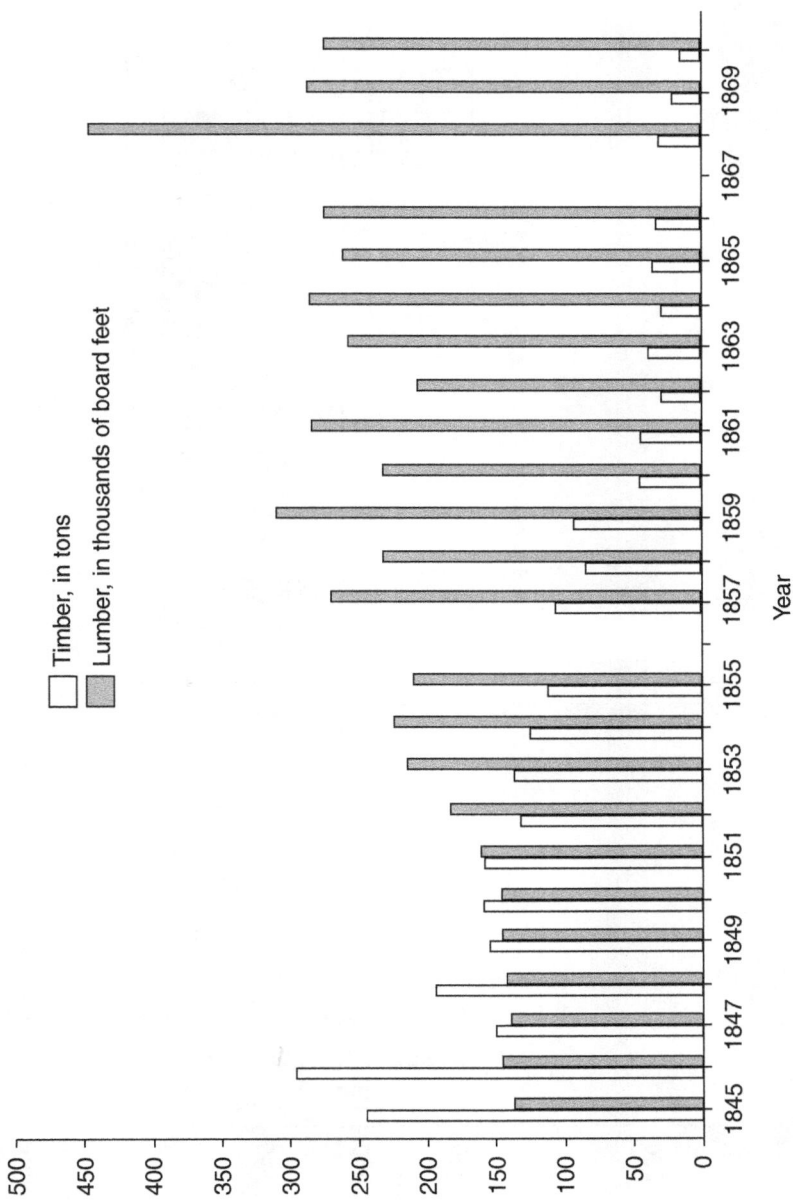

Figure 3. Quantities of timber and lumber exported from the port of Saint John, 1845–70

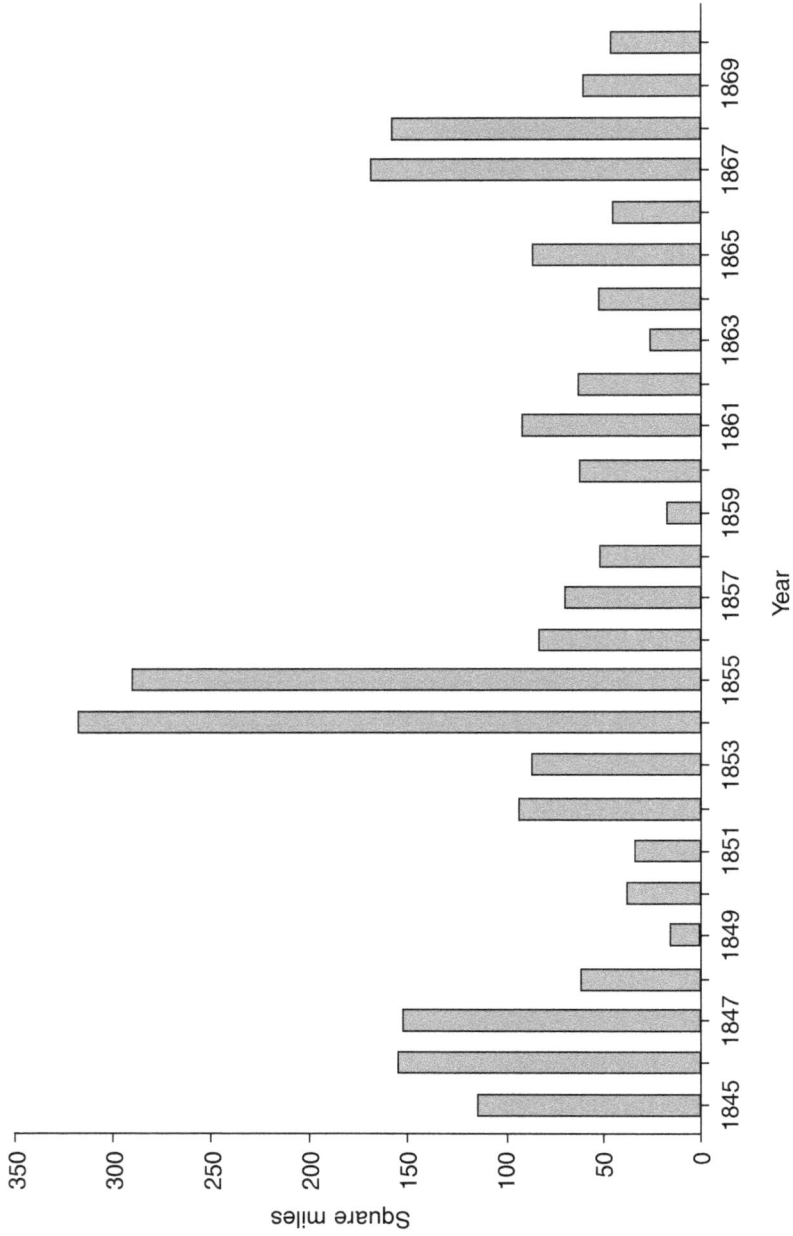

Figure 4. Timber licences in the Saint John Valley, 1845–70

The lack of production figures makes it even more difficult to determine what took place on the Maine side of the Saint John River basin. Indirect evidence suggests that the industry there was unstable as well. Townships or township sections of timberland could change hands several times in the course of a year. Buyers and sellers were always the same people, and the property was soon back in the hands of its original owner until the next round of sales.[32] This cycle suggests acute cash-flow problems, which implies that industry volatility existed in the American territory as well as in the British one.

The forest industry brought significant changes to the Upper Saint John Valley. It forced the resolution of the boundary issue, significantly changed patterns of migration, and altered the local social structure. Equally important, it tied the region to the continental and Atlantic economies. Britain purchased timber, U.S. cities needed lumber and shingles, the fisheries and the West Indies wanted barrel staves and other packaging material. Markets also shifted over time: as the overseas market for ton timber shrunk, the continental market for sawn lumber expanded. In addition, the industry involved local and external capital, suppliers, and labour, both before the treaty and after. In the early period, logging was conducted by small teams working independently or outfitted by outside merchants. The secondary literature on New Brunswick and Quebec argues that those small operators were gradually marginalized or eliminated in the course of the nineteenth century.[33] The situation on the Upper Saint John was less straightforward: large scale operators quickly dominated the industry after the treaty, but never monopolized it. Logging was carried out by a hierarchy of entrepreneurs, all the way down to the farmers who cut on the side.

The Lumberers

Big Men

Lumber operators shared one common characteristic: extreme vulnerability. Some were large operators whose presence spanned a long period of time and others were gone almost as soon as they arrived.[34] Dwarfed by the lumberers whose names surfaced repeatedly in the sources were mid-sized operators, whose businesses could be equally long- or short-lived. Finally, the small farmer–lumbers of the previous generation had never disappeared entirely.

Lumberers came from southern Maine and even from Massachusetts, from southern New Brunswick, especially Sunbury County, and from Lower Canada.[35] Some operators were complete outsiders who worked through local agents – like Pingree, who owned an enormous acreage of timberland in Maine,[36] or Rankins from Saint John, a branch house of Pollock, Gilmour and Co. of Glasgow, which conducted its business through Bedell of Fredericton.[37] Some, like James Tibbits, moved to New Brunswick and to the valley to conduct their business, kept a close look on activities on the Upper Saint John, and then went back home. Tibbits, a Quebec shipbuilder, engaged in lumbering and steam boating on the Saint John River, was elected to the New Brunswick house of assembly, became a member of the provincial executive and legislative councils, but nonetheless retired at Quebec where he died.[38] Other operators were state or provincial large-scale entrepreneurs who were directly involved in the day to day operations of their company, like John and Stephen Glazier from New Brunswick[39] or Shepard Cary from Maine.[40]

John Glazier (or Glasier), a native of Lincoln parish south of Fredericton, was the descendant of pre-Loyalist settlers.[41] In 1843 Glazier, in partnership with one of the main Bangor lumbermen, John Veazie, cut 4,800 tons in the territory in dispute between New Brunswick and Lower Canada on the uppermost Saint John.[42] The following year, Glazier and his brother Stephen began a lasting partnership. They started rather modestly but by 1847, they paid stumpage fees on 3,787 tons. The crisis of 1848 forced them to scale down, but over the next ten years, Glazier logged heavily on the uppermost Saint John.[43] In 1853, John and Stephen Glazier held the permits to log between the headwaters of the Daquaam and Saint John rivers, as well as on the heads of the Little and Big Black rivers, in the part of the former disputed territory awarded to Lower Canada.[44] After 1858 Glazier seems to have moved his operations elsewhere, possibly to the U.S. side, where he had purchased some timberland in 1849.[45] He had already cut timber on the Pingree land during the 1855–6 season. According to Richard Judd, Glazier's U.S. operations peaked that season, as afterwards there was less and less saleable timber to fell.[46] By the early 1860s, Glazier was going over some previously logged land, cutting the leftover smaller trees for sawn lumber. His New Brunswick operations could have been affected by the same shortage of timber-grade pines, and wound down for the same reason. The 1872–3 crises seems to have put an end to the Glaziers' lumbering operations. They only managed to keep their farm, which was heavily mortgaged. Even large operators were not immune to a reversal of fortunes. The same crisis brought down the powerful firm of Jewett of Saint John and its partner, Jewett and Pitcher of Boston, which went bankrupt in 1876, and brought down in their wake several substantial operators of long standing.[47] But by that time, Glazier had gone into politics: he had been elected a member of the house of assembly of New Brunswick in 1861, where he voted in favour of New Brunswick's entry into the new Canadian Confederation in 1867. He was appointed to the Canadian Senate in 1868 by the Conservative government of the time, and died in Ottawa in 1894.

Shepard Cary was one of John Glazier's American counterparts. The son of one the first settlers at Houlton, Maine, he initially trained as a carpenter and worked in New Brunswick, before opening a store in Houlton in partnership with his brother-in-law, Collin Whitaker, in 1826. Like most frontier storekeepers, Cary supplied lumbermen and accepted timber in payment. In the mid-1830s he went into lumbering himself, cutting with a state permit. His operations centred on Seven Islands, on the upper reaches of the Saint John River, some 80 miles above Fort Kent, where his brother Holman had established a farm and a supply depot. In the mid-1840s Cary opened a store at Fort Kent to secure supplies, and discovered that the farmers would not accept payment in truck: they wanted cash, and Cary had to comply. Cary's scope of operation seems to have been similar to Glazier's. Like Glazier, Cary went into politics, first at the state level for thirteen years, and then at the federal level for a term in 1861. By 1850 Cary had begun to divest himself of his timberland, and had started various manufacturing businesses in Houlton: a foundry, a furniture shop, and a clapboard mill.[48] Cary went out of business in the mid-1850s.[49] The Fort Kent store was sold in 1857 to William Cunliffe, who had worked for Cary since 1846. Cunliffe went into partnership with Shepard's brother Holman between 1865 and 1873, when Holman moved to Minnesota. Shepard Cary died in 1866.

The Glaziers' and Cary's difficulties were not unique. Lumbering was a speculative venture, and no one could take his solvency for granted. The northern Aroostook registry of the deeds details a number of episodes of rapid turnover of timberland: one or several owners first mortgaged whole sections or a township, then sold them at very low prices. A few months later, the sellers were buying back their property or similar ones, sometimes on credit. Glazier bought and sold in 1849; Cary in 1853–4. The turnovers highlight the fragility of the industry. They also shed some indirect light on the lumbermen's culture: they may have pounced on each other's misfortunes like a pack of wolves, but they made no visible efforts to drive anyone permanently out of the business. The loser at today's game was expected to be a player again tomorrow, with a bit of help from yesterday's creditors. In the game, reputation and a strict adherence to unwritten rules of conducts were critical. Dun and Co. actually rated the various lumberers in terms of their business integrity. Wiggin similarly underlined the moral qualities of some of the men in the biographies he wrote. He described Seeley as 'a man of strict business integrity, a gentleman of rich culture, a warm hearted, whole souled, honest man.' Among lumberers, reputation was the only secure capital.[50]

The organization of the industry also displayed some old-fashioned, if not archaic, characteristics. Lumbering was not treated as an on-going business, but as a series of single seasons independent of the others. Glazier returned in May or June the supplies he had not used that season to storekeeper and supplier John Emmerson and purchased similar items again three months later. He settled his account with Emmerson after he had sold his timber, which translated into accounts running for more than a twelve-month period but did not necessarily include the expenses for the following season, which were listed in a separate account. There was no J. and S. Glazier Co. that produced timber and lumber on a continuous basis, but two men who produced commodities on a yearly one. They did not capitalize their business and do not seem to have understood the concept of amortization. In any case, their way of inputting all expenses against the gross of the current season would have made this difficult. This practice also made calculating profits confusing; one wonders whether the Glaziers could tell how much they were really worth at any given time.

The Glaziers shifted some of the risks inherent in timber producing onto their supplier, storekeeper Emmerson, who had to supply them on credit. Cary for his part shifted some of the risks onto the workers, who were paid after he had sold his timber, and had to agree they would not sue for wages until then. If the wood was slow in selling, wages were slow in coming. Cary's hiring contracts also reflect an old-fashioned vision of labour relations. His employees were quasi-indentured servants. They agreed to work wherever Cary wanted at whatever tasks he ordered until they were discharged. They also agreed to forfeit their entire season's wages should they leave without permission, and to be liable for compensatory damages. They were to be paid in notes on any New Brunswick banks, not in species.[51] Cary's workers were bound to him, a practice which was not yet obsolete, but was fast becoming so.[52] His precautions may have been in response to recent labour problems. In 1845 his brother William, after bragging that he had hired men as cheaply as he could, confessed that he had to give them advances on their wages, and that one had not even shown up at the camp. 'I do not know what the law would call the transaction but I should call it swindling.' He had also heard that a man from one of their camps had gone over to another lumberer.[53]

Small Operators

Larger operators like Glazier and Cary did not drive the small operators out of business. Several individuals bound themselves to deliver ton timber to Cary in the 1840s; others got provincial licences, or bought stumpage rights from owners of timber tracts or from large licensees. Small operators also continued to be found in the provincial timber licence records. Between 1845 and 1871, the proportion of small-scale licences normally ranged between one quarter and three quarters of all licences. The distribution appears random, which is not very surprising as the numbers of licensees were small, never exceeding twenty-five. The main difference between large- and small-scale operators was the location of their activities. Large operators tended to move upriver and into the Allagash and Black River valleys. Small operators tended to be concentrated on the timberland at the back of the Saint John Valley settlement.[54] Presumably, large operators were not interested in those tracts, which had likely been culled of their best timber some time ago. Small operators, on the other hand, did not have the resources to venture far from the settlements in their search for timber.

Like their larger counterparts, smaller operators were a varied lot. They included people like John Emmerson, a Yorkshire native who became one of the valley's leading merchants (Emmerson is discussed in more detail in chapter 5). Emmerson's logging was inconsistent: in 1847 he cut 1,000 tons; in 1846, 2,233 tons. In later years his operations remained limited in scope and most of his permits were for between four and six square miles, never exceeding twelve square miles. Emmerson's timber operations may have been rather modest because they were secondary to his other activities: he opened a store near the junction of the Madawaska and Saint John Rivers around 1845.[55]

Messrs Rice, Beckwith, and Coombs are another example of small-scale entrepreneurs; the three became business partners in the 1830s. Charles Beckwith arrived at Madawaska sometime between 1831 and 1833.[56] He appears regularly in the provincial archives, playing hide-and-seek with Crown land agents who disbelieved the legal origins of his timber. He died within a decade. Elizabeth Ann Beckwith, who was granted land in the settlement in 1845, appears to have been his daughter. She married a Coombs at some uncertain date. Francis Rice was an Irish Catholic who moved to the Upper Saint John Valley in the 1820s. He married a woman from a charter family and became a farmer and schoolteacher. Immediately following the 1830 Catholic Emancipation Act, Rice was appointed justice of the peace for the Madawaska territory; he presumably was one of the few local residents who both knew English and was literate. He also became a militia adjutant. Rice does not seem to have done any lumbering outside his partnership with Beckwith and Coombs. In 1850, he was elected to the provincial legislature and was subsequently nominated to the provincial legislative council by the governor of New Brunswick. Rice also became a judge of the Inferior Court of Common Pleas, and a lieutenant colonel of the militia in 1864. Born with the century, he died in 1867.[57]

Leonard Coombs was the most involved in lumbering of the three. He moved to Madawaska about 1829 and purchased a piece of land with a stream for £300. As it was a British grant, he could legally cut its timber and bring it downriver. Coombs was commissioned as a militia captain in 1824 and promoted to the rank of lieutenant colonel in 1846. He also farmed.[58] He was involved in some sort of business at an early date because in 1832 he was sued for £1,200 ($4,800); his creditor wanted to seize his land. Coombs managed to placate him, but his cash-flow problems continued. In 1836 he had to mortgage his three lots at Madawaska to a Hugh Johnson. One of the lots had previously belonged to Peters and Wilmot, two Fredericton lumberers and millers who had tried to set up sawmills at Madawaska in the early 1820s and had gone bankrupt in 1828. Johnson was the creditor who had foreclosed on them. Coombs was both acquiring the same pieces of property and relying on the same lender as the previous timber firm.[59] In

1845 Coombs received a licence to cut timber on the Madawaska River. By the following year he applied for a position as provincial timber inspector, claiming that he had given up the trade. There is no evidence he secured the appointment.[60]

Coombes entered into a partnership with A.B. Hammond (who will be discussed in chapter 4). In 1845 Hammond and Coombs mortgaged 750 acres of land on the New Brunswick side of the river to Quebec timber merchant James Tibbits. The loan was to be repaid by 1852. In the late 1840s Coombs and Hammond lent money to a number of local people and foreclosed on most of them.[61] When the lumber trade ground to a halt in 1848, Hammond sold his share of the foreclosed properties to Coombs and pulled out. The same day, Coombs sold a part of a 670-acre lot south of the river to Tibbits and the rest to an Abraham Coombs. Tibbits seized some of Leonard Coombs's land the following spring to recoup a $2,500 debt but Coombs still managed to escape bankruptcy.[62] In 1851 when British agronomist J. F. W. Johnston visited the province at the invitation of the government, he visited Coombs, who was by then a militia colonel and gentleman farmer.[63] Before long, Coombs was appointed sheriff. As long as he was involved in the timber trade, Coombs seem to have spent his time staying one step ahead of his creditors and of disaster. The crisis of 1848 may have scared him into looking for more stable sources of income: farming and public appointments. His former partner Francis Rice was already following that route. Mid-size lumberers appear to have been a very vulnerable lot, and spent most of their business life desperately trying to avoid bankruptcy. However, lumbering did provide many of them with the visibility and stature necessary to get into politics or to secure government appointments.

Farmer-lumberers

Locally born farmers were also members of the lumbering brotherhood and they too fared unevenly. Several of them crossed the pages of Emmerson's account books; others can be found in the pages of the ledger of the Dufour store, which was situated next to the church, a few miles below Emmerson's.[64]

The farmer-lumberers supplied by the Dufour brothers did not fare too well. This may have been a matter of timing: the Dufour store ledger covers the depression years between 1844 and 1848. Nonetheless, at the end of 1846, not a bad year by any account, three of the ten farmer–lumberers supplied by the Dufour brothers had a negative account balance for the year.[65] Two were carrying over debts from the previous season and five had to give the Dufours promissory notes to cover their deficits. Their balances ranged from $45 to $400. One of the men, Joseph 'Quetoune' Michaud (identified in the parish register as a lumberman and different from Captain Joseph Michaud of the previous chapter) owed the Dufours $441 in 1846. At the end of the season, his seventy tons of pine and 4,000 feet of spruce brought in £64 ($256). He also had to pay £8 8s. 7½d. for rafting the wood. When his account was settled, he still had to give the Dufours a note for $176. Michaud started purchasing supplies again in March 1847, and the Dufours took a mortgage payable in November on the three pieces of land granted to him under the treaty. He defaulted, and the Dufours bought two of his lots, one for $50 and one for $1, well below their value.[66] By January 1848, Michaud owed £86, and had to sign another promissory note. Joseph Michaud was significantly impoverished by his participation in the timber trade, in large part because of his spending habits. His account with the Dufours was not limited to shanty supplies; Michaud was also buying larger quantities of household goods than most. Although Michaud owned land, he seemed to be trying to support his family through his income as a lumberman. It did not work: he was in difficulties even before the crisis of 1848. By 1850 he was landless, and the census lists his occupation as labourer. In 1860 he did own a modest farm on a good tract of land, but he was not enumerated in the agricultural census.[67]

Hilaire Levasseur was logging in partnership with the Dufours in 1846.[68] He continued doing business on his own during the 1852–3 season, between 1855 and 1859, and again between 1860 and 1864, supplied by Emmerson. His permits specified lots of two to four square miles at the rear of the Green, Rockway, and Quisibus rivers.[69] Levasseur himself lived at the mouth of the Green River. We know how much he cut between 1858 and 1860 from his account with another Glazier brother, Duncan, for the towing of his timber between Fredericton and Saint John: 594 tons of pine and 12,738 feet of logs in 1858; 45 tons in 1859; 496 tons and 730,000 feet of logs in 1860.[70] Although Levasseur seems to have done well, he also tried to pull out of the timber business. Like Michaud, he acquired land but had difficulties keeping it. Levasseur had purchased two half farm lots in 1847, perhaps with his timber profits, but had to sell one along with his treaty lot in 1848. He bought two neighbouring lots in New Brunswick in 1852 and 1858 and one in Maine in 1860, which he sold within a year to his brother; he also sold the last of his 1847 lot in 1863.[71] In 1861 Emmerson, who was operating as a wholesaler as well as a retailer, sold Levasseur a large stock of goods that reads suspiciously like a store inventory. The sale was on credit and Emmerson took a mortgage on Levasseur's farm to secure it. The store appears in no surviving records. Levasseur not only failed to repay the mortgage on time, but failed to pay the interest: in 1866 his store account at Emmerson was debited almost $50 for three-and-a-half year's interest. Levasseur's farm was sold at public auction to Emmerson's brother-in-law in 1866.[72] A rather cryptic entry in one of the Emmerson store ledgers seems to suggest that Levasseur rented his old farm for £15 a year until 1868, but was later buying it back on credit. In 1871 Levasseur was listed as a proprietor in the census, but no entry in the county land registry supports this claim. He did very well as a farmer, growing hay in large quantities. Levasseur landed on his feet, but only when he got out of lumbering and trade and turned his hand to commercial farming. Lumbering had been a springboard to nowhere for him. He ran for a seat in the provincial house of assembly in 1863, but was defeated.[73] His only civic appointment was as a justice of the peace in 1865.

The Albert brothers, Louis, Hubert, Sevère, and Joseph, did a little better than Levasseur. Louis (aka Louison) Albert owed the Dufours $400 in 1846, despite finishing the year with a profit of £77 ($308). But he had accumulated debts the years before and in August 1847 Abraham Dufour sued him for $460. The following January, Albert sold the Dufours half his properties, at below market price. He was left with a single one hundred-acre lot.[74] By the 1853–4 season he was logging again, on the New Brunswick side of the Green River, with his three brothers. It seems he was logging Emmerson's berth (Emmerson had a licence for six square miles). Emmerson sold supplies to Louison and his brother Sevère and, along with lumberman L. J. Brown who also had licences for the Green River tract, sold their timber in Saint John. The lot of wood, of unknown size and composition, fetched £1,176 10s. The brothers paid £215 to Brown, £42 to the Fredericton Boom Company where the wood was held and sorted, £23 to Duncan Glazier for towing, and £93 to Edwin Fisher, a timber broker in Saint John. They also gave their brother Joseph £56 for his share of the wood. After settling their store accounts, they were left with a joint sum of £435 8s. Their brother Joseph was logging independently and sold his timber to Brown for £306.[75] His balance, after settlement of his account, was £45. Despite a successful season, the Alberts did not continue logging, and reverted to farming.

Louis Albert lost some of his property in 1848, but none of his brothers seem to have suffered the same fate. Hubert, who was still a young man, owned none when he was lumbering with his brothers. The Alberts did nothing out of the ordinary with their lumbering profits. None went into any kind of business and Louis never acquired any land besides the two lots granted to him by Maine.[76] Joseph acquired all his land before 1852; Sevère had been granted a lot which he sold in 1847[77]; and the last two brothers may have acquired land after the 1853–4 season, but unfortunately some of their purchases went unreported – they sold land at a later date whose acquisition was never recorded in the register of the deeds. Louis and his brother Sevère did have an opportunity to go into business. They had married two sisters whose widowed mother, Angélique Martin, had a life interest in a lot at the mouth of the Rockway or Iroquoise River. The site was ideal for a mill and the lot was to revert to Angélique's heirs after her death. In 1849 Louison and Sevère sold their wive's rights to the lot to Denis Thériault, another of Angélique's sons-in-law.[78] Denis became a miller. Except for the few seasons when they worked in the woods, the Alberts were run-of-the-mill farmers. This was probably a wise move: lumbering was a gamblers' industry and in the long run, one was more likely to lose than win. But they could have used the profits earned in lumbering to underwrite other businesses, and apparently did not.

Conclusion

Timber was a staple commodity, but it created few backward linkages, with the exception of commercial mills (discussed in chapter 4). Large-scale lumberers did not invest in the region and rarely in the province or state. James Tibbits, who ran a steamboat service on the Saint John River, tried to establish one above Grand Falls. The venture failed, and the boat was dismantled, rebuilt below the falls, and finished its days plying the Lower Saint John.[79] John Glazier apparently ran a store for a time, and invested in the Fredericton Boom Company, a holding area for timber rafts waiting to be towed to Saint John that was run by his brother Duncan. Shepard Cary went into manufacturing, not in the region where he had made his money, although still in the same county.

The production of timber was also an old-fashioned form of business that bound workers to operators in a type of master-servant relationship. It was not a business organized to facilitate capital accumulation. It operated in the short term – the length of a season – and lumberers tried to shift as many of the risks as they could onto others: storekeepers, who provided them with supplies on credit, and workers, who were bound for the season and could not claim their wages until the timber they had cut had been sold.

Despite the risk-minimizing strategies, the forest industry was not a road to riches for lumbermen. Why then did so many engage in it? It is unlikely that they viewed trade as an economic activity governed by reasonably predictable rules (as later economists claimed), that made long-term, rational strategies possible. Like their eighteenth-century counterparts, they appear to have perceived trade and economic activities as so many discrete opportunities to reap a windfall. The trick was to know when to play and when to pass. The timberland turnover documented by the northern registry of deeds is evidence that sometimes one was forced to fold by the other players, who raked in all the chips and then would lend one the means of getting back in the game. The game required strategy but also luck and the right instincts. This gambling mind set, as much as the volatility of the trade, made the forest industry a poor agent of development in Madawaska and elsewhere. C.S. Clark, a Bangor lumberman who owned large tracts of timberland on Temiscouata Lake and the Madawaska River, was also the largest operator in the St Francis drainage basin of the Eastern Township in the mid-1850s and the 1860s. Clark did poorly in the late 1860s, and almost went under after 1875. He stayed afloat because he repeatedly logged or floated the logs illegally, and 'forgot' to pay his licence fees to the province. J.I. Little concluded that 'the history of C.S. Clark and Cie. had as much to do with political power as it did with market place imperatives.'[80] In the Upper Saint John Valley basin, non-economic factors were also more likely to contribute to the fortunes of lumber operators than was the marketplace.

Nor do smaller lumber operators seem to have derived much direct benefit from the timber trade. Lumbering was a 'discrete adventure' among others for them; the same applies to farmer-lumberers, who were probably no more successful in making a living from the avails of lumbering than 'Quetoune' Michaud. Most of these men improved their economic standing, or at least their economic security, when they stopped producing lumber and moved on to other activities. To what extent did these other activities benefit from their involvement in the timber trade? The Alberts were able to make a comfortable profit that they may have invested in their farm. On the other hand, lumbering did not provide Hilaire Levasseur with adequate capital for his later activities. Farmer-lumberers do not seem to have fared any better in the long run than their neighbours who stayed clear of the trade. When contemporaries claimed that he who farms and logs cannot do both well and goes to his ruin, they probably had people like Michaud, and Levasseur in his younger days, in mind.

4 Sawmills, Gristmills, and Lumber Manufacture

A mill working two saws employs four first rate millers or sawyers, four second rate and two ordinary men, 34 common labourers accustomed to the woods, the water and the axe, one surveyor of lumber and occasionally for a millwright, a carpenter, a blacksmith, 20 oxen and two horses

Crown Land Commissioner Thomas Baillie, 1831[1]

Mills that manufactured lumber and processed wood by-products into lath and packaging material were the main linkages created by the timber trade. To historians such as Graeme Wynn, Richard Judd, and Alan Taylor, as well as nineteenth-century observers and antiquarians, such mills were key factors in the economic development of the sparsely settled parts of Maine and New Brunswick.[2] Mills that catered to the staple trade, however, may have played a lesser role in regional development than the ones that targeted a local or regional clientele.

Thomas Baillie, the man in charge of administering the province's public land, claimed that large sawmills gave rise to settlements that housed millers, labourers, blacksmiths, and carpenters. Those settlements then attracted the shoemaker, the store, the public house, and finally the gristmill. Although sawmills were fairly expensive to build, they were not beyond the reach of a small entrepreneur. According to Baillie, a sixty- by forty- by twenty-five-foot mill, including the dam, cost less than £1,000 ($4,000). The machinery was very simple and made of wood; iron machinery was too expensive and impractical as no engineer was available to repair it. Since mills were water-powered and therefore idle during the winter months, men needing another source of income could work in the woods, and they could have farms and raise animals. Thus, according to Baillie, large mills not only stimulated the growth of settlements, but also the clearing of land and the development of farming.

Lumber mills were also bridges that connected isolated communities with the larger economy. They produced a region's first export in the shape of small quantities of square timber, clapboards, shingles, or laths, which were floated downriver to the nearest port. Millers who wished to engage in the lumber trade, even on a small-scale basis, needed raw materials and they encouraged the formation of winter logging parties drawn from the local farm population. They also collected logs from farmers and from independent logging parties. Mills thus played a pivotal role in integrating the agricultural and the lumbering sectors of the economy. Lumber mills were the commonest form of linkage generated by the timber trade. They also required that capital be tied up in infrastructure. This made 'capitalists' of millers in a way that lumber operators, who risked other people's money, rarely were.

The picture of the miller that emerges from the literature is of a man who moved to the frontier in search of economic opportunities and became a catalyst of settlement, his mill a locus of exchange between local and outside goods. Frontier adventurers were agents of development. Baillie's vision of the mill as a factor in the promotion of settlements was not inaccurate, but a bit optimistic. Some northern Maine sawmills were indeed the nuclei of later settlements, but seldom on the scale he described.[3] In the Aroostook Valley, the mill closest to that description belonged to Dennis Fairbanks, who settled in Caribou about 1832. He claimed 640 acres, erected a saw- and gristmill, five houses, a tavern, store, and school.[4] Fairbanks's was one of the larger complexes; more common was the situation in Ashland, where George Buckmore (the Maine state agent encountered in chapter 3) built a saw- and gristmill in 1838, soon joined by a public house, and then by a store. Elsewhere, as in Fort Fairfield and Washburn, also in the Aroostook Valley, the sawmill became an important focal point for the surrounding farmers because the miller also ground grain and carded wool, but these mills did not become magnets for other country businesses.[5]

Sawmills did not exist solely to feed the staple trade and did not all manufacture commodities for export. Settlers needed lumber, irrespective of the demands of international trade, and some mills were built exclusively to satisfy the local market. Custom mills supplied farmers with sawn lumber for their construction needs, or processed the farmers' timber. As the demand for lumber was limited and sporadic, the custom millers diversified their operations, adding grindstones and a carding/fulling machine to their equipment. Mills became a social centre where the farmers exchanged news and gossip while their timber, grain, wool, or cloth was being processed.[6]

At Madawaska, the situation was different. Settlers preceded the arrival of the millers, especially millers engaged in the lumber trade (henceforth referred to as 'commercial mills'). However, most of the commercial mills were concentrated in the western end of the settlement, where they attracted a larger than average non-farm population. By midcentury, Madawaska millers fell into one of two groups. The first was made up mostly of outside, Anglo-Protestant men with contacts in Saint John and access to capital, and who catered primarily to the staple trade in timber, lumber, and shingles. The other was made up of local, overwhelmingly French individuals providing services to their growing community.[7] The latter stood less chance of becoming very wealthy but they were also less likely to be wiped out by a downturn in the business cycle. Lasting success was more likely to reward those who kept their distance from international trade.

Staple Producers

The Baker Mill

The first commercial sawmill in Madawaska was probably the one built by either Nathan or John Baker. The Bakers, who worked as timber cruisers for Fredericton merchant Samuel Nevers, claimed land at the mouth of the Meruimticook. In 1831, John had only seven acres cleared on his one-hundred-acre claim, all planted in hay. In 1833 he had no crops, and reported none for the preceding years.[8] The brothers had not come to the Saint John Valley to become farmers; they intended to make their fortune logging and making lumber. As Americans, they were not able to get a grant for the land they occupied.[9] In 1824, Samuel Nevers had applied for a grant for the Baker property, which included a house, a barn, and a grist- and sawmill. It is not clear whether he got it – a marginal comment on the application states that 'the location being described is vacant and unapplied for Crown land.'[10] Nevers nonetheless behaved as if he considered himself owner of at least part of the Baker property. In 1825 he sold half of it to the Fredericton lumbering firm of Peters and Wilmot, and in 1828 he sold another half to a Fredericton widow, Phoebe Copperthwaite, who seems to have been in the business of collecting potentially profitable properties in the province, for £200.[11]

The mill disappears from the records until 1847 when Enoch, John Baker's son, sold the mill, the water privileges, and the mill lot (#67) to Frederick Hatheway, a Saint John merchant, for £500. The subsequent story of the mill can be glimpsed at in the county registry of the deeds. Glimpsed at but not followed, because it is quite plain that all the transactions involving it were not recorded. What we can witness is nonetheless revealing. Over the next twenty years, the mill, or undivided shares of it, was sold no less than twenty-eight times.[12] Buyers and sellers included a wide array a persons: Hatheway, Wiley and Burray of Madawaska, Turner and Whitney from Maine, Jesse Wheelock, one of Baker's original confederates, Hilaire Pelletier, a local French lumberer, Collins Whitaker, brother-in-law of lumberer Shepard Cary from Houlton, Edward Jewett from the lumbering firm of Jewett and March of Saint John, who paid $5,000 for the property, Prudent Gagnon, a local merchant and miller, as well as several members of the Baker family: John, his wife Sophia, his sons Enoch and John, Enoch's French-Canadian wife Madeleine Ouellette, and the younger John's wife Sarah. Most of the transactions involved one of those three women. Somewhere along the way, one mill became two: In the 1871 census, Prudent Gagnon is listed as owning a gristmill under repair worth $1,100 on this site, and Baker a sawmill worth $1,000 on the same site.

What can we conclude from what looks like a game of hot-potato? First, money-making properties (or shares thereof) changed hands very frequently, like timberland. Second, they attracted the interest of outsiders, who were as likely to be Americans as Provincials, like Hatheway, Whitaker, and Jewett. Third, the local family who originally built the mill had the greatest difficulty keeping it in its hands. And fourth, prices were absolutely erratic, suggesting speculative ventures. Whitaker and Jewett, who had deep pockets, paid $5,000 for the property (Jewett bought from Whitaker). We do not know what Jewett did with it, but five years later, half of the mill was being sold by Sarah and Madeleine Baker to Prudent Gagnon for $300.

Were people constantly forced to sell because they were experiencing cash flow problems and had run out of credit? Were outsiders then stepping in, willing to pay large sums when they thought the trade was favourable, and dumping the property at fire-sale prices when they discovered they had made a wrong bet, allowing the local people with less capital to regain the property? Though this explanation is plausible, it cannot be proven, and it is also unclear why the Baker women played such a prominent role in the transaction history of the mills.

The Fish River Mills

On the American side of the river, the situation was similar. The 1850 census lists two sawmills in Hancock plantation. The mills were heavily capitalized (an average of $10,000 each), and the total output was valued at $17,000. They were located on the Fish River about one mile above its junction with the Saint John, in the newly named village of Fort Kent.

One of the mills had a long history, having been started up by the Peter and Wilmot firm in 1825 before it went bankrupt. By 1836 the mill was in the hands of Nathaniel Bartlett, another of John Baker's companions. Bartlett sold it to Hatheway for £200.[13] In 1845 Hatheway sold it to Niles, West, and Soper, an Old Town lumbering firm (Old Town is in central Maine, next to Bangor). Soper sold his share right away, and after going through the hands of Bangor and Old Town men (and women) as well as a Massachusetts bank, the share ended up in the possession of a Bangor merchant, James Jenkins. West and Niles moved to Fort Kent, removed the Savage mill and built a new one, which contained an up-and-down saw and two clapboard and two shingle machines. Soon they added a store, a smithy, and a boathouse, as well as a house each on the property. Finally, they constructed a bridge across the river.[14]

Silas Niles died in 1852, and Henry West entered into partnership with Charles Jenkins. In 1854 a freshet washed out the whole compound except for the mill, and cut a new channel for the river. The partners rebuilt a new six-saw mill to manufacture deals for the British market. The 1850 census lists West and Niles as owners of a mill valued at $8,000, producing sawed lumber from logs and employing forty-five men. They produced $8,000 worth of boards and clapboards and $15,000 worth of ton timber. In 1866 the mill was sold to Asa Smith of Bangor, and shortly afterwards to George Seeley, a New Brunswick-born Fort Kent merchant. It burned in 1868 and was never rebuilt.[15]

The West and Niles mill was located on the east side of the Fish River. In 1847 Cyrus Bodfish from Gardiner in southern Maine and Colonel David Page of Waterville, near Gardiner, who may have come with the Maine militia, purchased from West and Niles the part of the lot that lay on the east side of the Fish River, with half the dam and water privileges, and built a mill. When the partners ran out of capital, Bodfish mortgaged the property to a Waterville man and finished the mill, which he equipped with one saw and clapboard and shingle machines. In 1848 William Dickey, another Gardiner man, bought the property. In the 1850 census, it is listed as the Bodfish and Dickey mill, worth $12,000. It had employed twenty men to produce $9,000 worth of boards and clapboards. Dickey added a gristmill to the property and sold it in 1854.[16]

The mill was purchased by Levi Sears, who happened to be married to Silas Niles's widow. The Fort Kent industrial schedule of the 1860 census has not survived. Sears is listed as a lumberman in the personal census; his real estate is worth $ 8,000 and his personal estate $15,000. He lived with his wife, two step-children, his daughter, a servant, and sixteen unmarried male labourers. In 1870 Sears was still in business; he owned a five-saw mill with clapboard and shingle machines estimated at $2,000, and a gristmill with two runs of stones worth $1,000. The output consisted of 2 million shingles worth $16,000, 15,000 feet of clapboard worth $ 1,000, $ 10,800 worth of boards, and $ 11,500 worth of flour. He employed twelve men.[17]

There are similarities between the history of the Fish River and Baker mills. In both cases, the sites and the properties built upon them attracted the attention of outside investors and before 1842, of the same outside investors: Nevers, Peters and Wilmot, and Hatheway. Outside investors teamed up with men residing on the site, like the Bakers, or moved to the valley themselves, like West, Niles, or Dickey. Mill ownership could be very unstable: as well as a means of making a living, mills were quasi-liquid assets. The mills at Fish River also played the role Baillie and later historians ascribed to them: they attracted settlers, provided wage earning opportunities for a considerable number of men, and became the nucleus of a small service centre. In 1860 according to the census, Sears and West were neighbours to Samuel Stevens, hotelkeeper, Joseph (José) Nadeau, inn-keeper, George Seeley, dry good merchant, and William Cunliffe, who ran a variety store. The four men were still in business in 1870, and had been joined by another merchant. By 1870 Fort Kent was also the township with the highest proportion of households not headed by a farmer. But although the mills spurred settlement and development, they brought uncertain rewards to their owners. The value of the mills declined markedly. In the case of the Sears mill, it collapsed to one-sixth of its value over twenty years, this despite extensive additional machinery.

The Hammond Lumber Manufacture

The third commercial mill was located at the other end of the settle-ment, and by 1870 was the largest lumbering business in the valley. This mill successfully reduced its dependence on the staple trade, and engaged in the manufacturing of lumber products for the regional market instead. It was started by William Cook Hammond, who was born in Kingsclear near Fredericton in 1818, and worked first in the lumbering business of his uncles Abraham and Charles Hammond. In 1841 he married Leonard Coombs's sister, and bought a farm across the river from his brother-in-law. Shortly afterwards, Leonard was lumbering in partnership with Abraham Hammond and with James Tibbits of Quebec. William Cook made a living farming, logging, trading and manufacturing lumber, at times in partnership with his brother-in-law.[18]

In 1848 Coombs sold a large lot that had been granted to him by the state of Maine in Van Buren to Abraham Coombs (perhaps his son), and four years later, Abraham sold his aunt Caroline (William Cook's wife) 260 acres of that lot for $1,500.[19] Maine had enacted a Married Women's Property Act a few years earlier, and selling the property to Caroline, as opposed to William Cook, put it out of reach of his credi-tors. Nonetheless, William Cook mortgaged the property immediately to Charles A. Hammond, his childless uncle who was an innkeeper in Grand Falls, a few miles downriver. It is not clear what William Cook was doing for a living at the time, but there was a mill on the property. In April 1859 William Cook was sued by a W.H. Smith of Bangor for $2252.49. William Cook turned over twenty acres of the Van Buren property, which was appraised at $2311.70, to Smith. Smith sold it the following year to John and Stephen Glazier for $100.[20] In the meantime, Smith probably ran the mill through an agent or relative: a G. Smith is listed in the 1860 census in possession of a mill worth $800 and employing eleven men. It produced $6,000 worth of boards, shingles, clapboards, and sashes, the latter a new manufactured product. As for William Cook, he is listed in the same census not as a mill owner, but as a farmer; his farm was valued at $ 4,000 and he grew astronomically large quantities of hay and potatoes.[21]

In 1861 William Cook contracted with the Glaziers to deliver 8,500 board feet of spruce logs over the next four years, and received a loan of $300 from them, secured by a mortgage on his wife's property. The mortgage was discharged in 1866. William Cook though did not do all the cutting himself, and subcontracted some of it to a J. Bourguoin in 1862. Bourguoin was to deliver $135 of spruce logs within twelve months, and the contract was secured by a mortgage on Bourguoin's farm, which was discharged in 1867. In the meantime, Caroline Hammond bought the mill back from the Glaziers for $2,000.[22] William Cook also possessed a few other pieces of real estate including a smithy, which he seems to have sold when he needed to raise cash. By 1870 William Cook was a farmer in a neighbouring township. His son, William Cook junior, on the other hand, was listed as a merchant and manufacturer of boards and shingles (not as a miller) in Van Buren. He was 26, married, and perhaps a partner with his father in W.C. Hammond and Co, worth $12,000. The company owned a mill equipped with two up-and-down saws, a hedger and a trimmer, two clapboard, two shingle, and two lath and picket machines. It employed ten workers. The output was evaluated at $19,100, half of it in clapboards.[23] Within ten years, the business had expanded and acquired property in Montana under the name Hammond Lumber Co.[24]

The Hammond story presents some variations on the preceding two. The Hammonds were relative latecomers to the Saint John Valley, and they came in part to take advantage of the timber trade in which the family was already involved. William Cook Hammond occasionally experienced cash-flow problems, and his property stood the risk of permanently slipping through his fingers on several occasions. The Hammond mill, as opposed to the Baker's, was only briefly owned by people outside the family. The Hammonds did not bring with them capital or credit lines, like the Fish River mill owners. They raised capital through family connections, and through mortgaging land. Caroline Hammond's property specifically seems to have been used as collateral to raise money. The Hammond Company was very much a family business, built over several generations, whereas the Fish River and Baker mills were disposable assets for the majority of their owners. The Baker and Fish River mills focused mostly or exclusively on timber and lumber manufacturing, whereas the Hammond mill diversified, producing items that were more than semi-processed commodities, such as sashes and mouldings. The Hammonds were still producing lumber in 1904. One of William Cook's sons was a director of the Bangor and Aroostook Railroad, and owner of the Van Buren lumber company (1901–1918), one of the largest lumber mills in northern Maine.[25] The Hammonds also tried to stay one step ahead of the economy; in the 1870s they started up lumber operations in Montana, and later in California.[26] The family was a different type of entrepreneur than Hatheway, Bodfish, and West and Niles, who seem to have merely ridden economic opportunities for as long as they could and then moved on. The Hammonds were budding industrialists, whereas the others were merely mining their environment for profit.

Custom Millers

Commercial mills were in the hands of outsiders who moved to the Saint John Valley to take advantage of the opportunities offered by the timber trade. Occasionally, these men engaged in other ventures (gristmilling, general trade, smithing), and they likely did some custom milling as well. Some were birds of passage, some stayed permanently. However, they did not push local men out of milling, any more than large lumberers had pushed local men out of lumbering (see tables 3, 4, and 5). Local men were far more likely to engage in activities primarily serving the needs of their community. The custom gristmills and sawmills, the carding and fulling mills were theirs. Although some of the mills seem to have been primitive, poorly capitalized affairs, it does not necessarily follow that local men were adverse to innovation. In 1870 the only Upper Saint John Valley mill that could boast a circular saw was a custom mill at Grand Isle owned by Michel Martin.[27]

Custom mills tended to belong to members of the charter families and even to a very limited number of interrelated charter families whose members had had the foresight to lay claim to appropriate sites in the early years of the settlement. With few exceptions their owners were large landowners, or men who had obtained the mill or a site from their father who was a large landowner. Custom mill owners had usually benefited from the patient accumulation of assets over two or three generations, and until the 1860s customs mills were rarely sold outside of the extended family.

All in the Family: Milling and the Thibodeau Clan

Our old acquaintance, Firmin Thibodeau, one of the millers identified by land agents Deane and Kavanagh, was related to no less than ten different Madawaska millers. Milling was in his blood: according to Thomas Albert, his grandfather Pierre had operated a mill in old Acadia.[28] Firmin was a nephew of the Jean Baptiste Thibodeau who milled in Montmagny (see chapter 1).[29] Milling continued down the line, mostly among Firmin's descendents. Firmin's double uncle Paul Potier had started the first Madawaska mill around 1790. Firmin's first cousin David Dufour, whose daughter Marie Edith married Firmin's grandson and namesake in 1842, had taken it over. The younger Firmin owned the Mill Brook site in Saint Leonard, which he sold to a David Pickett in 1860. Pickett operated a mill on the site, and six years later sold it to Isaac Bijeau, one of Firmin's great-nephews, for $ 750.[30] (All the mills and mill sites discussed in the remainder of this chapter were located at or very near the mouth of tributaries of the Saint John river)

One of the elder Firmin's three sons, François (born 1804), acquired the Bellefleur mill in 1835. He sold it to his daughter Julie and her merchant husband Jules Lévesque, in 1864. He also sold them the mill his father had owned in 1831. In 1867 the Lévesques sold the mill on credit to Joseph Corriveau for $500.[31] Corriveau's wife Flavie was a first cousin once removed to François Thibodeau's wife, a third cousin to Julie Thibodeau-Lévesque, and a second cousin to Barbe Bijeau, Isaac's mother. As for Michel Martin, proud owner of the mill with a circular saw, his mother was one of Firmin's daughters (Firmin had given her a granted farm as a wedding present).[32] His father, François-Xavier, who was labelled *écuyer* or esquire in the parish register, was a second cousin to Joseph Corriveau, and to Denis and Lévite Thériault, who will be discussed in the next section. François-Xavier's second wife was also a daughter to Firmin Thibodeau's second wife, making him a double brother-in-law to Vital Thibodeau. Past, present, and future millers must have been endlessly bumping into one another at weddings and funerals.

The elder Firmin's son Vital similarly owned several mills during his lifetime. In 1846 he bought a sawmill at Violette Brook for $900 from one Isaac Mace. His new mill was located next to a gristmill he already owned; three years later, he purchased another mill in the vicinity from his father. He exchanged the first mill in 1868 for a life annuity of $320 from Israel Michaud, who was not related to him. Michaud's father, a Canadian migrant, had managed to marry a Cyr, and thus ally himself with a charter family. In 1870 Michaud was running a grist- and sawmill on the south bank of the river. Vital sold the second mill to his son-in-law Firmin Cyr in 1862.[33] Neither the elder Firmin nor Vital ever resided on the site. They lived together at St Basile, on the New Brunswick side of the river. François lived at Grand Isle, where one of his mills was located.[34] Clearly, these men had to hire mill hands to run their mills; they could not do it themselves. In addition, they owned considerable acreage, far more than they could cultivate on their own.

Several of Firmin's descendents went into local politics. François, who had been a militia lieutenant since 1840 and a New Brunswick justice of the peace, was a member of the Maine state House between 1849 and 1852; he was succeeded by his brother-in-law Paul Cyr. Joseph Nadeau, innkeeper at Fish River, replaced Paul until 1857 when Firmin's grandson, the younger Firmin, took his place. Then Paul Cyr replaced him from 1859 to 1861. What is peculiar here is that François was a New Brunswick justice of the peace the same year he was elected to the state House.[35] François's wife was a religious patron who financed the erection of a shrine over an allegedly miraculous spring in Grand Isle, on the American shore. François was important enough for the bishops of Boston to stay at his home when they were conducting their pastoral visits in American Madawaska.[36] Two of his daughters were among the dozen or so pupils boarding at the St Basile Convent School in 1871.[37] In 1858 Thibodeau and Firmin Cyr took part in the county Republican convention, which elected former storekeeper and cousin Abraham Dufour as party vice-president.[38] Large-scale landownership beginning with the elder Firmin, had led to business, and both had been stepping stones to politics.

A Small Empire: From Country Miller to Politician

Régiste (also François-Régis or Régis) Thériault did not end up the worse for his foray into lumbering. He had an annual licence to cut on two square miles on the Rockway River from 1850 to 1852, and again in 1861. His son Lévite did the same in 1861 and 1866.[39] Lévite also purchased the old Madawaska seigneury around Temiscouata Lake, to ensure a steady supply of wood for his mill.[40] In 1861 Registe owed $10,000 worth of real estate, making him the richest landowner in the valley; he had three servants living with him. Lévite attended school at the collège Ste Anne de la Pocatière. He was census enumerator in 1861, a patronage job. In 1867 Registe sold his son a small lot on the Iroquois River for $ 1,400.[41] When Registe died in 1868, his real estate was valued at $8,000 and included a sawmill, a gristmill, a carding mill, a fulling mill, a tannery, and a blacksmith shop. In addition, his personal estate was estimated at $2,000.[42] Lévite, who was the only son, inherited the industrial equipment.[43]

The Rockway is a particularly winding river, and three lots at its mouth were suitable mill sites. In 1841 Registe had purchased one of the three mill sites on the Rockway River on credit from Joseph Martin the elder, father-in-law to his brother Bénoni, for £315. Soon afterwards he was operating a triple saw-grist-carding mill on the premises. In 1861 55-year-old Bénoni was listed in the census merely as a farmer, but his son Denis, the one who had bought the rights to one of the Rockway river lots from the Alberts, was a miller. In the 1850s Denis purchased from his father several pieces of land at the mouth of the Green River that could also have been used to build a mill.[44] In 1866 Bénoni sold the rest of his landed property to his other son Louis for $1,000. A brook that discharged into the Saint John River flowed through the property, and the northern half of the lot was described as in the possession of Israel Michaud.[45] There was a third mill on the Rockway, according to the 1861 census, run by Pierre Plourde, who also had had a licence to cut on the river in 1852–3, and was one of the farmer-lumberers in the Dufour ledger. In 1871 Lévite and Denis Thériault and Pierre Plourde were all operating mills. Lévite's reported gross output from the carding- and sawmills was $ 2,350; Denis's from the saw-, grist- and carding mills, $6,230, and Plourde's saw- and gristmill brought in $1,200.[46] Lumbering could be a profitable proposition, if the activity was pursued to supply a custom mill, instead of trying to sell to timber merchants. Lévite's wealth made a political career possible: he was returned as a member of the provincial legislative assembly in 1867–8 and again in 1870–82 and 1886–94; he was a member of the provincial cabinet in 1871–2. He was also secretary of the Victoria County agricultural society, member of the board of agriculture of the province, and registrar of deeds for Madawaska from 1894 until his death in 1896.[47] Lévite's father Régiste also had a commendable record of service to the community. He reached the rank of major in the militia in 1865 and was appointed justice of the peace in 1854. The other Thériaults appear to have eschewed community leadership.

Divisions

Although custom and commercial millers, storekeepers, and lumberers functioned primarily at different levels of the economy, they appear to have shared a commonality of interests or a common view of their social and economic roles. Francis Rice from Madawaska and James Tibbits from Andover were declared elected to the provincial legislative assembly in 1854. The vote was close: 422 for Tibbits, 420 for Rice. Charles Watters from Andover was the loser, with only 392 votes. At the opening of the session, the assembly was presented with three separate petitions from Victoria County. Tibbits, who instigated one, claimed Rice had been illegally elected through violence, influence peddling, and corruption. Mgr Langevin, the St Basile priest, alleged that irregularities had taken place at the Andover poll, where unqualified people had voted – for Tibbits. Langevin claimed that Watters should have been elected. Leonard Coombs, Firmin Thibodeau, and Léon Bellefleur, for their part, denounced the violence perpetrated by Watters's supporters at the St Francis, Madawaska, St Basile, and St Leonard polls. Tibbits's electors had been driven away at St Francis, and the trouble makers came from the state of Maine. Tibbits's petition was signed by 87 individuals, none bearing a French name. Coombs's was backed by 308 people, including a fair number of individuals from the local business class: merchants like Emmerson, P.C. Amiraux and J. Hodgson, lumberers like the four Glaziers, the three Beardsleys, millers or future millers like Joseph Cyr and P.O. Byram, innkeeper Augustin Perron, Simonet Hébert and sons Vital and Béloni, Squire Firmin Thibodeau, Francis Thibodeau, Joseph Cyr, and several Bellefleurs. Langevin's petition had the greater number of supporters (342), but included only three leading men: physician Florent Fournier, Joseph Hébert, and Régis Thériault. The other names all appear to have been farmers.[48]

Madawaska businessmen, whatever the nature and scope of their enterprise, their ethnicity, or their religion, rallied as one man to support the election of one of their own, lumberer James Tibbits. A large number of farmers, led by Mgr Langevin, opposed him. Langevin was the same priest who had been the target of a misconduct petition five years earlier. Apparently he had regained some ascendancy, but his earlier supporters were now aligned against him. No Madawaskayan appeared ready to challenge the election of the third candidate and one of their own, Francis Rice. Neither national origin, language, or religion seem to have played much of a role in the constitution of political factions; rather it was politics that divided businessmen from farmers, local men from outsiders, and split extended families. Incidentally, Watters was returned in the next election in 1857.[49]

Conclusion

Lumber production led to the creation of large commercial sawmills, but with the exception of the Hammond mill, they did not become genuinely autonomous operations and therefore were unsuccessful linkages. They remained extensions of the lumber trade and subject to its vagaries. They produced a greater variety of goods including deals, planks, staves, clapboard, shingles, and laths, which sold on overlapping but not identical markets (according to Baillie, Britain and the West Indies requested different types of deal). This reduced but did not eliminate their vulnerability to trade fluctuations. However, their dependence on large export firms to market their products left commercial sawmillers at the mercy of the latter's fortune, and their owners were as prone to bankruptcy as lumberers. When the forest industry declined in the later part of the 1880s, so did commercial milling. Wiggin, collecting histories at the end of the century, captured the sense of the decline conveyed by his informants: 'In those days no gayer place could be found in all the state that Fort Kent, and none where money was more plentiful, or was spent with a freer hand for everything that pertained to social enjoyment ... those days of exceptional business prosperity and of easy money making have long since passed away and with them many who were then active businessmen in the town.'[50]

   Commercial lumber mills promoted only limited economic development. Development appears to have centred on the smaller-scale custom mills. As the population grew, so did the custom mills' markets, and consequently their number and the scope of their operations. They could become the nucleus of a congerie of related businesses: every possible form of milling in the case of Thériault, gristmilling and baking in the case of Bijeau. They could also underwrite family upward mobility, as in the case of the Thériaults and Thibodeaux. Custom millers were also better equipped to lay the ground for modern entrepreneurship. They operated within a smaller, concrete universe, whose actors were known to all. They could then begin to conceptualize the economy as a system ruled by mechanisms that could be understood. Economic decisions could, on the whole, be rational ones. This stood in sharp contrast to the staple trade, which remained characterized by unfathomable randomness and shortage of timely and adequate information. Custom millers consequently did not so much engage in series of discrete successive adventures, as in a continuous process of capital accumulation and economic diversification, sometimes over several generations. They were the ones who transformed demand into local markets. Custom millers were also obvious political mediators. Electors in Maine and the governor and council in New Brunswick selected them, or their immediate relatives, for political offices. Sheila Andrew has argued that no self-perpetuating elite emerged at Madawaska nor elsewhere in Acadian New Brunswick during the second half of the century; she identifies Régis and Lévite Thériault as 'one of the few examples of a two generation elite family.'[51] However, underpinning this elite and constantly feeding it, was a permanent layer of well-to-do farmers and local businessmen, a layer that was largely self-perpetuating.

Custom millers embodied two paradoxes. First, they were better equipped to evolve into capitalists than lumberers since they were not involved in distant trading networks that taught them that the economy was a lottery. Second, mutuality was a better stepping stone to entrepreneurship than individualism. Financial capital was usually insufficient to become a successful custom miller, it had to be reinforced by social capital. It is probably no accident that a large number of mills remained in the hands of people closely related to each other, or that the Hammonds, who treated their businesses as family assets, were the ones who made the transition to manufacturing. Custom millers relied on networks of family relationship and also a reputation for fair dealing. If the rumour mill was accurate, Thibodeau, the generous squire who put up with trespassers 'to keep the peace,' laid down a better foundation on which his descendents could erect businesses and become leading men than the tighter-fisted Héberts. Mutuality should not be viewed as necessarily standing in the way of emerging market economies, but as a possible facilitator, a phenomenon not unique to the Saint John Valley.[52]

5 General Stores: Capitalism's Beachheads or Local Traffic Controllers?

John Emmerson, an Irish Protestant, lived there also. He was a very worthy man, and from good habits and close attention to business, accumulated considerable property. The beautiful houses that embellish the rising village of Edmundston, erected by his sons, are evidence of a father's thrift.

William Thomas Baird, 1890[1]

John Emmerson had indeed been a very successful man. He was worth more than $100,000 when he died in 1867. He had lumbered off and on but made his fortune from retailing, wholesaling, and landlording. He was also an efficient linchpin between Madawaska and the outside world. General stores, like custom mills, catered to a local clientele, but they were also links with the outside, much like commercial mills. Historians of rural areas usually stress this latter function.[2] Initially, they identified the stores as critical nodes in exchange networks, and as playing the same role in agricultural communities as saw millers did in lumbering districts: they presided over the movement of country goods outside the community, of credit and manufactured and exotic goods into it. The store was where the community could secure consumer goods, including goods they could have produced themselves or acquired from neighbours.[3] Rural merchants acted as necessary linchpins between rural communities and the larger, increasingly capitalist economy.[4] It was in their stores that local commodities were collected to be forwarded to distant markets; it was in their stores that rural people could purchase goods manufactured elsewhere, as well as exotic commodities such as sugar, tea, and rum. Without them the 'capitalist penetration of the countryside' would not have been possible. Their role is summarized by Gregory Nobles: 'They [the merchants] were economic and cultural innovators, the central agents of social transformation in their communities. They represented the human link to the wider world of export and exchange, the main conduit for commodities, credit and consumer goods. Thus, they had considerable influence on the emergence of new consumption patterns and market oriented activities among their neighbours.'[5]

Later historians broadened the view of storekeeper's role to include mediating exchanges in the local market through the buying and selling of local goods to local people, and through third-party transactions (A would buy something from B and would pay by allowing B to purchase goods at the store on A's account). Currency shortage made ordinary business or commercial transactions difficult; barter between two parties could work only if each wanted something the other had to offer. The merchants' book credit, operating like local letters of exchange, allowed more complex transactions among a larger number of people. Merchants in this way facilitated the operation of the local markets.[6]

Stores were also factors in community growth, and even development. They provided needed services and critical financing without which the process of settlement would have faltered. Douglas McCalla draws attention to the fact merchant credit was not limited to consumer credit, and that even some consumer credit was an indirect form of investment into production. In frontier areas farmers needed credit to stock and equip the farm that would eventually support them; they also needed credit to survive while they were clearing land. Pioneering would have been extremely difficult without the line of credit allowed by the merchants that substituted for start-up capital. Merchants, in short, underwrote the expansion of agricultural settlement.[7] The store was a centre of social activity, a place to go to meet others, to hear the latest gossip, and to pick up useful information.

In contrast, contemporary elites appear to have had a poor opinion of country storekeepers. Merchants did not produce anything: they merely shuffled goods around and thus were parasites. They also encouraged men to loiter on the premises, neglect their work, drink to excess, and get into debt.[8] In other words, contemporaries as well as historians have fit country merchants into either Dwight's or Taylor's definition of leading men.

The Upper Saint John Valley had no shortage of stores, starting with Lizotte and Duperré's trading post. Identifying storekeepers is easy; determining how they ran their businesses means gaining access to their books, most of which have not survived. Fortunately, the records of two midcentury Madawaska stores, the Dufour brothers' and John Emmerson's, have been kept.[9]

Dufour and Emmerson's stores did not play the expected role in the local and regional economies. Neither was an exchange node and neither channelled local commodities towards outside markets. They were not a 'human link to the wider world of exports' and they did not play a significant role in local exchanges between farmers or farmers and labourers, or in financing land clearing. They nonetheless acted as important intermediaries. They were conduits for North American food staples and imported consumer goods (this role is analysed in chapter 9). They provided employment: goods coming from the Canadas needed to be sleighed over the Grand Portage in winter, and other goods had to be picked up by boat or sleigh at Grand Falls. The stores also played a critical role in articulating the region's farm economy to the timber trade through cash exchange, demonstrating that the valley was well on the road towards a monetized economy by midcentury. Finally, Emmerson's store encouraged the advent of a cash-based trading culture.

Storekeepers

The activities of most early stores merchants is usually hard to document, and the Upper Saint John Valley is no exception. Scant information exists about the number of valley stores until the 1850 and 1851 censuses; Deane and Kavanagh identified three storekeepers in 1831 – Thibodeau, Bellefleur, and Soucy. After 1850 the censuses provide names, but the lists are not necessarily complete. There were half a dozen storekeepers in 1850–1 and nineteen in 1870–1, eight on the U.S. side and eleven in New Brunswick. Merchant-storekeepers closely connected with the lumber trade reported the highest values of real and personal estates in the 1870 U.S. census. The number of lumberers who owned stores suggests that the type of strategy Alan Taylor found in southern Maine may have occurred here as well: millers and lumberers may have opened stores and given credit to farmers to coax or coerce them or their sons to work for them.

Edward Wiggin's thumbnail sketches of Aroostook merchants shed some additional light on the relationship between the two economic sectors, at least as far as the Fort Kent stores were concerned. Harrison Knowles from Bangor, who also traded in lumber, opened a store at Fish River in 1854 and sold it to George Seeley in 1862. Seeley had clerked for John Glazier, who owned a store in New Brunswick, 10 miles above Fort Kent. Like Knowles, Seeley traded in dry goods and lumber. In 1866, he purchased an entire township and the halves of two others; he also bought one of the Fish River mills. Merchant B.W. Mallett's 'career' was typical of the Americans. He moved from Portage Lake to Fort Kent to St Francis and back to Fort Kent again and engaged successively or simultaneously in various related activities: lumbering, milling, manufacturing clapboard, trading in shingles, storekeeping, and farming. He also worked as a scaler for lumber operators. Mallett carried out business on both sides of the boundary and was linked with the Saint John firm of Jewett, which in turn had business partners in Boston. He was a partner of William Cunliffe, and under the name B.W. Mallet & Co. 'did a large business in trading, buying and shipping shaved cedar shingles which at that time was an immense industry upon the Upper Saint John,' writes Wiggin. Mallet was wiped out by the Jewett failure in 1876. Finally, Samuel Stevens, who clerked at the Jewett and March hotel, bought the premises and a store from his employers in 1848; he handled their account afterwards, but left the business in 1860 to become deputy collector of customs.

Even when not engaged in lumbering or commercial sawmilling, those men shared the career pattern of lumberers and commercial millers. They learned their trade clerking for a few years, then went into business for themselves, either alone or in partnership. They all relied on a network of peers to advance their business concerns. Those not directly dependent on lumbering appear to have had a better survival rate than those who were. But not all storekeepers followed this model; those who left records differed from it in several ways.[10]

The Dufour brothers, Abraham and Simon, had been born in the valley; they were sons and grandsons of millers, and each owned a farm. They tried their hands at a variety of money-making opportunities: they cut wood,[11] traded their own and other people's timber, and for a while they operated a general store next to the church, which they had purchased on credit from Antoine Bellefleur in 1844.[12] The records of the Dufour store are limited to a single ledger that begins in the middle of 1844.[13] The brothers appear to have run a tight ship. Accounts were settled at irregular intervals, but usually at least once a year. The Dufours charged interest on accounts that ran for more than a year without substantial payments, and demanded promissory notes from large account holders. These safeguards failed to protect them when the world collapsed around them as a result of the timber trade crash of 1847–8. The price of lumber and shanty supplies plummeted, customers could not pay their accounts, and the Dufours started suing them. They were in turn sued by their clerk, who claimed that they owned him in excess of $400.[14] It appears that the store closed or was handed to another person in 1848. The only transactions recorded in the ledger for that year were settlings of accounts. Some of the accounts were turned over to a southern Maine merchant, W.P. Vinal, who does not appear in either the 1850 U.S. or 1851 New Brunswick census.[15] The Dufours had tried their hand at storekeeping at the wrong time: the crisis in the timber trade killed their attempt at enterprise.

Some of the Dufours' business activities were apparently not reported in the store ledger. For example, the brothers organized the transportation of large quantities of oats and hay to various lumbering sites, but the fodder they record as purchased falls short of the amount they transported. In 1846, for instance, they organized the transport of 33,120 pounds of hay to various locations, but according to their ledger they had bought only 6,191; in 1847 they forwarded 189,956 pounds, 133,342 of which was listed as purchased. Evidently lumber operators purchased fodder at the farm gate and arranged to have it delivered to their camps and the Dufours orchestrated the deliveries. Although many people were credited for carting, sleighing, and boating fodder in the ledger, no one was charged for those services and no lumbermen operating at the sites the Dufours serviced had accounts with them. Obviously, the Dufours' forwarding activities were entered in a different account book, perhaps along with other transactions involving the lumber trade.

John Emmerson, a Yorkshire native, had moved to New Brunswick in 1818, according to the 1851 census; he was about sixteen at the time. He first lived in Lincoln parish, the birthplace of John Glazier, before moving to the Saint John Valley around 1828, where he began improving two lots with his brothers. In 1833 he was living with his father, and had no stock except one horse. Why did he choose this French settlement? The only Anglo-Protestant provincials who moved to the valley in the 1820s and 1830s were looking for timber to cut. Emmerson was likely acquainted with Glazier. The men were contemporaries and raised in the same parish so Glazier or his family may have told him about the prospects upriver. By the time he arrived, however, logging had been made illegal, although the province turned a blind eye to land claimants who sold the logs they cut, or allegedly cut, on their claims. After the signing of the 1842 treaty, large operators quickly moved in the region, including John and Stephen Glazier. The beginnings of Emmerson's storekeeping activities coincided with the renewal of lumbering on the upper reaches of the Saint John and with the start of the Glaziers' activities. The Glaziers needed enormous amounts of supplies and clearly were not interested in acquiring them themselves. Emmerson became their supplier; he was from their parish and had picked up some French in the intervening years. His earliest record, the delivery book, starts in 1845 with a list of barrels of flour, pork, beans, fish, and molasses received from Lower Canada and forwarded to John Glazier. Emmerson did not clerk or work for anyone before opening his store, perhaps because of his advantage in being one of the earliest English-speaking storekeepers in the valley. He died in 1867, and the store was subsequently run by his brother-in-law until his sons were old enough to take over. A series of daybooks that starts in the middle of 1873 and a new ledger that begins in October 1873 likely indicate when the younger men took over.

Like the Dufours, Emmerson had his fingers in many pies. In addition to his trading and store-related activities, he owned farms, town and wood lots, and got into the lumbering business as a supplier of logging teams, as a lumberer himself, and as a lumber broker; he acted as a purchasing agent for others, ordering goods and organizing their transportation and delivery to the client's door. He housed the post office, staffed for a while by his brother-in-law, and the telegraph office. The presence of the post office also allowed him to run a limited mail-order business: he sent some small items to distant customers through the mail, and they likewise sent their payments back.[16] Like the Dufours, he forwarded fodder to lumber camps. Emmerson also acted as a payroll officer and a banker. For instance, the commissioners who surveyed the interprovincial boundary in 1853 opened accounts at the store for their employees. Some workers simply withdrew cash from their accounts without making any purchases. Government payments such as cheques on the treasury and school warrants were also cashed at the store; the recipients used some of the money to balance their accounts, and either left the rest on account or withdrew it. Some men, especially those involved in lumbering, also left large amount of money on deposit at the store for safe keeping, identified in the books as money 'to be called for later.'

Emmerson died a wealthy man by local standards.[17] His estate included sizeable properties and investments in bank stock. The Dufours and Emmerson followed a different path into business than the Fort Kent storekeepers described by Wiggin, but once they had opened a store they adopted the same pattern of activities: they did not specialize in trade, they farmed, they were directly and indirectly involved in the forest industry, and they were vulnerable to business cycle downturns.

Storekeeping

The commercial books left by the Dufour and Emmerson stores are rich in information about their activities, but present some serious limitations. The ledgers listed accounts opened by customers who came to pick up merchandise when they needed it, and paid when they could. Arranged by customers' names, the accounts itemize all purchases and often give a unit as well as total price and provide the date and value of the transaction. They also list the dates and amounts of payment and their nature but the Dufour and Emmerson ledgers were never balanced. Emmerson also left a series of memorandum books organized by customer name. These were not drafts of the ledgers; customers had an account in the ledger, the memo book, or both, but the memo books do not duplicate transactions in the ledgers. Accounts were settled in the memo book roughly four times a year. The Dufour book lists 294 individuals with an active account in 1846, as opposed to 219 in Emmerson's in 1853 and 211 in 1863. These numbers do not include farmer-lumberers, inn- and storekeepers, lumberers, and in the case of Emmerson, clients who appear only in his receiving or delivery books. Customers were not limited to one side of the river – they came from Maine, New Brunswick, and Lower Canada, most from the vicinity of the stores.

The composition of the two stores' clientele was diverse. In 1846 almost all of the Dufours' customers were ordinary local households of farmers and rural craftsmen. Ten were farmer-lumberers, local farmers who cut timber as a side occupation or, like 'Quétoune' Michaud, neglected their farm to cut wood. One was the priest, who was selling the grain he collected from tithes and drawing money from his account. Emmerson had a greater number of non-farm customers: in 1853 fifteen accounts were for lumber operators, outside entrepreneurs who came to the Madawaska settlement to engage in the exploitation of local forest resources; three accounts were for land surveyors or boundary commissioners; and seven were for farmer–lumberers, including the four Albert brothers, who managed to have six accounts among themselves. The books also included a few innkeepers and the Victoria County Agricultural Society.

Like all stores of the period, these businesses operated on credit, and accepted payments in a variety of forms: cash, transfer to a third-party account, country products, manufactured goods, and labour. The values of the entries were expressed in Halifax currency (pounds, shillings, and pence), although transactions were occasionally recorded in dollars. Not all transactions were made on credit. Fabien Albert's 1863 memo book account shed some light on the way cash transactions could be carried. He purchased a slate, some fabric and thread, a book, and some leather. The storekeeper duly totalled the purchase: 6s. 5½p. He then added 6½d. worth of horse nails, and below the new total entered 'paid in oat.' Albert probably went to the store with a cartful of oats and a shopping list. When he discovered that his oats were worth more than his purchases, he added an item he could always use in order to make up the difference: nails. A few weeks later he showed up again at the store with seven bushels of oats, and a shopping list that included three glasses, lining fabric, cotton, thread, and buttons. He also needed horse nails, making the total 8s. 2d. His oats were worth 14s., so he picked up 5s.10d. worth of sundries to balance his account.

Not all store transactions were recorded. In Emmerson's account book some entries read 'balance on...' followed by a commodity and a lower-than-normal price. As the item is not listed as having been purchased at an earlier date, these entries suggest that the customer made a downpayment at the time of purchase and had the balance put on account. Other entries note 'left from oats' or 'left from order on J. Glazier', indicating that the customer had already received cash or goods in exchange for commodities or labour, and the difference was left on account. Bracketed and crossed-out entries different from the 'your account is now settled' lines also appear in Emmerson's memo books. The value of those transactions was not included in the settling of accounts and probably represented purchases the store-keeper entered in the book before realizing the customer intended to pay on the spot. The lack of precise entries coupled with the fact that customers did not limit their purchases to a single store makes it impossible to use the store books to uncover individual consumption patterns.

Rosemary Ommer has found that Gaspé merchants used differential pricing: people who paid cash were charged less than those who put goods on account.[18] Storekeepers made profits through manipulating prices. It is impossible to tell whether Madawaska merchants adopted the same practice, because cash purchases are entered in the books only rarely. Even if a record of cash purchases was available it would still be impossible to determine if there were differences in pricing since most items were available in a variety of prices. For instance, Emmerson's post mortem inventory lists paper collars at 8, 10, and 18 cents per dozen, umbrellas ranging between 30 cents and $1, and Indian rubber shoes at $1 to $1.50 a pair. If someone purchased collars at 8 cents, an umbrella at 50 cents, and rubbers at $1.20 and paid cash, was the price a discounted one or what anyone would be charged for those specific items? Moreover, people who ordered barrelled goods such as flour, fish, and mess pork, which were standard commodities, and paid for them in advance were not charged less than customers who put the same goods on account. The number of such cases is limited, and it is impossible to spin grand theories from a dozen trans-actions.

By 1858 Emmerson was acting as a commissioner – he charged 6 per cent above the value of goods and the cost of transportation – and wholesaler, and most of the storekeepers he supplied were located on the U.S. side of the river at Fort Kent. Emmerson supplied some of his business clients from his inventory, or ordered goods for them and had them delivered. These transactions appear in his delivery book that covers the years 1845 to 1868. Not everyone listed in the delivery book had an account in the ledger or in the memo books. Emmerson's receiving book of 1849–59 listed twenty-six individuals who received goods from him in 1853, in addition to the lumberers. Of these only four had accounts in the ledgers, eight in the memo books, while two had an account in both sets of books. The activities of one customer illustrate how the cash and credit system worked. In March 1853 Joseph Nadeau, the innkeeper at Fort Kent, gave Emmerson £2 10s. ($9). In July his ledger account was charged for two barrels of flour at

35 shillings each and for their freight (5 shillings). He immediately mailed in the payment. He was then billed for the freight on 25 barrels of flour, which he paid in-person in September. The receiving book, however, shows that Emmerson took in six barrels of flour for him in July and twenty-five barrels of flour and two of pork in August. No further charge beyond the freight is recorded for the cost of the flour. Nadeau very probably paid for the goods when he ordered, and also paid most of the freight in advance, closer to the delivery date. Nadeau, incidentally, is the gentleman in chapter 1 who received fabric from Quebec through the shoemaking brother-in-law of a carpenter brother-in-law. Despite the obvious convenience offered by Emmerson's services, Nadeau maintained his own supply and information channels.

Customers ordered flour, pork, molasses, and fish by the barrel, as well as a wide variety of other goods. A blacksmith ordered a set of tools; three people placed orders for stoves; Placide Thériault ordered a cabriolet; innkeeper Prudent Gagnon ordered three barrels of wine and three of port; innkeeper Michael Maloney ordered ten barrels of liquor, paid in cash. There is no alcohol recorded anywhere else in the ledgers and memo books. True to stereotype, the Irishman went for hard liquor, and the Frenchman for wine.

In 1846 Emmerson's ledgers listed eight lumberers plus Glazier who ordered shanty supplies. The eight purchased 22 barrels of pork, 246 of flour, 6 of herring, 3 of meal, and 1 of molasses. Glazier, for his part, needed 20 barrels of pork, 84 of flour, 6 of herring, 7 of molasses, 27 of meal, and 8 of beans. In addition, Glazier received tea, soap, axes, ropes, various tools, blankets, and dry goods. In 1853 there were only two lumberers in the receiving book; the others are in the ledger. Peter Clare, who also ran an inn, ordered 25 barrels of flour, 14 of sundries, and 1 of sugar. Glazier's operations required an astronomical quantity of goods: 313 barrels of flour and 78 of pork, plus the expected fish, molasses, tea, and tools, as well as casks, boxes, and chests whose contents were not identified.

Initially, Emmerson's ledger and memo book customers were not the same. As far as can be determined, the great majority of the 1853 memo book customers were ordinary householders: farmers, craftsmen, widows. Ledger account holders were most often businesspeople: lumberers, store- and innkeepers, and millers. This characteristic was more pronounced by 1858. The number of ledger business customers dropped from seventy to fifty, and the regular households from thirty-nine to sixteen. In 1863, on the other hand, there is no obvious difference between the people who had an account in one set of books and the other. Almost all customers were found in the ledger, and only forty-two in the memo books. Memo book accounts were carried over into ledger D, but in a pinch when Emmerson ran out of space in ledger D, he carried over some of the accounts into memo book J. In 1863 individuals who would have been found in the ledgers a few years before, like Augustin Peron, the Degeli innkeeper, were now found only in the memo book. Emmerson was no longer making a distinction between his use of the two types of books.

Other changes were taking place in his bookkeeping. In the earlier years, ledger account holders were privileged clients. Memo book customers settled their accounts about four times a year or stopped putting purchases on account, but ledger account holders settled less frequently. They were allowed to accumulate large balances, and could go for long periods with limited payments and no interest. Leon Belle-fleur, erstwhile farmer, who supplied the teams surveying the boundary line between Lower Canada and New Brunswick in the early 1850s, was allowed to draw supplies from the Emmerson store for almost two years without making any significant payment. He eventually settled his account with a check on the treasury. John and Stephen Glazier had a balance ranging between $1,000 and $2,000 every summer. Emmerson does not seem to have pursued delinquent accounts very aggressively in the 1850s. He did not charge interest and seldom collected notes or took mortgages on his reluctant clients' properties. His practices became less lenient in the 1860s when he began charging interest on ledger and memo book clients alike. One ledger customer left the province after an exasperated Emmerson seized his stock.

Emmerson may have changed his business practice because some of his clients, especially earlier ledger clients, were abusing their credit. Emmerson's post mortem inventory includes a list of book debts that comprises 694 entries, each referring to a ledger or a memo book.[19] Ledger debts account for 79 per cent of the total, despite the fact that the 233 ledger customers make up only 34 per cent of the list. Of the bad debts 81 per cent refer to ledger entries. The worse offenders were lumberers. By comparison, only 43 per cent of the debts that refer to a memo book entry are identified as bad debts. (The ledger entries are skewed towards the earlier period, as opposed to the memo books, which are predominantly from the mid-1860s.) The debtors include an

Irish priest who moved to another parish leaving behind a $624 debt and members of the well-heeled Martin and Thibodeau families who were in no hurry to settle their accounts. The fact is that memo book clients were less likely to default. In the early 1860s Emmerson finally realized that distinguishing between customers with a lot of collateral who could be given extended credit for large sums, and the smaller fry who either paid promptly or were denied further credit, did not help his bottom line as much as he thought it would. The well-to-do were not necessarily better at paying their debts. As a result, he tightened the rules for almost everyone: pay up or be charged interest and be denied further credit. In this context separating the customers between two sets of books was no longer very pertinent, and Emmerson began to keep people's accounts in whatever books had pages to spare.

Profits?

Despite the fact not all their customers made a payment, Dufour and Emmerson both collected enough in a given year to balance the debits of active accounts, while some inactive and unpaid accounts lingered in the books.[20] Some customers, on the other hand, made payments but bought nothing, and not all payments applied to purchases made during the year in question. This is particularly true of farmer-lumberers and lumber operators who ran up large debts buying supplies in the fall, and settled their account the following summer or later. The Albert brothers were given in excess of $6,000 worth of credit at Emmerson's in 1853, settled their accounts in the summer, and went out of lumbering altogether. Excluding farmer-lumberers, lumberers, and store- and innkeepers supplied by Emmerson, the average debit was quite modest: $7 at Dufour's; $17 at Emmerson's in 1853 and $16 in 1863. Emmerson's debt book shows that 80 per cent of the 170 accounts in his memo book J owed him less than $20; 66 per cent owed less than $10 and 14 per cent less than $1. No account had a balance exceeding $200 except Glazier's. Neither store was underwriting agricultural expansion through credit to new farmers, but Emmerson's granting of interest-free credit to lumberers, sometimes over several years, was akin to providing them with free financing. Emmerson was subsidizing the forest industry, and more specifically John and Stephen Glazier and their acolytes.

It is unclear how much profit storekeepers made in a given year – they never drew up balance sheets and some accounts were allowed to run for years with minimal payments. In addition, the figures derived from Emmerson's receiving book, delivery book, and ledgers and memo books are impossible to reconcile. Neither storekeeper drew up a year-end inventory. Their books were designed to record who owed how much to whom and nothing more; they do not show which goods sold best, and what the profit margin was on each category. Emmerson's records indicate that the gentleman had no concept of accounting: his bookkeeping was imprecise, inconsistent, and useless as a management tool. The Dufour and Emmerson books resembled those of Samuel Jacob, the late-eighteenth century Richelieu Valley merchant. Allan Greer has noted that though Jacob did an adequate job at keeping track of credits and debits, he never prepared a balance sheet. Greer concluded that the store owner 'never knew precisely where his profit was, overall, or on any particular enterprise.'[21] The Dufours and Emmerson were also apparently content to have more money in their pocket at the end of the year than at the beginning. They sold goods over the counter and hoped that when their own bills were due, they would have money to pay them. The storekeepers had not developed the modern concept of profit and had an uncertain control over their cash flow. They based their business decisions more on gut feelings than on accurate economic data.[22]

Exchange Nodes or Agents of Development?

Country stores operated on credit, and credit was usually given for country products or labour. Historians believe that the shortage of small denomination coins and bills coupled with the seasonality of the economy led to elaborate systems of book debts to avoid the exchange of currency.[23] When accounts were settled, credits and debits were usually close even if the volume of business had been large, and little currency had to change hands.[24] Money played a limited role in the settling of accounts in Upper Canada. Douglas McCalla estimates that before union, cash accounted for between 3 and 30 per cent of customer credit. Payment was mostly in the form of wheat, pork, rye, barley, ashes, lumber, and tobacco.[25]

A heavy reliance on payment in kind turned country merchants into marketing agents for their clients. They needed buyers for the various commodities left at the store and through storekeepers, farmers linked with various external markets. The Dufour and Emmerson stores, however, did not function in this role (see tables 3 and 4). The Dufour store initially appears to fit into this pattern. Country products accounted for almost half of the credits, both in terms of value and frequency of payment. Cash played a limited but not negligible role, accounting for 10 per cent of credit and one quarter of the customer payments. Oats and hay were the largest category; oats alone represented 35 per cent of the total payments. However, the Dufours collected almost no country products outside of fodder and third-party payments accounted for a mere 10 per cent of payments. The store was not, then, the locus of exchanges between the members of the local community, nor was it a place where country products were swapped for imported goods and then forwarded to outside markets. Oats and hay stayed in the vicinity, but fed a transatlantic industry. Customers also got a significant amount of store credit for transporting goods to the shanties: One-third of the Dufour's customers engaged in this activity, representing 13 per cent of the value of all credit.

Emmerson was not very interested in collecting country products: they accounted for a mere 6.6 per cent of all credits and only one-quarter of the customers used them as a form of payment in 1853. Oats represented 3.7 per cent of all credit; by comparison butter and eggs represented 1.3 per cent. In 1863 country products were still used by only a third of the customers. The proportion of credit represented by that category, however, had tripled to 17 per cent. Oats and hay were up to 7.6 per cent but freighting for the storekeeper earned the customers at least as much. Customers earned an average of $7.75 from freighting in 1853 and $12.74 in 1863.

A shift also occurred in third-party payments between 1853 and 1863. In 1853 they were randomly distributed among the accounts holders but by 1863 this was no longer the case. Only a small number of customers received credit for the products of their industry. These included two hunters who paid in pelts, three Native women who made moccasins and snowshoes and dressed hides, a blacksmith who manufactured wrought iron items, a farrier, two tanners, a fuller, a saddler, and a maker of spinning wheels and loom parts. These individuals received credit by selling their products to Emmerson, doing work for him, or receiving credit for work done for others. Third-party payments were otherwise few and far between that year, if we exclude payments made by lumberers on behalf of others. The artisans were the exception. The hunters sold their furs to Emmerson outright, or left them with him on consignment with the promise that Emmerson would get the best possible deal for them. In 1863 he sold some furs to Henderson and Renfrew in Quebec City and the ledger also includes a reference to an unclear transaction with William Hosa, fur merchant in New York City.

Cash was the leading form of payment at Emmerson's in terms of frequency and proportion of total credit, representing 58 per cent of the customers and 41 per cent of the credits in 1853, down to 42 per cent and 25 per cent in 1863.[26] Those figures are striking for two reasons. First, cash was an important source of credit. It appears to have played a more important role in store transactions in the valley than in Upper Canada, despite the Upper Canadian stores being located along a major waterway. On the other hand, cash had been a common medium of exchange at the late eighteenth-century Nova Scotia stores investigated by Wainright.[27] The second point worth noting is the counter-intuitive decline in the use of cash.

Emmerson may have encouraged the use of cash. He collected a relatively small quantity of country products, perhaps as a result of a deliberate policy. Collecting and disposing of dribs and drabs of local products – two dozen eggs here, three bushels of buckwheat there, a thousand shaved shingles elsewhere – clearly was not the way he wished to conduct business, and he may have actively discouraged this form of payment. He bought almost all his eggs, butter, and poultry from a limited number of people, suggesting that he identified suppliers for goods that he was planning to resell locally. With the exception of maple sugar, the country products Emmerson took as payments were resold in the valley; they were not forwarded to outside merchants. The extensive use of cash at the Emmerson store was not an isolated practice. At the Morneault store across the river in Grand Isle, cash was also the primary method of settling accounts.[28]

Cash was available, although it is uncertain in what amount or what form it took. According to the Madawaska priests, the valley suffered from a money shortage until the opening of the lumber camps in 1824–5.[29] The camps provided markets for fodder and employed the locals. In addition, some farmers harvested trees independently. All these activities could have given those engaged in them access to money. The forest industry then could have channeled money into the valley in the form of specie, notes, or scrip, any of which the store-keepers might have labelled 'cash.' As many lumberers were American, valley residents may have had access to an adequate supply of U.S. dollars. However, in the 1840s the Mainer Shepard Cary was paying his men in New Brunswick bank notes, which he obtained by selling his timber in Saint John.[30] And in 1846 one priest informed his bishop that 'our paper is all from New Brunswick.'[31] Conversely, in 1858 Emmerson was swapping dollars for British North American notes with Rivière du Loup merchant and forwarder George Pelletier. Clearly, both New Brunswick bank notes and American money circulated in the valley. If customers had no cash, they could work for Emmerson, either labouring at the store, on one of his farms, or, more commonly, transporting goods. There were always barrels, crates, kegs, and boxes to haul from Rivière du Loup, work to do in the warehouse, and supplies to deliver to lumber camps or other merchants. Lesser quantities of goods came upriver from Saint John and had to be picked up at Grand Falls. Between 1846 and 1867 Emmerson's own supplies averaged 573 barrels a year, not to mention bags, chests, casks, and other containers. Add to this total the orders for the lumberers and a lot of men were needed to haul the goods. Customers who freighted for Emmerson to earn store credit saved him the cost not only of a permanent or semi-permanent crew of hired men, but also of a sufficient number of sleighs, boats, carts, and horses. Farmers could supply the labour, the animals, and the equipment, and as most of the carrying was done in wintertime, they probably welcomed the opportunity to get out of the house and exercise the horses. According to the receiving book, which includes labour costs, a man earned 25s. ($5) for bringing 4 barrels from Rivière du Loup (according to Emmerson's records, 4 barrels was the normal carrying capacity of a sleigh). Some men, however, appear to have brought two sleighs each loaded with 3 barrels on any given trip. A large proportion of the freight carriers may have been paid on the spot. The receiving book lists eighty-five individuals who transported goods between Rivière du Loup and the store in 1853; only eighteen of them had an account at the store and of those, only eight were credited for 'hawling.'

In the face of economic downturn, Emmerson would need to adapt his trade practices. The year 1853 was a good one for the forest industry, and by extension, for the valley; 1863 was not (see chapter 2). Fodder prices dropped to an all-time low: oats fetched 1s.8d. or 25 cents a bushel instead of the customary 50 cents. The Central Bank of

New Brunswick failed. Farmer had difficulty selling their cash crops, and earned little when they did. Reduced income was only one of the problems that plagued valley trade that year. The other was the American Civil War, which had a detrimental impact on the money supply. American coins lost their value and in 1863 the Canadian post office stopped accepting them at face value. Greenbacks also quickly depreciated; Emmerson took them at 75 cents on the dollar.[32] In order to sustain trade, Emmerson had little choice but to accept country products. He did so at his own risk – though he took in country products at the reduced exchange rate, he may not have been sure he would be able to resell them. Emmerson thus operated as a partial buffer between his clients and the larger economy, perhaps hoping to earn their loyalty. He also tried to reduce the local specie shortage: in December 1864 he went to Quebec City where he obtained $500 worth of silver (presumably in Lower Canadian currency) from one of his main suppliers.[33] Emmerson likely intended to put the silver into local circulation since he used other forms of currency for his own payments. Cash reasserted its preeminence once the crisis was over: 80 per cent of the payments credited in the 1871–2 daybook were in cash. Emmerson's actions seem more those of a proto-Keynesian interventionist than a stereotypical predatory capitalist. He fed the local economy with cash to try to keep it from stalling, clearly acting as if he believed that his fate was bound up with that of his customers.

Country merchants also acted as agents of development when they underwrote start up farms with long credit, although neither the Dufours nor Emmerson played this role. Members of charter families are overrepresented among account holders, especially at Dufours; recent immigrants are conspicuously absent. Newly arrived settlers who were clearing a piece of land could not expect to receive credit from the brothers. They either needed to have money to put on the counter or goods to swap some on the spot for what they needed, or they did without. Emmerson was occasionally more inclined to give credit to newcomers, but only on a short-term basis. Neither shopkeeper underwrote the agricultural development of the frontier with long credit, but they were agents of development in other ways. Both facilitated the trade in local goods by transporting fodder to the shanties. Emmerson helped his customers weather an economic downturn: he became more flexible about the nature of payments despite increased risks for him; he acted as an intermediary between an emerging artisanal sector and its cash-strapped customers; and he fetched specie from the outside to alleviate a local shortage of unde-preciated currency.

One Step Forward and Two Steps Back:
Emmerson and the Banking System

Country storekeepers were not only important players in the local economy; they were also smaller players in the wider state, provincial, or international world of trade. British North American banks had been established in large part to facilitate transactions between mer-chants. They provided short-term credit through the discount of com-mercial paper, increased the money supply by issuing notes, and could provide customers with drafts or cheques. A reliable bank increased the safety of business transactions and smoothed out short-term cash flow problems.

At the time of his death, Emmerson was a shareholder of four banks: the Banque du Peuple, the Quebec Bank, and the Montreal Bank, all in Lower Canada, as well as the recently defunct Bank of Upper Canada. His inventory also lists a few hundred dollars on deposit in three Lower Canadian saving banks and an additional $3,000 in unidenti-fied banks. Emmerson, who strove to reduce barter at his store, seems to have been eager to adopt up-to-date ways of doing business when dealing with the outside world, relying on the services of several banks. The evidence is misleading. Emmerson's account books instead reveal a man who was surprisingly reticent to use banks and the serv-ices they could provide him with. He relied more heavily on tradi-tional ways of transferring money such as cash, bills of exchange, and drafts on individuals' accounts, and on the services of trading houses. At the first sign of trouble, he reverted to the safest medium he could think of: British sovereigns.

Emmerson's business clients – the lumberers, farmer-lumberers, innkeepers, and storekeepers – were responsible for most of his store's gross income. In 1853 he collected $14,186 from lumberers alone. In 1863 he collected only $2,608 from them, but Saint John timber broker Edwin Fisher also collected $22,656 on his behalf. The business customers paid in cash, financial instruments, and/or wood products. In 1853 four farmer-lumberers paid exclusively with timber. H.W. West and Co., merchants and sawmillers at Fish River, paid in timber, cash, bank notes, and drafts. Lumber was the only 'country' product, along with maple sugar, that Emmerson collected to ship outside the valley. Lumber operators paid in cash, bank notes, and cheques, drafts from Saint John's timber brokers, or transfers to Emmerson's accounts in Saint John or occasionally Quebec City. Other forms of credits such as returned goods and services such as towing and freighting were marginal.

Emmerson also found himself doing more and more business with Fisher. In 1858 the lumberers were already settling the bulk of their accounts with 'cash from Fisher on timber' or with 'receipt from E. Fisher' or 'by timber sold by John Emmerson in St. John as per bill from E. Fisher.' Fisher handled only a portion of Emmerson's financial affairs in Saint John. The majority of Emmerson's dealings were with J.J. Hegan, a Saint John textile importer who quickly became his main supplier and 'banker.'[34] Emmerson sent him the various papers he received in payment and Hegan sent him specie, notes, and other instruments in return, all by mail. Emmerson entered some of his transactions with Hegan in his ledgers (see table 5). The accounts are obviously incomplete; they do not balance and the value of the goods sent does not correspond to what is listed in the receiving book. They nonetheless suggest the broad outlines of Emmerson's financial strategies. Commercial papers and orders for payment from his own debtors provided him with an important source of credit. He collected relatively little paper money or cheques, unless they were subsumed under the heading 'cash.' Treasury orders and school warrants, on the other hand, represented significant amounts. In return for these, Hegan sent Emmerson money (specie and notes), commercial papers, and goods, and paid some of his bills in Saint John or Fredericton. Until 1860 notes from the Bank of British North America, a London concern with branches in Saint John and Quebec City, represented a large part of the money thus received. The notes would have been useful in Quebec City, where Emmerson placed large orders. After 1860 bank notes were replaced by sovereigns: Emmerson's response to the Civil War was to retreat to British gold.

Emmerson's books never indicate he asked a bank to discount his commercial paper: it appears that his orders were payable on demand. He rarely used cheques or bank drafts and when he did, he obtained them from Hegan. Hegan, like Fisher, provided Emmerson with the services one normally expects from a bank: he exchanged currency, provided him with bank notes, bills of exchange or payment orders, cashed various forms of financial papers, and settled his local accounts. Emmerson even deposited money with Hegan: at his death, Hegan held $4,000 of his money, which had earned $240 in interest.

Emmerson wanted money: he paid his suppliers promptly – at least twice a year, and more frequently within a month of receiving goods – and mostly in cash. Most of his business in Saint John was with suppliers who, according to their advertisements in the New Brunswick Almanac, accepted only cash, or gave favoured terms to those who paid in cash.[35] Quebec City merchants were no different. In 1849 Emmerson obtained a 5 per cent discount from Methot and Chinic, hardware merchants in Quebec City, for cash payment.[36] Plenty of suppliers still operated on credit, so Emmerson paid cash because he chose to do so, not out of necessity. His accounts in Saint John were settled with specie, various financial instruments, or payments made on his behalf by his larger creditors, such as lumber baron John Glazier. Emmerson's largest supplier was H. J. Noad in Quebec City, who provided him with foodstuffs. Emmerson was sending him money ('cash by mail') every fortnight. In 1853 his invoices totaled $13,961; in 1858, $ 10,820. After Noad's successor, Jeffrey Noad and Co., went out of business, Emmerson bought his staples from Ross and Co., also in Quebec City. His payments became less frequent, but more varied. In January 1864 he sent them $955.15 worth of sovereigns by mail. Shortly afterwards, he paid them $200 in person. In July he sent two drafts on the Bank of Montreal totalling $617.50; in November, he sent $428.67 worth of gold by mail. In December he delivered $686.42 in cash in person and received in return $500 in silver. Emmerson's ideal business world was a cash world.

Conclusion

The Dufour and Emmerson records shed light on two related issues: what role did general stores play in the local economy and how similar or different were storekeepers from other entrepreneurs? Neither store was a place where country products were exchanged for either services or for imported goods, although the stores did supply the region's lumber camps with locally grown fodder. By not functioning as the locus of exchange between local goods and imported goods, the two stores played a different role in the local economy than their counterparts in rural New England, Quebec, Nova Scotia, or Ontario. This fact did not prevent them from being the place where the local economy made connections with the world economy. At both stores local people took advantage, directly or indirectly, of the lumber trade to acquire the wherewithal to purchase outside products. Oats and hay, which made up the lion's share of the country products brought to the stores, were lumber-camp supplies. The main local source of cash was the timber trade: people secured cash or credit working in the woods, directly supplying the camps, or selling goods to the families of shanty workers or to new farmers. Transportation represented another significant source of income connected with the lumber trade. Oats, hay, transportation, cash, and wood products represented 72 per cent of the payments at the Dufour store and 62 per cent at Emmerson's in 1853 and 48 per cent in 1863, lumberers, farmer lumberers and storekeepers excluded.

Clearly the timber trade rather than the general stores was the mediator between the local and the outside economies. It brought to the region the money that allowed storekeepers and local people to escape the constraints of the barter system. The valley economy was heavily monetarized compared to other regions, thanks to the presence of competing lumber operators in the area. When the timber trade failed, as in 1848, storekeepers could find themselves in dire circumstances, because their customers lost their ability to pay. The Dufour store was brought down for this very reason. In 1863 another recession in the timber trade forced Emmerson to accept increased payments in kind from farmers. Long distance trade therefore shaped the modalities of local exchanges, although in a more complicated way than historians have suggested so far.

Storekeepers aided the transition to a monetarized economy by discouraging payments in kind and pressing for cash, or at least for something that they personally needed, like labour. They had their own reasons to prefer payments in cash and at the time of purchase. Cash payments were more efficient and more profitable; Emmerson, however, may have favoured them to ensure the security of his enterprise. His bookkeeping was such that he could not accurately estimate his profits, but he could have learned a lesson from the Dufour failure: cash flow problems could bring a store down. Emmerson wisely collected as much cash as he could, tried to get people to pay in a timely fashion, and avoided debts to his own suppliers. This in turn allowed him to secure better prices from the supplies. Although his bookkeeping was inadequate for accurate cash flow management, Emmerson always managed to have enough on hand to make his own payments and he died debt free. His more 'modern' business practices were not imposed on him by the spread of capitalism or by a desire to maximize profit, but by observation, common sense, and a pressing desire for survival.

Emmerson was a man with a foot in two very different universes, the timber trade and the retailing of consumer goods. The traditionalism of timber trade may have helped him to get a start in business. The Glaziers could have done business with Emmerson because they were from the same parish and Emmerson could have felt morally indebted to the Glaziers for his start in business. But the Glazier connection was both an opportunity and a potential danger. The Glaziers were by far Emmerson's biggest customers, responsible for at least half of his gross income. Emmerson's fate was tied to just one lumberer concerns – should they fail, so would he. The Glaziers also expected long credit on their account. They used the store in the same way historians claim farmers did. They collected goods when they needed them and paid after they had sold their crop, in this case, wood. They were also rather miserly; they once sent Emmerson a cow hide for credit and in May or June they would return the supplies they had not used that winter, also for credit. The culture that permitted the continuation of indentured contracts between lumberers and their men was also a culture that created privileged but clearly hierarchical links between men from the same parish. If the Glaziers felt they had to give priority to a countryman, they believed that in return they were entitled to favourable treatment. Emmerson, after benefitting from the Glaziers' 'benevolence,' felt duty bound to them for as long as they wanted his services.

The Glazier account yielded an indirect benefit to Emmerson: economies of scale. The Glaziers were very big clients and this made Emmerson a very big purchaser. He could deal with the mercantile firms at the top of the pyramid and cut out the middlemen. He actually became a middleman himself. By comparison, the Dufours were getting their supplies from second-tier wholesalers on the Lower St Lawrence (at least, those are the ones who sued them in 1848). Emmerson could probably negotiate better prices and had access to a wider range of products. The size of his orders justified his travelling to Quebec City and Saint John to visit potential suppliers. Emmerson's motivation was not profit maximizing, but risk minimizing, and his dependence on the Glaziers made such strategies even more urgent.

His sons took the business a step further. First, they do not seem to have had connections with lumberers. The Glazier-Emmerson relationship may have had a personal dimension that prevented Emmerson from parting company with the lumberers, despite the risks involved. William and Thomas Emmerson walked away from the patrons-and-clients culture. Second, the young men kept their books according to the rules: they balanced the columns; they kept daybooks; and one of the surviving ledgers contains only the accounts of their waged employees who put their purchases on account until they were paid. Unlike their father the young Emmersons did not throw different kinds of accounts together in the same book. All outstanding accounts were settled in December. The young men probably received some formal training in bookkeeping but though they followed the forms, they may not have understood the spirit. From the few surviving books, it appears that they could draw up a balance sheet if they were so inclined, but they never did. They had the tools to calculate their profits but they did not do that either. Bookkeeping was not yet an analytical tool. In this respect the Emmerson brothers were no different from Robert Connors, a merchant from the New Brunswick side of the river opposite Fort Kent, whose books from the 1870s have survived. Connors's books also superficially appear as if he kept them according to the principles of accounting: double entries, separate groupings for different types of transactions, yearly settlements. But in attempting to get an overview of his activities, it becomes obvious that nothing squares, that some transactions are missing, that nothing comes close to a balance sheet, and that there are no yearly inventories.[37]

In the new Dominion of Canada, merchants designed their accounting systems by the book, but had not yet developed the calculating habits of capitalists. They made a living rather than profits. But the haphazard bookkeeping and back-pocket management of a John Emmerson, who engaged in all and sundry business ventures that came his way, died with his generation. The younger Emmersons appear to have engaged in a narrower range of activities than their father. They only occasionally engaged in lumbering. They continued to accumulate real estate, which may have been an insurance against the consequences of commercial failure. In Emmerson's case, the timing was perfect both in symbolic and business terms. Emmerson died a month after the creation of the Dominion of Canada, which was intended to replace staple-producing colonies with an industrialized affiliate of a global empire. He also died a few years before the recession of 1873 wiped out the old generation of lumberers and timber merchants.

6 A Tale of Two Markets: Frontier Farming

Few people in the world live better than the farmers of New Brunswick. By their industry, they raise an abundance of agricultural produce: and they have been censured for their extravagance in consuming the food that would bring a high price in the market, and by the sale of which their gains would be increased.

Abraham Gesner, 1847[1]

Great crops have been raised in Madawaska for several years past – latterly sufficient for their own consumption and the support of emigrants thither, besides exporting four or five thousand bushels to Canada.

John Baker and James Bacon, 1827[2]

The only market now existing in Aroostook for ordinary agricultural production is that created by the lumbering operators. This is generally a good one to an extent sufficient to absorb the surplus which the settlers now tilling the soil have to dispose of; but it is by no means a uniform one, varying as it necessarily must, with the fluctuations of that interest (proverbially uncertain) which creates it.

Secretary of the Maine Board of Agriculture, 1857[3]

These three quotations convey contradictory images of the valley and of New Brunswick farmers. Were they subsistence or market oriented, and if the latter, in what markets did they participate? Like the secretary of the Maine board of agriculture, many historians of Canada have noted the existence of a close, almost symbiotic relationship between agriculture and the forest industry in peripheral regions. The picture is usually not a cheery one: lack of outside markets forced farmers into subsistence agriculture and winter employment in the shanties to survive.[4] New Brunswick agriculture has similarly suffered from a poor reputation among historians, in part because the province has always been a net importer of food. New Brunswickers allegedly spent too much time fishing, cutting and floating timber, or building ships, than tending their fields. Farming would have been reduced to growing a large garden, a potato patch, some buckwheat, and a bit of hay for the family cow. Raising a few pigs would have rounded up the agricultural activities of the typical rural family and all this production was meant for family consumption.[5] Most rural Maritimers would thus have belonged to two distinct worlds: subsistence farming, where activities were geared towards on site consumption and not to markets, and where exchanges were purely local and limited in value, and the forest and fishery industries, heavily dependent on the international market, and subject to its fluctuations and constraints.

Madawaska agriculture would seem at first glance to have fared as badly. Farmers frequently relied on cash to settle their store accounts, and storekeepers collected few country products with the exception of fodder. John Emmerson did not ship agricultural commodities outside the valley, but he imported considerable quantities of flour, meal, biscuits, mess pork and fish, not all of it for the lumberers. In 1853, not a peak year, he purchased over 774 barrels of flour. A barrel of flour weighed 196 pounds and a pound of flour makes a pound of bread. Emmerson had then brought enough flour to make about 152,000 loaves. Assuming a one-pound loaf per day, this amount would feed 416 persons for a year. His purchase more than doubled the following year, which would seem to indicate that by the 1840s at least, agriculture was unable to feed the local population and was reduced to being the handmaiden of the forest industry.

However, most contemporary reports on the province's agricultural potential and even on the performance of the farmers are positive and, like Abraham Gesner's comments, contradict the vision of later historians. Baker and Bacon even present the surprising image of a region that exported to Lower Canada. Sources of information about Madawaska agriculture are surprisingly abundant. Writings exist about farming in general in New Brunswick, and later in northern Maine. Many of those texts were usually produced by individuals trying to promote the province or the county to potential immigrants and they naturally tended to make their region sound like a farmer's paradise. Nonetheless, their description of pioneer farming techniques and their recommendation as to crop choices seem reliable enough: Crown Land agents, agricultural societies, and private settlement companies had every interest in helping people to succeed. They certainly understood the constraints of farming in the province better than some of the European experts who deplored at length the fact that North Americans stubbornly refused to follow the example of their own farmers. Abundant but unsystematic information is scattered in the accounts of travellers who visited the Madawaska settlement or went through it en route to other places. The descriptions of the Upper Saint John were similar to descriptions of New Brunswick: marvelous potential and splendid crops, despite indifferent farming techniques. Farmers had an easy life – too easy. New Brunswick and Madawaska farming deserve neither all this praise, nor all this criticism. Farming could be profitable, but at the cost of a lot of hard work, and always at the mercy of some natural calamity. The existing sources describe Madawaska as a thriving farming region engaged in commercial agriculture from the 1820s onwards. It produced wheat surpluses until the mid-1830s, when a series of natural disasters forced farmers to seek alternative marketable commodities. They then turned to producing supplies for the lumber camps.

Frontier Farming

Farming in the Saint John Valley was subject to a set of unavoidable limitations: the local soil and climate on the one hand, and the nature of pioneer farming on the other. Both put limitations on the choices farmers could make.

The Physical Environment

Most of the soil of the Saint John Valley is good by Maritime and New England standards, which means less than first rate. The best soils are classified as category II in the Canadian soil classification scheme. Part of the upper and middle Saint John and Aroostook River valley runs through a large stretch of Caribou loam, a light, well-drained soil suitable for potatoes. In the eastern half of the Madawaska Territory a gravelly loam prevails. The soil of the hills that frame the valley is thin, yielding good crops of stones every spring. When not too sloping, hillside land is suitable for pastures. The main asset of the Saint John River resides in the intervales and bottomland that line its banks all the way to the Bay of Fundy. Made up of fine fluvial deposits, in their natural state the intervales were covered with deciduous trees that, unlike conifers, produce humus. Some intervales flooded every spring, which contributed to their fertility.[6] In parts of the valley including the eastern half of the Madawaska settlement, the intervales can be three miles deep.

The valley climate is continental: short, hot, and fairly dry summers; long, very cold winters, characterized by heavy snowfalls. The growing season averaged 120 days in the nineteenth century, with killing frosts until the third week in May and frost starting again in the third week of September. The frost-free period was barely enough to ripen nineteenth-century wheat.[7] To make matters worse, the intervales are low-lying pieces of land, more susceptible to late and early frost than the hills.[8] These days, frosts hard enough to kill tomato plants can occur in late August.[9]

The climate of the valley varied over time. Peter Fisher, the first historian of New Brunswick, has provided a description of climatic conditions until the late 1830s. The century began with a period of mild winters and cool summers, interrupted by the famous 'year without a summer' in 1816. The weather gradually improved until 1822, when bumper crops were harvested throughout the province.[10] Drought struck in 1825, so severe that the entire Miramichi Valley went up in flames, destroying thousands of acres of timber. The reverse problem affected the early 1830s: the summers were cold and wet, even frosty. Two unusually cold winters in 1835–6 were followed by an excessively dry summer, which almost destroyed the pastureland.[11]

Baron and Smith's records of killing frosts for Maine show that the length of the growing season fluctuated widely.[12] Between 1829 and 1845, the only pre-1900 period for which data is available, the growing season in northern Maine ranged between 75 and 200 days. The seasons were unusually long in the early 1830s, dropped precipitously to between 80 and 85 days in the middle of the decade, increased to an average of 140 at the end of the 1830s, and dropped again below 100 days for the rest of the period for which data exists. I have not found other detailed descriptions of the climate for the later period, but this example is sufficient to demonstrate that farmers were vulnerable to the vagaries of the weather. Dry or wet summers reduced yields, early frost prevented timely sowing, and late ones could destroy crops before they had been harvested.

The shortness of the growing season also limited opportunities to stagger the planting of crops. The farmers had to play with the different ripening times of the various field crops and with the urgency of their harvest. In general the farming season began in May. Potatoes were put in the ground between the beginning of the month and early June. Wheat and other grains were then sown and by the end of June, the grass was strong enough to support the stock. The grain harvest started in the middle of July. Wheat, which looses its grains shortly after maturity, could not wait and had to be harvested as soon as it was ripe. The grain harvest extended through the middle of August and overlapped with the haying season. Barley and oats were harvested after the wheat was in, but no later than the first of September. Corn, when it was grown, was cut in September. Potatoes and turnips were dug in the middle of October, and even later if the weather allowed it. Milk cows and horses were brought in in November, and the rest of the stock the following month. It was then butchering time, as the hard frost allowed farmers to freeze the meat for a few months.[13]

Pioneer Farming

Pioneering imposed its own constraints on the farmers: improved acreages were tiny and cluttered with stumps for several years. Pioneer farms were also usually underequipped and understocked and thus lacked manure for fertilizer. These factors all limited production levels. The first thing a would-be farmer did after taking possession of his lot was to cut some of the trees to erect a shelter. The first house was normally made of round logs fifteen to twenty feet in length and chinked with moss or clay. The roof was covered with boards, and then with birch or spruce bark held in place with poles and ties. A wood-framed chimney lined with clay provided a source of heat. The typical New Brunswick pioneer log house had one window and one door with a sash window. There was a root cellar under the floorboards and a loft above. Later, the farmer would build a frame house and convert the log building into a barn or storage shed.[14]

Once a shelter had been built, the pioneer felled more trees that he either burned for heat or used for fencing (there is no reference to the practice of tree girdling in New Brunswick or Madawaska). According to Thomas Baillie, a farmer could clear four to six acres a year.[15] This figure seems exceedingly optimistic: one or two acres a year is more realistic.[16] Stumps could not be removed until they had rotted. Baillie believed the big roots took five years to decay but intervale land seems to have been faster to clear.[17] The New Brunswick and Nova Scotia

Land Company claimed that the roots of hardwood and spruce decayed fairly quickly and could be extracted after two years 'with a little additional labour,' whereas 'pine and hemlock seem to require an age.'[18]

Until the stumps were removed, farmers could not plough their fields. They simply broadcast their seeds over the surface and covered them either with a triangular harrow drawn by horses or manually with a hoe.[19] The New Brunswick and Nova Scotia Land Company maintained that three good successive crops could be had by using this method on upland without any manure and also that intervale land never required fertilizer. Wheat, oats, and potatoes planted in hills and tended with the hoe constituted the first three recommended crops. Afterwards, the field was left in grass until the stumps were removed. The company suggested mixing grass seed in with the last grain crop to raise some late hay after the harvest. Indian corn, pumpkins, cucumbers, peas, and beans were hilled like potatoes, whereas other grains, turnips, hemp, flax, and grass seeds were broadcast and harrowed over. Baillie only mentions two crops that were planted before the stumps were removed: first potatoes and then wheat mixed with grass.[20] Bouchette described potatoes as a sure crop on imperfectly cleared land, requiring 'no labour but that of a hoe.'[21] Mainers followed a similar strategy. They planted wheat, oats, or corn on newly cleared land. In the second year oats followed wheat, wheat followed corn, and oats followed oats. In the third year, they planted oats or buckwheat, and afterwards left the field in grass until it could be cleared of stumps.[22] Pioneers also tended gardens where they grew salad greens, kales, and asparagus. Beans were susceptible to frost so were only grown in gardens, but peas were a field crop, especially in the French settlements.[23]

Not all would-be farmers were able to move onto a clearing lot when they wanted to. Capital was required for tools, farm implements, stock, seeds, and provisions. Perley's *Handbook for Emigrants* estimated that an initial capital outlay of £100 was needed, in addition to the cost of land. Baillie and later Edmund Ward suggested that emigrants hire themselves out to farmers to learn how to farm in the new land. Like the millers and the storekeepers, farmers could serve an apprenticeship with others as they tried to save some start-up capital. Ward claimed that one could save enough in five years to establish oneself. Baillie suggested renting a cleared farm as another step towards the accumulation of the necessary capital.[24] The result, according to Baillie, was that 'after ten years, he has a new log or frame house with stone chimney, a frame barn, 25 or 30 acres cleared admitting in many places the plough, a horse, two oxen, a pair of steers, two cows, a calf, eight to ten sheep and half a dozen of hogs.'[25]

Baillie was trying to attract emigrants to New Brunswick, and his calendar seems to have been a bit optimistic; this result would be more likely to take fifteen year to achieve. The amount of stock was particularly generous for a farm still encumbered by stumps.

If building up a farm took a minimum of ten years, the farmer's options were limited. He had to earn money, support his family, buy stock and equipment, but could not expand production to meet his needs. For all practical purposes, he could only plant the fields that had been cleared in the past two years, the others being under grass until the stumps could be removed. Despite Baillie's generous estimates, those fields were not likely to cover more than fifteen to twenty acres. This pace of growth was especially true of farmers who had to work in the woods during the winter.

Contemporary observers, seldom farmers themselves and often Europeans, were not impressed by New Brunswick husbandry, or by the farmers' habit of winter work in the woods. If we can believe James Robb, mid-nineteenth century New Brunswick farmers practised the same kind of agriculture as seventeenth- and early eighteenth-century New Englanders: they cropped the same piece of land for six or seven years, then turned it into pasture for the same length of time.[26] Some sort of crop rotation was in effect, but it was not sufficiently scientific for Robb, who refers to 'an indifferent alteration of crops.' Farmers knew about fertilizers; they manured their potatoes, and began to use mineral fertilizers such as plaster of Paris, lime, and alluvial deposits in the 1830s.[27] Maine farmers also knew about green manure, but the board of agriculture criticized them for allowing their manure to deteriorate before they had a chance to apply it.[28] There is no way to know how widespread the use of organic and mineral fertilizers was, especially as farmers seem to have relied on bringing new land under cultivation to maintain production levels. Robb described the process: 'Thus a virgin soil can cheaply produce at any time, and when it has been once exhausted by cropping, the field may be laid down to pasture until fertility is restored, with another piece of the forest brought in to undergo the same treatment. This may not be the best method, but at all events, it is a natural one for poor men to follow inasmuch as it involves least outlay of skill, labour or capital.'[29]

Even Robb, who looked down his nose at New Brunswick agriculture, recognized that the practice was rational, if deplorable. Continuous cropping followed by several years of recovery with the land left in grass was also the norm in Maine.[30]

Even those observers who sneered at New Brunswick husbandry reported high, and even very high, yields per acre: 20 to 30 bushels of wheat and bread grains on new land; 30 to 40 bushels of oats; and 250 to 300 bushels of potatoes.[31] Maine yields were equally good. Of course, the commentators were putting the region's best foot forward: the Provincials were writing for European emigrants who would not have been impressed by lower yields, and the Americans were trying to convince farmers that Maine, not the west, was an agricultural El Dorado. Even if crops on virgin land were as high yielding as they claimed, yields soon fell to the North American norms of 10 to 15 bushels of wheat an acre.

Characteristics of Madawaska Farming

The Visitors' Testimonies

Madawaska farmers likely practised the same type of husbandry as their colleagues in other parts of New Brunswick, and probably in most parts of the northeast frontier. Comments by contemporary visitors to the region do not suggest otherwise. For instance, Alexander Baring (the future Lord Ashburton), who came across the valley in May 1796, observed good land under cultivation – 25 bushels per acre of wheat among the stumps.[32] The first traveller to put his impressions down on paper was Park Holland, who visited the settlement in 1790 while surveying the Bingham purchase. He wrote of the settlers: 'They have a Church and priest, cattle, horses, sheep and hogs, raise wheat, oats, barley and peas, and flax, and tobacco, which, though of a poor quality answer for smoking, make their own cloth, etc... Their houses are built of logs, and those we entered were neat and in order. They make their meat into soup to which they add onion and garlic, which grow wild upon the banks of the river.'[33]

The following year, Patrick Campbell found agriculture thriving at Madawaska. Farmers raised 'the strongest crops imaginable of wheat, barley, oats, and vegetables of most kinds (except Indian corn) in great plenty.' The settlers had gardens in which they grew onions, turnips, cabbages and 'other garden stuffs.' Campbell commented that the settlers had everything they needed except money, and added that 'where they could get that I am at a loss to know.' The nearest market was, in his estimation, 200 miles away, a great impediment to selling farm produce.[34] In 1812 Mgr Plessis, bishop of Quebec, made similar comments when he visited the Saint John Valley. The settlers were prosperous, but access to market was a problem. 'Les habitans ont plus de 30 lieues à aller au fleuve St Laurent et 60 à aller à Fredericton. Voilà néanmoins leurs seuls débouchés. Comment tirer parti de leurs denrées. Les frais de voyages n'en absorbent-ils pas presque tout le profit.'[35]

Young lieutenant John Le Couteur of the 104th Foot crossed the settlement with his regiment in 1812, on his way to Quebec. He described Madawaska as an 'insulated settlement [...] entirely separated from the busy world.' The inhabitants told him that 'they went down to Fredericton once or twice a year, to sell or barter their fur for what commodities they require.'[36]

Surveyor Bouchette visited the valley for the second time between 1826 and 1829 and reported that it was growing large surpluses of wheat, which was milled into flour and sold in Fredericton. He described the intervales as particularly suitable for hay and pasturage, and supporting numerous flocks and herds, which the settlers could not take to market for lack of appropriate means of communication.[37] Bouchette's comments echoed the statements made by Peter Fisher in 1825 in his history of New Brunswick: the land was of good quality, Indian corn would not grow on account of the latitude, but 'wheat, oats, grains, etc... flourish there in great perfection. The inhabitants are all farmers, and generally raise more than they can consume, having a surplus of grain to sell to traders in the settlement or to take to Fredericton.'[38] John Baker, however, had the settlers selling their surpluses in Lower Canada.[39] The three men's comments suggest that a trade in grain and flour developed in the Upper Saint John Valley between the War of 1812 and the early 1820s, when Fisher was writing his history.

The next description of local economic activities dates from 1831 by American land agents Deane and Kavanagh. Their observations suggest that there had been few qualitative changes in the local husbandry practices and way of life since the days of Park Holland. The crops were the same ones listed by Holland, with the addition of potatoes. The stock consisted of 'small boned cattle, Canadian horses, large bodied, coarse woolen sheep, and swine.'[40] The latter were presumably the ubiquitous razorback variety, described thirty years later by

J.F. Johnston as 'long snouted, long legged, ravenous looking brutes,'[41] and in another of his books as a cross between an alligator and a giraffe: it had the snout of the former, and the legs of the latter.[42] The razorback did not grow very fat, was mean tempered, but managed nicely on its own when turned in the woods to browse.[43] The inhabitants purchased their cattle in Lower Canada[44]; the most common type of cow in the province was a small, thrifty animal that was nonetheless a good milker – a good choice for people with limited resources.[45] The Canadian horse, which the valley settlers raised, enjoyed such a good reputation that Lower Canadians bred it for export to the United States.[46]

Up until the 1830s the settlers practiced a type of mixed agriculture, and grew as wide a variety of crops as local conditions would allow. The stock was similar to that found in Lower Canada and the crops grown could be found all over eastern Canada and the northeastern United States. The Saint John Valley agriculture was unexceptional in terms of types of crops and stock and flock varieties. In 1831 many of the settlers hunted in the fall and some produced large quantities of maple sugar in the spring. Those who did claimed sugaries or hunting grounds.[47] The phenomenon was not likely new: the two activities had likely been going on since the beginning of the settlement. Housing, on the other hand, had improved since 1790. Most settlers lived in one- or two-room houses made of square timber; some were painted or clapboarded. The early log shelters were converted into barns.[48] In 1831 the settlers imported their edge tools from British North America but made other farming implements themselves. They tanned their own leather and made their own shoes and cloth.[49] In his *Notitia of New Brunswick* published in 1837, Fisher noted that 'log huts, some of which are very large, being comprised of two buildings joined together' were still common, but frame houses were coming into style. Clothing was locally made and consisted of 'coarse cloth, kerseys and linen.' In the early 1840s some Madawaska-made clothing was sold in Fredericton.[50] The settlers procured their salt and manufactured goods from Fredericton and Canada.[51]

The observations of visitors to the Saint John Valley from the late 1830s to the early 1850s point to a shift in crops varieties. In his autobiography, William Baird reminisced about a visit to the Madawaska settlement in 1838 and describes loaves resembling 'huge knots sliced from a tree, and the bread dark but sweet.'[52] This obviously was not wheat bread. In 1851 Johnston mentions the extensive cultivation of buckwheat in New Brunswick 'since the wheat has become so precarious a crop.' Although Johnston claimed that buckwheat pancakes were delicious and as nutritious as bread, he deplored the cultivation of the plant; it was too easy to grow and therefore encouraged laziness among the farmers, and it forced women to cook everyday when they should have been more productively employed doing something else.[53] He believed that if wheat would not grow farmers should replace it with rye or oats, which could be made into real bread. Buckwheat was not solely a subsistence crop. Aroostook county historian, Clarence Day, citing a mid-nineteenth century state surveyor's report, described it as a staple crop in the Aroostook and Saint John Valley, 'used to fatten hogs and poultry, feed horses and oxen, and ground into flour.'[54] The Maine board of agriculture also described it as a source of food and fodder, the finer flour for humans and the coarser remainder for the animals.[55] Buckwheat had become to northern Maine farmers what corn was to their Midwestern counterparts: an all-purpose commodity. This could explain why it was in high demand, so much so that Wiggin claimed it was a commodity currency, always accepted as payment by the local stores.[56]

Lumbering also seems to have created a substitute market for local products and visitors identified the lumber camps as a source of employment for local people. Edmund Ward stated in 1841 that the valley boasted several farmers who raised substantial quantities of oats and grains 'with which they supply the lumbering parties in their immediate vicinity.'[57] Johnston also noted in his remarks on the agricultural capabilities of New Brunswick that lumbering offered 'a more ready market for farm produces. It kept prices up and gave employment to idle hands.'[58] The importance of the lumber camps as a market for the entire northern part of the state of Maine (which became Aroostook County after the signing of the 1842 treaty) was noted by local newspapers and by the county agricultural society. In 1857 the Maine board of agriculture noted that the lumber camps were the only existing market where Aroostook County farmers could dispose of their surplus. Ten years later, a local newspaper was echoing those comments: 'The farmers will share in the harvest [of lumber] by creating a demand and market for everything he can raise. As long as lumber is high, hay, oats and all kind of farming produce will be high also. The winter will be as productive to him as the summers [...] Raising most of his supplies, the farmer of Aroostook can convert the heavier and bulkier articles, such as hay, oats, buckwheat, potatoes and all the coarser kinds of grain, which will not pay the cost of transportation to a distant market, into lumber which will float down the St. John to a market.'[59] Members of the board of agriculture did not find this situation ideal, as the shanty market was notoriously volatile. Furthermore, as the animals spent their winters in the woods, a large part of the manure they produced was lost.[60]

Reliable accounts of Saint John Valley farming are scarce after 1850. American tourists, government officials, or journalists frequently visited the Madawaska Territory, but they were so convinced that the French were living in a time warp that they invariably saw uncontaminated or backward peasants (depending on whether they took their cue from Longfellow or Darwin) living the life and eating the food of their seventeenth-century French forbears. The Provincials generally ignored the French, perhaps suggesting that there was nothing remarkable about the place, its people, and the way they conducted their business. The reports of the Maine and New Brunswick boards of agriculture are less informative than they might have been. The French appear not to have joined the agricultural societies upon whose reports the board relied. The board members for northern Aroostook, for instance, were from Fort Fairfield in 1857 and 1858 and from Houlton, even further south, in 1876.

The last relevant document that describes the valley is a description of Victoria County written in 1872 by Charles Lugrin, secretary of the agricultural board of New Brunswick, and appendixed to the journal of the provincial legislature. Victoria County included the New Brunswick part of the Madawaska Territory as well as several Catholic and Protestant Irish civil parishes.

Lugrin listed hay, oats, buckwheat, peas, and potatoes as county staple crops. Wheat production had increased somewhat, but had not regained the importance it had in local agriculture at the beginning of the century. Farmers blamed successive crop failures for this state of affairs; Lugrin believed that bad farming practices, which had exhausted the soil, were to blame. Buckwheat had replaced wheat, a development Lugrin deplored. He did not think the grain was a very good food source, but it ripened quickly. Peas formed 'a staple article of food, particularly among the French with whom pea soup is a deservedly favourite dish.'[61] Oats were usually excellent, and 'the whole county, but particularly the lower parishes (That is the Irish ones), cannot be surpassed in their adaptation to the growth of potatoes.' Intervale land and islands produced excellent hay, although the quality had lately declined. Flax was grown mostly among the French 'who are expert at weaving good, strong and durable linen.' Like many observers, Lugrin noted that Victoria county farmers practiced extensive agriculture; like most, he disapproved: he thought this was not the most profitable use of their time.[62] Lugrin similarly criticized the farmers engaging in lumbering and shingle making, which he saw as 'speculations' that could only lead to lifelong debt. He was nonetheless enough of a realist to understand it could not be eliminated entirely, and advised farmers to limit themselves to small-scale logging. He also recognized that the lumber camps were the only cash markets accessible to local farmers, and were insufficient to absorb the entire surplus local production. Farmers had to make shingles or have small lumbering operations of their own to prosper.

Lugrin's account of agriculture in Victoria County is particularly useful for his detailed description of existing stock. He found fault with the animals, which he deemed ill-adapted to the wants of the people. The horses lacked strength: they were descendents of the 'hardy little French horses' imported from Canada at the beginning of the century, but the stock had unfortunately been weakened through indiscriminate cross-breeding. On the positive side, the horses had 'nerve, energy and speed'; they were small enough to be economical, but not to the point of being useless on a farm. Horses were not always the best choice of draught animals, though, and Lugrin believed the French kept too many of them. Poorer farmers would be better off with a team of oxen, which could have done the same amount of work for half the cost. Horned cattle were described as small, but good milkers; sheep as average in size and fleece, and 'the common breed of pigs in the French parishes is very long in the leg, with an immense frame, and rather difficult to fatten.' Cross-breeding easily improved the pigs, however, and turned them into heavy porkers.

Lugrin's thorough descriptions are interesting on several counts. First, with the exception of crop mixes and markets, not much seemed to have changed between 1830 and 1870. The stock descriptions especially are quite similar to those of Deane and Kavanagh and Johnston. Second, Lugrin was visibly unimpressed by Victoria County agriculture, be it French or Irish, in either its Catholic or Protestant varieties. However, nothing he found could not be easily remedied with a bit of manure here, a more judicious crop or stock selection there, and widespread cross-breeding with better stock. Victoria County agriculture was distinguished by neither its vices nor its virtues. It had great potential, and was held back by poor communication more than by the deficiencies of the farmers. Like his neighbours in Aroostook County, Lugrin believed the arrival of the railroad would herald an era of prosperity for the region.

He had a point. Isaac Baker's report to the Maine board of agriculture in 1876 noted the impact of the railroad in his area. Houlton was connected to the New Brunswick and Canada line, which was inching its way up the Saint John River. It was now possible for southern Aroostook farmers to ship large quantities of hay, oats, and potatoes to Boston. Ten to twelve potato starch factories were now operating in the county, each consuming between 50,000 and 80,000 bushels annually. The northernmost starch factories were in Fort Fairfield and Presque Isle. Baker also believed that most farmers would be better off switching to dairying, and noted the presence of three cheese factories in the county. The northernmost again was in Presque Isle, and catered to the local market where cheese sold for 12 cents a pound. The Houlton factory, which produced twice as much, sold cheese on the Boston market for 12 to 15 cents a pound.[63]

A Statistical Overview

Visitors to Madawaska encountered a prosperous agricultural community that after the War of 1812 engaged in both subsistence and market farming. Stock seems to have remained the same throughout the period while crop choices evolved. Wheat appears to have become a commercial crop after the War of 1812, and to have been abandoned by the late 1830s. Quantitative evidence corroborates and refines this picture. It suggests that crop production was normally very good, and of a sufficient amount to support a rapidly growing population. A cursory analysis of existing quantitative sources[64] allows the construction of two series that show average quantities per productive farm,[65] and average quantities per household (see tables 6 and 7).[66]

Table 6 suggests that farm production was quite high. Bread grain production never fell below 46 bushels per farm, and was as high as 125 in the early 1830s. Bettye Hobbs-Pruitt in her study of eighteenth-century Massachusetts estimated that a farm growing at least 34 bushels of grain had reached subsistence level, and one growing 45 or more was producing for the market.[67] The average Madawaska farmer never grew less than twice the minimum required by his Massachusetts counterparts to cover his household's needs. Average production

1 *Travel on the St John River on the way to Quebec in January or February* (1815) (New Brunswick Museum, Saint John, N.B., W6798). Note the bread oven on the outside of the house to the left. The house is also displaying a characteristically French-Canadian curve. The team escorting the two gentlemen is wearing French-Canadian hooded coats, ceintures fléchées, and high cut moccasins. The following description of a party leaving the Dufour's inn at Madawaska in 1829 could apply to this picture : 'January 15th. - A party of persons had collected for the purpose of proceeding with out guides towards Quebec; and so we all started together ... The picture of our caravan was now totally changed. A dozen persons of various descriptions had joined our party, some at the end and some at the beginning of their respective journeys. They pelted each other with snowballs, and sang and whistled, smoking and hallowing ... The guides had procured dogs to draw the toboggans, and several of these great creatures, from the coast of Labrador and Newfoundland, were loose and followed in our train.' (George Head, Esq. *Forest scenes and incidents, in the wilds of North America: being a diary of a winter's route from Halifax to the Canada , and during four months' residence in the woods on the borders of Lake Huron and Simcoe,* London: John Murray, 1829)

2   One of the resting places on the Grand Portage route between Rivière du Loup and Lake Temiscouata was *Camp Saint Francois*, north of the Lake (note the wide bridge and the traveller on a cart). (Milicent Mary Chaplin Fonds, watercolor, July 1842 ; LAC, negative C-000919)

3 *Tow Boats on the Madawaska*, c. 1840, by Mrs Arianne Saunders Shore (Beaver-brook Art Gallery, Fredericton, 1969.23). By the 1840s, the British had some sol-diers stationed at the Dégeli, at the junction between Lake Temiscouata and the Madawaska River; the individual in the central yard between the buildings is wearing a red coat; goods were carried in small boats in summer. This type of boat was ubiquitous in the region, and remained in use till the late nineteenth century, as the following description by Wiggin indicates: 'formerly the larger portion of the supplies for the lumber camps and also for the stores along the river was boated up the river from Fredericton. The boats used were large, flat bottomed scows with a cabin built upon the after end in which the boatman ate and slept and upon the top of which the helmsman stood and steered the boat by means of a huge rudder. Some of these boats are capable of carrying 200 barrels of pork and are drawn up the river by horses' (Wiggin, *History of Aroostook*, p. 194).

4 *Long farm on Lake Temiscouata*, ca. 1815 (LAC, Peter Winkworth collection, e-001201329). Although the Long farm was on Lake Temiscouata, the style of the buildings and the layout of the farm were not significantly different from the ones of the farms along the Saint John. The Long farm also served as a relay and inn for travellers up and down the Grand Portage. The peacefulness of the picture belies the activities that went on when travellers stayed over for the night. Rest was not guaranteed, as George Head discovered: 'January 16th. At last we arrived at the house of Mr. Long, situated at the extremity of Lake Tamasquatha … We found a new set of travellers, who had established themselves in the house; and these being reinforced by our numbers, a confusion of tongues prevailed in our room which set at defiance all description. We had thirty six persons in it, besides six or eight large dogs belonging to the tobogins. We were obliged to lay on the ground like so many pigs. My next neighbour was a major in the army, whom I never saw before and have never met since; he seemed more fatigued than I was, and did nothing but groan all night. The dogs disturbed us; for they ran about and trod upon us; they growled; and twice before morning, there was a battle royal among them, with the whole room up in arms to part them by throttling and biting the ends of their tails. What with the noise, and the shouting, and the swearing in bad French, we were in a perfect uproar. For this, the natural remedy, of course, would have been to turn the dogs out; but the masters would not allow it, as they were of too much use by far on a journey. The gabble of tongues, the smell of tobacco smoke, and the disturbance altogether, was really dreadful; and there was, besides, a truckle bed in the room, on which two women reposed – the mistress of the house and her sister' (Head, *Forest Scenes and Incidents*).

5 The Grand Falls in 1840. This watercolour shows the extent and nature of
the forest. The platform is part of Sir John Caldwell's mill. (Alexander Cavalie
Mercer, watercolour, 1840, watercolours fond, LAC negative C-035944)

6   This is Simon Hebert's farm at the Petit Sault (now Edmundston) around
1836. It then served as an inn. The other two pictures (opposite) show the same
location in 1865 and 1880. Some of the original buildings were still there in 1880.
(Philip John Bainbridge, watercolour, 1836, LAC negative C-011852; CDEM
PC2-15; PC2-40)

7   The Grand Falls were a formidable obstacle to the log drives, as this picture from the 1880s clearly shows. (Provincial Archives of New Brunswick, George Taylor, photograph, P5-185, 1882)

8   By the end of our period, the trees which used to line the river had all been cut down and replaced by a continuous string of farms. (PANB, Ketchum collection, P4 1-35. Four miles above Grand Falls)

9   The three houses on these two pages show clearly how housing evolved as farms got more established. The first picture shows a typical clearing, with a house under construction, and a shanty in the yard. On the second one, an 'American' and a 'Canadian' house stand side by side on the bank of the river. The Canadian houses were built parallel to the river, and the 'American ones' perpendicular to it. By 1848, many houses built at Madawaska were similar to the O'Neill house in the last picture: a one story building with the roof projecting over a gallery, and side utility building. (CDEM, PB1-16; PB1-12; PA1-15)

10   This is the Emmerson house referred to in the quote at the beginning of chapter 5. Built in 1867, it later served as Edmundston's city hall. (CDEM, PC-83)

11   This unexpectedly candid picture postdates the period covered in this volume, but such pictures are extremely rare, and the activities pictured here (women doing the laundry, a man doing mundane yard work) are unlikely to have changed much since the middle of the century. This was probably a 'trial picture' – the photographer's blackroom on wheels is even visible at the side. (Courtesy St Francis Historical Society)

Madawaska Sept 3.

12   This sketch is the only picture of any kind of pre-photographic era Mada-waska costume. The women wear tops with the mutton sleeves in fashion at the time, neckerchiefs tucked into the front of their short gowns, plain petticoats, wrap around aprons, and mocassins. The head gear does not look at all like the ones contemporary Acadian women in the Maritimes were wearing; In fact, this costume could fit a description of Lower St Lawrence women's dresses: 'the women wear in summer printed short gowns reaching to the middle and blue or red petticoats with a broad brimmed straw hat, and in winter, they often wear a grey coat like the men.' (Sir James Edward Alexander. *L'Acadie, or Seven Years' Exploration in British North America,* London, 1859, vol II.p. 55. LAC C-135256)

13   Some typical 'backwood consumers,' Elie Thibodeau and his wife Seconde Jalbert, circa 1875. Elie was a comfortable, but by no means rich farmer in St Francis (Me.). Seconde is dressed in her best clothes for the picture, and her dress and hat reflect the fashion of the time. Elie is wearing a very crisp white shirt, clearly cut from factory made fabric, a small bow tie, and thick homespun pants. His hairstyle and full beard are also typical of the period. (Courtesy St Francis Historical Society).

14   And here is the 'Acadian Maiden' diligently weaving the 'homespun' referred to in chapter 8. The contrast between this fashionable adolescent and the
rustic loom on which a bed rug is in progress suggests the picture was set up.
(Pullen: *In Fair Aroostook*)

per household (table 7, total production divided by the number of households, including those classified as non-farm) was also high. The average production of grain per household never fell below 38 bushels except in 1833. It peaked at 170 in 1870.

By 1850 wheat had been superseded by hay, oats, potatoes, and buckwheat, which remained the major crops for the next twenty-five years. The shift from wheat to fodder did not coincide with the opening of the lumber camps in the 1820s, but with their legalization in the 1840s and the expansion of logging in the following decade. There were good reasons why a farmer would not want to produce for the shanties, as long as he could grow wheat with a reasonable chance of success. In the early 1830s wheat yielded about 12 bushels an acre and normally sold locally for 6 shillings ($1.20); oats yielded about 18 bushels an acre and fetched 2s.6d. or 50 cents. If the crop was being grown on new land, the farmer could collect an extra shilling per bushel of wheat, but only 4 pence per bushel of oats. As New Brunswick was a net importer of wheat, the market was guaranteed. Madawaska farmers could have been undercut by western grain: the price of flour did go down in the valley, from the 40 shillings a barrel ($8.00) reported by Baillie in 1832 to a low of 35 shillings a barrel in the mid-1850s. The local price of wheat also went down from 5 to 10 shillings in the late 1830s to 5 to 8 shillings around 1850, and 6 shillings around 1860. Western competition had a slightly depressing effect on local prices in the long run, but prices fluctuated wildly, and the fluctuation did not always reflect the ups and downs of prices in Upper Canada. Wheat was a better choice as long as it grew well, but by the late 1830s successful wheat crops could no longer be taken for granted.

The culprit was the natural environment. Madawaska farmers did very well in good years, but their prosperity was fragile. Madawaska agriculture was very vulnerable to climatic vagaries because of the extreme fluctuations in the length of the local growing season. Consequently, the settlement was plagued with several climate-induced crop failures in the first fifty years of its existence. Crops failed in 1787, 1797, 1814, 1816–17, 1828, possibly in 1832, dramatically in 1833, and again in 1836, the mid-1840s, and 1855.[68] The Hessian fly damaged the wheat crops in 1792.[69] The crop failure of 1833 was a disaster, which forced the territory to ask the provincial government for relief.[70] Before the settlement had fully recovered, wheat midges, rust, and potato rot swept through the area. The wheat midge and rust repeatedly devastated the wheat crops from the mid-1830s to the late-1850s, and were still problems in 1876.[71] They defeated the farmers' attempts at growing large quantities of wheat: production per farm stagnated at 35 to 45 bushels, and then collapsed entirely. The Aroostook County Agricultural Society in northern Maine dated the midge's first appearance to 1834 or 1835; in 1859 it noted that a natural predator of the midge, the ichneumon fly, had appeared in Canada and New York.[72] British agronomer Johnston traced the progress of the midge in New Brunswick from the southern part of the province in the early 1840s to the Upper Saint John Valley by 1846–7 and dates the appearance of rust to 1848.[73] Farmers and agronomers were equally at a loss in the face of the situation. Johnston gave farmers contradictory advice. He advocated early sowing against rust, so that the grain would ripen before the critical mid-season, but he also recommended late sowing, so that the grain would not ripen until the midge had laid its eggs. Farmers relied on a time-honoured countermeasure: they shifted crops. Johnston mentions that in the Saint John Valley the midge problem led to the substitution of oats and buckwheat for wheat. In the Saint John Valley farmers had first tried barley and potatoes as substitute crops, but the potato blight struck New England and the Maritimes in the early 1840s. In 1859 the board of agriculture of Aroostook County observed that it had blighted the crop for the past fifteen or twenty years.[74] Although the secretary of the state board claimed that the impact of the disease was uneven and that 'for ten years past, not over a quarter of the crop had ever been lost from the rot in any locality,' a quarter of a crop is not unsubstantial.[75] Farmers did their best to counteract these calamities, and by 1850 the Saint John Valley farmers had settled on the mix of crops they continued to cultivate until the arrival of the railroad made large-scale potato growing profitable: oats and buckwheat, hay and potatoes.

By the mid-1830s the wheat boom was over, not because farmers had exhausted their soil (there was plenty of virgin land left, even on old farms), but because of problems beyond their control. Farmers groped for a few years for a solution. Only when logging was legalized after the 1842 treaty and then expanded did they find one: supplying fodder to the shanties. Farmers adjusted to environmental constraints through crop and market shifts. Lumber camps, which loom large in the life of northern Maine and northwest New Brunswick in the second half of the nineteenth century, did not impose their needs on local agriculture. Farmers turned to them as a substitute market only when it became painfully obvious that wheat growing was a thing of the past. Instead of trapping farmers in a depressed economy, the agro-forestry system gave them a new lease on life.[76]

The lumber camps were not the farmers' only markets either. Baker and Bacon noted that there were three outlets for the territory's agricultural production: on-site consumption, sale on external markets, and the 'immigrants thither.' Newcomers whose farms could not immediately support them constituted a market. And there was no shortage of newcomers. Immigration was considerable in some years. Only a minority of households owned an operational farm in the early 1830s, that is, a farm with crops in the ground. In 1831 one-quarter of the lots enumerated by Deane and Kavanagh had been in cultivation less than five years, and one farm in five had less than five acres cleared. In 1833 only 158 of the 402 households listed by Maclauchlan lived on an operating farm; the others had land, but hardly any stock and little or no crop.[77] When immigration slowed down in the second half of the century, the non-farm population increased instead. In New Brunswick Madawaska, the number of non-farm households grew from 23 to 30 per cent between 1861 and 1871 and on the U.S. side from 23 to 36 per cent between 1860 and 1870.[78] This local market presented two advantages: it was less unstable than the shanty market, and it purchased a wider range of commodities. The lumber camps that had accounts at Emmerson's store only bought fodder locally; the rest of their supplies came from Lower Canada. The non-farm population and the new arrivals bought local surplus meat, potatoes, peas, as well as perishable commodities such eggs and poultry.

Although the repeated failures of the wheat crop forced farmers to look for alternative crops, they had less impact on the settlers' diet. Well into the 1850s, deeds of maintenance, the contracts thereby an elderly couple exchanged their farm for support, listed no bread grain other than wheat. When wheat was not listed, it was replaced by equivalent quantities of store flour (*farine du magasin*).[79] People raised on wheat bread were unwilling to change their habits. Baird's dark bread may have been only one type of bread the settlers' wives put on the table. So were the famous buckwheat pancakes that remained a staple of the local diet till the Second World War and are still popular today. Women could continue making white bread because they could purchase wheat flour.

Inexpensive imported flour appeared in the region in the 1830s.[80] Madawaska wheat was hardly competitive when flour sold for $6 a barrel, and the farmers may very well have concluded that the difference in price was not sufficient to justify the risks.[81] And as mentioned in the previous chapter, Emmerson brought large quantities of flour into the valley from the mid-1840s on, and biscuits after 1848. The market had come to the rescue of the cook. Purchases of flour would have increased the need to sell other commodities on external markets. Self-sufficiency was clearly not paramount, and was subordinated to dietary preferences. The records are not always complete but there seemed to be a relationship between poor crops, signalled by high prices, and the quantities sold. Crop failures drove both prices and purchases of flour up. Madawaska households coped with crop failures by going to the store.

Gesner was obvious exaggerating when he claimed that New Brunswick farmers were among the better off in the world, but they were not among the worst off either. The same could be said of Madawaska farmers who, barring a climatic disaster or the appearance of a pest, could easily cover their needs and be left with surpluses for the merchants. But he was wrong to believe that farmers preferred fattening their bellies to fattening their purses. Farm households were not interested in self sufficiency: they sought markets as outlets for their production. They also did not hesitate to turn to markets to buy what they could no longer grow, even when local substitutes were available. Not all farmers were in the position to take part or profit from market activities. Some were clearly more market-oriented than others.

7 A Hierarchy of Farmers: Saint John Valley Agriculture

It has been said and apparently with truth, that the progress of agriculture may be measured by the desire shown by the cultivator of the land for improved implements and agricultural machinery. Machines are devices for economizing power and applying it to the best advantage

John Robb, 1856[1]

In 1799 Madawaska residents wanted a resident priest. The twice-yearly visitations from the Kamouraska or Ile Verte priests did not satisfy them. They believed that the bishop refused their request because he was unconvinced that the area could support a resident pastor. In attempting to address the matter, they included in their petition an enumeration of their tithes.[2] It turned out that many farmers produced in excess of their own needs. Simon Hébert was one of the largest tithe payers. His 8 bushels of grain corresponded to a production of 208 bushels, well beyond the 45 bushels needed for a farm to reach commercial levels. Only fourteen farmers out of fifty-five petitioners tithed 1 bushel or less. Nineteen tithed 2 bushels, and another twenty-two 3 bushels or more. The 1799 tithing list raises intriguing questions. First, some farmers were producing much more than others. Did they have significantly larger families to feed, or a desire to produce marketable surpluses? Second, if most Madawaska farmers were already commercial farmers with production exceeding 45 bushels, this early record belies the notion of an evolution from subsistence to market production. Were Madawaska farmers commercial as early as 1799? How did they weather the mid-century crisis and the crop shift? Who were the commercial farmers? How did they differ from the others? Did they fit Robb's definition of 'improving farmers'? And how did this interest in markets affect their society? J.F.W. Johnston's description of a two-tiered society echoes Christopher Clark or Allan Kulikoff, who claimed that in the United States the spread of a market economy led to a division between farmers who succeeded in becoming 'capitalists,' that is, produced for outside, impersonal markets, and those who 'reverted to subsistence.'[3] The more recent historiography suggests a different impact: everyone engaged in market production and farms spread along a continuum ranging from near subsistence, to heavily commercial.[4] If commercialization had split early Madawaska farmers into two groups, the tithing household distribution would have been bimodal; instead, the data presents a skewed bell curve, better fitting the Hudson Valley model. But did this pattern outlast the eighteenth century?

To answer those questions requires a change in methods. While the 34 to 45 bushel benchmarks used by Bettye Hobbs-Pruitt are useful yardsticks, they are not very precise, as they do not take into account the variations in household food and feed needs. The method developed by Marvin McInnis is conceptually very simple: subtract factors of production and food needs from farm production to get marketable surpluses, and regional food needs from total regional production to calculate regional surpluses. Once marketable surpluses are estimated, it is possible to calculate the proportion of farm production they represent.[5] (The procedure is explained more fully in Appendix I.) Clarence Danhof defined commercial farms as those that consume less than 40 per cent of production.[6] Expressed in another way, farms whose production corresponded to 250 per cent or more of their needs or a surplus equal or higher than 60 per cent of production were commercial. This is the definition used here. The definition can be extended to also consider commercial a region that is able to sell 60 per cent of its production outside of its boundaries (lumber camps are here treated as outside markets).[7] Danhof labels the other farms 'subsistence,' a confusing term most people equate with self-sufficiency and minimal involvement with markets. Yet a farming household that could market 50 per cent of its production was not exactly avoiding markets, and as Hobbs-Pruitt has shown, the low-surplus farm households could not have subsisted without engaging in market activities either. It is less misleading to refer to those non-commercial farms as small- to medium-surplus ones. There is also a considerable difference between a subsistence farm that just covers the needs of its inmates and one requiring only half its production to feed them. The farms with marketable surpluses below 60 per cent of production are here divided into low-surplus (surplus equal or lower than 30 per cent of production or production equal or lower than 125 per cent of needs) and medium-surplus farms. Commercial farms can similarly be subdivided into two groups: low commercial (surpluses between 60 and 79 per cent of production) and high commercial. Farms whose production is equal or less than 100 per cent of needs operated below subsistence levels.

Together the various documents give a picture of Madawaska agriculture that is surprisingly coherent and dovetails nicely with the qualitative evidence. What emerges from the calculations is a picture of a region that was borderline commercial for the entire period, but beginning to run into difficulties in 1870. The marketable surpluses were surprisingly high considering the reputation of Maritime agriculture or the customary image of farmers who engaged in the agro-forestry system. In 1860 Madawaska agriculture compared favorably with Ontario farming, but not everyone attained the same levels of commercialization. Most farmers huddled around the boundary between low commercial and medium surplus. At the high end, agriculture was very profitable. However, farmers with very high surpluses were not 'improving farmers.' They reached their production levels by doing more of the same, not by changing their techniques or investing in their farms. Madawaska farmers were market responsive, but traditionalists.

Early Surpluses and Early Differentiation

Surplus production began early on in the Upper Saint John Valley, but as the settlement was small, this was not much noticed by observers. The tithing record listed above is one of three that date from March 1799, July 1799, and August 1807.[8] The March 1799 document lists the total quantity of grain tithed by each individual household. The later 1799 and 1807 records do not break down quantities by household, but provide aggregate figures for each type of grain, for peas, and for potatoes.[9] Although they cannot be used to estimate total farm production and farm surplus, surpluses of bread grain, peas, and potatoes can be estimated. The numbers suggest that Madawaska was already feeding its population from within, and farmers had already begun to produce significant surpluses.

There were 55 households listed in the March 1799 tithing record, totalling 331 persons. According to the family reconstitution cards, there should have been 329 persons in those families, a remarkable agreement. However, 16 French-Catholic families who were residing at Madawaska in 1799 according to the family reconstitution cards are not mentioned in the tithing record, a total of 87 persons. Either these families had crops and did not fulfill their obligations towards the priest or they had nothing to tithe. For the sake of argument, they will all be assumed to have had no crops. The 55 listed households tithed 157 bushels of grain, which corresponded to a total production of 4,082 bushels. This was enough to feed all the tithing families and leave them, after putting aside seed and paying the miller, with a surplus of 1,466 bushels, or 27 bushels per household. The total grain needs (food and seed) for all 71 resident families amounted to 3,222 bushels. If the unlisted families had no production, the others could have fed them and been left with a surplus of 860 bushels. Some of that grain would have been used to feed the stock, but feed needs cannot be estimated as tithing records do not mention stock numbers.

The summer 1799 record provides additional information as it gives total figures for each type of crop (see table 8). This time, production corresponded to about 99.5 per cent of the entire population need for bread grain, 88 per cent of its requirements for peas, and 94 per cent of its need for potatoes. The adequacy of oat production cannot be estimated. Despite those figures, there may not have been a food shortage if the non-tithing families indeed produced some crops. Garden production of roots, legumes, and vegetables may also have compensated for a small shortfall of field crops. Although the settlement was self-sufficient in grain, peas, and potatoes, not all the farmers were. Production was unevenly distributed among farm households. In March 1799 16 per cent of the tithing families did not cover their food grain needs, 31 per cent had a surplus of at least 40 bushels, and 9 per cent a surplus exceeding 100 bushels. The situation in August 1807 was better. Wheat production alone covered 126 per cent of the entire population's needs for bread grain. Pea and potato production exceeded estimated needs by 40 and 60 per cent respectively.

The figures derived from the three tithing records, besides highlighting the variations in crop size from year to year, suggest that the valley could already feed its entire population from within. Regional surpluses were small, but farm surpluses were not. Less than twenty years after felling the first trees on their land, some farmers were producing enough to feed all, and in good year would have some left over for merchants. Simon Hébert not only grew a large surplus, but as a miller he collected a proportion of the milled grain as payment (in Lower Canada, a miller customarily received one-twelfth of the grain). Local exchanges could have involved swapping grain for pelts, the current commodity currency. But no matter how significant the surpluses were for those who produced them, they were not large enough in absolute terms to generate a noticeable volume of trade. The inclination to produce in excess of need is also not surprising since both the Acadians and the French Canadians had been part of commercial economies before moving to the Saint John Valley. Louis Mercure had bought a mill site from Michel Martin and sold it to Pierre Duperré, who by 1806 had sold the lot and a double mill to Fraser and Robinson. Hébert was no oddity. Fraser and Robinson's willingness to pay lots of money for the Duperré mill also suggests they expected the area to soon develop into a significant wheat growing region, and it did.

There are neither tithing records or census-type sources for the period between 1807 and the Maclauchlan survey in 1833, but a glimpse of farming activities between 1818 and 1831 can be had from the grain bonus schedule.[10] Those documents provide a picture of a region engaged in intense clearing activities, and growing large quantities of wheat. Table 9 summarizes the information available from the grain bonus schedule. Two items here are striking. First, the majority of farmers who collected the bonuses were producing above subsistence level, if the 34 bushels per household yardstick is used and even if those farmers grew no other grain. Not only was this proportion high, but it kept increasing, as did the number of farmers collecting the bonuses. The proportion of farmers who reported more than 100 bushels on new land doubled between 1821 and 1822 and tripled by 1824. By 1826 almost half the bonus farmers were in this situation, although the proportion subsequently declined. The highest amount of bonus grain reported was also fast increasing: 350 bushels in 1825 and a staggering 559 bushels in 1830.[11] The peak year in terms of individual production was 1826; nine bonus farmers out of ten reported crops of at least 34 bushels. The peak year in terms of aggregate production was 1827; that year the provincial government paid bonuses on a total of 9,888 bushels of grain, mostly wheat. The increase in the amount of eligible grain and consequently the increase in acreage cleared, closely followed the immigration peak of the mid-1820s. The quantities of grain eligible for the bonus later diminished, although a record number of farmers collected in 1831.

Being the recipients of large bonuses contributed to some farmers' economic success. Fourteen men reported harvests in excess of 200 bushels of grain grown on new land between 1824 and 1831. Two cannot be identified: their names appear in no other records.[12] The careers of the others reveal a great variety of experience. Three collected the bonus once, three collected it twice, and one, three times. Two brothers, Hilarion and Dominique Daigle (sons of the younger Joseph) collected it seven and eight times respectively. Together, they received slightly over £100 ($400) from the government. The Daigle brothers were living in the western part of the valley, where most of the lumbering activities were taking place; for them, land improvement and grain growing were probably linked with timber making. The Daigle brothers became substantial landowners. In 1831 Hilarion claimed three farm lots, two of which he had acquired in 1826 and 1827. David Cyr, who happened to be Simon Hébert's adopted son, collected the bonus four times for a total of £32 4s. 11d ($129), the last time for 559 bushels in 1831. He was an innkeeper who claimed three lots in 1831 and had a large stable of draught animals that would have been useful in the woods. Michel Martin received the bonus only twice, reporting 443 bushels of grain in 1827 for which he received a total of £28 3s. 10d. ($112) from the government. In 1831 he claimed four lots and had cleared 176 acres. In 1833 Martin, with the Hébert brothers, was one of the three largest stock owners in the settlement. Not all beneficiaries of government subsidies did this well; some individuals who collected substantial sums from the government were listed as requiring assistance in 1833. Wealth could evaporate quickly and prosperity was obviously not a linear or irreversible process. Although fragmentary, the evidence from those two sources unmistakably point towards one conclusion: a significant proportion of Madawaska farmers were market oriented, and the settlement was able to export agricultural commodities very early.

From Wheat to Fodder

Agriculture in the Heyday of Wheat Production

The impression of a thriving pioneer community busy clearing land while growing large quantities of wheat is confirmed by the sources available for the early 1830s. According to the Deane and Kavanagh and the Maclauchlan records, only a minority of households owned an operational farm in the early 1830s, that is, a farm with crops in the ground. These farms were nonetheless capable of feeding the entire resident population, and still were left with a surplus that could be sold to lumber camps or more likely outside the valley

Table 10 shows the size of the farm surpluses by commodity, based on the people and animal population reported in the survey. Peas, potatoes, beef, and mutton were all produced at commercial levels (more than 250 per cent of needs). Beef and mutton production was extremely high, boasting a surplus of 80 per cent. The regional surplus was also impressive. Bread grain came close to commercial level: the surplus was worth 57 per cent of production. The average farmer could boast a 68-bushel bread-grain surplus, almost all of it wheat. Farmers grew small quantities of rye and barley and no corn nor buckwheat. The size of the surplus was such that the leftovers could not have been incidental. They had to have been planned, as it required five to six acres of land at 10 to 12 bushels an acre to grow 68 bushels of wheat. In addition, the average farmer also planted more than twice as much potato and pea crop as his family needed.

The quantities of bread grain reported by Maclauchlan are corroborated by the Deane and Kavanagh report. According to Deane and Kavanagh, the valley tithed on average 500 bushels of wheat, and as much as 900 bushels in some years. This amount corresponds to a production of 13,000 to 23,000 bushels. Conversely, other commodities may have been under-tithed. Deane and Kavanagh reported tithes of 100 bushels of peas, 150 bushels of oats, 700 bushels of potatoes, and small quantities of barley, corresponding to productions of 2,600 bushels of peas, 3,400 bushels of oats, and 18,000 bushels of potatoes. It is possible that farmers substituted other forms of payments for field produce; Father Dionne may also not have been grateful to receive 1,500 bushels of potatoes.[13]

The farmers' surplus calculated from the Maclauchlan survey was more than enough to cover the food needs of the entire population and leave some substantial surpluses for sales outside the valley (see table 11). Baker and Bacon claimed the valley exported 4,000 to 5,000 bushels of grain to Canada. It was certainly capable of doing so. The surplus that can be calculated from the Maclauchlan report amounts to 6,000 bushels, enough to produce about 1,000 barrels of flour if it was milled locally. By 1830 the valley was one of the provincial bread baskets.

Farmers did not make it a practise to grow surplus feed. The animals reported in the 1833 survey would have required 2,632 tons of hay and 20,550 bushels of oats to be fed according to mid-century Lower Canadian practices, and much more according to contemporary agronomists' standards.[14] The valley grew 3,559 tons of hay in 1833 (there is no hay figure for previous years), leaving a surplus of 927 tons. By comparison, only 11,404 bushels of oats were produced in the early 1830s. Oats were not the only available feed: potatoes were used as fodder and the potato surplus, combined with the bran left from milling wheat into flour for the settlers, could have bridged the gap.[15] If the loggers were using local animals instead of bringing teams in, there would be no need to increase production beyond the requirements of the local stock. Madawaska farmers' routine of improvising their animals' feed was typical. North American farmers as a rule adopted a casual approach to stock feeding. McInnis, MacNeil, and Bitterman found that feeding practices in Nova Scotia and Ontario fell short of the standards recommended by the literature of the time.[16] And the literature on early New England farming consistently refers to the underfeeding of animals during the winter.[17]

Farmers could have adjusted the quantity of livestock to available oat supplies, but the majority seems to have done just the opposite, maintaining rather large numbers of draught animals. Operating farms reported a considerable number of horses and oxen: 56 per cent of the farms had at least three horses or oxen and 9 per cent had at least six draught animals. Horses, like sons, were a source of wealth. They were needed to clear the land on which bounty-earning grain could be grown. Land clearing was also a profitable operation in and of itself, as the trees could be sent downriver to be sold. Lumbering, especially deep in the woods, required animals. Judging by the number of draught animals in the valley, it seems that anyone who could was busy harvesting trees, and the activity was not yet proving detrimental to farming. Those who did not log themselves could rent their animals to logging parties for the winter.

The average total farm surplus would have been about $320 (see table 12; for prices see appendix 2). This amount was considerably larger than the profits that the Albert brothers made from their lumbering season. The surplus was also ample in the context of local land prices and wage levels. Between 1830 and 1834 a 200-acre farm on granted land sold for an average of £138 ($552). Ungranted land fetched about half that price (about £70 or $280).[18] In 1843 the priest was renting out a well-located farm belonging to the church for $60 a year.[19] In other words, a farmer renting a holding and producing average surpluses could have saved enough to buy an established farm within five years, which made farming more profitable than wage work. In the 1840s male labourers earned about 2 shillings a day (40 cents) or 25 shillings a month ($5, including with room and board) when hired by the month. Men who were hired for the entire year earned about £15 or $60.[20] Farmers' potential earnings were not insignificant when compared to the earning power of labourers or to the price of land. And farmers who collected grain bonuses or sold timber did even better.

Market availability, good commodity prices, government subsidies, and a fairly high immigration level had a predictable impact on land prices. The few deeds entered in the York and Carleton county registries that indicate both price and acreage suggest that the land market was sensitive to economic conditions. Prices were high in good economic times and not so good at other times. The post-1814 wheat trade pushed prices upwards, but this was nothing compared with the impact of the opening of lumber camps. If indeed lumberers brought money into the valley, they may have triggered inflation: land prices went through the roof (see figure 5). The crisis of 1833–4 had a detrimental impact on prices, but did not lead to a collapse and the price increase resumed soon afterwards. Land was clearly a commodity, and may have been a commodity as far back as the War of 1812.

The Fodder Years

Calculations similar to those done for the early 1830s reveal a steady decline in the size of farm surpluses after 1850, with few exceptions: oats increased steadily, although less in New Brunswick than on the U.S. side of the river. The decline is partly a source artefact and partly evidence of growing difficulties that had little to do with farming techniques, climate, or markets, and a lot to do with trying to farm land unsuitable for the purpose. (See tables 10 and 12) Table 10 measures farm production in terms of its ability to cover the needs of the farm population and its animals, broken down by type of commodity. Table 12 shows the average value of net farm production, the average surplus value, and their ratio. The numbers behave as predicted. As explained in appendix I, farm surpluses should have declined, as the

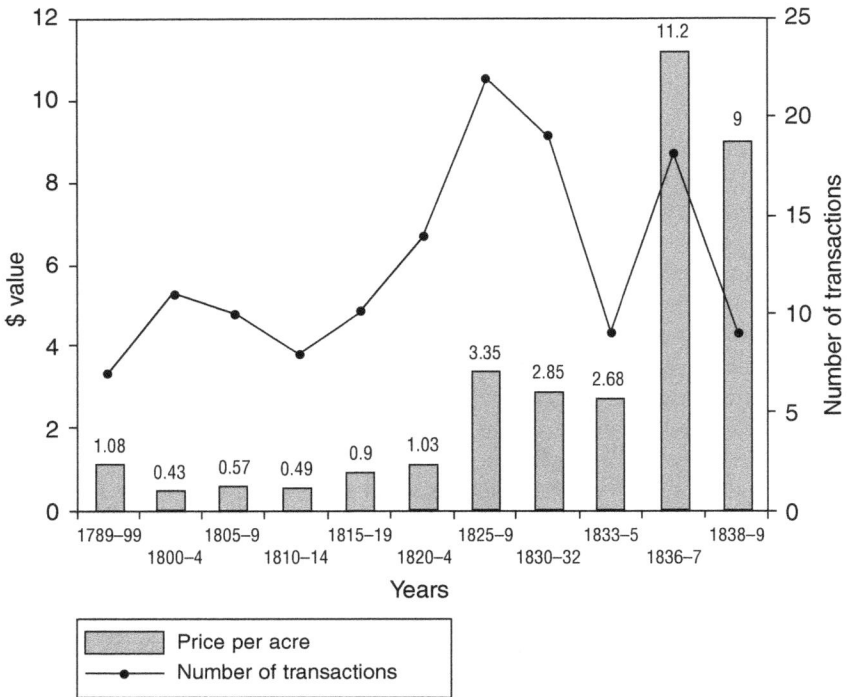

Figure 5. Price of Land, 1789–1839 ($ per acre)
Sources: PANB, York country registry office, 1785–1833; Carleton county
registry office 1833–40.

data includes an increasing proportion of low-production farms. Although by 1860 Madawaska farmers seem to have slipped below commercial production levels, they were not reduced to true subsistence-level production. Even New Brunswick in 1871 could still sell one-quarter of its production, and a 27 per cent surplus hardly seems to fit the description of an incidental leftover.

How much of this decline is due to the nature of the sources? One way to disaggregate distortions caused by the sources from real trends is to look at what is comparable: farms valued at $500 or more.[21] These numbers unfortunately exclude the 1871 data, as this census does not list farm values (see tables 13 and 14). Collectively, farms worth at least $500 were classified as commercial farms and remained so over the twenty-year period, although their ability to generate surpluses decreased slightly over time.

Foodstuff production was decreasing, with the exception of bread grains, which stabilized. Pork production dropped. Potato production increased noticeably in New Brunswick in 1871, but this may simply have reflected a bumper crop that year. Fodder production increased, especially on the U.S. side. It seems that the better-off farmers were slowly shifting their efforts from food production for the local market, but also for themselves, to commodities destined for outside markets. However, the shanty market was also shrinking because of the decline in the lumber industry. Increased fodder production could not compensate for decreased foodstuff production; the strategy ultimately did not work very well. The value of farm production declined, but even when it was stable, as between 1860 and 1870, the value of the surpluses continued to go down.

The poor performance of New Brunswick farms in 1861 could be attributed, at least in part, to bad weather and pests. The census marshal for the eastern part of the settlement reported wormy wheat, frozen barley, and rusted potatoes. If the barley froze on the stalks, the entire valley had to be affected by the cold snap and other crops had to have suffered as well. This could explain the poor hay crop and the potatoes, normally picked in early October, could have been harvested in the snow, reducing the size of the harvest and its ability to keep. The spread of agriculture on marginal land can also explain why the farm population as a whole generated smaller surpluses in the 1870s than at mid-century. The decline was more pronounced in New Brunswick, where the number of farms went from 435 to 871 between 1861 and 1871; on the U.S. side the number of farms increased from 667 to 775 and farm surpluses shrank less. This fact does not account for the decline among higher valued farms. Soil exhaustion due to continuous cropping could be the underlying reason, except that the riparian farms, which were the first to be settled, were the least likely to show a decline.

The size of the regional surpluses should have increased between 1850 and 1870, given the greater proportion of farms included in the later censuses. In fact, this only happened between 1850 and 1860 (see table 14). The smaller regional surpluses in 1861 could be blamed on the weather. The explanation does not hold for the 1870s. The increase in the proportion of non-farm households could be a factor in the decline of regional surpluses: the local market was growing. However, the surplus decline cannot be explained by population growth alone. Aggregate farm surpluses were apparently diminishing – the farmers had less to sell and more local people to sell to, which reduced the quantities available for external markets. It is possible that the quantities of farm commodities that farmers were able to put on the market had not really diminished because they were buying food to feed themselves, as was the non-farm population. Surpluses would then only seem to have diminished because the calculations assume that farm households fed themselves and overestimate on-site consumption. Whatever the explanation, the net result was the same in terms of income. The value of the difference between farm output and food and feed need had diminished. Collectively, farmers were worse off in 1870 than they had been in 1850. It seems that by 1870 the type of mixed agriculture practised in Madawaska had reached its limit. The land available for the expansion of the cultivated area was becoming poorer and poorer and the shanty market was faltering and would collapse soon. The opportunities to market various commodities outside the region being made possible by the railway working its way upriver, did not come a moment too soon.[22]

The Saint John Valley: A Comparative Perspective

How well did Madawaska farmers fare compared to their contemporaries? Marvin McInnis has estimated the surpluses on Ontario farms for 1861. His findings are summarized in table 15 and paralleled with comparable data for Madawaska in 1860 and 1861, as well as for the northeastern United States in 1860. The Madawaska average farm surplus was lower than the Ontario one; however, the distribution of farms was different. There was a greater proportion of deficit farms at Madawaska, which depressed the average. The Madawaska region had a large number of deficit farms because it was still a pioneering region. When the deficit farms are excluded from both regions, the gap is narrowed considerably. Madawaska's top farms especially on the U.S. side were producing surpluses above Ontario levels. Comparing one region to an entire province is a tad artificial, but the data shows that Madawaska farmers were not underperforming Ontario ones.[23]

Madawaska does not come out as well when compared with the United States. Atack and Bateman have estimated the marketable surpluses on farms in 102 townships in the American northeast in 1860. Surpluses were negative in 19 per cent of the townships and in another

19 per cent they ranged between 0 and 150 bushels or corn equivalent (Atack and Bateman converted the entire farm production into corn equivalent). In 62 per cent of the townships there was a surplus exceeding 150 bushels of corn equivalent. Madawaska farm surplus (not regional surplus) would have fit into the 0 to 150 bushel range. The average value of the surpluses on northern farms was $360 in 1860, as opposed to $172 at Madawaska. Madawaska looks a little less dismal when compared with New England. The average New England surplus was $370. One of the six townships in the Atack and Bateman sample had a surplus in the $150–299 category; four were in the $300–449 category; and one in the $450–599 category. In addition, there were even fewer deficit farms in New England than in Ontario, reflecting the age of the settlement. Once deficit farms are excluded from calculations, Madawaska agriculture becomes typical of the region. The productive capacity of the Madawaska established farms and their earning capabilities were well within northeastern U.S. norms. What differed was the fact that Madawaska was still a frontier zone in 1860, whereas the New England townships were not.

The evolution of Saint John Valley agriculture between 1830 and 1850 paralleled the evolution of agriculture in New England and Lower Canada in other ways. Crop failures and the unreliability of distant markets prompted farmers to give up wheat growing as a commercial venture, seek markets closer to home, and adjust production accordingly. The shift from wheat as a dominant commodity to more diversified field crops was also not unique: a similar pattern characterized the Midwest in the 1860s and 1870s. New farmers grew large quantities of wheat because they badly needed cash to stock and equip their farms, and switched to a safer mix as soon as they were established.[24] Marketable crops were grown in addition to those the household could consume, not instead of them, with a few exceptions.

Hierarchies of Farmers

McInnis also noted that the size of the marketable surpluses varied among farmers: 16 per cent were deficit farmers and 16 per cent could feed an additional three families. Most clustered in the middle of the range.[25] The distribution at Madawaska was similar throughout the century. The expansion of wheat production and the later crop shift did not change this situation.

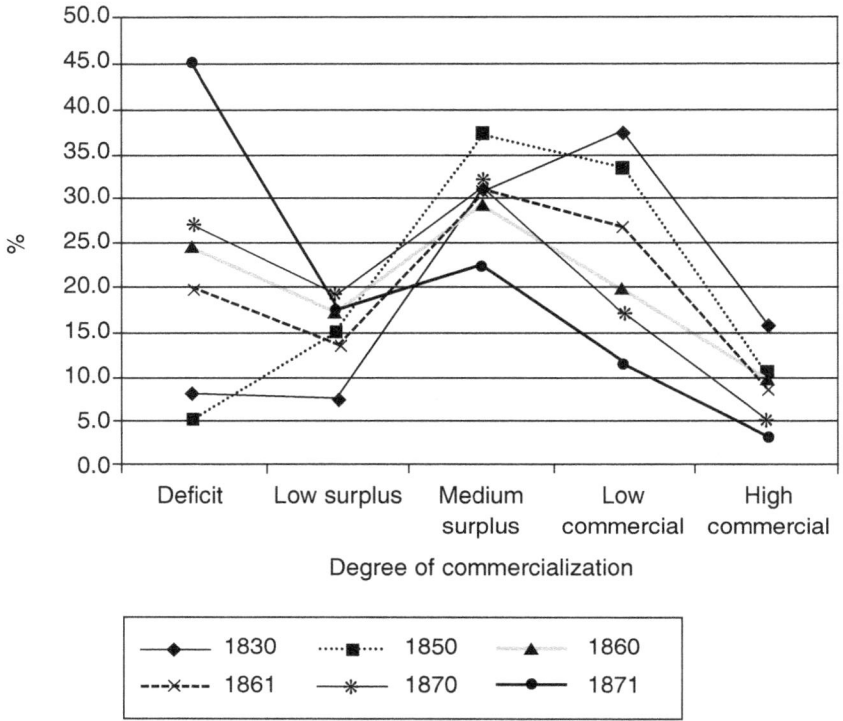

Figure 6. Distribution of farms, by degree of commercialization all farms, 1830–71

In the 1830s almost 3 out of 4 productive farms belonged to either the medium surplus or the low commercial categories. A not negligible 16 per cent was high commercial (see figure 6). Commercialization led to a clearly stratified community, but not to the division of the settlement between subsistence and commercial farms; the farms without crops were likely to come on stream within ten years, replaced by another group of start-ups. Some individuals started out farming with certain advantages. An individual was more likely to be a commercial farmer if he belonged to a charter family, owned granted land, or if his household included more than one adult male. What mattered most was belonging to a family that had resided at Madawaska for a long period of time and had secured one of the coveted granted lots. The crisis of the mid-1830s did not have a levelling impact, nor did it exacerbate existing inequalities. The tithing record for 1835, like its predecessors, reveals an uneven distribution of households, with most clustered in the middle of the curve.[26] Because it is not possible to determine the size or composition of the households enumerated in these records and no data exists on their stock numbers, their surpluses cannot be calculated. I reverted to Hobbs-Pruitt's benchmarks for this reason. However, more than a quarter of the parishioners were not liable for the tithe on grain, and a comparable proportion tithed on 100 bushels or more (see table 16). Well-to-do farmers maintained their relative position through the crisis.

Wheat production had generated a stratified farming community characterized by a large midde group of farmers. The distribution of farms appeared different in the second half of the century. At first glance, the shift to fodder and foodstuff production seems to have split Madawaska farmers into two distinct groups. A closer look at the data does not support this hypothesis. From 1860 onwards the farm distribution is bimodal (two peaks), with the split more pronounced in the 1870s than previously. However, this distribution does not reflect an increasingly sharp division between low and medium surplus and commercial farms. The first cluster is made up of farms below subsistence level, and the second of mostly medium surplus farms. The proportion of farms in the first cluster increases significantly over the years. So does the proportion of low valued farms in the population under observation. One phenomenon can be the result of the other. An examination of the distribution of farms valued at $500 or more suggests that the difference in the composition of the various farm categories is in part responsible for the apparent growth in the proportion of deficit farms (see figure 7).

The distribution of farms worth $500 or more varied little between 1850, 1860–1, and 1870 and is similar to the distribution of 1830 operational farms. It assumes the shape of a slightly distorted bell curve. Most non-deficit farms (71 to 75 per cent depending on the years) were either medium surplus or low commercial ones. The farms worth at least $500 were not sharply differentiated, but neither were they a homogeneous group. They included a small proportion (10 per cent) of deficit farms and a slightly larger one (9 to 15 per cent, depending on the year) with surpluses in excess of 90 per cent of production.

The increased division of the farm population into two categories is partly a source artefact, resulting from the exclusion of non-productive farms from the 1830 and 1850 data. Farm communities always in-

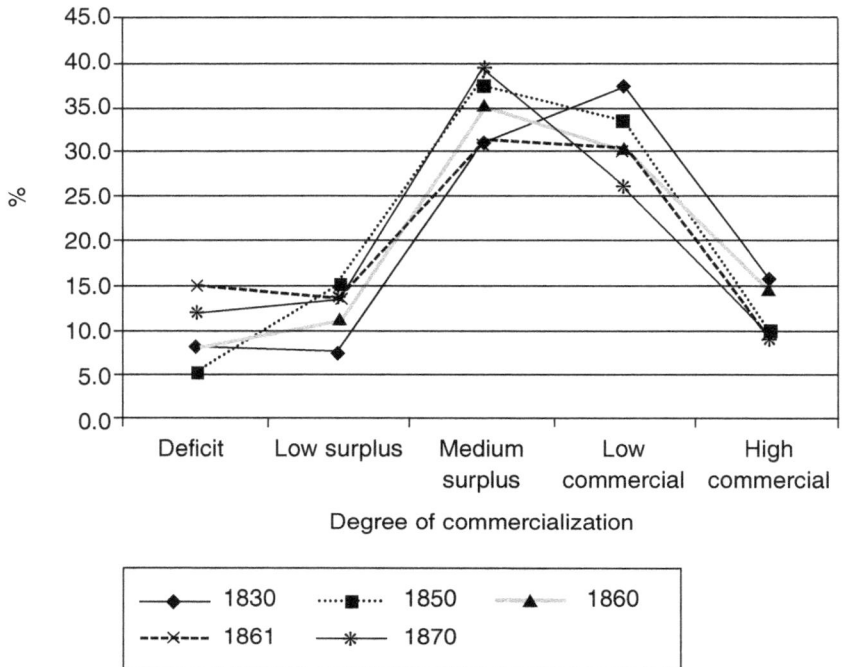

Figure 7. Distribution of farms worth at least $500, by degree of commercialization, 1830–70

Note: 1830 farms are the ones listed as having had crops in the years before in the Maclauchlan report; farms in all other years are listed as worth $500 or more in the census.

cluded a proportion of deficit farms: new farms at the clearing stage; farms established on marginal land; or farms too small to support a family but adequate as an income supplement for wage earners. However, the fact that almost one-half of the 1871 New Brunswick farms were at less than subsistence level also suggests that their growth reflected a new reality. New Brunswick Madawaska was growing more rapidly than its U.S. counterpart between 1860 and 1870. The population growth seems to have exaggerated a real phenomenon: by 1871 farm expansion could only occur on marginal land not really suitable for agriculture, at least for field crops. These farms could never fully support their owners. Madawaska arable agriculture had reached its ecological limit.

Madawaska farmers neither chose nor avoided commercial agriculture, leading to a community divided between market oriented and subsistence oriented farmers. Farmers all strove for a competency and most achieved it, with surpluses ranging between 30 and 50 per cent of production. A small group managed to go further, but this ideal was beyond the reach of a growing number of families who were carving out farms in back settlements. They may have found that mere subsistence was the most they could achieve.

Production Strategies

Some farms produced much more than others and more importantly, they were able to generate proportionally larger surpluses than others. How did they achieve these results? Conventional wisdom dictates that increased production and productivity must have resulted from improved technology, defined broadly to include not only machinery but also hybrid seeds and pedigree animals and the use of inorganic fertilizers and soil conditioners. Investing in improvements to increase productivity and profit was a capitalist strategy – using money to make money. Craig and Weiss, however, have challenged the role of mechanization in increased productivity. They argue instead that northeastern farms became more productive in the 1860s because women increased the amount of time they devoted to farm work by about 25 per cent, and boys and girls by 13 and 17 per cent. Men also worked harder: the time they devoted to farm work increased by 29 per cent. These changes were in large part due to increased demand for commodities traditionally produced by women and children: pork, dairy products, poultry, fruit, and vegetables.[27] Were Madawaska commercial farm owners pursuing capitalist strategies, did they work longer and harder, or did they simply put more people to work, especially more sons? In the last case, commercial farming would merely have been a phase in the life cycle of the household.

Land productivity was higher on commercial than on small and medium surplus farms; the ratio of farm net production value per improved acres increased with farm categories and holds true for all periods. However, higher yield may not have been the cause of increased production until after 1870. Yields can be calculated for a limited number of crops, and the results for 1861 are inconclusive. In

1871, on the other hand, potato and hay yields were higher on commercial farms. If the trend revealed by those crops is representative of the entire range of field crops, then commercial farming led to increased yields, not the other way around. Farmers were also slow to modify their techniques. Higher yields were not the result of the introduction of new plants in the rotation or the use of improved seeds. Less than 10 per cent of farmers reported production of turnips, mangel-wurzel, and grass seed, and their distribution does not show any significant patterns. Turnip or grass seed was as likely to be found on small and medium surplus farms as on commercial ones. Neither were higher yields the result of mechanization. Commercial farms had more equipment but it was not necessarily more elaborate or more varied than that of other farms. The 1871 census does not report the value of the equipment, but it does list the type of machinery or tools owned. The 875 farms owned 923 ploughs, 5 harvesters, 35 horse-drawn rakes, 19 threshing machines and 129 screens. Less than half of the deficit farms reported a plough and most the farms that reported more than 1 plough belonged to the commercial and medium surplus categories. But fully one-quarter of the commercial farms reported no plough at all. Of the 19 threshing machines 17 were owned by medium surplus or low commercial farms; so were 29 of the 35 horse-drawn rakes. None of the high commercial farms owned a harvester, and 1 of the 5 machines was owned by a deficit farmer, who may have made a living harvesting other people's fields for shares. The number of pieces of equipment apart from ploughs is so small that it cannot be considered a significant factor in increased productivity and commercialization; however, mid-range farms were the most likely to own the new equipment. Commercial farmers clearly used the same farm techniques and technology as their neighbours.

The existing data does not indicate that middle-aged farmers with adolescent or adult sons were in a better position to increase production and generate higher surpluses (see table 17). There is no correlation between the number of males 16 and above in residence and a farm's degree of commercialization. In fact, commercial farms seem to have suffered from a chronic shortage of labour.[28] It was the deficit farms who were the most likely to have idle hands. Men on commercial farms may have worked harder or longer hours, or even conscripted their womenfolk for some tasks usually considered men's work. The data on reported wages from the 1870 census suggests that commercial farmer alleviated on-site labour shortages by hiring workers, but not by hiring live-in hands (few wage payers had servants). The more commercial a farm, the more likely it was to have hired labour during the preceding year. High commercial farms also spent more on labour than others. The overall production of a farm was not determined by a family's capacity to work the land, but by its ability to hire additional workers.

Other changes signalled the emergence of a labour market. Storekeepers Emmerson, Dufour, and Connors paid for specialized work at a higher rate than for general labour. They also ceased to treat the day as the basic unit of labour; Robert Connors paid workers by the task – so many portaging trips, for instance. Employers gradually shifted from hiring daily men to buying a specific type of labour in specific amounts, which might explain why live-in servants were not very common. The hiring trend may only have affected certain type of work; the value of general labour remained impervious to changes and held at 50 cents a day through the period.[29]

Unfortunately, the sources are deficient on the operations of the labour market. The census data shows that live-in farm servants were adolescents and young adults below marriagable age, found in households short of young people in that age group. Some censuses also indicate whether a household had hired labour during the year, but do not detail when and for what purpose. One storekeeper kept track of the people he hired for a multiplicity of tasks; another did not unless they were taking fodder to the lumber camps for him. The account book of a mid-century carpenter records the money he advanced to his *engagés*, but not the total amount he paid them.[30] And that is it. Only limited conclusions can be drawn about labour from existing sources: families with no adolescents borrowed young people from the neighbours, but whose neighbours? It is almost impossible to identify the family of origin of the servants in the census or of half the workers in the account book. Even who the farmers' live-out help was is unknown. Were they people who had to sell their labour and were they exploited? Or were they adolescents from large households sent to work for the neighbours to get them out of the way? The carpenter's account book suggests that quite a few of these young men and women spent a fair amount of their earnings on themselves. Were the sons and daughters of well-to-do households hiring themselves out as wage-earners for a few weeks or months? In that case, did they belong to a different class than their fathers, who hired other families' adolescents? And what about the fathers themselves, who may have freighted for the merchants during the winter? In addition, some people had to work because their holding was not self-supporting, but how many of them were unable to secure a larger farm later in life, even through rental? The sources do not allow the distribution of households between a wage earning and an employing class, and the boundary between the two is by no means clear. The two groups seem to have overlapped and membership in one or the other depended on shifts in life cycle. Capital and labour, meaning employers and employees, morphed into one another within the economy of the household. The impossibility of identifying workers in terms of age, marital status, family of origin, or conditions of hiring makes it impossible to discuss the labour market.[31]

Commercial farmers seem to have responded to market incentives by increasing labour inputs – they hired more workers. Increased land productivity was achieved at the expense of labour productivity. Towards the end of the period, commercial farmers appear to have been able to raise yields as well. None of this made commercial farmers improving farmers by the standards of the time, as described by James Robb.[32] Madawaska farmers were not yet capitalist either. They did not invest in machinery, pedigree animals, and perhaps not even better land to achieve higher levels of production. Instead, they responded to markets by doing more of the same. They were closer in nature to the Civil War-era farm families than to the machine-hungry individuals common in an older literature.

There was another change afoot that census data cannot capture. Until the midcentury, commercial farmers were almost always members of a charter family or had married into one. This was no longer the case in 1870–1. By then, barely half of the commercial farms belonged to a charter family, even when traced through the female line. Charter families were still over-represented among commercial farmers, but they had lost their quasi-monopoly. Millers, for their part, were usually commercial farmers as well: Registe, Denis, and Benoni Theriault and Isaac Bijeau were low commercial farmers in 1861; Vital Thibodeau was a high commercial one; Jules Lévesque was in the medium surplus category; and Corriveau was a deficit farmer. Ten years later Bijeau had the highest net farm production value in the entire valley, Vital Thibodeau, Lévite Thériault, his cousin Denis, their milling neighbour Pierre Plourde, Jules Lévesque, and Michel Martin were all high commercial; and Benoni Violette was low commercial. Millers diversified their manufacturing activities, but not at the expense of farming.

Conclusion

In 1870, Madawaska farming was significantly different from what it had been a quarter of a century before: gone were the thick patches of wheat among the stumps that used to line the river. And gone too was the dense forest on the hills, which the early settlers would have used to supply themselves with wood or sugar. One of the most significant changes in the period was the shift from wheat to fodder production. This change was the consequence of a series of factors that were largely beyond human control: a shortening of the growing season at midcentury, the spread of plant pests and diseases that neither farmers nor experts knew how to fight; the arrival on the local market of western flour at competitive prices, and the expansion of an alternative market. The second significant change, the increased proportion of households that derived a precarious living from their hill farms or who owned no farm, was a consequence of population growth, and of the inability or unwillingness of the poorer people to move south to the New England mill towns, or to the western farming frontier. These farmers could barely escape subsistence levels of production, and pulled production averages down. But population growth and the aggregate decline in agricultural production left the better-off farm households unaffected. The performance of farms valued at $500 or more remained unchanged. Those were also the households likely to benefit from the slow impoverishment of new farmers, who provided their better-off neighbours with a source of labour and a market for their goods. Social stratification intensified: the poor were getting poorer, even if the rich were not getting significantly richer. There was nothing unusual in this development. Twenty years ago, synthesizing the recent and abundant literature on the 'little communities' of early America, Darett Rutman had suggested that they underwent the same type of changes: initially, the ratio between population and resources (usually land) was favourable. As population grew, the ratio reversed and the growing shortage of suitable land led to outmigration, unless the community could diversify its economic base and no longer rely entirely on agriculture. Growth and development also intensified social stratification. Madawaska followed this model.[33] But stratification no longer closely reflected the division of the population between charter families and more recent arrivals as it had up until midcentury. As immigration slowed down and the children of earlier immigrants reached adulthood, non charter members began to rise in the social hierarchy. At the same time as outsiders were buying mills and mill-sites from old residents, non-charter family farmers were elbowing their way into the ranks of commercial farmers.

In other respects, many similarities existed between the earlier and later periods. Madawaska settlers usually became self-sufficient as soon as their farm was established (which could take ten to fifteen years), but were seldom content with mere self-sufficiency. Most established farmers grew significantly more than they needed as early as the 1830s, and possibly earlier. They sold what they could and tried to cater to the market that offered the best prices and the greatest stability. Farmers preferred the provincial bread-grain trade to the shanty supplies market, and did not neglect the local market in foodstuff created by new farm households. Commercialization did not depend exclusively on access to distant, especially export markets. The bread-grain trade was provincial and did not rely, like the shanty trade in fodder, on an external demand for another commodity, in this case wood.

Commercial farming did not preclude farmers' participation in other activities. In the early 1830s Madawaska farmers took advantage of all available money-making opportunities and rode each as long as they could. In this respect, they resembled contemporary business-men: they too pursued discrete adventures. They grew large quantities of wheat, sold the surpluses, and collected provincial bounties for wheat grown on new land; they cleared land, sold the timber, and in the process increased the value of their holding. But they stretched themselves thin. Animals were fed whatever was handy and yields were low. North American husbandry was sloppy by European standards; Saint John Valley farming was no exception. Colonial New Englanders' and most frontier farmers' practices were the same. But primitive techniques and remoteness were not incompatible with large volume production and market involvement.

This casual approach to farming was a rational choice. Farmers spent more time clearing land than tending their fields because they could get a higher return for their labour that way. They also increased their capital: cleared, fenced, and stumped acreage was worth much more than unimproved land. Not everyone benefitted equally from commercialization. Some men were able to accumulate wealth, pass their social position on to their children, and even branch off into manufacturing. Others went nowhere despite the opportunities available to them. The inability of some farmers to take advantage of market opportunities did not result in a polarized society. Farms distributed along a bell curve, they did not split into two distinct groups. This distribution survived the midcentury crop shift. Through the period, most farms fell into the medium surplus or low commercial categories once they were past the first few years.

In the second half of the century, Madawaska could not boast the most productive agriculture in the northeast, but it was far from the worst and withstood the comparison with Upper Canada, which Canadian historians always use as the yardstick to measure the performance of other provinces before Confederation. Madawaska farmers were reasonably prosperous by North American standards because they managed to balance production for subsistence, production for a predictable and captive local market, and production for a more profitable but also more volatile market embedded in the Atlantic economy. Most commodities could either be sold or consumed on-site. Some commercial crops targeted the shanties, which were initially an outreach of the Atlantic mercantile economy, and gradually became part of the continental trade in sawn lumber and building materials. Foodstuffs and textiles were consumed on the premises, and sold on the local and even regional market. Farmers also relied increasingly on the continental market for flour, mess pork, and fish.

Commercial farming did not exclude self-sufficiency. Because agriculture remained unspecialized, households continued to cover their own food and feed needs if they were so inclined. However, they did not maximize self-sufficiency. Farm households were willing to turn to the market for necessities they could not produce, but also goods that had available substitutes (wheat flour), that enhanced the quality of their diet (fish), or that allowed them to minimize disagreeable chores (pork). Established farm households could revert to food self-sufficiency simply by adjusting their diet to their production. They used the market to buy food, but were not truly dependent on it.

Market production did not lead to narrow specialization in part because of this market for foodstuffs. Technological constraints also made it unwise to abandon diversified production. Animals were the main source of fertilizer, and had to be kept whether there was a market for their products or not. The short growing season left no time to plough the fallow: sheep, much less finicky eaters than cows, kept it clean and turned the weeds into manure. Pigs, malodorous and ornery but intelligent, were only good for meat. As soon as mess pork was available in the stores, farm households reduced the size of their pig stock. Households also had to stagger their harvests to adjust for the size of their labour force, and the short growing season meant planting crops with different harvest times. Consequently, with the exception of surplus size, little distinguished commercial farmers from others. The one difference was that as overall output increased, fodder production increased proportionally faster. Market crops were grown in addition to the others, not to replace production for subsistence. The 'subsistence/non-commercial' to 'commercial and specialized' shift did not occur here. Madawaska went from diversified and market-oriented to diversified in a different way as it became oriented towards other markets.

Neither did commercial farming lead to any form of modernization. Farmers successfully responded to ecological constraints and market opportunities, but they showed little willingness to change their farming techniques. The sources provide scant evidence of technological changes: almost no new crops, little machinery, and almost no use of purchased seeds and fertilizer. In 1870 there were few 'improving farmers' at Madawaska; they were still using techniques that would have been familiar to their grandfathers. Farmers responded to market opportunities by increasing labour input, even if this meant hiring extra hands.

Although Madawaska farmers were directly and indirectly dependent on the forest industry as an outlet for their production, they do not appear to have suffered from this precarious relationship for several reasons. First, unlike many Canadian farmers caught into the agro-forestry system, they were not farming marginal land before 1871. Second, they had a choice of market: if the shanties failed or did not offer fair prices, there was the local subsistence market, and if absolutely necessary, some goods could be shipped downriver. In 1848 at the peak of the forest industry crisis, the price of oats at Madawaska plummeted from 2s.6d. to 1s.8d., half its value two years earlier. But oats could still be sold; the price did not go from 2s.6d. to nothing, which would have been the case in the absence of a local market. Third, no lumberer had a monopoly on the regional forest industry, like the Prices in the Saguenay or the Hamiltons on the Lower Ottawa River. At Madawaska, lumberers were in competition with each other. The most powerful took advantage of their position, not to fleece the local population, but to sideline their rivals. 'Big John' Glazier was known for paying in gold, most likely in order to skim the market of the best supplies and workers. Farmers must have learned very quickly how to play one operator against another.

The lumber camps and the market for foodstuff also remained distinct from each other. The shanties obviously determined the local price for fodder so when demand was high, start-up farmers ended up paying more for oats for their horse. The camps probably had less impact on foodstuff prices, because lumberers were fed a diet significantly different from the one of the local farmers. Glazier ordered white flour, oatmeal, cornmeal, molasses, beans, herring, cod, tea, and mess pork for his men through Emmerson. Madawaska people neither grew nor purchased beans, preferring pea soup. They ate mixed-grain or white bread and buckwheat pancakes, but never bought cornmeal (corn did not grow this far north). They purchased very little molasses, clearly preferring maple sugar and West Indian sugar, and they ate beef, veal, and mutton, none of which graced the tables of the lumberers. The only food common to both groups was fish, rice, mess pork, and white flour, all brought from outside the region, and their prices reflected not local demand but conditions in the Canadas. The shanties did not buy local food except possibly potatoes, and thus could not drive prices up. A downturn in the forest industry could depress local food prices by restricting the amount of money buyers had to spend. The available price data is too scattered to draw a definitive conclusion: fodder prices did fluctuate with the condition of the forest industry; flour prices and prices for other bread grains and bread-grain products fluctuated too, in response to prices in the outside markets. The prices for the food consumed locally (fresh meat, eggs, and butter) appear to have been more stable, but they were slightly lower in 1863, a bad year in the forest industry, than in 1853, which was a good one. The three categories of commodities, shanty supplies, staple foods, and perishable commodities responded to the conditions in their respective markets. Local exchanges were also well on their way to constituting a market; not only did prices fluctuate, but wages were beginning to reflect skills and productivity as well as time at work. The absence of farm account books unfortunately prevents assessing the extent of this transformation.

A farm was also two economies in one: his and hers. He was responsible for field crops and cattle, for clearing land, digging ditches, building fences, and erecting buildings, alone or with the help of neighbours. She was in charge of the garden, barnyard, fowls, dairying, and textile making, also alone or in cooperation with neighbouring women. Historians do not agree on the impact of farm commercialization on women. They do agree that in arable and cattle-raising regions, women's role diminished and became marginal: women remained wedded to subsistence production and informal, non-commercial exchanges. In dairy regions, on the other hand, women abandoned some farm subsistence production and household textile manufacturing for commercial production of butter and cheese. Historians disagree on what happened next. Did men elbow women out of the way because market activities were a male prerogative?[34] Did women walk out of the dairy because the work was too hard and they had alternatives?[35] Or were Craig and Weiss right to suggest that 'women and children shifted their time from unmeasured household tasks to market activities or reallocated their efforts among farm and non farm market work,' a contention supported by other historians.[36] Madawaska was an arable region yet commercialization did not sideline women. Moreover, Madawaska demonstrates that the development of dairy or poultry production was not a prerequisite for farm women to produce for markets. Markets could exist for other female-produced commodities. The next chapter will shed some light on the distaff side of the economy.

8 The Homespun Paradox:
Domestic Cloth Production and
the Farm Economy

Presently the door was opened by an impassive little Frenchman with a melan-
choly face and dark blue homespun trousers, who ... ushered them into the pres-
ence of a pensive-looking Madame in plaited hair and blue woolen petticoat, and
a group of reserved and thoughtful children in blue ... from the wooden bottomed
seat, then, Penman thoughtfully contemplated the huge Canadian stove, six feet
high, that stood in the partition wall, so as to warm both rooms alike ... then
he looked at the loom and the spinning wheel, and thought of Longfellow's
Evangeline.

Charles Hallock, 1866[1]

In 1866 Charles Hallock took the readers of *Harper's New Monthly*
Magazine on an excursion to the 'primeval forests' of the Aroostook
and Madawaska and a visit to the prelapsarian Acadians who inhabited the region. The entire article was written to evoke Longfellow's
Evangeline. The loom, the spinning wheel, and the clothing of blue
homespun evoked the image of a people frozen in time. The article's
antimodern motives would soon be commonplace in tourism promo-
tional literature, especially that inviting English-speaking people to
visit French-speaking areas.[2] The perpetuation of domestic textile
production loomed large in this type of literature. Even texts that
intended to convey the image of a modern, enterprising people who
happened to be blessed with the privilege of living in a scenic,
unspoiled environment could not resist milking the image, or the
Evangeline connection, when the opportunity arose. Clarence
Pullen's *In Fair Aroostook*, published in 1902 by the Bangor and Aroostook Railway, opened the chapter on 'Maine Acadia' with a quote

from *Evangeline*: 'The wheel and the loom still are busy / Maidens still wear their Norman caps and their kirtles of homespun.' The chapter is illustrated by a photograph of an adolescent girl at the loom. She wears no Norman cap or kirtle of homespun, though, but a white shirtwaist, a pleated plaid skirt, and a frilled, paisley-print apron. And she is not weaving homespun but a bed rug (*catalogne*). Poor Mr. Pullen could never quite decide whether his Acadians were quaint relics of bygone days or enterprising Americans.[3]

Tourism promoters saw the continuation of domestic textile production as a positive good. In parts of rural Quebec, women sold tourists the goods they allegedly produced as part of their 'self-sufficient' economy, untainted by the stains of trade and consumerism.[4] Present-day historians, facing evidence of late farm-based manufacturing, are much less impressed. In the course of the nineteenth century, agriculture commercialization was supposed to have displaced household manufacturing. Atack and Bateman for instance claim that 'The relatively rapid demise of home produced clothing, furniture and similar items in farm and other rural households indicates that a developing industrial-agricultural economy was emerging in the northern border states.'[5]

After 1870 home manufacturing represented a negligible proportion of farm income. Textiles declined first. By the 1830s the production of hand-made cloth was dead or moribund in the United States. In British North America the situation was different. Domestic cloth production declined in Upper Canada only after midcentury and increased in Lower Canada and the Maritimes between 1850 and 1870. Madawaska was one of the regions where domestic cloth production was important in the second half of the nineteenth century.[6] Historians first attributed late farm-cloth production to a stagnant agriculture. Households made their own cloth because they could not afford factory-made material.[7] The fact that cloth production persisted in the Maritime provinces, a region not reputed for its thriving agriculture, had seemed to corroborate the hypothesis.

This explanation fitted the transition to capitalism paradigm but it became problematic when Canadian cloth production was placed in the North American context. If Ontario agriculture outperformed that of New England why did Ontario farms continue weaving long after New Englanders had given it up?[8] Madawaska agriculture was no worse than Ontario's yet Madawaska was a high producer of domestic cloth until very late in the century. The growth of cloth production at Madawaska parallels an increase in the proportion of poor farms, but was there is a link between the two phenomena? Correlation is not necessarily sign of causality, and poverty can be dismissed right away as a possible cause. In 1871 there was no negative correlation between the value of net farm production and cloth production at farm level. The higher the value of net farm production, the higher the production of cloth, and the more likely a household was to report cloth to the census taker. The proportion of farms that reported cloth production increased with the degree of commercialization and then declined. It peaked among medium surplus farms with 88 per cent reporting textile production (see table 18). Beyond a certain production level, women had to choose between weaving and helping the men. Among households that produced cloth, quantities increased with degrees of commercialization: high commercial farms produced twice the average amount. If self-sufficiency was the goal of textile production, only the well-to-do could achieve it. Madawaska does not appear to have been an anomaly. The same phenomenon occurred in other eastern Canadian regions in 1871.[9]

Canadian historians have recently proposed alternative explanations to late farm cloth production: women wove because it was worth their while. Carding mills and factory-made warp speeded the process of textile production, and there was a market for the finished product.[10] Kris Inwood in particular has noted that homespun was a niche product, and that a long-distance trade existed in this commodity.[11] Adrienne Hood found a similar situation in Pennsylvania at the beginning of the nineteenth century, suggesting that is was not a typically Canadian phenomenon.[12] Madawaska fits into this revised view of homespun production.

In Madawaska domestic cloth production was neither a practice born of poverty, nor a folk activity perpetuated by a people untouched by modernity. Instead, it was evidence of women's responsiveness to the opportunities offered them by available markets, and as Inwood has suggested, it was facilitated by industrial developments.

Market-dependent Production

Madawaska domestic textile production was not market independent. Local exchanges provided weavers with some of their raw material (wool and flax), and outside markets provided them with the other (cotton warp).

The 1871 census reported the number of sheep owned and the amount of wool, flax, cloth, and linen produced by each farm household. The same information exists at parish level only for 1851.[13] Madawaska had enough sheep to produce the woollen yarn required for its fabric output in 1851 and 1871; however, individual weavers were not necessarily self-sufficient in wool. In 1871 there was a close relationship between the number of sheep and the amount of reported wool, but no relationship between cloth or flannel production and the number of sheep or amount of wool reported in the census. A significant proportion of sheep owners never reported any cloth and 3 per cent of the households reporting cloth had no sheep, although one reported 150 yards of flannel. The ratio of wool to cloth varied widely from household to household. There was no more relationship between flax and linen production than between wool and cloth production. Domestic cloth production obviously relied at least in part on local exchanges of wool and flax.

The weavers' work was facilitated by access to carding mills, despite the fact Madawaska carding mills did not officially process enough wool to satisfy the needs of the local weavers. According to the various censuses, there were four such mills at Madawaska in 1871, three on the Canadian side of the river, and one on the American side; three of them had processed a total of 5,500 pounds of wool; the production of the fourth was not reported.[14] According to the aggregate tables, there was another carding mill at Saint Leonard, but it is not listed in the manufacturing schedule. No fulling mill was reported in the valley; nonetheless, in 1866 John Emmerson paid Joseph Corriveau, the owner of the American carding mill, for fulling cloth.[15] The U.S. census does not report Corriveau as owning a fulling mill. Levite Theriault inherited a fulling mill from his father in 1868, but he is listed merely as gristmill and sawmill owner in the census.[16] Census takers, for some reason, overlooked fulling mills.

Madawaska weavers probably acquired wool from neighbours who did not weave themselves; they also used factory-made cotton warp. Cynthia Wallace-Casey mentions that advertisements for cotton warp and offers to buy homespun appeared in the Saint John newspapers as early as the 1840s.[17] J.J. Hegan, Emmerson's suppliers, who advertised their wide range of British imports in the Saint John city directory in 1863, also drew attention to the fact they sold warp

Particular attention is directed to our stock of domestic made warp
In white, blue and fancy colours, grey cotton etc...
Wholesale and retail[18]

Both the Dufours and Emmerson sold cotton warp. In 1846 the
Dufour brothers sold 189 pounds to 47 customers (21 per cent of their
clientele). This quantity was enough to make between 1,140 and 2,000
yards of cotton warp/wool weft cloth, or an average of 27 yards per
purchasing household.[19] In 1853 Emmerson sold warp to 38 account
holders (19 per cent of all clientele). Regular warp was worth between
5s.3d. and 6s.3d. for a 5-pound bundle. Blue warp at 10s. a bundle and
red warp at 2s.6d. for half a pound were purchased by 11 and 1 customers respectively. Emerson's 38 account holders purchased a total of
270 pounds, or 4.75 pounds each, slightly less than the Dufours' customers. Besides warp, store customers were also purchasing ingredients for fabric dye: mordants, such as saleratus and alum, and pig-
ments such as indigo and copperas. Households that purchased warp
also bought factory-made cloth, mostly cotton, a bit of silk, and small
amounts of woollen material. Purchases of cotton warp are additional
evidence that store-bought fabric did not displace home-made material. Increased consumption of store-bought fabric did not necessarily
mean decreased consumption of home-made material, or vice versa. In
fact, at the Dufours', purchases of fabric tended to increase with purchases of cotton warp. There is no clear relationship between the two
at Emmerson's. The data, however, does not lend itself to firm conclusions. The purchases reported in the store books did not necessarily
represent all household purchases; customers could patronize other
stores, and an unknown proportion of purchases was paid in cash on
the spot. Nevertheless, the data does not support the contention that
domestic weaving was a cost avoidance strategy.

The Civil War had an adverse effect on the supply of cotton warp,
and consequently on prices. At Emmerson's, prices soared from an
average of 5s.6d. ($1.50) a bundle in the 1850s to 20s. ($4.00) in 1863–6.
The price gradually decreased, but as late as 1872 a bundle still retailed
for 10s. Between July 1871 and July 1872, Emmerson's sons sold 161
pounds of cotton warp (89.5 of white, 29 of blue, and 5 of red, and the
rest unspecified) to 33 account holders, an average of 4.87 pounds per
account holder. Customers were buying more cotton than before the
war, despite the sharp price increase, which suggests that cotton warp

was a necessity, not a luxury. At the Connors store across the river from Fort Kent, cotton warp sold for between $2.25 and 3.00 in 1875–6. By that time, colour does not seem to have made a difference in price. The 44 Connors customers purchased an average of 5.79 pounds of cotton.[20]

Much more interesting is Emmerson's receiving book for 1849–58, because it itemizes the warp and fabric he was receiving from Hegan. The quantities were not negligible, averaging a little over 1,000 pounds a year, with a peak of almost 3,000 pounds in 1856. That 1000 pounds of cotton would have been enough to make 6,250 yards of mixed fabric of the type commonly produced in New Brunswick.[21] Including the American side of the river there were about twenty stores in the area in 1870–1;[22] Emmerson's imports were probably not the only cotton warp available in the valley. Merchants like Emmerson or the Dufours attest to the existence of well-established distribution networks for factory-made textile products reaching far into the countryside. The large quantities of warp sold at Madawaska are evidence that cloth production was not independent of the market economy. The use of factory-made warp could also explain why homespun production increased after 1850. If more warp was becoming available locally, more fabric could be made.

The Uses of Domestic Cloth and Factory-made Material

Fabric was mostly used for clothing and household linen and also served for horse blankets, sacking, and bolting cloth. A reasonably precise picture of the composition of Madawaska wardrobes can be gathered from local deeds of maintenance. These agreements were signed when an elderly couple turned over its farm to a younger one in exchange for support. The nature of the support was spelled out and until the 1860s was in-kind.[23] Support included clothing allowances for the elder husband and wife.[24]

In the first quarter of the century, women routinely received a suit of homespun, an under-petticoat, a suit of calico or the equivalent amount of fabric, a calico *mantelet* (a sort of loose blouse) or the equivalent in fabric, a yard of muslin or a muslin cap, one or two yards of cotton or one or two aprons, two to three linen and flannel shirts, stockings, mittens, footwear, and cotton handkerchiefs.[25] Other items could include silk handkerchiefs, silk bonnets or material to make them, cotton stockings, umbrellas, shawls, and petticoats (a petticoat was a skirt; an under-petticoat was the name of the undergarment). Women also wore homespun aprons.

A woman's wardrobe would naturally include more items than she received yearly, and worn out clothing was recycled. The new suit was likely to be used for Sunday best, and last year's Sunday best became this year's everyday costume. Last year's weekday suit could be worn for doing dirty work. New homespun aprons were requested so rarely that old gowns and petticoats were probably converted into aprons. Cotton aprons were easier to wash, but homespun ones offered greater flame resistance as they were at least partly made of wool, and were thicker. They would have been more appropriate for work around open flames such as laundry and soap making. Children's clothes could also be cut from the good parts of adults' used garments. Worn woolen garments could be used for patches, cut into strips and used as weft in the fabrication of bed rugs, or when beyond recycling, be thrown into the wool churn to be shredded, respun and woven into blankets. The best parts of used cotton garments could be turned into aprons, caps, kerchiefs, towels, baby shirts, and weft for bed rugs; the worse ones became rags. Socks and mittens were darned, refooted, and finally sent to the wool churn.

This wardrobe resembles the contemporary Acadian female costume in the Maritimes, including Madawaska, described by Scottish traveller James MacGregor in his account of his travels in Eastern Canada in 1826–7.[26] MacGregor describes women wearing woolen, vertically striped petticoats, widely pleated at the waist and stopping about six inches above the ankle, 'small, neat calico caps' sometimes covered with a tied handkerchief, and blue cloaks reaching halfway down their bodies and fastened by a brass broach. He observed that women in Chaleur Bay were beginning to wear gowns instead of the traditional two-piece garment. The only depiction of Madawaska female costume dates from 1836 (see illustration 12). Women were then wearing short gowns with fashionable mutton sleeves and kerchiefs tucked into the neck, straight, ankle-length skirts, aprons, mocassins and distinctive headdresses.

A typical 1830s supply of men's clothing included a suit of homespun, two flannel and two linen shirts, an extra pair of homespun trousers, possibly under-trousers or drawers made of wool, socks, mittens, hats, and footwear. Cotton and silk handkerchiefs, broadcloth waistcoats or the material to make them, beaver hats, and overcoats were delivered every two, three, or sometimes four years. Men usually received a greatcoat upon their retirement that was to last them the rest of their lives.

Firmin Thibodeau, who retired in 1831, had much more sophisticated sartorial tastes. In addition to the usual suit of homespun and extra trousers, he wanted a complete suit of superfine cloth yearly, half a dozen homespun and as many fine shirts, five pairs of moccasins, shoes, and boots, a beaver hat and a silk one, and two cambric and two cotton handkerchiefs yearly. His wife did not request anything unusual except black worsted stockings and six shirts instead of the customary three, but she wanted her clothes to be made of the best material.[27] If the Thibodeaux were typical, well-to-do men were apparently much fancier dressers than their wives. As early as the late 1820s, a prominent man frequently wore fine cloth and shirting, a beaver hat, and a silk tie (handkerchiefs were used as neckties). This wardrobe fits MacGregor's description too: Acadian men throughout the Maritimes wore 'round' blue jackets with straight collars and metal buttons, blue trousers, and blue and scarlet waistcoats. On Prince Edward Island, men who wore coats of English cut were teased endlessly, but on the Bay of Chaleur this new style was becoming more acceptable. Obviously the same was true in Madawaska.[28]

Cotton apparel had appeared in women's wardrobes as early at the turn of the century, but only for small items such as handkerchiefs, muslin caps, and calico nightcaps. One exception was Frosine Martin, who requested a calico gown or petticoat and short gown as early as 1805. Her request was for one 'forever': this was not an article for daily wear.[29] By the 1820s cotton suits and *mantelets* were becoming normal parts of a woman's wardrobe, along with cotton aprons, and by the 1850s linen shirts for men and women were being replaced by cotton ones. Silk appeared in the 1820s, but only for bonnets and handkerchiefs or neckerchiefs. It took one to one and a half yards of silk to make a bonnet, which suggested quite a few ruffles and flounces; a muslin cap required only one yard.

By the midcentury a shift in style had taken place. Petticoats and *mantelets* were still common, but suits were increasingly replaced by frocks and gowns in the lists of requested clothing. A winter gown was increasingly likely to be made of merino. Stays and corset appeared at about the same time, although they were rare. Shawls became more common, suggesting that the real article replaced folded squares of ordinary fabric, and women's mantles or manto (overcoats) began to be mentioned. New styles were creeping in from the outside, but apparently mostly for Sunday clothes. Style changes were slow: in the 1870s the clothes requested in the deeds of maintenance were the same as in the 1850s. Women were selective in what they adopted: corsets, as mentioned, were rare, and Hallock in 1866 was struck by the fact women did not wear hoop skirts. Impractical items or styles were apparently ignored, or reserved for non-working days. This attitude could explain the choice of material for clothes. It seems that women chose convenience over fashion for their everyday clothes, and continued wearing their short skirted, two-piece, loose outfits for work. This does not mean Madawaska men and women were indifferent to their clothes. Hallock referred to the universal blue of the clothes, and indigo was a common dye sold in the stores. The commonest colour of the cotton fabric sold at the Dufour and Emmerson stores was yellow – solid, striped, checked, and printed. Yellow silk neckerchiefs were also common and yellow is the colour most likely to set off indigo blue. Conservative styles should not be assumed to imply lack of taste, or a disinterest for appearances. As discussed in chapter 10, Madawaska people were not impervious to fashion. They just did not let it run their lives.

These lists of clothing illustrate the respective uses of store-bought and home-made material. At midcentury, everyday clothes were made of durable homespun. In summer, women replaced their woollen garments with lighter cotton ones. Men continued wearing woollen pants. Emmerson also sold Coburgs or cotton pants and storekeepers sold heavy, utility cotton material. Orleans, a cotton warp/worsted weft fabric would also have been suitable for pants. Summer shirts for men and women were also made of cotton. Women protected their clothes with cotton aprons, and their headgear was always made of purchased material. Silk was limited to accessories. Good clothes for men included a broadcloth waistcoat and a suit of purchased material if they really wanted to look the gentleman. Women dressed up after midcentury in merino gowns, or by changing the cut of their Sunday clothes to partly reflect outside fashion. The young lady in Clarence Pullen's book who posed for the picture dressed in factory-cloth finery while sitting at the loom was the ultimate result of this trend.

Production for Exchanges

Elizabeth Mancke's study of late eighteenth-century Nova Scotia suggests that the textile products made by women were not solely intended for self-consumption. Cynthia Wallace Casey also found that women did not weave exclusively to cover the textile needs of their households. Woven goods were exchanged with neighbours or taken to the store. Madawaska textiles similarly entered exchange networks.[30]

Not everyone produced cloth; a quarter of the farms did not. A further 15 per cent did not produce enough for the needs of a couple and 14 per cent produced more than needed for self-sufficiency (100 yards or more). Local sales of fabric have not left any traces in the sources. The Dufours and Emmerson bought very little homespun and ready-made garments, but in 1853 a peddler named Robert Connors bought dozens of homespun shirts and pants from Emmerson, apparently the same Connors as the later store-keeper opposite Fort Kent. Connors could also have gone from farm to farm buying women's goods. Some material also reached extra-local markets. The only direct evidence of this trade are the memoirs of a former Saint John Valley resident, Isaac Stephenson, who spent his childhood and youth on the Saint John River at Hartland, about 100 miles below Madawaska. Stephenson remembered that in the 1840s 'At Hartland and Spring Hill [about mid-river] I saw as a child, the products of the forest go by in an endless stream of rafts, the towboats laden with supplies for the farms, the canoes of the Indians and white men, the pirogues of the Acadians carrying to market the woolen garments made from their own flocks of sheep and maple sugar obtained in the woods.'[31] Madawaska residents wove and made clothing that they sold downriver, either because southern merchants gave them better prices or proposed a more interesting variety of goods in exchange. How late in the century Madawaska settlers took their goods to Fredericton is not known, but the Lower Saint John market for home-made textile products remained strong until the 1880s. In the 1880s southern New Brunswick newspapers still carried ads asking for woollen yarn, homespun, mitts, socks, and hats in large quantities.

In June 1880 A.A. Miller advertised in the *NB Reporter and Fredericton Advertiser*:

Look Sharp

Buy your cotton warp at

A.A. Miller and Co

and make up

Homespun cloth, socks, mitts, etc.

Early in the season, and you can be relieved

of all such domestic goods at the store of

A.A. Miller and Co, opposite city hall,

in exchange for dry goods.

We want about

4000 yards of cloth.[32]

In September of the same year, A.A. Miller and Co headed their ad with the words: 'Woolen goods in great demand.' They were looking for 'homespun cloth of all kinds in large quantities, also 2000 pairs of socks and mitts, 1–2 ton woolen yarn, over socks, home knit drawers, shirts, pants etc.'[33] In November they asked for 'all the homespun cloth, socks, mitts, yarn etc. made in York county' (Fredericton was in York County).[34] By 1881 Miller's stock had been purchased by Tennant and Davies, whose ad also ended with a call for socks, homespun, mitts, and yarn. They advertised 'camp supplies for lumbermen, camp blanketing, grey blankets, knit shirts and drawers, socks, over socks and mitts, horse blankets, our own make.'[35] In return for their products, knitters and weavers could select from a bewildering array of goods imported from England, the United States, and the rest of Canada: shawls, silks, velvets, tweeds, and the latest novelty dress material. Similar ads can be found for other Fredericton merchants and in newspapers from other New Brunswick cities as well.

The demand for domestic cloth and knitted goods was high, and Madawaska people who could not sell their production locally to neighbours or to lumbermen would have had no problem finding purchasers outside the valley. Madawaska weavers made linen in addition to flannel. English-speaking parts of New Brunswick produced none or very little; linen was made almost exclusively in the Acadian districts, and the Saint John Valley was apparently famous for its linen production at the beginning of the century, although this is more a matter of local knowledge than of hard evidence. Flax was apparently turned into a towelling material called crash.[36] How far it was marketed is not known. New Brunswick stores did not place ads calling for homemade household linen, but J. J. Hegan carried 'Genuine Domestic Linen...hand dressed and manufactured from flax in this province, entirely free from the process of machinery and chemicals.' His advertisement in 1866 boasted that 'it was stronger and more durable than any goods of the same kind. Should be purchased by every housekeeper.'[37] If the hand-processed linen he advertised was a Madawaska product there is no way of knowing.

Women's Labour Opportunity Costs

Demand for the product is only part of the explanation for the continuation of domestic cloth production in New Brunswick. Weavers also had to find the activity advantageous and Madawaska women had two incentives to weave. First, their family needed the material for work clothes. Second, they could sell some of their production on local and regional markets. It would have been very profitable for them to do so: domestic cloth was worth making. The Dufours and Emmerson paid 80 cents a yard for the little they bought and sold it for $1.00. Connors sold it for $1.00 to 1.25 in 1875–6. The Madawaska data does not provide enough information to calculate profits, but Judith Rygiel and I were able to estimate the weaver's added value for Charlotte County in southwest New Brunswick. The 122 county weavers listed in the county's manufacturing schedule reported making fabric worth an average of 70 cents a yard and containing 35 cents worth of raw material. Weavers averaged 3.5 yards of fabric a day (months worked divided by output). There was not much variation in the production per day from one weaver to the next. The weaver's added value, the difference between fabric value and raw material value, ranged from 35 to 40 cents a yard throughout the county.[38]

At Madawaska, cotton warp sold for 40 cents a pound in 1871. Madawaska weavers made the same type of material as the Charlotte County weavers, and if wool cost the same, they would have added a value of 42 cents a yard if they sold the material 80 cents, and 62 cents if they sold it for $1.00. If they made 3.5 yards a day, their gain would have been at least $1.40 a day. Weavers would have equated added value with profit. Modern day accountants and economists factor depreciation of equipment, the use of space for the loom, inventory, and marketing costs into the calculation of profit. Nineteenth-century farmers had little concept of those hidden costs – it is not even certain that accountants had yet developed them. Weavers would have considered the $1.40 a day as earned income, which compared very favourably with contemporary women's wages: farm servants earned

$2.50 a month plus room and board at the time. Even female teachers earned less, between $12 and $18 a month in 1859. Most men did not earn as much as the weavers. Farm labourers made 50 cents a day; craddlers earned $1.00 a day at harvest time, as did log drivers. Lumberers earned $15 to $20 a month with room and board, before the mid-1860s. In 1875–6 Connors paid his workers $10 to $25 a month.[39]

Why did men not weave if it was such a profitable occupation? On an individual basis it might have been worthwhile for them to learn the craft, but by so doing they would have deprived the women of a source of income and impoverished the household. Men were better off seeking employment outside the home, even if they earned less than the women on a daily basis. Why, then, did not more poor households weave? Possibly weaving may have been less profitable for them because the hidden costs would have been more burdensome. They would have had to acquire a loom if they did not already own one; they were likely to own fewer sheep and thus produce less wool; and they would have had to purchase more raw material. The expense would have been proportionally greater for them than for their well-to-do neighbours. People with money idle in a jar did not miss it when they invested in tools or raw material. The poorer the weaver was, the more she missed her pennies. Store credit was less likely to solve the problem for the poor than for the well-to-do, because they received less or no credit at all from the stores. And they had smaller houses and would have been inconvenienced by the presence of the loom in a way the well-to-do, who had space, were not. The poorer the household, the less hidden the hidden costs were. Nineteenth-century people may not have had an abstract concept of costs, but they knew their impact. A lot of poorer farm households clearly concluded that the cost and inconvenience of putting together the necessary resources in time, equipment, and material to make cloth placed this activity beyond their reach.

The strong regional demand for domestic cloth and its profitability were not enough to induce Madawaska people to specialize in cloth production. The largest cloth producers were all households that were engaged in farming and possibly in other activities. Only one Madawaska weaver was a professional, that is, listed as a weaver in the personal schedule of the census, and she was not a household head, but a married daughter of the household head. Very few weavers made more than 150 yards of fabric per year. Households that produced large quantities of fabric included more adult females than the norm, but the reverse was not true. An average of 1.3 females over the age of sixteen lived in households producing less than 25 yards of fabric, and 2 in households producing more than 200 yards. The two households that produced 1,000 yards of fabric included 4 and 2 females over the age of sixteen. In other words, a greater number of women translated into larger quantities of fabric, but households did not necessarily specialize in fabric production just because they included a large number of women. Weaving was integrated into the diversified production of the farm household, and as a rule did not generate huge surpluses. In this respect, domestic cloth resembled the other commodities produced by Madawaska farms. Landed rural households took advantage of existing opportunities, but not to the point of specializing in either farming or manufacturing.

Weaving cloth to sell was not the only way women could become involved in commercial textile production. The papers of John Emmerson provide a glimpse of those activities. There is no indication that Emmerson himself was interested in domestic cloth as a commercial item: he bought and sold little of it. But his household consumed domestic cloth and did not produce it, or all of it, but instead farmed out the various phases of its production to local people. In 1865 and 1866 Emmerson gave work to two spinners, a Mrs St Onge, sometimes referred to as 'the old woman,' and her daughter Marie. Lucie St Onge was a sixty-year-old widow in 1871, who lived a few houses from the Emmerson store with her sons Alexandre, twenty, Eugene, twenty-two, Achille, seventeen, and her daughter Marie, twenty-three. Alexandre was a day labourer who occasionally sold shingles to Emmerson. Achille was Emmerson's hired boy in the mid-1860s. In 1865 Emmerson gave the women 63 pounds of wool to spin; in 1866, 58.74 pounds; in 1867, 9.5 pounds; and in 1868, his widow gave them 33 pounds. The women were paid 25 to 33 cents a pound for spinning (a pound of wool takes about two days to spin). Emmerson was also charging them 20 cents a month for the rental of the spinning wheel. This fact suggests that the women were spinning for other households, since they would not have continued to rent the wheel month after month even when they were not spinning for the storekeeper. The relationship was apparently not one of mutual help between two groups of women, but a strictly commercial one between a wealthy household and a labouring one. The Emmersons hired spinners the way they hired harvesters.

In 1853 Emmerson hired Benoni Beaulieu's wife to make 33.5 yards of linen towelling at 16 cents a yard and 45.25 yards of cloth at 25 cents a yard. The price difference reflects the fact that towelling was only 12 to 15 inches wide, whereas cloth was 30 to 36 inches wide. As Emmerson was also taking homespun as payment on account from other people and giving 80 cents a yard for it, Mrs Beaulieu evidently wove with Emmerson's yarn and the prices entered in the ledger are for her labour only.[40] It is possible to weave several yards a day, which means that Mrs Beaulieu was better paid than the St Onge women or even male day labourers. Woollen material may subsequently have been sent out for finishing. In 1866 Emmerson paid Corriveau $9.80 for 'carding and fulling,' but it is not known how much fabric was processed. Once the cloth or linen was made, Emmerson would hire women to sew. In 1853 Charles Fournier's wife sewed two shirts at 25 cents and three pairs of breeches at 33 cents; Mrs Joseph Martin, who had an account in her name despite the fact her husband was alive, regularly bought cotton warp from Emmerson and regularly sewed for him. She may have been a seamstress.[41] She received 60 cents for making trousers, $1.50 for making coats, and 50 cents for making waistcoats. Mrs Baptiste Michaud, whose husband was also alive, had an account in her own name and in 1853 bought cotton warp from Emmerson as well as a few sundries and paid by making three coats at 50 cents, six cotton shirts at 25 cents, and doing some general labour at 40 cents a day.[42]

Ledger entries show how Emmerson had some or all of his textile needs met: giving wool to women to both card and spin; giving wool to spin to a day labourer's household whose women probably spun for others as well; and giving wool to card and cloth to full to a local mill. Some local seamstresses sewed outer clothing for the men in Emmerson's household and also seem to have woven for their own accounts. The ladies of the Emmerson household may have made their own clothing: Emmerson did not order ladies' garments from the local seamstresses. Emmerson's widow ordered a sewing machine through the store in 1871 and his sister-in-law also owned a machine: she ordered needles and bobbins through the store. The Emmerson household relied both on the labour of its own women, on local hand carders, spinners, weavers, and seamstresses, and on local carding and fulling mills to provide its clothing. The Emmerson's history also shows that even when local exchanges aimed to satisfy the needs of the household, they were not necessarily forms of barter based on use or value, but could be strictly commercial. And there is no reason to believe Mr Emmerson was the only well-to-do head of household to hire women to card, spin, weave, and sew.

Conclusion

Madawaska farmers responded to market opportunities by intensifying production for which there was a demand. Their wives did likewise. The market provided women with a profitable outlet for their goods and also facilitated production. Local carding mills and distant spinning mills increased women's productivity and facilitated their response to the market. Women were then participant in the rural market revolution as producers and consumers. Marjorie Cohen has argued that in Ontario, men elbowed women out of dairy production when it became truly commercialized: market activities would not have been suitable for women.[43] Madawaskayans do not seem to have perceived women engaging in market activities on their own as problematic. However in Ontario, wheat growing was declining and men needed to find a substitute commercial activity. In Madawaska, men had no reason to want to replace women at the loom. Textiles were one of the commodities produced by the household, like oats, potatoes, or butter. Home production could cover the household's needs for woollen cloth if they wished, like the production of buckwheat or meat could allow them to be self-sufficient in bread grain and protein. Households were no more desirous to be self-sufficient in textiles than in foodstuffs. Textiles were produced both for home use and for the market, and the market was a source of food and textiles.

Women's response to market incentive was no more uniform than the men's. Only 11 per cent of weavers produced large quantities of fabric, at least 18 yard per capita or in excess of 250 per cent of needs. This output averaged out to at least 110 yards per household, which was worth about $46. Most weavers followed less ambitious strategies: one-third of them and one-quarter of all households produced enough to cover the needs of an average family – their per capita production ranged between 7.5 and 18 yards. About 40 per cent wove between 50 and 150 yards. This production would not have entailed an undue amount of extra work, two to six weeks of labour over the course of the year, plus the time spent spinning, if needed. Selling 50 yards of fabric at 80 cents could net the weaver $20 and allow her to make quite a few purchases. Most women were not output maximizers trying to produce as much as possible for the market. Like the men, they occupied a space at the limit between medium surplus and commercial production. Farm women were not underworked, and maximizing profit meant an increased workload for them. Like the men, the women were utility not profit maximizers. On the other hand, they seem to have understood the opportunities offered by the high price of homespun. Industrialization and local infrastructure reduced the labour required to produce cloth by providing weavers with prepared warp and some of their carded wool. Women responded positively (per capita fabric production went up between 1851 and 1871) but sensibly to those opportunities. Producing for the market was worth their while to a point, and they responded, to a point. The trick was to balance the need for material goods with the need for time for other tasks, or even leisure.

If women had sold their homespun and garments made of this fabric directly to consumers, they could have acquired money for cash purchases at the store, hiding their participation in the market economy. The cases of Mesdames Michaud and Martin also seem to indicate that women could control their own earnings and even receive store credit in their own name, husband or no husband.

Craig and Weiss's claim that 'women and children shifted their time from unmeasured household tasks to market activities or reallocated their efforts among farm and non farm market work' during the Civil War year can also describe the situation at Madawaska.[44] Some women responded positively to a demand for their products by intensifying production. As a group they wove more, and a greater proportion of households appear to have woven as well. To do so they may have shifted their time away from other activities. Weaving increased at the same time as the number of pigs per farm declined to the point where many farms suffered from a deficit in pork production. As soon as mess pork was available at the store, women reduced their numbers to the bare minimum. Women reallocated their time from an unpleasant outdoor task to a clean indoor one, supported by a market that supplied them with raw material, tools, food, and an opportunity to sell their handiwork.

Men and women were thus sensibly market responsive. They produced for self-sufficiency as well as for markets, and they appear to have been able to place a price tag on their time. But why did they seek profits in the first place? Some historians would argue that commercial activities in and of themselves were not proof of a commercial mind set. Farmers, they would argue, entered the market spurred by social imperatives – to establish their children and perpetuate a customary way of life rooted in economic independence. To do so they had to accumulate assets, especially real property, which they gave their sons as they came of age or married (girls were given chattel and other moveables). Finally, aging parents exchanged the farm for mainte-nance from a son, who also was responsible to compensate any sib-lings for whom provision had yet to be made. Once cheap land ceased to be available, families had to engage in commercial activities to raise the money to buy property for the next generation. In other words, they used the market to reach non-market goals. In the process, however, they often undermined the very socio-economic system they were trying to preserve, if market forces beyond their control had not already began to dissolve it. Parents began to place the competitive-ness of the farm as a business above family obligations; land ceased to be a patrimony and became a commodity. Madawaska families sought the market long before they ran out of cheap land. As I have shown elsewhere, their system of property transmission bore the mark of a commercial agriculture and of the commoditisation of land.[45] Mada-waska men and women did not enter the market to keep changes at bay. But entering the market allowed them to join a growing category of individuals: consumers.

9 Consumption and the 'World of Goods'

... skirts guiless of hoops.

Charles Hallock, 1864[1]

Owes Régiste Thériault:
Lining and balance on hoops to Christine ...... 2/6.[2]

Emmerson ledger C, 1863

Owes François Lagacé

1844	report from Folio I, p. 146			5/9
January 2	1 barrel			7/6
1845	Goods delivered to his daughter Marie			1/6
February 5	credit for 1 pr. slippers from Marie	2/3		
	¼ yd gingham			4d
July 26	Marie begins her time at 12/6 per month			
August 26	credit for Marie's salary	12/6		
	1 pr. French shoes			8/
	1 yellow silk kerchief			5/
July 13, 1847	1 pr. suspenders			1/
	1 scythe to son			10/
August 7	By hay in the field	£1 5/		
	10 ½ pounds of bacon at 10d			
	Interests on 13/6 from May 1st,			
	1845 to present			2/0½
	Total debit			£3 17/4½
	Total credit		14/9	
	Balance due and transferred to W.P. Vinal		£3 2/7½	

Dufour ledger 1844–8

In 1863 three accounts at John Emmerson's – Régiste Thériault's, Herménégilde Couillard's, and Isaie Martin's – were debited for the purchase of hoops, a necessary accessory if one were to follow the latest fashion. Thériault was the miller discussed in chapter 4 and Christine was his twenty-three-year-old daughter, Couillard was a schoolteacher, and Martin a commercial farmer. Martin was debited twice with the purchase of hoops that year; he also bought a pair of spectacles. His two oldest daughters were twenty and seventeen. Four sets of hoops in a population of about 10,000 do not indicate a craze, and any farm boy worth his salt could probably have fabricated hoops with material at hand. But they show that remoteness was no obstacle to knowing what was in style – and to wanting it. The skirts innocent of hoops commented on by Hallock were not worn by women living in a world uncontaminated by the demon of fashion, but by women who could not afford a hoop skirt, or who did not want to be bothered by this cumbersome contraption, at least for their workaday clothes. Hoops were for show, and it is probably no accident that the three account holders were men whose wives and daughters could spare enough money for an unserviceable skirt, or enjoy sufficient leisure to sport it. Or, at the very least, had little outdoor work to do, as was the case of the teacher's wife. Even girls of more modest means could pretty themselves up, as Marie Lagacé's purchases in the Dufour ledger show. The gingham could have been used to trim a garment made of homespun. Her wages were used to pay for a pair of fancy and expensive shoes, and an equally expensive neckerchief. Marie's 12s.6d. would have gone further had she satisfied herself with cobbler's shoes at 3 shillings and a plain cotton kerchief at 1 shilling; the remainder would have bought enough cheap cotton for a gown. But Marie obviously did not fancy plain shoes or plain kerchiefs and she was willing to work for a month at the store to get what she really wanted.

Marie Lagacé and Christine Thériault bring the 'world of goods' and consumption to the fore. Consumption is a recent topic of interest among historians, whose approach has undergone a marked shift in orientation in the past few years. It emerged in 1982 with the publication of McKendrick, Plumb, and Brewer's *Birth of a Consumer Society*.[3] Consumption historians were initially interested in what was being consumed, by whom, as well as when and where new patterns of consumption emerged. They viewed consumption as both the cause and the consequence of a more diversified and more abundant supply of ready-made goods. Consumption was a companion of the Industrial Revolution but it also entailed an attitudinal shift. Objects were now acquired for non-utilitarian reasons even by non-elite individuals without much money to spare, and could be discarded before being worn out simply because they had ceased to please. The desire to emulate one's betters apparently played a limited role in the rise of consumption; consumption first increased among the 'middling sort,' including storekeepers and artisans, but they were not purchasing knocked-off versions of the items gracing the homes or wardrobes of their betters. Consumption patterns were instead class specific. The discovery of this shift in attitude towards objects, and of the non-emulatory nature of consumption led historians away from economics and into the realm of culture: consumption was a meaningful activity.

Consumption emerged as a paradoxical behaviour. On the one hand, it increasingly became a way to express one's individuality, especially as far as clothing was concerned, to the furore of moralists and of some members of the elite who wanted clothing, and to a lesser extent other material possessions and eating habits, to firmly establish the boundaries between the various ranks. On the other hand, various groups, including social classes, developed specific patterns of consumption, which became part of their collective identity. The middle classes, for instance, consumed to signify respectability, if not moral refinement and superior tastes. By the eighteenth century, inexpensive linen had made crisp, white shirts, shifts, caps, neckerchiefs, and aprons outwards signs of personal cleanliness, and indirectly, of moral rectitude. White linen was replaced in the nineteenth century by cheaper, easier to launder cotton, which no longer needed to be white either. By the nineteenth century, clothing had become but one category of goods imbued with symbolic meaning. Furniture, home decoration, food (what was served, how it was prepared, how it was served), reading material, the use of one's leisure, all that can be subsumed under the generic 'lifestyle,' could be used to project an image of the self, to define one's group identity, and to signify one's adhesion to specific values and moral standards. One was what one ate, drank, used to cover ones' nakedness, or to furnish one's dwelling. Consumption was an economic activity laden with symbolic meaning and the study of the world of goods could no longer be limited to production and distribution, nor even to class-bound patterns of acquisition.[4]

Consumption was also a highly gendered activity. At the most basic level, men and women consumed different goods. Men bought neckties and cigars, women thread, thimbles, and fancy hats. But female consumption also held greater significance since women not only consumed for themselves, but supervised most of the consumption taking place in their household. Many of the new consumer goods belonged to categories whose purchase and use was the responsibility of women: food, linen, clothing, children's toys and educational material, and among the elite, culture. Women constructed the family's public image in part through consumption, and they were held responsible for this image. An ill-clothed woman was unfeminine and lacked taste; ill-clothed married men were the victims of their wives' shortcomings; ill-clothed singletons obviously needed to get married. The middle class defined itself as respectable and morally superior partly through the use its women made of consumer goods. The key role women played in this process made contemporaries uncomfortable; they demonized the female consumer as a vain, selfish, spendthrift creature who drove her husband to ruin, threatened the country's trade balance, and undermined social hierarchies. And the tourist literature which idealized certain part of rural North America, stressed the women's self-sufficiency and like M. Hallock, indifference to fashion. Male consumers were not the target of such ire; one could almost doubt that such a creature ever existed. Consumption was a typically female vice.[5]

Studies of the world of goods and the meaning people gave their possessions have focused largely on urban areas and on the middle and upper classes. Not much has been written on consumption among rural North Americans although the North American countryside was not untouched by the world of goods. Historians of the nineteenth century consider consumption to be part of the emerging commercial economy. Storekeepers offered a broadening range of goods to their customers; farmers began to specialize and to purchase the goods they used to make themselves.[6] Women shifted from the production of goods for the households to the production of goods for the market.[7] For economic historians, the commercialization of agriculture 'naturally' led to consumption. Women historians, however, either hint or state bluntly that women produced for the market in order to consume, a reversal of Elizabeth Mancke's conclusion that in the eighteenth century, women consumed to produce.[8] This theory also suggests that there was nothing preordained in the emergence of a consumer society: people had to want to consume and the people whose attitude mattered may have been women.

Colonial historians would take exception with the notion that the world of goods did not emerge until the nineteenth century. Imported goods were common in the eighteenth century, to the extent that T.H. Breen has argued that they contributed to 'anglicizing' the colonies.[9] Carol Shammas, Adrienne Hood, Laurel Ulrich, and a few Canadian historians demonstrate that colonial households could not have been self-sufficient even if they had wanted to, because they lacked most of the necessary tools; they also argue that British colonials had no desire for self-sufficiency in any case, and relied matter-of-factly on artisans and stores, in addition to their own efforts, to supply their needs.[10] Alan Taylor even depicts Maine frontierspeople who clearly preferred store goods to anything they could make.[11] The consumer revolution like the transition to capitalism is a process whose timing varies depending on the historians investigating it.

The study of North American consumption thus presents a few challenges. Timing is the first one: when did the world of goods appear? Agency is the second: was the emergence of this world of goods the ineluctable outcome of some law of economic development, or the result of decisions and choices that could have been different? And who propelled the rural households into this world of goods: merchants, undifferentiated households, or gendered men and women? Most of the existing work broadly sketches behavioural changes: Joan Jensen comments that women engaged in market production in order to buy manufactured goods. But which women? What goods did they buy? When and where were they purchased? More detailed studies rely on probate records that list who owned what at death. Aside from their bias in favour of the better off, the records do not capture the flow of goods through a household. They are good sources for material culture, but not as useful for the study of consumption patterns.

How can Madawaska shed some light on these questions? Here was a commercializing rural economy where women produced for the market and occasionally had their own store accounts. What did the people of the valley consume? Did consumption patterns change over time? And who consumed what? Those questions can only partly be answered. The main source, the store ledgers, does not allow the identification of individual consumption patterns. People had a choice of store, did not limit their shopping to one or two, and paid cash for some of their purchases. Purchases on account are not entirely indicative of consumption. The store books nonetheless list what was sold and, assuming cash payments were random, it is possible to rank the various commodities in order of importance. Emmerson's receiving book sheds additional light on the topic, as it lists what he purchased from wholesalers, as opposed to what his customers put on account. The receiving book is not as detailed as it might be: 'sundries' is a particularly unhelpful category. Evidence from this material can be supplemented with two merchant's inventories: Emmerson's from November 1867 and John Costello's, an Edmundston merchant who died in 1865.[12]

A Conduit for Consumer Goods?

As discussed in chapter 5, neither Emmerson nor the Dufours appear to have shipped much produce outside the valley. They did, however, bring large quantities and a wide variety of products into the region. The role of the store as a local distributor of outside commodity is easier to grasp using Emmerson's delivery and receiving books.[13]

Emmerson purchased enormous quantities of staple food for his store, always in Lower Canada. Flour came from various mills in Upper Canada through Noad of Quebec City (often the producing mill was identified). Staples came almost exclusively from the Canadas. Emmerson purchased most other goods from Saint John merchants, who described themselves as importers in their almanac advertisements. Hegan and Co., who soon provided Emmerson with all his textiles and notions, depicted themselves in 1864 as 'importers of British and Foreign dry goods of every description.' William Tyson was an 'importer and dealer in China, glass and earthenware.' W.A. Adams presented himself over two pages as an 'importer of all descriptions of English, American, German and French hardware.' He also ran a nail factory. Hasting Brothers were importers of British and foreign dry and fancy goods, including tea and West Indian goods. Their terms were 'moderate,' they gave preference to cash purchases, but there was 'no second price' in their establishment, a modern practice. Lockart and Co. operated a 'fashionable cheap hat, cap and fur store'; they manufactured hats and imported dry goods. Fellow and Co., who published their entire catalogue in the 1864 almanac, were druggists, chemists, and sold seeds. They imported from London, Glasgow, and Paris. And finally Sheffield House imported English gold jewellery, silver and electroplated ware and ornaments, fishing rods, archery and cricketing goods, watches, cutlery, and cabinet hardware.[14] Some of those wholesalers deliberately targeted country merchants: Hegan and

Co. announced in their 1855 advertisement that 'personal attention will be given to the selection of goods for all wholesale and retail orders received from the country.' So did F. Clementson, another of Emmerson's suppliers, who dealt in China, glass, and earthenware and had a showroom in Saint John. Clementson sold wholesale and retail and prepared 'crates packed to order for the country trade.'[15] These wholesalers and the country merchants they serviced became key relays in the flow of goods from the manufacturing centres of Europe and the United States to remote rural communities.[16]

Emmerson was not content with ordering his inventory from two or three suppliers, nor was he particularly faithful to most of them. The only ones who reappear in the receiving book for 1849, 1853, and 1858 were Noad, Hegan, Adam of Saint John who sold tools and hardware, Hasting of Saint John, William Avery, stationer in Saint John, and Parson and son, shoemakers in the tiny mid-Saint John Valley town of Woodstock. In the late 1840s Rankins had been one of Emmerson's suppliers of British textiles; he was still doing business with Rankins in 1858, but Rankins was supplying him with molasses instead of Scottish tweeds. The number of suppliers also fluctuated: from 38 in 1849, to 44 in 1853, and 25 in 1858. Some of the purchases were highly specialized: Lockhart and Co. from Saint John supplied Emmerson exclusively with felt hats; Richard Shaw of Quebec with cartwheels and horse gear; Francis Clementson with crockery and chamber pots; James Jarvis of Saint John with manila ropes; Sheffield House (a cashonly business) with cabinet hardware, scissors, and cutlery, and the list could go on.

Emmerson shopped around. He personally went to Quebec City and to Saint John once or twice a year and kept an eye out for useful technical innovations. In 1858 he bought a sewing machine for £26 and purchased lamps, shades, and lamp oil from the New Brunswick Oil Work, which had begun to advertise in the almanac in 1858. The oil work manufactured paraffin lamp oil and advertised 'liberal discounts for wholesale dealers.'[17] Emmerson received a 25 per cent discount on his first order and he reordered twice during the year. The product was more popular than he had expected.

Emmerson was in a position to acquaint his customers with the new products available in Quebec City and Saint John at the wholesalers he patronized. He could also sell them at competitive prices. The Dufours and Costello similarly could act as conduits for consumer goods, but as the Dufours supplied themselves from merchants on the Lower St

Lawrence rather than directly from importers, their selection may have been more limited, and their prices less advantageous. Not everything found a market in the Saint John Valley, so what exactly was retailed in valley stores from the mid-1840s to the late 1860s, and how popular were those goods?

I have regrouped the bulk of goods sold at Dufours' and Emmerson's into twenty-two categories and calculated the proportion of clients purchasing goods in each category at least once, as well as the proportion of total debit represented by each category after eliminating cash remittance and interest from the debits (see table 19). Few categories of goods were purchased by the majority of customers (fabric, maintenance, notions, and tobacco at Dufours'; fabric, food, household supplies, notions, and tobacco at Emmerson's. And few of those categories were purchased by more than half of the clients either. Little difference exists between the high- and low-debit customers. In the aggregate, the purchases of customers with a debit equal to or higher than $10 display almost the same distribution as the purchases of those with a debit less than $10. But rich and poor did not necessarily have the same needs. First, low and high debit need not equate with poor and rich and second, the different categories comprise a wide range of products that may have been purchased. Some necessary goods not found on many accounts, such nails or thread and needles, are further evidence that people patronized more than one store.[18] Customers had choices, and took advantage of them to shop around. Saint John Valley customers did not behave any differently from those in Upper Canada.[19]

The low value and infrequency of purchases related to farming confirms some of the previous chapters' conclusions: techniques remained very traditional, and farmers made little use of purchased seeds or fertilizer. Abraham Dufour's purchase of a barrel of lime is responsible for the entire fertilizer category at Emmerson's in 1863. Emmerson sold a few plough points and harrow teeth, but this is the extent of his trade in farm machinery. Articles of hygiene also were infrequently purchased. Medicine and culture were bought more frequently at Emmerson's than at Dufours'. The latter comprised mostly ABCs in French and English, slates, pencils, and paper, and were primarily bought by schoolteachers, who either loaned or gave supplies to their pupils. On the other hand, the two moccasin-making Amerindians are prominent among the buyers of school supplies. The distribution of goods in terms of frequency of purchase is otherwise without surprises.

The same categories lead in both stores in terms of value: food, followed by fabric, clothing, and footwear. Hand tools and maintenance materials came next at Dufours'; household equipment and supplies at Emmerson's. The Dufours sold significantly more material to assist textile production (almost 5 per cent of total debit) than Emmerson. Emmerson also sold proportionally less fabric than the Dufours. In 1863 Emmerson sold almost no cotton warp and much less fabric; the culprit was the Civil War. In 1853 Emmerson offered cotton as cheap as 8 pence a yard (13 cents); in 1863 the cheapest was 1s.3d. (25 cents).[20] Emmerson's 1863 prices and the ones found by Douglas McCalla in Upper Canada in 1861 were surprisingly close. It might be assumed that prices would be higher in the distant Saint John Valley and significantly lower along the St Lawrence. In fact, what mattered was not distance from the nearest port, but distance from the source of supplies. The Saint John Valley was closer to Liverpool and Boston than was Upper Canada, even if it was quite distant from a port.

Elizabeth Mancke argued that men produced to consume and women consumed to produce.[21] In the Saint John Valley, almost all accounts were settled with the products of men's work or with men's labour. Men produced to consume, but it could also be said that men often produced with the assistance of women (at hay or harvest time, for instance). Female purchases were also in the major categories (food and textiles, supplemented by textile production and notions) and required additional female labour to be useable. Many items grouped under the 'household' category were also female tools like pots and pans, crockery and cutlery, or ingredients of household activities such as wicks for candle making or various chemicals for cleaning and scouring. Women definitively consumed to produce. They produced food, clothing, and a home furnished in a given way and cleaned to specific standards. Men mostly consumed to produce as well. Tobacco, the ultimate article of consumption, represented less than 5 per cent of all debits and only one client out of two put any on account. In fact, women used tobacco too, and matches had other uses besides for lighting pipes. Shirts, pants, cravats, and neckties represented a small fraction of total purchases. Men purchased tools, hunting and fishing gear, raw material such as iron and leather, paint, nails, glass panes, putty, hinges, latches, and locks, all production inputs or means of production. Even the horse, which could be a symbol of masculinity (a man was not a man until he owned a good looking and well-kept horse) and a status symbol, was also a working animal. Clearly both sexes consumed to produce.

The Rural World of Goods

It is from the details of the categories that the story of rural consumption emerges. The aggregate figures alone do not reflect the very utilitarian approach to the world of goods of Madawaska consumers. Staples (flour, mess pork, fish, meal) represented the bulk of food purchases. At Dufours', flour accounts for 10 per cent of all debits. Emmerson retailed the same products, but the leader at his store was not flour, but the cheaper and locally produced buckwheat meal, purchased by 16 per cent of customers and making up 8 per cent of debits. Flour followed with 10 per cent of the customers. However, flour buyers may have been in the habit of ordering a barrel or two from the store and paying cash. Poorer people were more likely to buy meal rather than flour and were also more likely to make piecemeal purchases of fifty pounds or less and put them on account.[22] Biscuits were a product Emmerson appears to have carried from the day he opened his store (they are listed in his receiving book in 1845) and were purchased by 15 per cent of the customers. Emmerson seems to have sold more fish to more people than the Dufours (10 per cent of the customers in 1863). Customers bought cod by the pound, herrings by the dozen, or ordered a whole barrel or half barrel of salted fish or a box of dried cod. Similarly, 15 per cent of his customers purchased pork, mostly by the pound. Other customers may have ordered barrels of mess pork in the same way they ordered barrels of flour and paid cash for them.

The Dufours sold very little sugar, which does not seem surprising as the region was a producer of maple sugar. Emmerson, on the other hand, sold sugar and molasses (25 per cent of the customers in 1853; 18 per cent in 1863). His store seems to have been the site of a curious *chassé-croisé*. He rented sugar kettles out and bought maple sugar from local people. Some of this sugar he shipped to George Pelletier, the forwarder at Rivière du Loup who relayed his orders from Quebec City. He also sold maple sugar back in the valley: his inventory lists more than 2,000 pounds of maple sugar in November, well after the end of the sugaring season. But he also purchased sugar loaves and molasses from his Quebec suppliers as early as 1849, as well as from George Pelletier. Collectively, Madawaska people were swapping local sugar for the West Indian variety, an exchange for which a possible explanation will surface below.

Baking techniques were evolving with the availability of leavening agents. The Dufours sold pearl ash and saleratus to 6 per cent of their clients while Emmerson sold saleratus, baking soda, and baking powder to 10 per cent of his. However, he had 410 pounds of soda in stock at his death; a storekeeper would not keep that much stock of a moisture-sensitive product if the demand was limited to one consumer in ten. Saleratus and soda were inexpensive goods that were better bought frequently to keep the supply fresh, and for which the housewives probably paid cash. Emmerson also sold a few baking pans in 1863, and his inventory lists three tin bakers at $1.50 each.

Drinking habits also seemed to be changing. Neither store retailed alcohol, but in the period under consideration, liquor sales were regulated both in Maine and New Brunswick. Twenty-nine or 11.5 per cent of the Dufours' customers bought tea; none bought coffee. Chocolate, a late eighteenth-century treat, was on the way out, with only four people purchasing any. Emmerson had some in stock in 1867, and sold none on credit in 1863; the same was true of coffee (he had 30 pounds in stock in 1867, and none was put to account in 1863). Tea, on the other hand, was bought by 20 per cent of Emmerson's customers for a total of about 36 pounds. Qualities were not differentiated in the store accounts or in the inventory. Here tea was tea. In other parts of British North America storekeepers distinguished between different types of tea, and Emmerson's suppliers seem to have done so. In 1849 he received 'Hyson tea' from Fabien Boule in Quebec City but later, tea is lumped into the uninformative category 'sundries.'[23] Both Emmerson's and Costello's inventories include teapots (cheap tin ones and pricier earthenware ones), tea kettles, cups and saucers, and teaspoons. The growing fondness for tea may explain the swapping of sugar. Maple sugar, like molasses, is fine with robustly flavoured food, but tea calls for white sugar. And if Madawaska people had not sweetened their tea, they would have had no use for teaspoons.

Fabric was one of the two main categories of purchase charged to accounts, and most of the recorded purchases were for cotton, both in terms of total value and in terms of frequency of purchase. Both Dufours and Emmerson sold a wide variety of material. At the Dufours', the most frequently sold was inexpensive cotton at 20 to 30 cents a yard). Cheaper cotton at 10 to 20 cents a yard was less commonly purchased. The store sold very little of the higher priced cotton material and woollen material was purchased by even fewer customers and in lesser quantities. However, store customers favoured high-end woollen products at 60 to 80 cents a yard over cheaper ones. Factory-made material was generally purchased in small pieces, usually insufficient to make a complete garment. The yardages, like Marie Lagacé's quarter-yard of gingham, suggest that most fabric was used for caps and bonnets, aprons, trimmings, and in the case of woollen material, cuffs, lapels, and fronts of waist-coats. Silk purchases were extremely rare, and at Dufour's people who purchased silk usually purchased at the same time a sheet of cardboard, hat ribbon, buckles, and stiff wire: hat-making materials. Emmerson's customers displayed the same buying pattern in 1853, except for favouring the cheapest cotton over the mid-priced. Emmerson received an extensive variety of fabric from his Saint John supplier. In 1851, by no means a high volume year, he took in 2,287 yards of fabric, plus some pieces of flannel of unspecified yardage. The largest category was grey cotton[24] (725 yards), fol-lowed by a dozen different inexpensive cotton prints totalling 526 yards. He retailed very little luxury fabric, and did not carry much in his inventory. Emmerson also stocked ribbons, laces, inserts, edging, and banding in equally large amounts, as well as buttons and hooks and eyes by the gross. Lace and other trims varied widely in price, colour, and possibly material. Women who used to trim their clothes with bits of purchased fabric may have changed to ready-made trims that were easier to use and probably more varied in look than fabric. The pieces of fabric purchased in 1863 were also longer, although by no means extravagant. For instance, twenty-eight customers bought calico: half bought less than 3 yards, the minimum yardage for a woman's short gown. Only five bought at least 6 yards, enough for a petticoat. Plain cotton was bought in pieces from half a yard and up (half a yard could make a shift for an infant). And although several people bought merino, none bought enough for a dress, despite the low cost of the material (1s.8d. to 2s.6d. a yard). Cloth was similarly purchased in smallish pieces, large enough for a waistcoat or unstructured jacket for a medium-sized man or a woman. Lining, which started at 7½d. a yard, was a rather popular item. It could have been used to make scratchy homespun jackets more comfortable. By contrast, Costello carried the fancy stuff Emmerson did not stock: silk lining, 'Scott' plaid, delaine, kersey, 'casener' (kerseymere?), silk gros de Naples, and imported linen (brown holland and Onasbruck). Emmerson retailed relatively little fabric, especially high-end fabric, perhaps because other stores had begun to specialize in this line. He may have decided to focus on low-end cotton material, for which he could have obtained quantity discounts from Hegan.

Tools, hardware, and maintenance products did not change; the same ones had been available for centuries with one or two exceptions. Both stores carried an assortment of hand tools, a wide range of nails, tacks, spikes, and the curiously named 'sparrow bills,' a sort of fastener; paint was available in various colours, as well as oil, turpentine, paint brushes, varnish, coal tar, and putty. All sorts of metalware was sold that could hinge, close, fasten, or lock various containers or cupboards. Emmerson stocked tarpaulin, oilcloth, and 'patented' oilcloth, a product with new and improved claims over the usual variety. There was some sandpaper in the Emmerson inventory, but I found few purchases at 3d. a sheet. Sandpaper had no use in carpentry or even in the rather rough joinery that characterized early Madawaska furniture; it was a tool for the cabinetmaker who sought the smooth finish necessary for the application of varnish. Screws and screwdrivers were new items in the 1863 account book and the inventory. Screws were born of the Industrial Revolution as threads were difficult to make by hand. They eventually replaced dowels, being easier to use. Monkey wrenches, also available at Emmerson's in the 1860s but not at Costello's, were another new tool and used a machined threaded rod. These came from the United States; had they come from Britain, they would have been called spanners. The male world of goods does not appear to have changed much over time, but it did incorporate time-saving innovations.

The world of household goods was another story. The very few Madawaska post mortems available suggest very spartan homes. The common room contained a stove, table, seats, chests, a few pots and pans, and a limited amount of crockery and cutlery. It also housed women's tools and served as women's workshops. Here they carded wool, scutched flax, spun, wove, sewed, mended, knitted, and cooked. The 1845 inventory of J.B. Cyr, a sawmiller who drowned in the river in 1843 leaving a wife and four children, lists two bedsteads with bedding, a bedstead settee, an iron stove, three tables but no chairs or benches, and three chests. To cook and serve food, Marguerite Cyr had a tea kettle, frying pan, soup kettle, iron kettle, six spoons, forks, and knives, as many plates, cups, and saucers, a decanter, and an oval dish. One could also find in the house two smoothing irons, a candle mould, four tubs, a kneading trough, a spinning wheel, a reed, and the mechanical parts of a loom (but apparently no loom frame). There was also a candlestick, a looking glass and a $10 clock. The beds excepted, this reads more like the description of a scullery than a home. Marguerite Cyr was also obviously a busy woman, spinning, perhaps weaving, baking bread, moulding candles, and ironing clothes. She could keep track of her time with the clock, and steal glances at her appearance in the mirror.[25] The 1860 inventory of B. Madore, a well-to-do farmer, lists a single and two double stoves, four beds with bedding, a dresser with crockery, two big and one small pot, two bake pans, two kettles, two tables, seventeen chairs, one chest, a churn, a frying pan, two firkins, one loom with reeds and pulleys, and two flax wheels. There was no spinning wheel, despite the presence of 40 pounds of wool. The only luxuries were two looking glasses. The total value of these items was $146.40. The collection included some new items: a dresser and more crockery than the administrator cared to itemize, enough stoves to heat at least three rooms and two of a better sort than the Cyr's, and seats with backs for everyone and more. The double stoves made oven baking possible, hence the baking dishes.[26]

The Dufours sold few household items; what they sold was basic, and similar to the items found at J.B. Cyr. Their most commonly sold article was candlewick. The Madore inventory suggests a less-than-spartan lifestyle, and Emmerson's account books and the two store inventories indicate that the goods required to achieve it were available in the 1860s. Both merchants offered a wide range of cookware including griddles, frying pans, dippers (sauce pans), and tin bakers, as well as crockery, cutlery, and a variety of glassware at different prices. Emmerson offered blanketing and counterpanes, as well as cotton batting or wadding that could be used for quilts, and he was still selling this in 1863 despite the high price of cotton. Emmerson stocked flat irons, and Costello smoothing irons. Costello's inventory lists two 40-yard pieces of carpeting at 80 cents and $1.50 a yard, as well as two qualities of carpet tacks and a piece of tablecloth fabric. Emmerson sold both in 1863 (8 yards of carpeting at 10s. or $2). Neither the inventories nor the ledger mention curtains, drapes, or blinds; Costello, however, kept ten window blind pulls, as well as latches for window sashes. Wallpaper could be purchased at both stores: Costello had 88 rolls in stock, and Emmerson one lot of room paper. Costello offered brass candlesticks and chandeliers (28 cents and 12 cents), and even two plated ones at 50 cents a piece. Looking glasses could be had for prices ranging from 12½ to 50 cents. Emmerson did not carry brass items, but sold furniture: two 'show cases' at $20 and $30, and shelves. The inventory gives lot but not individual prices for the shelves, and they are high, from $45 to $75, suggesting prices in the same range as the showcases. Few of those goods appear in the 1863 accounts, but as they were durable or semi-durable, this is not surprising. A flat iron was probably a once-in-a-lifetime purchase, and even carpeting was not replaced every year. Some items retailed at Emmerson are not listed in the inventory, probably because their turnover was high: candles (9 per cent of the customers), lamps and accessories such as chimneys and wicks (7 per cent of the clients), and oil (23 per cent of the customers and 9 per cent of the debit).[27]

The store accounts and the two inventories also indicate that a wide range of not very utilitarian, but usually inexpensive items had become available in the 1860s, and were being purchased: whalebones, skeletons for bonnets at 5 cents a piece, hoops for skirts, neckties and cravats instead of the traditional neckerchiefs, paper collars at 8, 10, and 18 cents a dozen, paper cuffs, spectacles at $1.50, razors and shaving boxes, hairnets (a few cents a piece), hair oil, fancy or toilet soap, playing cards, flypaper, starch and bluestone, cigars (Emmerson had 380 in stock at his death), umbrellas ranging from 30 cents to $1 and parasols at 75 cents, stove polish or stove blacking, and India rubber shoes at $1 to $1.50 a pair. The stores were beginning to look like dime stores rather than mere warehouses. Emmerson and his colleagues did their best to acquaint their customers with new products. Nonetheless, there were products advertised by Saint John merchants that Emmerson never purchased. Unsurprisingly he carried no archery or cricket equipment in his store, and did not bother with damask, English gold jewellery, or fancy ladies' work-baskets.[28] But he also did not buy seeds (except grass seed), agricultural machinery, or ready-made gents' clothing. Had he vainly tried to sell those items or did he believe his customers would not buy them? Emmerson stuck with the utilitarian and the traditional. If a Madawaska resident fancied writing desks, silver-plated cutlery, or an English-made frock coat, he would have to go to

Saint John and get it himself. Emmerson was a conduit for consumer goods but not for everything the new world of goods had to offer. Surprisingly, as Emmerson appears to have owned the largest store in the valley, many of the fancy goods were found elsewhere, at his near neighbour Costello. Did the storekeepers begin to specialize, Emmerson going for higher volumes of cheaper goods, and Costello trying the high end of the market? Or were the fancy fabric and brass items in Costello's inventory the results of errors in judgement, leftover goods he could not sell?

More Work for Mother

New objects were more than a matter of numbers. Their ownership sooner or later led to a reorganization of the interior space of the house, and to a different use of this space. They also led to a reorganization of women's time. Outdoor footwear has to be left at the door of a carpeted room; a space to swap footgear thus had to be provided, as well as slippers or indoor shoes. Starched and pressed clothes cannot be kept in a chest, where the pressure of the other garments would rumple them again: they must be hung or carefully folded and laid in small piles on shelves in a wardrobe. More pots, pans, glassware, crockery, and cutlery make a dresser necessary: a simple shelf by the stove and a few hooks no longer suffice. Hairnets, shaving boxes, toilet soap, hair pomade, and shoe blacking all call for drawers. So do school supplies. These new commodities could not be accumulated in a house furnished merely with a table, and a few benches, chests, and beds. Homes increasingly needed wardrobes, cupboards, dressers, and chests of drawers to keep the clutter under control, and perhaps showcases to show off the best pieces. The plain painted pieces of furniture of the previous generation may have begun to look a tad rustic: joiners were beginning to varnish, or at least sand, their work.

Oil lamps similarly brought changes to home and work. They allowed people to do some work after dark; the women could knit, spin, sew, or mend, the men could mend shoes, fix hand tools, or whittle toys. Families were no longer forced to go to bed soon after dark for lack of chores that could be done by candlelight. Longer working evenings encouraged the use of more comfortable seats: the advantage of chairs over benches became painfully obvious. Cushions for the back and small stools to lift the feet were also useful. The new light made work more visible but also made the inside of houses more visible from the outside. Curtains, drapes, and blinds suddenly became useful, and for some, necessary items to protect privacy.

The new goods had minimal impact on men's work or, like screws, were time-saving improvements. The same was not true for women. Flour and meal, whether bought from the store or produced on site, required the same amount of kitchen time. Mess pork saved the housewife a lot of work, salt fish created more (especially dried cod, which has to be soaked in several waters to be edible). But other household goods were no time savers. The common use of flat irons made rumpled clothes less and less acceptable, and starch appeared in the store too, to ensure really smooth finishes. Bluestones added to rinse water made whites looks whiter and dazzling whites became at least an ideal by which to judge the women whose laundry was drying outdoors. Shoe blacking meant shoes had to be polished. Carpets had to be brushed regularly and stains removed. Brass required regular polishing. The availability of stove blacking made dull, stained, and rusted stoves signs of slovenly housekeeping. Even oil lamps were no blessing: now that it was possible to knit, sew, spin, and mend after dark, there was no reason not to.

The new commodities made the common room cosier and more inviting and they allowed women to display a sense of aesthetics. But all was not progress on the home front. Women may have saved time sewing garments out of store-bought fabric instead of weaving their own, but they lost the advantage when they began to blue, starch, and iron the fabric. Purchasing manufactured articles did not necessarily free women's time for more productive activities. The room that no longer looked like a workshop, once cluttered with the candle-making tools, spinning wheels, and loom perhaps relegated to another room or shed, required more work from women. This may be what led them to reserve the front parlour for special occasions, like funerals or visits by the priest. As opposed to bread- and candle-making, spinning, and weaving, maintenance work became visible only when not done. Soon women would have to choose between being producers or homemakers, because there would not be enough time to be both.

Consuming Adolescents

Marie Lagacé worked for a month to buy a pair of fashionable shoes and a silk kerchief. The usual image of nineteenth-century adolescents, however, is that of working for their family and turning over their wages to their parents. Marie worked for her own benefit and she may have been more typical than supposed. Carpenter Joseph Audibert hired a succession of young helpers in the early 1850s, whose wages ranged from $6 to $18 a month for his twenty-year-old brother-in-law Simon Martin.[29] The young workers borrowed money from Audibert, or bought goods on his account until they were paid. Audibert recorded the debts in his account book. The young men spent a lot of the money on themselves; they bought clothing or fabric for men's clothes (red shirt flannel, for instance), tobacco, and drinks. They played cards, which seemed to require the buying of 'treets' or drinks by some players for the others. Pierre Albert spent 12 cents on tobacco and matches, twice 25 cents on drinks, 25 cents on liniment, and bought a pair of pants for $2.50, which left him with $2.53 at the end of the month, less than half his wages. Elie Jannot, hired at $7 a month at the beginning of November, was charged in December with a pair of shoe soles at 50 cents, and 'four glasses playing cards' on 1 December, three glasses for the house on the 9th, three glasses 'for the women' on the 15th, and one for himself on the 18th.

Tamis Bouchard, first hired in March 1851 and rehired in June, spent during those first three months 24 cents on tobacco, $1.47 on rum and 'glasses,' 70 cents for a black silk neckerchief, $3.25 for a pair of boots and stockings, $2.00 for three and half yards of red flannel and $2.50 for a shirt. The total was $10.16 out of $21 worth of wages. Most of the money Tamis spent went on his back. Audibert's brother-in-law Simon Martin spent his money on the same things: card-playing 'treets,' alcohol, neckerchiefs, boots, and red flannel. In March he was charged for goods that may have been for his parent's household: three and a half yards of satinet, three yards of woollen, two and a half sheets of batting, and fifteen yards of striped cotton. The box of shooting caps, silk kerchief, hat, opeldidock, and oilcloth suit at $2.50 he bought the same month were likely for him. The grand total was $12.90. Like Marie Lagacé, these young men bought clothes; they also smoked, played cards, and apparently paid for a round of drinks when they lost. Adolescents of both sexes were consumers.

Conclusion

New patterns of consumption emerged at Madawaska between 1846 and 1863 and more specifically between the late 1850s and 1863. Even a cursory look at the goods put to account in the various years points to change. The shift between 1846 and 1863 could reflect the fact that a different store and a more ambitious storekeeper had come on the scene. However, changes are palpable in the ten years preceding 1863: tea gained in popularity, for instance, and the little consumer items available in 1863 were not to be found five or ten years before. To be more precise, the consumer revolution at Madawaska took place between 1855 and 1860. It occurred against the backdrop of generally prosperous agriculture, the peak years of the forest industry, and a relatively abundant supply of cash. People could and did earn money, and they spent it at the store. They may also have spent it differently from their parents and grandparents. They certainly spent it on different kinds of goods.

In 1803 Frosine Martin had requested a cotton gown 'for ever' in her deed of maintenance.[30] The gown was not a true consumption item, to be worn, discarded, and replaced when it wore out or went out of style. It was something for display, a still-rare item not many women owned, and which she wore on special occasions, carefully storing it in between. Saint John Valley eighteenth-century store purchases, with the exception of the obviously utilitarian ones like salt or nails, may have been confined mostly to expensive but durable items intended for display. The scattered Hazen and White books need to be thoroughly analyzed to confirm this hypothesis, but the purchases of the Acadians during the Revolutionary War, such as high-end fabric and pewter, suggest this could have been the case. Jean Robichaud symbolized his rank in the 1770s through garments he took out of his chest on special occasions, and through a few pieces of pewter on his mantlepiece.[31] The goods the Robichaud brothers traded with the Natives in the 1790s belonged mostly to this category as well.[32] One distinguished oneself from the neighbours less by the quantities of goods owned, than by their rarity. Frosine Martin did the same by welcoming her guests on feast days in a calico dress and a white cotton bonnet, but perhaps also through offering them chocolate to drink. Consumables as well as durables could be marks of rank.

A generation later, Squire Firmin still understood the symbolic value of clothing. He sat in one of the front pews in church on Sundays, clad in broadcloth, a beaver hat on his lap. The suit and hat could be worn every week; they were intended to be replaced yearly, not to last a lifetime.[33] Firmin displayed his rank by wearing new or nearly new garments of the best material. His wife appears to have eschewed the culture of display – her clothing was ordinary. However, she requested half a dozen shirt a year, not likely to be worn out in a twelve month. She could then launder less often and when she did, a dozen or more shirts could be seen flapping in the breeze, as opposed to the two or three her less wealthy neighbours could put on the line. Wealth could also be displayed in roundabout ways.

Firmin and Eléonore Thibodeau stood poised between an older world of hospitality and display and a new one of using and discarding, of consumption. Fast forwarding to the 1860s a world had emerged where quality, durability, and perhaps cost had lost a lot of their symbolic value. Utilitarian items, like homespun clothes, were the durable ones. Sunday best increasingly had to be fashionable: gowns instead of traditional two-piece suits, with hoops, if one could afford it. Once, rank had been symbolized through the possession of scarce, high-priced, but durable goods. By the mid-nineteenth century, industrialization was putting on the market a greater variety and quantity of relatively cheap goods. What became desirable was no longer possessing a few treasured items, but acquiring novelties before everyone else, and acquiring a large number of goods. People could have continued to prefer quality to quantity and novelty. The fact they did not shows that there was more to the new patterns of consumption than new ways of showing off. Consumer items now did more than help people define their social identity; they also gave the individual greater choices, greater control over their lives, and a greater means to express their individuality. They also made life easier, more comfortable, and more fun.

Consumption patterns began to shape the role of the stores in a number of ways. First, stores supplied customers with almost indispensable manufactured objects: crockery, cutlery, pots and pans, tools, thread, needles and pins, paint, glass panes. Even oil lamps and chamber pots, though not strictly speaking necessities, became indispensable almost as soon as people tried them. Second, the stores provided their customers with items that supplemented their home production. Households covered most of their food needs through their own work and exchange with the neighbours and they made their own clothes, even if they hired a seamstress to do the work from store-bought fabric. The store made the house more comfortable with carpeting, for instance, the diet less monotonous with spices, fish, and hot drinks, and the bread better-tasting with white flour. They improved the serviceability of wardrobes with umbrellas, shawls, and shoes, and allowed people to follow fashion if they were so inclined. Variety took preference over ostentation, for the most part. Customers bought a growing variety of inexpensive fabrics rather than larger amounts of expensive ones: women preferred two calico gowns to one silk one. A similar trend was reflected in purchases of household items. The narrow range of moderately priced items available in 1846 broadened, but even in 1867, expensive crockery and cutlery were still not available in local stores. Emmerson's supplier advertised silver plated items and other luxury goods in the New Brunswick Almanac, but the new items that began to crowd Emmerson's shelves were more likely to be modestly priced ones.

The emergence of a consumer society at Madawaska translated into the ability to purchase cheap, semi-useful trifles almost at will: cotton stockings, horn combs, earthenware teapots, perfumed soap. These types of inexpensive items got people into the habit of shopping for manufactured goods and goods produced outside of the region. Rural merchants were the conduits through which the products of industrial capitalism reached the countryside. However, the customers were more than a passive audience. They could have continued to favour expensive items for display; they could have put their money into durable consumer items like home furnishings, or into production goods, like tools. This pattern did continue to a point. But people also chose to become consumers, to acquire both goods they used up quickly, like hair oil or shoe polish, and quantities of fairly inexpensive items.

The sources fail to show whether the local elite consumed differently from their neighbours, or merely consumed more. They likely did both. Consumption was also mediated by age and sex. Adult males by and large purchased to produce, and their consumption patterns probably changed little over time. Women purchased to produce as well; they also purchased for the home, for the table, to raise standards of hygiene, and to improve appearances. Men had to tacitly approve those purchases, as they were the account holders. They must have agreed that carpeted floors, gleaming stoves, and saucers under the teacups were desirable, or at least have agreed not to interfere with how the women ran the household. Young people bought clothes for show, which they coaxed daddy into allowing, or which they worked for themselves. Young men appear to have spent their earnings freely and indulged their desires with little constraint. Merchants may have proposed goods and households may have disposed of them, but the households did not operate as undifferentiated blocks. Men, women, and children were not entirely free to make autonomous purchasing decisions, but neither were women and children entirely devoid of autonomy. The counter of the general store marked one of the limits of patriarchy.

Conclusion:
Domesticating the Economy,
Commercializing the Household

Geographically, Madawaska was a backcountry settlement situated on the frontiers of New England, New Brunswick, and the St Lawrence Valley. However, it was anything but insular or inward looking. It was linked to the outside world not only by its location astride a major communication route, but also by the settlers' web of personal connections, and more importantly, by trade. The valley engaged in the successive staple economies that connected the northeastern United States, British North America, and Britain with each other: the fur trade, the trade in ton timber, and the trade in sawn lumber. The region also played a role in the development of a continental economy, first as a supplier of bread grain, and subsequently as a purchaser of North American food staples such as flour, fish and pork. It also contributed to the growth of the western capitalist world, as a purchaser of factory-made goods.

The Madawaska economy was more than an extension of the staple trade, or a passive component of the emerging industrial-capitalist order. Its history highlights the blind spots of export-led models: local economies obeyed their own logic and local residents made their own choices, they did not merely react or adapt to changes imposed from the outside. Changes could be viewed as opportunities as well. Madawaska history was also more than a chapter in the usual story of the 'transition to capitalism.' The region's residents had never been averse to trade, and their participation in commercial activities predated their settlement on the banks of the Upper Saint John. Commercialism did not lead to wholesale capitalism here, even if some local capitalists could be found. The reasons for this situation varied with the economic agents concerned. Staple producers failed to dependably accumulate capital, showed scant interest in manufacturing, and sought safety in farming, government appointments, or politics. Farmers and their wives were utility rather than profit maximizers – and were also keen consumers. In addition, more than structural changes were needed to allow capitalism to emerge. The various agents needed to develop a different understanding of the ways economies worked – not as random sequences of events, not as moral systems, but as reasonably predictable mechanisms. Those who did develop this new understanding were local service providers and local producers of consumer goods. The Atlantic trade fuelled growth, but development occurred in the middle economic layer, the one between over-the-fence barter and export trade, and it is from there that capitalists emerged.

The Saint John Valley economy functioned at two different levels, three if neighbourhood barter is included, but barter has left few documentary traces, and may have already been in decline. At some indeterminate but early date, face to face exchanges had taken a distinctively economic turn, contributing to the emergence of local markets. Here barter had migrated from the sphere of material culture to that of economic exchange, as it had elsewhere.[1]

At the most visible level, international trade in the shape of the timber and lumber trade involved distant merchants, outside entrepreneurs who may have moved to the site of their activities; it also involved directly or indirectly almost all the local population. Labourers and adolescent farmers' sons worked in the woods in winter. Farmers could derive a significant proportion of their income from the shanty trade, and additional money or credit from freighting. Storekeepers supplied the shanties and acted as intermediaries between the lumberers and their suppliers, or as timber brokers for local operators. As participants in the timber trade, all those agents were subjected to its vagaries. A downturn in the timber trade translated into free falling prices for fodder, reduced employment opportunities, and lack of cash to settle store accounts.

In the long run, the timber trade was an unreliable source of income for labourers, farmers, and storekeepers alike. It was no more reliable a source of income for lumber operators, and many failed as a result. The timber trade was not the road to riches. It was not transparent and could only appear irrational to the men on the ground. Its vagaries could not be blamed on natural calamities like insect infestations or wet summers. Somewhere, faceless and nameless human beings clamoured for timber or left it to rot on the quays, for reasons imperfectly known. This was no encouragement to capitalist behaviour, no matter how it is defined. Lumber operators and timber merchants invested little locally and tried to shift at least some of the risks onto others, whether labourers or suppliers. The timber trade consequently generated limited linkages. It was also not likely to convince anyone that taking risks on impersonal overseas markets offered good opportunities for long-term profits. The trade looked more like a lottery that produced more losers than winners. Many of those who did take part appear to have done so with an eye to the earliest safe exit.

Madawaska did not participate in the Atlantic trade solely as a provider of staples. It was also a market for European manufactured goods, like the ones imported by Messrs Hegan, Clementson, Hasting, et al. in Saint John, or for foodstuffs, from Upper Canadian flour to Indian tea, gathered in the Quebec City warehouses of Noads and Cie and others. Merchants did not foist products onto settlers to force them to increase the production of commodities the stores could resell for a profit; they appear to have collected only limited amounts of country products. If Emmerson and Morneault were typical, by midcentury merchants preferred to be paid in cash. And as most of the labour provided by the merchants' clients was used to run the trade, securing labour for a personal business venture was not the main reason to go into shopkeeping. Merchants opened stores because retailing appeared to be a profitable activity.

Merchants operated as conduits for imported goods, but exercised only limited control over what went through their hands. They not only faced competition from other merchants, but settlers could learn about available goods, and even acquire them, through their own personal connections. Merchants necessarily followed consumer markets more than they constructed them, but the consumer market cannot be explained in purely economic or structural terms. People did not only buy necessities they could not produce themselves or goods that saved them time, money, or labour. It is understandable why cotton, which was cheap, easy to wash, quick to dry, and comfortable in all temperatures would be preferred to linen. It is also understandable why chamber pots would be preferred to pails or trips to the barn. There is no practical reason that explains why women who could afford it did not invest in a good silk gown and paisley shawl, which would have lasted them twenty years or so, except that they no longer viewed their best clothes as investments. Nor are there practical reasons why collars should be stiff as cardboard, why white fabric was blued to look even whiter, why tea was served in cups and saucers rather than mugs, or why farmers should need clocks. People chose to buy these things not strictly because the purchase made economic sense or increased their level of comfort, but because they enjoyed the sense of ownership or imbued the goods with specific meaning. Ownership could emphasize their individuality, signify wealth and success, or signal respectability, urbanity, or modernity. These factors took consumer decisions out of the control of local merchants, who could merely try to offer the goods they thought would sell. Consumer decisions were also uncontrollable – and unfathomable – by Bradford or Liverpool fabric makers or Sheffield cutlery manufacturers. How could they guess that red flannel shirts of the type issued by Poor Law overseers in England would be a must-have item among Upper Saint John Valley dandies?

Merchants did not just import European or North American consumer goods. Madawaska people mostly bought inputs, goods that were used to produce other goods: fabric and notions, of course, but also weaving yarn, cookware, hardware, tools, steel, and iron. Country storekeepers operated within different levels of exchange, and provided links between them. They participated in a commercialized local economy by orchestrating exchanges of goods and services among their clients through third-party transactions. They made it possible for a rural population to trade products that then entered continental or Atlantic trade networks, and to acquire cash with which to buy foreign finished products. Stores were also the sites for the exchange of inputs. At Madawaska, the stores collected inputs for an export-based activity, such as fodder for the lumber camps, and supplied the raw materials, semi-finished products, and tools their clients used in craft production and household manufacture.

The trade in forest products was not irrelevant to the valley's economy, but its importance was mostly confined to bringing people and money into the region. Between the world of over-the-fence barter and the rather mysterious Atlantic trade emerged a lively local and regional commercial economy that was partly dependent on the other two and involved almost the same people. Farm households produced food and textiles with or without the help of labourers, and fed and clad those who were unable to provide for their own needs; the goods and services of the millers, artisans, and storekeepers were used by all. Many labourers and new farmers depended on the forest industry for a large part of their income, local and regional markets were not entirely independent of fluctuations in international trade, but they were not its handmaiden either. They obeyed a different logic: support the region's households both by providing them with necessary goods and services and by the sale of local commodities on suitable markets. The inability to meet the demand of a given market did not spell longterm disaster either; throughout the nineteenth century Madawaska settlers were able to find substitutes for goods in decline. Wheat was replaced by fodder, ton timber by sawn lumber, and at the end of the century on the American side, potatoes and their by-products replaced fodder as the main commodity linked with distant trade. The distant markets, however, were more frequently continental ones.

Proximity made the local and regional markets fairly transparent and understandable, although not entirely predictable. Crops could fail, downturns in the timber trade could reduce the income of a significant proportion of the population, but these were variables that farmers and others could factor into their strategies. One knew what people did when their income shrunk; one knew what happened when a crop failed. Farmers, artisans, millers, and storekeepers could develop contingency plans.

Rational business decisions did not then lead to profit maximizing; valley people showed no inclination to acquire the tools to accurately evaluate their profits. Farmers did not keep books, storekeepers and artisans were only interested in keeping track of active and passive debts. On the other hand, their lack of analytical tools did not stand in the way of their making rational decisions concerning quality of life. People knew when they had worked more than they wanted for a given result. Scientific management tools were unnecessary for utility maximizing. A good understanding of the functioning of the local and regional markets, commercialism, and rationality did not turn most people into capitalists, in the sense of using money to make money. Farmers who invested in better equipment, better seeds, and better stock were still very rare in 1871. Instead, they responded to market demand by working more or hiring labourers, not by altering their way of farming, or ploughing back profits into the farm. Farmers were not without ambition, but most channelled it into other directions: stores, mills, and other businesses that catered to a local clientele.

Entrepreneurship developed at the meeting place between the three economies. Farmers who stepped up production targeted two markets, trying to avoid excessive dependence on the shanty trade, but not rejecting it altogether. Lasting economic developments occurred in the regional economy, but they drew upon the profits made from farming. The agents of development were the local entrepreneurs like the custom millers, who kept as much distance as possible between themselves and the staple trade. They patiently accumulated social and financial capital over the years, if not the generations, and slowly built a lasting local infrastructure. A few became regional manufacturers. Custom mills, craft shops, and to a lesser extent stores, were in the hands of locally born individuals, often from successful farm families. Professionals (physicians, lawyers, surveyors, and teachers) who appeared later were by and large children of those same families, who had money to spare for their education outside the valley (or in the case of the girls, at the Saint Basile convent). Some used their economic prominence as stepping stones to political careers, which gave them, if not influence over decisions taken in Fredericton or Augusta, at least a better knowledge of the world in which they had to operate. It is also striking that the New Brunswick government appointed to local office people from the same small group of families who provided Maine Madawaskayans with candidates for elections. The 'top down' and 'bottom up' political systems both recognized and rewarded the same few prominent families.

The boundary between the barter economy, the local/regional market, and long distance trade was porous; so was the boundary between farming, rural entrepreneurship, and the professions, especially if politics is included as a form of profession. The local elite emerged not from among those with the closest ties to international trade, but rather those who had best been able to draw on the whole range of available markets; they personally increased their distance from the Atlantic economy, focusing instead on providing goods and services for the valley's population. New farmers who provided the more established ones with a reasonably predictable and profitable market allowed the latter to take the risk of working for the timber trade. But the local/regional market was fed by timber trade money, acquired through wage work, trade, and barter. These three spheres operated interdependently; their symbiosis makes untenable the oppositions between the allegedly antithetical worlds of capitalism and household economy, or between the two diametrally opposed economic sectors of capitalist trade and subsistence farming. It also calls into question the concept of a transition to capitalism. The three economies could not exist without one another, and operated as various levels of a single economy.

This interdependence also highlights the inadequacies of export-led models. The regional economy mattered, and it mattered a lot. It is here that linkages were created and a lasting infrastructure was developed. And it is from here that the local elite emerged. The transformations that characterized the Madawaska economy in the nineteenth century should not be seen in terms of the valley's progressive integration into the Atlantic economy. Madawaska had always been part of it. The lumber trade mattered, but it was less a transforming influence than a relatively short-lived source of opportunities and dangers, later replaced by others. The real centre of the story is the local men and women who tried to pursue their own material, psychological, or social advantages by making use of all the options available. In the end, development was primarily the result of endogenous forces, and human agency played a not insignificant role in the process. The economy was an extension of the household, not the other way around.

In the course of the nineteenth century, those men and women also developed new ways of viewing economic activities and market transactions. The nature of entrepreneurship, the understanding of business changed, and both evolutions were linked. In the still hierarchical turn-of-the-century society, men were expected to know their place, unless elevated by their betters. Economic resources were controlled by the 'better sort,' who allocated them to groups and individuals according to their station and the perceived needs of the larger community. The economy was still understood in moral terms. Acadian settlers were entitled to farms in a remote location because the British needed to protect the mail route. Louis Mercure deserved a mill site on account of his revolutionary war services. On the other hand, Dorchester, and later the post-1815 New Brunswick government, seem to have concluded that Pierre Duperré was a self-serving upstart whose services could not be completely avoided, but who should not be encouraged into thinking he was important. Frontier speculators and men who elevated themselves through their own efforts disrupted the existing social hierarchy, and needed to be kept in check. Mercure lost favour when he was suspected of being a speculator. In this context, entrepreneurship was suspect, and even potentially subversive. It may not have been an accident that Louis Bellefleur, the first recognizable capitalist in the valley, was a merchant with a pedigree, backed by the leading trader on the Upper Saint John and a high ranking Loyalist who was provincial treasurer and president of the province's first bank. For a while, Bellefleur and his sons bridged two worlds. In the end, they were thrown back into the eighteenth century, in a world where estate holding and government patronage defined one's social status and determined one's wealth. This was not a world conducive to a modern vision of business or the economy. The economy has come to be conceptualized as an autonomous system governed by identifiable laws. Eighteenth-century men still viewed it as an aggregate of activities that could legitimately be organized from the top down to reflect and reinforce the existing social order. Turn-of-the-century merchants and other men of business did not view their activities as a series of discrete adventures, did not chase the elusive windfall because they had not read Adam Smith and were ignorant of economic reality, but because they understood the system in which they operated only too well.

The next generation was a mixture of old and new, and often what made them old forced them to be new. Labelling these men a transitional generation does not do them justice. Theirs was the generation affected directly or indirectly by the timber trade. The timber trade depended on distant markets, out of the reach of the local producers and hence opaque and unpredictable. This randomness in turn could only reinforce the notion that the economy was not a rational system, an impression further reinforced by the fact that the timber trade and the forest industry were also political constructs. Colonial timber's access to the British market was initially protected by tariffs, and New Brunswick merchants were very much aware of the consequences of changes in the tariff structure. In the 1820s and early 1830s, British–born Crown Land Commissioner Thomas Baillie wanted to sell the province's timberland to wealthy capitalists, even from outside of New Brunswick, and use the proceeds to endow a permanent fund. The fund's revenue would have been put at the disposal of the British-appointed governor and his council, to render them independent of the legislative assembly (a bunch of merchants and upstarts who did not know their place). Baillie's scheme failed, and instead provincial Crown land was placed under the control of the assembly in 1837.[2] The provincial merchants and lumbermen who controlled the assembly chose not to alienate the timberland, but to auction off cutting rights. Within ten years, the assembly passed a labour act that made it possible for prospective settlers to acquire title to a farm lot upon the performance of work on local roads. Politics, not the laws of the market, still determined access to resources, and the assembly chose to make

those resources accessible to people with little capital. Maine also facilitated the acquisition of farmland by bona fide settlers but sold off
large tracts of timberland. Maine's forest resources fell into the hands
of men with capital.

Operators still treated their lumbering activities like so many discrete adventures, hoping for a windfall or a government appointment,
if they were British. They strove to minimize dangers through networking and partnership with their peers, through connections with
large-scale merchants, and through shifting risks to those they viewed
as their dependents. Their success at networking rested on their reputation for fair dealing and integrity, at least with their equals, which
inhibited any profit maximizing aspirations they may have had. Personal loyalty was also part of this culture and forced all, suppliers and
wage earners, to share the risks. Lumber operators were cultural
traditionalists but they were not archaic. As Naomi Lamoreaux has
shown, mutuality, networking, reliance on family labour (even when
the nephew or cousin's performance was less than ideal), adherence to
a common code of ethics, and strong emphasis on personal integrity
shaped the culture of early nineteenth-century merchants and manufacturers, and defined their economic strategies.[3] Glazier, Cary, and
even Emmerson shared the same understanding of proper business
behaviour as their contemporaries on the eastern seaboard, or even in
England. The moral economy was not dead, but it was less obviously
tangled in political patronage. Lumber operators were not agents of
economic modernization, though. They were still wedded to mercantile capitalism.

By bringing cash into the region, the timber trade also spurred the
emergence of a cash economy, a definitively modern phenomenon.
Storekeeper Emmerson's decision to maximize cash transactions was
likely a solution to an immediate, concrete problem: how to minimize
the dangers of failure. Cash-based trade was a safer option. Emmerson
could withstand a bad season and ease his clients' terms of payment if
he did not have to worry about a visit from a writ-carrying sheriff. Traditional storekeeping, based on a chain of credit from wholesalers to
country customers, was vulnerable to the failure of any link of the
chain, as the Dufours learned at their expense: they found themselves
in court, as plaintiffs and defendants. By trying to remain solvent,
Emmerson brought modern retailing practices into the valley. He also
likely intuitively grasped that cash-based trade was more profitable.
His own willingness and ability to pay cash gave him access to a wider

range of suppliers, and allowed him to secure competitive prices. He appears to have passed the savings on to his clients, who would take their business to him rather than to his immediate competitors. To benefit from better prices, his customers also had to pay relatively promptly and preferably in cash.

As a local entrepreneur, Emmerson, like the custom millers, was grasping with concrete problems whose terms were clear, even if the underlying causes were not, and whose solutions were commonsensical, even if they were difficult to put into practice. Local traders and businessmen could protect themselves to a point from the vagaries of the larger economy by planning and developing long-term strategies. To develop a manufacturing complex by gradually adding a carding machine, fulling mechanism, tanning pit, or smithy to a custom grist- and sawmill business needed an understanding of the nature and scope of local demand for those services. Accepting potatoes rather than eggs for credit and preferring cash to in-kind payment rested on the same type of understanding. Lumber manufacturing and storekeeping gradually ceased to be adventures and became stable providers of services to an identifiable clientele with a reasonably predictable behaviour. Farmers probably relied on similar business strategies. They tried to benefit from the forest industry without being overly dependent on it. Growing fodder for the shanties was a gamble, but in a good year could bring a windfall. Selling foodstuffs or textiles on the local market may have been less profitable, but it was also less risky.

Producers' understanding of the nature of markets shifted with the markets for which they produced. But more than people's attitudes towards market production were undergoing a change; so were their attitudes towards consumption. In the deferential society of the eighteenth century, access to economic resources were privileges bestowed by the elite upon their clients, and consumption was a way of signifying rank and signalling one's position in the social hierarchy. In the mid-nineteenth century world, when fewer personal mechanisms allocated resources, consumption became a way to convey the respectability that no longer was derived from affiliation with a powerful patron. It was simultaneously a marker of group identity and a way to assert one's individuality.

What individuals like Messrs Bellefleur, Hammond, and Emmerson, and even Mr and Mrs Average Farmer show is that the modern economy was not lurking in the wings, fully formed and ready to spring on the stage at the first opportunity. It was the result of the actions of myriad individuals groping for solutions to problems whose causes they understood imperfectly. The concept of transitional types, of individuals in a system but not of it does not work. Emmerson was not poised between two existing systems, one where retail was based on a chain of credit, and another of fixed prices and cash payments. He brought the second system into being through his decisions. He was a sculptor, not a bridge, shaping a new order out of the material at his disposal, without really anticipating what his actions were going to create. And the same was true for everyone else in the world of nineteenth-century Madawaska.

APPENDIX 1: SOURCES AND METHODS

Family Reconstitutions, Demography, and the Study of Migrations

This study is based largely on a series of databases created over the years for a series of projects. The reconstitution of all the Catholic families who lived in the Upper Saint John Valley in the late eighteenth and first half of the nineteenth century came first. Family reconstitutions collect the information contained in the baptismal, marriage, and burial registers. French-Canadian parish registers are highly detailed and allow the study of many demographic milestones. Infants were baptized within three days of their birth. In the case of emergency, the midwife or a person confirmed in the church had a duty to administer an emergency baptism, which would subsequently be recorded in the church records, even if the child died immediately afterwards. In this way, parish registers are a good substitute for birth registers. Baptismal records include the name of the child, the date of birth or age at baptism, the first and last name of the father and his occupation, the first name and maiden name of the mother, and the residence of both parents. Godparents are also listed, occasionally with their relationship to the child. Marriage records include the name of the bride and groom, their occupation, and residence, and the names, occupation and residence of their parents. In the case of the mothers, the maiden name is almost always indicated. The record indicates whether the parties were cousins, and had received special permission to marry and lists the names of the witnesses and their signatures. Burial records for unmarried people contain exactly the same information as their baptismal records. In the case of married people, the parents are not listed, but the spouse is.

The thoroughness of the records make family reconstitutions (and genealogy) easy and highly reliable. There are now computer programs to reconstitute families for demographic or genealogical purposes, but those were not available when I conducted this research, and I did the work by hand on family reconstitution cards (FRC, see figure 8). The underlying principle behind using family reconstitutions to study migrations remains the same, whether the data is computerized or not. The primary use of FRC is demographic. I found them most useful to study migrations (the database can be used to date fairly precisely arrivals and departures)[1] and kinship networks within the community. The FRC and existing genealogical material connects

Husband's name:
Husband's ID:
Birth:
Census ages:
Death:
Father:
Mother:
Residence at Mg-Groom:
　　　　Father:
Occupation:
Other spouses:

Marriage:
Date:
Place:
Consanguinity:

Signature:

Wife's name:
Wife's ID:
Birth:
Census ages:
Death:
Father:
Mother:
Residence at Marriage-bride
　　　　father
Occupation:
Other spouses:

| Name of Child | Birth date | Occ. father | census ages | | | Spouse | Marriage | Res at Mg | Spse res. | Father's occ | Death |
			50/51	60/61	70/71						
1											
2											
3											
4											
5											
6											
7											
8											
9											
10											
11											
12											

NOTES:

Figure 8. Family reconstitution card.

Madawaska families with families in the Lower St Lawrence, and links Madawaska families with pre-deportation Acadians.[2] Surprisingly, family reconstitution becomes problematic after 1850. Burials are under-registered, especially the burial of infants (there are years when no baby is reported buried). And the new priest of Sainte Luce, the Belgian-born Father Sweron, did not believe in listing the names of the bride and groom's parents.

The FRC can also be linked with population lists and censuses, the first of which is the Deane and Kavanagh report (1831). This report comprises three sections: a nominal list of land claimants, including acreage claimed and improved, buildings, date taken, ways the claim was acquired, and additional information the land agents deemed relevant; a general description of the settlement; and a head of household census indicating the number of males and females in the household. The first two parts were published by W.O. Raymond in the *Collections* of the New Brunswick Historical Society. The third section has not been published and is available, like the rest of the report, at the Maine State Archives. Almost all the Catholic households listed by Deane and Kavanagh can be linked with the FRC. The second list is the Maclauchlan report, which is really a head of households and agricultural census of the 402 households residing in the Upper St John in December 1833 (see Farm Production and Marketable Surplus below). Again, almost all Catholic households in this report can be linked with the FRC and the two reports with each other. The discrepancies between the information provided by these three sources are negligible, so that reliability of the two reports is high. However, linkages between the FRC and the lists of people granted land in 1845 (in the United States) and 1848 (in New Brunswick) under the terms of the 1842 border treaty are quite imperfect: the population is larger and there are many people who bear the same name. One can still link families, but not individuals. In other words, one can link groups of individuals when one can identify at least two of them, usually the husband and the wife. Linking the family reconstitution cards with the 1850 U.S. census and to a lesser extent the 1851 New Brunswick census was a frustrating exercise: the census-takers were English-speaking, and, especially on the U.S. side, mangled many names beyond recognition. For the same reason, linking the 1850–1 censuses with those from 1860–1 was not a very productive exercise. By 1870–1, names are more clearly recognizable; census marshals are usually local people, and even if they are English-speaking, they have some idea how to spell the French names. But the population is much larger, and between omissions, migrations, or moves across the river between the two census years, a lot of people are lost. (1870 New Brunswick residents who moved to Maine during the year were counted by neither jurisdiction).

Property Ownership and Transmission

The second database includes all real estate transactions registered in the pertinent county registry offices and at the northern Maine registry of the deeds. I found 3,474 real estate transactions relating to the Upper St John registered in New Brunswick or Maine between 1790 and 1870; only 274 related to the pre-treaty period. I used these records to reconstitute the transactions of each property owners, following the same principle as for family reconstitution. Instead of listing births and death, I listed grants, purchases, sales, and mortgages on landholding cards bearing the name of the persons involved. Each transaction is therefore transcribed twice, once on the grantor's card, and once on the grantee's. The cards also identify the land granted under the 1842 treaty. Transactions normally refer to lots or portion of lots identified with reference to the 1845, 1848, or subsequent land grants. Because acreages are not systematically indicated, I measured the land in lots using midcentury grants as the standard unit. Midcentury lots and subsequent state or provincial lots were relatively uniform in size, about 130 to 150 acres. Significantly smaller or larger properties are counted as fractions or multiples of lots. For example, the 'northern half of lot 234' is counted as one-half of a lot if it is bounded by the 'southern half of lot 243,' and as one-third of a lot if it bounded by the 'middle part' of the same lot. As few farms were sold in bits and pieces, this system works reasonably well. Once all the acts were regrouped in this fashion, I linked the landholding cards with the family reconstitution cards and when possible with the censuses.[3] Most land record cards can be reliably linked with family reconstitution cards. Wives' names are listed in case of a sale, as women were routinely asked to relinquish their dower rights to the property. Linking these cards with the agricultural schedules of the various censuses is not an easy task. Censuses, even agricultural ones, list households, which may own more than one piece of land or, in the case of tenants, none at all. Properties are not always clearly identified in land registry books. 'Old Michaud's lot up Green River' does not help us very much, even if contemporaries knew exactly what was being described. To make matters worse, this population had a rather casual attitude towards registering deeds, which was rarely done at the time of the transaction. Delays averaged three years; I have seen registration more than thirty years after the fact. As a rule, if a transaction was not registered on the spot, it would not be until the property changed hands again. Some families' wheelings and dealings are so messy that it is impossible to figure out what is going on. The county registry office records were also the source of the maintenance deeds database. Maintenance deeds (*donations entre vifs*) were contracts signed between a retiring couple and a younger one taking over their farm; the contract specified the annual goods and services the young couple was to deliver to the older one, 'or half to survivor'; later in the century, goods and services were replaced by annuities. Maintenance deeds are a particular good source to determine what people were eating.

Despite its shortcomings, the real estate database is not useless (see my several articles on property transmission), and as it clearly suggested Madawaska intergenerational property transmission patterns were typical of commercial agricultural societies, my next step was to look at farm production and more particularly at marketable surplus production.

Farm production and Marketable Surpluses

This was both easier (someone else has already devised a method to do so, and provided me with comparative material) and more complicated, because I wanted to cover the pre-census period as well. And in the census age, the territory is divided between the United States and New Brunswick. Two different jurisdictions took the census of the north and south banks of the river, asking different questions, and on different years.

Depending on the period under investigation, we can rely on:

- tithing records;
- grain bonus payment records;
- Warden Maclauchlan's 1833 report, which can be linked with Maine land agents Deane and Kavanagh's 1831 report;
- the agricultural schedules of the 1850, 1860, and 1870 U.S. censuses;
- the agricultural schedule of the 1861 New Brunswick census;
- the appropriate schedules of the 1871 Canadian censuses;

- the agricultural schedule of the 1851 census has not survived for Madawaska; only the aggregate figures published in the Journal of the legislative assembly in 1852 are available.[4]

Tithing Records

Records of tithes for the entire valley exist for March 1799, July 1799, and August 1807.[5] The March 1799 list is most likely a record of tithes paid, and the other two of tithes due. They provide us with a snapshot of field crop production in the last year of the eighteenth and the first decade of the nineteenth century. The March 1799 document lists the total quantity of grain tithed by each individual household. As the population is still very small, this list can be reliably linked with the FRC. The later 1799 and the 1807 records do not break down quantities by household, but provide aggregate figures for each type of grain, for peas, and for potatoes. The tithing year seems to have gone from July to July, but farmers apparently did not pay their tithes at a set time. According to a later tithing book, the priest estimated what was owed him and the farmers brought the goods at their convenience.[6] Tithing records are again available for the years 1835–7 and for the western parish of Sainte Luce in 1840–2.[7] By that time, the population had grown too large to accurately link households in the priest's records with the FRC.

Grain Bonus Payment Records

In 1818 the New Brunswick legislature passed a bill providing bonuses for bread grains grown on new land. To qualify, the land had to have been cleared in the last two years, and never born a crop.[8] The value of the bonus varied with the type of grain: wheat, rye, and corn fetched the highest (1 shilling a bushel, or 20 cents), and oats the lowest (4d, or about 6 cents). Nominal lists giving the name of the claimant, the quantities of each grain grown, and the amounts of money paid have survived for almost every year during which the program was in effect. The quantities reported are large. One may argue that they could have been inflated by the claimant. But quantities had to be sworn in front of a county magistrate, who presumably was familiar enough with the region to know what was realistic and what was not, and probably had been instructed to keep an eye for misrepresentation. In addition, farmers who claimed large bonuses for grain grown on new land also reported high crop averages to Warden Maclauchlan when he produced his quasi-census of Madawaska in 1833. The two documents thus support each other.

The Maclauchlan Report

The report owes its existence to the crop failure of 1833 that resulted from a wet summer and an early winter. The unfortunate inhabitants petitioned Fredericton for relief. Before taking action, the provincial government requested a report from Warden Maclauchlan. Maclauchlan proved extremely zealous. He visited every one of the 402 families still in residence, named the heads of the household, indicated the number of people of each sex living with them, and listed all the stock they owned. He asked how much they had harvested of each crop, qualified the answers with comments on their quality, asked how much they had sown of each commodity in the spring, and what the normal harvest in past years had been. Only a minority of the farms enumerated by Maclauchlan had reported crops in the past years (159 or 40 per cent)

Maclauchlan then sent an itemized table to Fredericton and the document had the expected results: supplies of meal were quickly – and expensively – forwarded to the Saint John Valley (detailed expense accounts have survived). The document is particularly useful because it lists not only the unrepresentative 1833 crops, but the previous year's averages. The estimates are quite high, and they may have been exaggerated to make the farmers' plight seem even more pitiable. But Maclauchlan had lived locally for at least fifteen years; he had been a deputy surveyor before being appointed warden of the disputed territory and would have known a tall tale if he had heard one. The figures he was given may represent averages from a good year, but are not likely to be unrealistic. And they are indirectly corroborated by Deane and Kavanagh. Their report also indicates the quantities of crops tithed and the crop sizes that can be calculated from those records are similar to those in the Maclauchlan report.[9] The acreage under cultivation can also be estimated from the quantities of seed sown, and the yield per acre by dividing the past year crop averages by the acreage sown in 1833. Not only are the resulting yields inexcessive, but they fall much below the ones reported by Deane and Kavanagh, which are obvious exaggerations:

	Wheat	Barley	Oats	Buckwheat	Peas	Potatoes
Estimated yields (bushels /acres)	11.9	14.6	17.5	8	13	132
Deane and Kavanagh's figures	20	25	30	n.d.	n.d.	250

In short, the Madawaska settlers could have grown the quantities they reported. Maclauchlan's document is internally consistent.

The Censuses

Agricultural censuses were taken in Canada and the United States every ten years from the mid-nineteenth century. But because the Saint John Valley was part American and part British North American during that period, and because the censuses on both sides of the river were taken a year apart from each other, we never get a full picture of the territory in any given year. We cannot aggregate the data, because production levels can vary a great deal from crop year to crop year. Besides, the United States and New Brunswick (and in 1871, Canada) did not ask exactly the same questions from exactly the same population. In 1850 only farms valued $500 or more were included in the agricultural schedule of the U.S. census, although but for unknown reasons, the census taker included some farms valued as low as $300. Apart from the heads of households reported as 'laborers' in the population schedule, there were 167 farms on the U.S. bank of the river in 1850. The state had granted 565 farm lots in 1845, but two-thirds of those lots were reported by the land agents as not yet improved.[10] The farms enumerated in the agricultural schedule in 1850 represent 36 per cent of the lots granted in 1845, a similar proportion to that of farms with crops in 1833. It is plausible that those 167 farms were the only operational ones on the south bank of the river in 1850. The others would still be at the clearing stage, and a literal-minded census taker would have listed their owners as laborers. The 1860 and 1870 censuses include all the farms worth at least $100. The 1861 New Brunswick and 1871 Dominion censuses include all holdings, including schools and convents that grew their own supplies of potatoes.[11] If we assume that the value of a farm reflects its productive capacity, the New Brunswick censuses should include a higher proportion of marginal farms than their U.S. counterparts, and the later censuses a greater proportion of such farms than the 1850 one. Average farm surpluses should therefore be lower in New Brunswick than in the United States and lower in 1860 and 1870 than in 1850.

Aggregate regional surpluses (what is left after the farm and non-farm populations have been fed) should evolve in exactly the opposite way. The 1850 census reports the production of only one-third of all the holdings on the U.S. side. Some crops had to be grown, and some animals kept on the non-enumerated farms. As the calculation of regional surpluses relies on the production of the farms enumerated in the censuses and on the size of the entire population of the valley, the greater the number of farms taken into consideration, the larger the regional production estimate and the estimated regional surplus.

Calculating Marketable Surpluses

The method followed here is the one devised by Frank Lewis and Marvin McInnis;[12] Rusty Bittermann has used a similar method in his work on Cape Breton.[13] Marketable surpluses are defined as the difference between net farm production and farm food needs.

Net Farm Production

Net farm production is the difference between gross farm production and factors of production. Gross farm production is the sum of field crops reported in the census, estimates of butter production using the Lewis and McInnis formula, and estimates of meat production based on:

- the number of animals reported in the census, adjusted for time of year;
- average local weight of animals at midcentury (from Johnston, *Report of the agricultural capabilities of NB*)[14]; and
- slaughtering ratios used by Lewis and McInnis for Quebec and Ontario.

Factors of production are seeds set aside, based on reported crop and contemporary seed/crop ratio, and estimates of fodder consumption, taken from Lewis and McInnis. Net farm production can then be measured:

- in pounds and shillings or in dollars, using contemporary local and regional prices for agricultural commodities (see appendix 2);
- in terms of some production unit defined by the researcher. Atack and Bateman, for instance, converted all farm production in bushels of corn-equivalent[15]; or
- in terms of calories. This is one of the approaches used by Bittermann, MacKinnon, and Wynn.

In my previous articles I have used the second method and I used the first one here. Both approaches led to the same conclusions, but leave out the following commodities:

Garden and orchard production (no data); eggs and poultry (no data); wool (under-reported); honey and sugar; wood products (only 1871 N.B. data available); domestic textile production (ibid); home manufacturing (only U.S. data available); fur trapping (only 1871 N.B. data available); farm improvements (no data); and potash and mineral production.

BREAD GRAIN CONVERSION

I converted all bread grains (wheat, rye, barley, and buckwheat) to a common unit: the bushel of wheat-equivalent. Conversion rates are derived from F.B. Morrison, *Feeds and Feeding* (20th ed.), as are those used by Atack and Bateman. They take into account both the different weight of each grain and the differences in nutritive content. For instance, a bushel of wheat weighs 60 pounds, of which 84 per cent (50.4 pounds) is digestible matter. One bushel of barley weighs 48 pounds of which 37.7 pounds is digestible matter. To calculate the wheat-equivalent one bushel of wheat = 50.4 / 37.7 = 1.33 bushel of barley.

	Weights used (from Johnston)	Conversion ratio
Wheat	60 lb	
Barley	50 lb	1.33
Buckwheat	48 lb	1.6
Rye	52 lb	1.1
Corn	59.5 lb	1
Oats	38 lb	2.2
Potatoes	60 lb	no object

FEED

Lewis and McInnis first estimates of oat and hay consumption in 1851 Lower Canada rested on the recommendation of contemporary agronomists. However, they found that the province did not grow enough to meet those requirements, with production covering only 50 to 70 per cent of need. I have adjusted their oat and hay estimates downwards to reflect Lower Canadian practices.

Annual feed estimates

	Hay, in tons	Oats, in bushels
Horses	1.52	53.7
Oxen	1.82	26.8
Milk cows	1.8	—
Young cattle	.86	—
Sheep	.15	3

Pig feed is estimated at nine bushels of various dry material; I settled on five bushels of potatoes and four bushels of the cheapest grain, under the assumption that farmers would try to spend as little as possible on feed. Potatoes were always cheaper than grain, and the smallest cull potatoes are not convenient human food.

Surpluses

Marketable surpluses are the difference between net farm production and the food needs of the farm household. The food needs are the adult food allowance times the number of adults or equivalent in the household. Children under sixteen are counted as half an adult, thus two children equal one adult-equivalent. Adult food needs are based on the requirements listed in the deeds of maintenance for Madawaska. Food requirements showed little variations in quantities and composition from one household to the next, with a few exceptions; some households required wine, rum, and brandy, and some requested a greater variety of spices than others. A few mentioned garden products, eggs, and poultry. There was no difference in food allowances for men and women.[16]

By the midcentury, wheat allowances had been replaced by store flour; fish (dry and green cod and salted herrings) was frequently mentioned as well. I used modal values to estimate yearly food allowance, which correspond to the following weekly allowances:

Potatoes	14 lb	Sugar	8 oz
Bread grains	7 lb	Dried fish	8 oz
Salt pork	2 lb	Butter	8 oz
Beef/mutton	1.5 lb	Lard	2 oz
Dried peas	1.25 lb	Salt	half a bushel
Rice or barley	1.5 oz	Tea	2 oz (the weight of 6 modern tea bags)

Milk, eggs, poultry, and vegetables could be added in season. There was no mention of cheese or honey. Pepper, the occasional spices (nutmegs and cloves being the most frequently mentioned), chocolate (enough for one cup a week when required), wine, port, rum, or brandy are listed. Beer, whisky, or gin are never mentioned. These food items in these quantities could provide a generous, but not excessive, number of calories for active persons living in a cold climate.

The figures represent adult consumption. Most historians distribute the population by sex and by age group, and assume increased consumption with increased age of children. I counted all children under age sixteen as half an adult. To test the accuracy of this simpler method, I calculated the number of adult equivalents in two control townships, first using Atack and Bateman's formula in *To Their Own Soil*, then McInnis's formula in 'Marketable Surplus in Ontario Farming,' and finally, my formula. The results were virtually identical.

Textile Production

Contrary to the U.S. censuses, British North American and Canadian censuses reported textile production until 1881. The New Brunswick census of 1851 included a question on fabric and loom ownership, and the aggregate results are included in the tables published in the journal of the house of assembly of New Brunswick in 1852. The 1861 New Brunswick census counted looms and asked for information on the value of the fabric produced. The Dominion census for 1871 included nine separate schedules: personal, death, buildings and equipment, field products, stock and animal products, manufacture/industrial, forestry products, mineral and quarries, and fisheries. Information about domestic cloth production can be found in three different schedules. The personal schedule reports people's main occupation. According to the instructions, women were to be listed as having an occupation only if they were individually paid for it. Schedule 5 (agricultural production) reports wool, flax, and cloth. Schedule 6 (manufacturing) lists 'industrial establishments,' described as 'a place where one or several persons are employed in manufacturing, altering, making up or changing from one shape or another, materials for sale, use, or consumption, quite irrespectively of the amount of capital employed or of the products turned out' in the census instructions. A profit was irrelevant; what mattered was the fact that 'raw material had changed form, and so much value had been added to it; and it is the fact to be recorded.'[17]. How the census takers understood their instructions is perplexing because weavers are not consistently listed in schedule 6. The key criterion for inclusion appears to have been the presence of a hired hand for at least part of the year. In the case of weavers, women who reported small amounts of cloth but who had paid help were listed in schedule 6; women who produced large quantities without such help were not. Schedule 6 indicates the nature, quantities, and value of input and output, the value of the equipment, the number of months worked, the number of hired hands, and their annual wages.

At Madawaska, no weaver is listed in schedule 6, not even Helene Michaud, identified as a weaver in the nominative schedule, and whose household reported 1,000 yards of cloth in schedule 5. The Bijeau household was similarly not listed in schedule 6 despite a production of 800 yards of cloth and 200 yards of linen. The narrowly defined commercial production (production for sale) of the census census clearly underestimates real production totals. Two other scholars (one a professional weaver) and I have published some research comparing Madawaska textile production with the one in two other eastern Canadian communities: Charlotte County in southwest New Brunswick, and the Argenteuil seigneurie northeast of Montreal. Weavers appear on schedule 6 for Argenteuil and Charlotte County, and I used our findings to fill in the gaps in Madawaska. Charlotte was settled at the same time of Madawaska; its economy was more diversified: agriculture, large-scale saw milling, fishing, and quarrying. Farming was poor; the soil was thin and stony.[18] The agricultural schedule for Charlotte County lists 1,101 cloth producing households. There were 122 weavers listed in schedule 6 (almost all women) and 145 weavers in the nominative census. Those discrepancies highlight the problems identified above. Charlotte County domestic textile appears to have had the same use as Madawaska's: the fabrication of work clothes and outdoor garments. As far as we can tell, Charlotte County homespun was similar to that produced at Madawaska.

Extrapolating some conclusions from one area to the other thus seems legitimate.

The Store Ledgers

The last databases were created from the books of two storekeepers in business in Madawaska before 1870: the Dufour brothers and John Emmerson. As an understanding of the nature of the sources is indispensable to follow the argument, they are described in the text. In theory, one should be able to link the lists of store account holders with the other databases, but again, this does not work very well, especially in the case of the Emmerson books. It is necessary to comb the entries in search of the mention of a spouse or child to be able to sort homonyms, for instance. The storekeepers also had difficulties keeping the various François Thibodeaux or Joseph Cyrs separate, and used nicknames ('Le maigre,' 'à la veuve,' 'à Chatacoin'). Unfortunately, we do not know whose nicknames were whose.

APPENDIX 2: PRICES USED FOR ESTIMATING PRODUCTION AND SURPLUS VALUES

Agricultural prices, 1830–71, in $

	About 1835		About 1850		About 1860		About 1870	
	High	Low	High	Low	High	Low	High	Low
Wheat/bushel	2.50	1.00	1.60	1.00	1.20	1.20	2.00	2.00
Buckwheat	.80	.80	.80	.60	.50	.45	.50	.50
Peas	2.00	1.50	2.00	1.50	1.50	1.50	3.00	3.00
Potatoes	.30	.20	.50	.40	.33	.33	.35	.25
Oats	.60	.50	.50	.30	.45	.33	.65	.50
Hay/ton	10.00	10.00	8.00	12.00	15.00	11.00	10.00	12.00
Barley	1.00	.80	1.20	.80	1.00	1.00	.50	.40
Rye	.80	.80	1.50	1.50	1.50	1.50	.75	.60
Beef/mutton/lb.	–	–	.04	.06	–	–	.05	.05
Pork	–	–	.13	.17	–	–	.17	.17
Butter	–	–	.17	.17	–	–	.08	.15
Eggs/doz	–	–	–	–	–	–	.13	.17
Sugar/lb.	–	–	.08	.08	–	–	–	–

Sources: Baillie, *An Account of the Province of New Brunswick* (1832); ACS/CSA, cahiers de dîmes de l'abbé Dionne (1835–7) F100/34/V, comptes et dîmes de Sainte Luce, 1842–3 F100/34/XIII, livre de comptes et de reçus, paroisse de Sainte Luce, (1836–51) F100/34/XXXVII; dîme de la paroisse de Saint François (1847–52) F100/34/XLII; Dufour ledger (1844–8); Emmerson ledgers, memoranda, and day books (1850–73); Emmerson inventory, 1867; Johnston, *Report on the Agricultural Capabilities of the Province of New Brunswick* (1850): *Aroostook Pioneer*, 1869.

APPENDIX 3: TABLES

Table 1 Saint John Valley population, 1790–1870

Date	Population	Increase	Annual rate of increase	Corrected population[a]	Natural increase[b]	Net migration[c] since previous reference year
1790	174	174		174		
1799	418	244	16%	418	i.d.	i.d.
1808	456	38	3%	456	i.d.	i.d.
1820	1171	715	13%	1160	481	+223
1830	2476	1305	11%	2249	638	+451
1833	2518	42	.5%	2403	336	−182
1834	2272	−246	negative	2170	98	−331
1840	3460	1188	7%	3227	869	+188
1850	6167	2707	8%	5580	1910	+457
1860 (est.)	9500	3333	5%	8400	3694	−874
1870 (est.)	14000	4900	5%	i.d.	i.d.	i.d.

Note: i.d. = incomplete data. Estimating population figures and calculating rates of growth for the Saint John Valley after 1842 is problematic. Until the signing of the 1842 treaty, provincial and American census takers visited both sides of the river. Afterwards, census marshals enumerated the population of their side of the valley only. Unfortunately, the US and NB counted their populations a year apart, so there is no available total population figure for any post-1850 census year.

It is still possible to calculate the population of Madawaska in 1850. The US took a census in 1850, and NB in 1851. The NB census includes the number of births and deaths that took place in the preceding year, and the year of arrival of immigrants. By adding the deaths and subtracting the births and the immigrants since 1850, a close approximation of the population in 1850 can be made.

In subsequent census years NB did not ask when people had entered the province. An approximation of the NB population in 1860 can be made by subtracting the 1861 natural increase from the census figure. The result is a slight overestimate of the population present a year earlier. Later parish registers were rather poorly kept; determining a reliable figure of the natural increase in 1871 is not possible. The population estimate for 1870 is exaggerated, but useful to illustrate the overall trends.

[a]These figures exclude non-Catholics who are identified through a linkage of the family reconstitution cards, the 1820, 1830, 1850, and 1860 population schedules, and the 1833 Maclaughlan survey. The 1834 provincial census and the 1840 U.S. census provide only aggregate population figures. I assumed the proportion of non-Catholics was the same in 1834 as in 1833, and estimated the 1840 proportion of non-Catholics by interpolation between the 1833 and 1850 figures.
[b]Natural increase = number of births less number of deaths; it can only be calculated for the Catholic population.
[c]Net migration = overall population increase in a given period less the natural increase over the same period.

Table 2 Real estate wealth, 1860–1

Value of farm	Non-charter families		Charter families	
	Number of farms	% of total	Number of farms	% of total
0	20	3	2	1
$1–299	218	35	38	21
$300–499	215	35	40	22
$500–999	117	19	56	31
$1000 or more	53	9	43	24
Total	623	101[a]	179	99[a]

[a]Do not add up to 100 due to rounding.

Sources: Value of farms: U.S. census, 1860; NB census, 1861. Family category: family reconstitution cards.

Table 3 Modes of payment, Dufour and Emmerson stores, 1846–63

	Year	Total credits, in $	Cash (%)	Country products (%)	% by 3d ranked mode of payment (or higher)	Third (or highest) source of credit
Dufour	1846	3611	10.8	42.9	13.7	transportation
Emmerson	1853	3593	40.8	6.6	12.1	labour
Emmerson	1863	3764	24.6	17.1	16.6	transportation

Table 4 Frequency of payments, Dufour and Emmerson stores, 1846–63

	Year	Total number of payments	Cash (%)	Country products (%)	% paying in 3d ranking mode of payment
Dufour	1846	208	28.4	40.7	34.1
Emmerson	1853	173	57.8	24.3	12.1
Emmerson	1863	162	42.0	38.7	27.6

Table 5 Transactions between John Emmerson and J.J. Hegan, 1854–64, as % of total annual value.

Received from Hegan

	1854[c]	1855	1856	1857	1858	1859	1860	1861	1862	1863	1864[c]
Cash		4.1		41.4	11.7	30.8	1.4				
Bank notes				12.5	22.3	10.9	45.6	6.7	37.2		
Unspecified[a]			29.5		15.5						
Cheques											
Financial instruments					0.9		1.4	0.6		18.1	
Drafts			17.7	3.9	16.1		34.4	8.1	25.5	2.1	
Merchandise		95.9	52.8	42.2	33.5	58.3	17.2	32.6	27.9		
Gold (British sovereigns)								52	9.4	79.8	100
Total value in $	0	4,358	6,831	7,730	15,473	5,845	14,484	5,974	5,484	7,763	4,404

Sent by Emmerson to Hegan

	1854	1855	1856	1857	1858	1859	1860	1861	1862	1863	1864
Cash		26.5	65.1	70.3	29.7	35.5	26	41.1	22.7	70.4	68.9
Bank notes		7.4		3.4	10	9.6	4.6	16.5	30.2	13.7	2.9
Unspecified[a]				6.9	16.4		9.7		47.1		24.5
Cheques											
Financial instruments	100	62.9	29.7	17.8	37.9	51.5	29.8	29.5		4.6	
Public funds[b]		3.1	5.2	1.6	4.5	3.4	10.4	12.9		5.5	3.7
Drafts on Emmerson's account					1.5		19.5			5.8	
Total value in $	1,245	2,151	7,488	11,619	14,408	14,554	28,662	15,117	2,985	10,240	4,907

[a]The listed amount includes cash and other instruments, without breakdown by category.
[b]Drafts on public treasury, public work, and school commission warrants.
[c]Incomplete years.

Table 6 Production per farm, 1799–1871, in bushels

Year	# of farms	Wheat	Buck-wheat	Bread grains[a]	Oats	All grains[b]	Peas	Pota-toes	Hay (tons)
1799	56	53	1	56	11	67	8	70	nd
1830s	159	111	3	125	74	198	39	356	nd
1833	159	37	3	46	29	75	13	229	16
1835	156	41	7	64	36	100	14	216	nd
1840*	41	38	22	100	55	154	28	268	nd
1841*	54	35	nd	69	90	159	24	232	nd
1842*	61	46	7	97	81	178	19	227	nd
1850[†]	167	8	142	176	134	310	24	171	21
1860[†]	667	6	93	122	89	211	15	133	13
1861[‡]	435	9	71	102	88	190	16	110	13
1870[†]	775	2	125	133	95	229	11	109	10
1871[‡]	862	6	73	85	73	158	10	121	7

Note: No data = nd.
* Sainte Luce only
[†] U.S. side only
[‡] NB side only
[a] including wheat and buckwheat
[b] total grain production (bread grains and oats)

Sources: 1799: AAQ, Lettres des prêtres missionnaires, 3 Mar. 1799; 1830s: Maclauchlan report, averages of past years; 1833: Maclauchlan report, current crops; 1835: ACS/CSA, Fonds Collège de Sainte-Anne, Fond Abbé Henri Dionne, Cahiers des dîmes de l'Abbé Dionne, F100/34/V; 1840: Lettres de prêtres missionnaires, 16 Sept. 1840; 1841: Ibid. 10 July 1841; 1842: Fond Abbé Henri Dionne, Cahier de dîmes de Sainte Luce, 1842–3 F100/34/XIII; 1850: MSA, U.S. census, agricultural schedule for Hancock, Madawaska, and Van Buren plantations, Aroostook County; 1851: PANB, Journal of the legislative assembly of New Brunswick, 1852, appendix 1, population returns and other statistics, Victoria County: 228–30 (the agricultural schedule was not preserved); 1860: U.S. census, agricultural schedule for St Francis and St John plantations, Glazier Lake (T17R10), Eagle Lake plantation, Wallagrass (T17R7), Fort Kent plantation, Allagash (T16R10), Frenchville plantation, New Canada, T14R11, T12R16, Madawaska, Grand Isle, and Van Buren plantations, Letter GR1, Letter LR2, Letter FR1; 1861: LAC, NB census, parishes of St Francis, Madawaska, St Basile, and St Leonard, M558 & M559; 1870: U.S. census, agricultural census for St Francis, St John, Eagle Lake plantations, unincorporated territory above St Francis, Wallagrass (T17R7), Fort Kent, Allagash (T16R10), Dickeyville, New Canada, Madawaska, Grand Isle, Van Buren, Connor plantation, Hamlin plantation, Cyr plantation, TRR1, T18R10, T17R6; 1871: Census of Canada, NB, parishes of St Francis, Madawaska, St Basile, and St Leonard, schedules 4, 5, and 6. C 10385 and C 10386.

Table 7 Production per household 1799–1871, in bushels

	1799	1807	1830s	1831	1832[1]	1833	1835	1840*	1841*	1842*	1850†	1851‡	1860†	1861‡	1870†	1871‡
# of households	72	100	403	475	113	403	[403]	140	175	250	466	550	880	621	1042	1166
Wheat	42	44	45	29	29	15	16	15	11	11	3	4	2	5	2	5
Buckwheat	1	nd	1	nd	nd	1	3	10	nd	2	51	59	34	34	94	55
Oats	9	11	30	6	10	11	13	24	28	20	46	61	41	42	73	55
All grains	53	inc	80	inc	inc	30	38	69	49	43	111	135	49	51	173	119
Peas	6	8	16	9	10	5	6	11	7	5	9	13	6	8	8	7
Potatoes	56	78	143	41	88	90	101	121	72	55	61	106	46	47	82	85
Hay (in tons)	nd	nd	nd	nd	nd	9	nd	nd	nd	8	8	nd	5	6	8	5

Note: nd = no data; inc = incomplete data
* Sainte Luce only
† U.S. side only
‡ NB side only

Sources: 1799: AAQ, Lettres des prêtres missionnaires, 22 July 1799; 1807: Ibid., 15 Aug. 1807; 1830s: Maclauchlan report, averages of past years; 1831: Deane and Kavanagh, 'Report'; 1832: Lettres des prêtres missionnaires, 16 July 1832 (Ste Luce parish only); 1833: Maclauchlan report, current crops; 1835: ACS/CSA, Fonds Collège de Sainte-Anne, Fond Abbé Henri Dionne, Cahiers des dîmes de lAbbé Dionne, F100/34/V; 1840: Lettres de prêtres missionnaires, 16 Sept. 1840; 1841: Ibid. 10 July 1841; 1842: Fond Abbé Henri Dionne, Cahier de dîmes de Sainte Luce, 1842–3 F100/34/XIII; 1850: MSA, U.S. census, agricultural schedule for Hancock, Madawaska, and Van Buren plantations, Aroostook County; 1851 PANB, Journal of the legislative assembly of NB, 1852, appendix 1, population returns and other statistics, Victoria County: 228–30 (the agricultural schedule was not preserved); 1860: U.S. census, agricultural schedule for St Francis plantation, St John plantation, Glazier Lake (T17R10), Eagle Lake plantation, Wallagrass (T17R7), Fort Kent plantation, Allagash (T16R10), Frenchville plantation, New Canada, T14R11, T12R16, Madawaska, Grand Isle, and Van Buren plantations, Letter GR1, Letter LR2, Letter FR1; 1861: LAC, NB census, parishes of St Francis, Madawaska, St Basile, and St Leonard, M558 & M559; 1870: U.S. census, agricultural census for St Francis, St John, and Eagle Lake plantations, unincorporated territory above St Francis, Wallagrass (T17R7), Fort Kent, Allagash (T16R10), Dickeyville, New Canada, Madawaska, Grand Isle, Van Buren, Connor plantation, Hamlin plantation, Cyr plantation, TRR1, T18R10, T17R6; 1871: Census of Canada, NB, parishes of St Francis, Madawaska, St Basile, and St Leonard, schedules 4, 5, and 6. C 10385 and C 10386.

Table 8 Estimates of crops, 1799–1800
crop year, in bushels

Wheat	2964
Buckwheat	78
Corn	52
Rye	52
Oats	598
Total grains	3744
Peas	468
Potatoes	3902

Source: AAQ, Lettres des prêtres
missionnaires, 22 juillet 1799.

Table 9 Grain bonuses, 1818–31

Year	1811	1819	1820	1821	1822	1823	1824	1825	1826	1827	1828	1829	1830	1831
Number collecting	1	3	14	33	32	nd	24	39	51	111	nd	nd	96	126
N of previous collectors	0	0	7	7	17	nd	8	12	24	–	nd	nd	50	28
Average bushels grown on new land, per claimant	15	46	39	45	58	nd	85	95	115	89	nd	nd	81	56
% reporting more than 34 bushels on new land	0	0	50	52	59	nd	83	79	92	87	nd	nd	85	63
% reporting more than 100 bushels	0	0	0	6	12	nd	37	31	47	29	nd	nd	25	18
Highest # bushels reported	15	65	90	113	204	nd	207	350	284	443	nd	nd	559	287
Total # of bushels reported	15	138	546	1485	1856	nd	2040	3705	5873	9888	nd	nd	7813	7050
Estimated # of acres cleared	1.25	11.5	45.5	124	124	nd	170	309	489	824	nd	nd	651	588

Source: PANB, Papers of the Legislative Assembly, Schedule of persons entitled to the bounty for raising grain on new land, 1818–31.

Table 10 Farm production as proportion of food and feed needs of farm population, 1830–71

Year	1830	1850	1860	1861	1870	1871
Bread grains	233	230	198	169	206	146
Peas	280	213	149	160	135	113
Potatoes	357	212	198	150	162	171
Oats	66	96	135	89	142	95
Hay	151	159	166	160	159	116
Beef and mutton	328	358	370	373	183	160
Pork	155	104	93	155	79	93
Butter	183	256	149	145	144	134

Sources: Maclauchlan's survey (1830s); U.S. censuses, 1850–70; NB censuses, 1851 and 1861; Dominion of Canada census, 1871.

Table 11 Farm production as proportion of regional needs, 1830–71

Year	1830	1850	1860	1861	1870	1871
Bread grains	147	138	180	125	150	119
Peas	174	118	126	111	95	91
Potatoes	214	110	167	103	113	139
Oats	50	96	135	82	142	95
Hay	135	159	166	121	159	116
Beef and mutton	204	248	300	240	120	127
Pork	103	47	76	102	52	78
Butter	120	95	121	95	95	105

Sources: as for Table 10.

Table 12 Value of farm production and farm surpluses, in dollars, 1830–71

Year	1830	1850	1860	1861	1870	1871
Value of net farm production	420	545	333	374	337	249
Value of surpluses	316	338	172	213	152	67
Surpluses as % of net production	66	62	52	57	45	27

Sources: as for Table 10.

Table 13 Farm production as proportion of farm needs, 1850–70 (farms valued at $500 or more)

Year	1850	1860	1861	1870
Bread grains	230	221	169	227
Peas	213	185	185	158
Potatoes	212	224	148	187
Oats	96	150	87	166
Hay	159	173	147	179
Beef and mutton	358	501	428	352
Pork	102	94	170	95
Butter	256	184	163	140

Sources: as for Table 10.

Table 14 Value of farm production and farm surpluses in dollars, 1850–70 (farms valued at $500 or more)

Year	1850	1860	1861	1870
Value net farm production	564	506	442	518
Value surpluses	382	324	264	311
Surpluses as % net production	68	64	60	61

Sources: as for Table 10.

Table 15 Value of farm surpluses in Madawaska, Ontario, and the northern United
States, 1860, 1861 (in dollars)

	Ontario, 1861	Madawaska NB,1861	Madawaska US,1860	NE United States, 1860
Average surpluses, all farms	210	192	212	451
Average for farms with positive surplus value	280	274	264	n.d.
Average surplus for first quartile (exceeded by 75%)	20	280	294	about 100
Median value of surplus	149	129	133	305
Average value top 25%	324	552	601	about 600
top 10%	639	780	951	1000
top 5%	830	935	1317	n.d.
% with deficit	16	23	16	8
% with surplus sufficient to feed three households	16	12	11	n.d.

Sources: Ontario: McInnis, 'Marketable Surplus in Ontario Farms'; United States, Atack
and Bateman, *To Their Own Soil*.
Note: McInnis included all the units enumerated in his calculations, not only those with
five acres of improved land; the other data in this table are based on the same criteria,
hence the slightly different averages than in previous tables.

Table 16 Distribution of tithing households, 1835

Calculated grain production, in bushels	None	less than 34	34–44	45–99	100–199	200–299	300–399	Total
Number in category	59	41	10	43	40	15	6	214
Proportion in category (%)	27.6	19.2	4.7	20.1	18.7	7.0	2.8	100
Farms with grain production only	38.1	26.4	6.4	27.7	25.8	9.7	3.9	155

Source: ACS/CSA, Fonds Collège de Sainte-Anne, Fond Abbé Henri Dionne, Cahier de dîmes de l'abbé Henri Dionne, F100/34/V.

Table 17 Farms with shortage or surplus of on-site labour, 1850–71 (as % of all farms)

Farm category	1850 Shortage	1850 Surplus	1860 Shortage	1860 Surplus	1861 Shortage	1861 Surplus	1870 Shortage	1870 Surplus	1871 Shortage	1871 Surplus	1870 % reporting paying wages
Deficit	50	33	9	28	14	21	20	37	16	27	4
Low surplus	42	25	21	17	22	15	32	35	28	19	6
Medium surplus	49	21	30	12	36	19	55	26	44	10	16
Low commercial	65	3	51	3	59	4	65	12	63	7	36
High commercial	91	0	76	0	60	7	81	12	62	4	59

Source: As for Table 10.

Table 18 Farm production and cloth production, Madawaska, 1871

Farm category	# farms in category	# house-holds producing fabric	% reporting fabric (linen included)	Average yds. of fabric per capita, by producer	Average yds. of fabric per producer (linen included)	Average value of cloth (linen excluded) per producer, in $
Deficit	391	272	70	5.25	54	32.50
Low surplus	87	77	88	6.87	55	34.80
Medium surplus	250	220	88	9.31	69	48.10
Low commercial	97	79	81	13.32	91	54.90
High commercial	29	20	69	36.44	157	96.60
All	854	668	78	7.83	67	40.70

Source: Dominion of Canada census, 1871

Table 19 Distribution of purchases by Dufour and Emmerson, by category, 1846 and 1863

	As % of customers buying goods		As % of value of all purchases	
	Dufour 1846	Emmerson 1863	Dufour 1846	Emmerson 1863
Farm equipment	1	4	1	1
Building materials	11	5	2	1
Clothing and accessories	37	40	9	12
Culture	17	31	1	2
Fabric	55	51	20	11
Fertilizer	—	1	—	1
Food	40	58	28	23
Hardware	12	31	1	6
Hand tools	28	31	6	3
Horse gear	11	38	3	2
Household	31	61	3	6
Hunting and fishing	13	17	1	1
Hygiene	17	17	1	1
Metal	20	22	3	2
Leather	12	27	1	5
Maintenance	50	42	8	3
Medicine	15	26	1	1
Notions	52	49	3	2
Seeds	1	3	1	1
Textile production	31	21	5	1
Tobacco	50	49	4	4
Other	25	54	6	10

Sources: Dufour ledger, 1846; Emmerson ledger, 1863.

Notes

Abbreviations

AAQ   Archives de l'archdiocèse de Québec
ACS/CSA Archives de la Côte-du-sud du Collège de Sainte-Anne
ANQQ   Archives nationale du Québec à Québec
CIHM   Canadian Institute for Historical Microreproduction
LAC   Library and Archives Canada
MSA   Maine State Archives
MSL   Maine State Library
NBM   New Brunswick Museum
PANB   Provincial Archives of New Brunswick
PNB   Province of New Brunswick
SMA   State of Massachusetts Archives
UMFK   University of Maine at Fort Kent
UNBA   University of New Brunswick Archives

Introduction

1 Mackintosh, 'Economic Factors in Canadian History'; Innis, *Essays in Canadian Economic History,* 3–16; Innis, *The Fur Trade in Canada*; Innis, *Problems of Staple Production*; Jones, *History of Agriculture in Ontario*; Ibister, 'Agriculture, Balanced Growth and Social Changes in Central Canada'; McCallum, *Unequal Beginnings*; Ouellet, *Histoire économique et sociale du Québec*; Ouellet, 'Le mythe de l'habitant sensible au marché'; Paquet and Wallot, 'Crise agricole et tensions socio-ethniques dans le Bas Canada'; Le Goff, 'The Agricultural Crisis in Lower Canada'; 'Response' by G. Paquet and J.P. Wallot, and 'Reply' by Le Goff. For a review of the debate on

French-Canadian agriculture, see McInnis, 'A Reconsideration of the State of Agriculture in Lower Canada.' For a relatively recent survey of the use of the staple thesis, see Gerriets, 'Economics and History.'

2 Séguin, *La conquête du sol au 19e* ; Séguin, 'L'économie agro-forestière'; Hardy and Séguin, *Forêt et société en Mauricie*; Willis, 'Fraserville and Its Temiscouata Hinterland.'

3 Lower, *Settlement and the Forest Frontier in Eastern Canada* ; MacNutt, *New Brunswick*; Troughton, 'From Nodes to Nodes'; MacKinnon and Wynn, 'Nova Scotian Agriculture in the Golden Age.'

4 North, *The Economic Growth of the United States*; North, 'Location Theory and Economic Growth'; McCusker and Menard, *The Economy of British America*; Perkins, *The Economy of Colonial America*; Hoffman, et. al., *The Economy of Early America*; Bidwell and Falconer, *History of Agriculture in the Northern United States*; Bogue, *From Prairie to Corn Belt*; Danhoff, *Changes in Agriculture*; Gates, *The Farmer's Age: Agriculture*; Shannon, *The Farmer's Last Frontier*; Russel, *A Long Deep Furrow*; Atack and Bateman, *To Their Own Soil*.

5 Atack and Bateman, *To Their Own Soil*, 6.

6 Already noted in 1984 by Richard Sheridan in his essay 'The Domestic Economy' in Greene and Pole, *Colonial British America*.

7 A 1996 U.S. volume summarizes: 'At the beginning of the XIXth century, a largely subsistence economy of small farms and tiny workshops, satisfying mostly local needs through barter and exchange, gave place to an economy in which farmers and manufacturers produced food and goods for the cash rewards of an often distant market place,' Stokes and Conway, *The Market Revolution in America*, 1.

8 In the United States, the debate has divided historians in two camps, one that can be labelled 'economic historians' or 'market historians' and the other 'social historians' or 'household economists.' For the former see: Grant, *Democracy in the Connecticut Frontier Town of Kent*; Lemon, *The Best Poor Man's Country*; Bushman, *Puritan to Yankee*; Wolf, *Urban Village*; Rothenberg, 'The Market and the Massachusetts Farmers'; Appleby, *Capitalism and a New Social Order*; Perkins, *The economy of Colonial America*; Rothenberg, *From Market Place to a Market Economy*; Lemon, 'Comments on James Henretta's "Family and Farm."'

For the second group see: Waters, 'Patrimony, Succession and Social Stability,' 'Family, Inheritance and Migration in Colonial New England,' and 'The Traditional World of the New England Peasants'; Mutch, 'Yeoman and Merchant in Pre-industrial America'; Merril, 'Cash Is Good to Eat'; Henretta, 'Families and Farms'; Clark, 'Household Economy,

Market Exchange, and the Rise of Capitalism in the Connecticut Valley';
Clark, *The Roots of Rural Capitalism*; Henretta, *The Origins of American Capitalism*. For a recent survey of the argument see Appleby, 'The Vexed
Story of Capitalism Told by American Historians.'

In the United States, the debate over the transition to capitalism has
segued into one on the 'Market Revolution' after the publication of
Charles Sellers's book *The Market Revolution*. See Ellis et al., 'A Symposium on Charles Sellers'; Johnson, 'The Market Revolution'; Gilje 'Special
Issue on Capitalism in the Early Republic'; Stokes and Conway, *The
Market Revolution in America*; Bushman, 'Markets and Composite Farms
in Early America'; Feller, 'The Market Revolution Ate My Homework.'

This debate has had only faint echoes in Canada. Canadian historians
are aware of its existence, and may refer to it, but have resisted using the
categorization of Canadian farmers as either pre-capitalist or capitalist as
the basis of their interpretations. The exception is Allan Greer, who
adopted the household economy model: Greer, *Peasants, Lord, and Merchant*. Gérard Bouchard's theory of 'co-integration' has not made any disciples either: Bouchard, *Quelques arpents d'Amérique*.

9   Kulikoff, 'The Transition to Capitalism in Rural America,' 143
10 Kulikoff, *The Agrarian Origins of American Capitalism*.
11 Bouchard, *Quelques arpents d'Amérique*.
12 Bushman, 'Markets and Composite Farms in Early America,' 364.
13 An early critique can be found in Buckley, 'The Role of Staple Industries
    in Canada's Economic Development.' See also McInnis, 'Marketable Surpluses in Ontario Farming,' 'Ontario Agriculture at Mid-Century,' and
    'Perspectives on Ontario Agriculture'; McCalla, 'The Internal Economy of
    Upper Canada,' and *Planting the Province*; Lewis and Urquhart, 'Growth
    and the Standard of Living in a Pioneer Economy.'
14 Courville, Robert and Séguin, 'The Spread of Rural Industry in Lower
    Canada'; Courville, 'La crise agricole du Bas Canada'; 'Un monde rural
    en mutation,' 'Croissance villageoise et industrie rurale dans les
    seigneuries du Québec,' and *Entre Ville et Campagne*, 40, 248; McCallum,
    for instance, credited wheat for Ontario's prosperity, but rejected the
    notion Quebec farmers' inability to take advantage of the wheat trade
    was the sole reason for their performance – the lack of urban markets
    was. McCallum, *Unequal Beginnings,* 4–5. Similarly, Bouchard did not lay
    the blame for the late commercialization of Saguenay agriculture at the
    feet of the forest industry, as did the earlier tenants of the agro-forestry
    system, but attributed it to the lack of regional urban markets.
15 McNeil, 'Early American Communities on the Fundy' and 'Society and

Economy in Rural Nova Scotia'; Acheson, 'New Brunswick Agriculture at the End of the Colonial Era'; Mancke, 'At the Counter of the General Store'; Gerriets, 'Agricultural Resources, Agricultural Production and Settlement at Confederation'; Bittermann, 'Middle River'; 'Farm Households and Wage Labour'; and Bitterman, 'The Hierarchy of the Soil'; Bittermann, MacKinnon, and Wynn, 'Of Inequality and Interdependence'; Inwood and Wagg, 'Wealth and Prosperity in Nova Scotia Agriculture'; MacKinnon, 'Roads, Cart Tracks, and Bridle Paths'; Lewis, 'Rooted in the Soil.'

16 A good example of such an emerging regional market is the Philadelphia region, studied by Lindstrom, *Economic Development in the Philadelphia Region*. For the colonial period, see Shammas, 'How Self-sufficient Was Early America?'; and Newell, *From Dependency to Independence*, whose thesis is similar to Innis, *Creating the Commonwealth*. See also Matson, *Merchants and Empire*. Three interesting recent studies spanning the eighteenth and nineteenth centuries are Wermuth, *Rip Van Winkle's Neighbors*; Bruegel, *Farm, Shop, Landing*; and Gruenwald, *River of Enterprise,* For earlier and influential work see Clark, *The Roots of Rural Capitalism*; Rothenberg, *From Market Place to a Market Economy*; Hobbs-Pruitt, 'Self-Sufficiency and the Agricultural Economy of Eighteenth-Century Massachusetts'; Vickers, 'Competency and Competition'; Taylor, *William Cooper's Town*; and Bushman, 'Markets and Composite Farms in Early America.'

17 For instance see McCalla, *Planting the Province*; Courville, *Entre ville et campagne*; Greer, *Peasant, Lord, and Merchant*; Rothenberg, *From Market Place to a Market Economy*; Newell, *From Dependency to Independence*; Clark, *The Roots of Rural Capitalism*; Wermuth, *Rip Van Winkle's Neighbors*; Bruegel, *Farm, Shop, Landing*; Lindstrom, *Economic Development in the Philadelphia Region*; Jensen, *Loosening the Bonds*. This selection is not meant to be exhaustive.

18 Taylor, *Liberty Men and Great Proprietors*, 103.

19 Barron, *Those Who Stayed Behind.*

20 Wynn, *Timber Colony*; Little, *Crofters and Habitants*, 134–55; Little, *Nationalism, Capitalism and Colonization*; Bouchard, *Quelques arpents d'Amérique*; Lewis and Urquhart, 'Growth and the Standard of Living in a Pioneer Economy.'

21 Sandwell, 'Rural reconstruction,' 6.

22 Ibid., 19.

23 In 1984 Jacob Price called demand 'the great unexplored frontier' of Early American history. Price, 'The Transatlantic Economy,' in Greene and Pole,

Colonial British America, 26. Obviously, his advice fell mostly on deaf ears. Breen reiterated the same idea a few years later. Breen, 'An Empire of Goods,' 467. For other studies of consumption in the seventeenth and eighteenth centuries see Breen, 'Baubles of Britain'; Shammas, 'The Domestic Environment in Early Modern England and America'; ' How Self-sufficient was Early America?'; and *The Pre-Industrial Consumer in England and America*; Ruddel, 'Consumer trends Clothing, Textile and Equipment in the Montreal Area.'

24 McCusker, 'Measuring Colonial Gross Domestic Product,' McCalla followed his study of producers in *Planting the Province* with work on retail and consumption: see McCalla, 'The Needs of Farm Households'; 'Retailing in the Countryside'; 'Consumption Stories'; and 'Textile Purchases by Some Ordinary Upper Canadians.'

25 Breen, 'The Meaning of Things,' 230.

26 Mancke, 'At the Counter of the General Store.'

27 Newell's *From Dependency to Independence*, 97–8, supports this claim.

28 De Vries, 'Between Purchasing Power and the World of Goods'; and 'The Industrial Revolution and the Industrious Revolution'; Weiss, 'Long Term Changes in U.S. Agricultural Output per Worker'; Jensen, *Loosening the Bonds*, 87–90; Osterud, *Bonds of Community*, 211; Craig and Weiss, 'Agricultural Productivity Growth During the Decade of the Civil War'; Boydston, 'The Woman Who Wasn't There'; Craig, 'Y-eut-il une "révolution industrieuse" en Amérique du Nord?'

29 McMurry, *Transforming Rural Life,* and 'American Rural Women and the Transformation of Dairy Processing.'

30 Clark, *Roots Of Rural Capitalism*, 160; McCalla, *Planting the Province*, 93; Courville, Robert, and Séguin, 'The spread of Rural Industry in Lower Canada'; Courville, 'Croissance villageoise et industrie rurale dans les seigneuries du Québec'; Vickers, 'Competency and Competition'; Newell, *From Dependency to Independence*, 99.

31 My definition of entrepreneur is the dictionary's: 'The organizer of an economic venture: especially one who organizes, owns, manages and assumes the risks of a business.' *Webster's Third New International Dictionary*, 1961.

32 Clark, *Roots of Rural Capitalism*, 166; Greer, *Peasant, Lord, and Merchant:* 175; Nobles, 'The Rise of the Merchant in Rural Market Towns.'

33 Courville, 'Villagers and agriculture in the seigneuries of Lower Canada'; McCalla, 'Rural Credit and Rural Development in Upper Canada'; Dépatie, 'Commerce et crédit à l'île Jésus.'

34 Martin, 'Merchants and Trade of the Connecticut River Valley'; Taylor,

William Cooper's Town; Bruegel, *Farm, Shop, Landing*, 163–6; Wermuth, 'New York Farmers and the Market revolution; and *Rip Van Winkle's Neighbors*, 52–62; Gruenwald, *River of Enterprise*. See also Martin, *Profits in the Wilderness*.

35 'Historiquement, il faut parler, à mon sens, d'économie de marché dès qu'il y a fluctuation et unisson des prix entre les marchés d'une zone donnée, phénomène d'autant plus caractéristique qu'il se produit à travers des juridictions et souverainetés différentes.' Braudel, *Civilisation matérielle*, 195. The notion of 'market economy' in the early modern period may seem strange at first glance, as various layers of government did not hesitate to step in and regulate marketplace activities. But as Braudel argues, many of the rules and regulations were meant to prevent a minority from cornering the market. In a sense, the rules against forestalling and engrossing proceeded from the same motivations as current antitrust laws or laws against insider trading. In addition, the authorities were far from micromanaging every activity in the marketplace. McCusker and Menard use the same yardstick to determine the existence of markets: 'Economists understand by the term *Market* ... the whole of any region in which buyers and sellers are in such free intercourse with one another that the prices of the same goods tend to equality easily and quickly.' Interestingly, the definition is a vintage one: McCusker and Menard get it from Alfred Marshall, who borrowed it from a nineteenth-century French economist. McCusker and Menard, *The Economy of British America*, 303, quoting Marshall, *Principles of Economics*, 324, who was quoting Augustin Cournot, *Recherches sur les principes mathématiques de la théorie des richesses*. Price synchronicity is also the criteria used by Rothenberg, *From Market Place to a Market Economy*.

36 Braudel, *Civilisation matérielle*, 2; and *Afterthoughts on Material Civilization and Capitalism*.

37 McCusker and Menard argue for broad price synchronicity between England and British North America by the eighteenth century, for instance. McCusker and Menard, *The Economy of British America*, 66.

38 Mancke, 'At the Counter of the General Store'; Carter, 'An Economy of Words'; Wallace-Casey, 'Providential Openings.'

39 Braudel, *Civilisation matérielle*, 4.

40 Bruegel, *Farm, Shop, Landing*, 3.

41 Appleby, *Economic Thought and Ideology in Seventeenth Century England*. See also Newell, *From Dependency to Independence*, pt 2.

42 Clark, *The Roots of Rural Capitalism*; Vickers, 'Competency and Competi-

tion'; Bruegel, *Farm, Shop, Landing*; Newell, *From Dependency to Independence.*

43 McCalla,'The Ontario Economy in The Long Run.'

44 Local government came very late to New Brunswick. Initially, local governance was patterned on the English system of quarter sessions. Parish officers and justices of the peace were appointed at the pleasure of the Crown. By-laws were passed by the provincial house of assembly, which also doled out funds for local work and services out of provincial revenues. Only poor rates were levied locally, except in Acadian districts where poor relief was left to the Catholic Church. An 'Act for the establishment of municipalities' was passed by the legislature in 1851, but the law was permissive only and did not require their creation. As taxation normally accompanied incorporation, local ratepayers made sure they did not take advantage of the possibility. Only in 1877 was an act passed requiring the incorporation of all counties, which operated as rural municipalities. Whalen, *The Development of Local Government in New Brunswick.*

45 Albert meticulously chronicles the religious history of the settlement in his *Histoire du Madawaska.*

46 Ganong, 'A Monograph of the Origins of Settlement in the Province of New Brunswick,' 103.

47 McCallum, *Unequal Beginnings*, 88; Lamontagne and Harvey, *La production textile domestique au Québec.*

48 Lamoreaux, 'Rethinking the Transition to Capitalism.'

49 A problem highlighted by Rothenberg in 'The Market and the Massachusetts farmer,' 4–5. Gloria Main is equally critical of this attempt at second guessing motives: 'Debates over the unknown and unknowable mental attitudes strike us as sterile.' 'The Red Queen in New England,' 125n16.

50 'Capitalist' and 'commercial' are not synonymous, as any historian of English medieval manorial economies will attest. See Beckett, *The Agricultural Revolution*; Cooper, 'In Search of Agrarian Capitalism'; Allen, *Enclosure and the Yeoman.*

51 This advice was given as early as 1986 by American historian Darett B. Rutman: 'Historians' efforts to characterize early American life should be directed not by an assumption about the mind of Anglo-America and its small communities, but by the broad social process underway to which those communities – or at least the studies of them – testify.' Rutman, 'Assessing the Little Communities of Early America,' 172.

52 Merril, 'Putting Capitalism in His Place,' 322.

1: People on the Move

1 University of Maine at Fort Kent, Acadian archives, Audibert papers.
2 Johnston, *Notes on North America*, 70.
3 Albert, *Histoire du Madawaska*, 76; Bernard, *Histoire de la survivance Acadienne*, 187–188.
4 Martin, Review of *Coalescence of Styles*, 610.
5 The terms 'emigrant' and 'immigrant' refer to people moving from one political entity to another. People who move within the same political entity are 'in-migrants' or 'outmigrants.' Those labels do not work in the valley. Immigrant is appropriate for pre-1867 newcomers from the St Lawrence Valley, as Lower Canada and New Brunswick were independent until that date. After 1867, however, Lower Canadians moving to the north bank of the river should be called in-migrants, and those moving to the south bank, immigrants. People moving from the south bank to the north and the reverse should also be called immigrants, but not before 1842. For the sake of clarity, I refer to all people moving into the valley from outside its boundaries as immigrants. People who moved back and forth between the two banks of the river before and after 1842 were merely moving around within their community. They were not migrating.
6 ANQQ, Greffes de Me N.C. Levesque, notaire à Québec. Contract for the sale of a sawmill between J.B. Thibodeau and J.B. Cormier of St Pierre de la Rivière du Sud, to J. de Saint Felix, Knight and Equerry of Saint Thomas de la Rivière à la Caille, 17 Jan. 1768. Genealogical information from Charbonneau and Légaré, *Répertoire des actes*, a transcription of all vital records in the Old Province of Quebec, supplemented by census data for the period. The printed version ends with the year 1765; the more recent CD-ROM version with 1800.
7 The 1783 Studholme report lists Cormier as having settled on the Lower Saint John sixteen years previously. Thibodeau is not listed. Raymond, 'Papers relating to Townships on the Saint John.' This work contains a transcription of the Studholme report, which lists the names of all the French inhabitants above St Ann's Point.
8 MacNutt, *New Brunswick*, 79–82; Ganong, 'A Monograph of Historic Sites in the Province of New Brunswick'; 'Additions and Corrections to Monographs' ; 'Papers Relating to the Townships on the Saint John'; Hannay, 'The Maugerville Settlement'; MacBeath, 'New England Settlements in Pre-Loyalist New Brunswick'; Young, 'Planter Settlements in the Saint

John Valley'; Raymond, *The River Saint John*; Moore, *Sunbury County, 1760–1830.*

9 The movements of the Acadians from 1755–85 are easier to trace than expected, thanks to an abundance of genealogical material. See Arsenault, *Histoire et généalogie des Acadiens*; Bergeron, *Le Grand Arrangement des Acadiens au Québec*; Charbonneau and Légaré, *Répertoire des actes.*

10 PANB, Land Petitions and Application Books, petition from François Violet, 28/Aug./1786, F1032; Petition from Joseph Terrio, 28/June/1786, F1032; Raymond, 'First Governor...'; Ganong, 'Monograph of the Origins Of settlements'; Raymond, ed., 'Papers Relating to Townships on the Saint John.'

11 PANS, Minutes of the Executive Council, RG1 v. 212, memorial from several Acadians, 29/Aug./1767; Ganong, 'Monograph of Historic Sites,' 268–70; and 'Origins of Settlements,' 67. Two Acadians were even formally settled on proprietors' land: François Cormier had 'a title from Lewis Mitchell through Capt. Ferguson, one of the grantees' and Oliver Thibodeau had a lease from a Richard Shorne, for 999 years.' Raymond, 'Papers Relating to Townships on the Saint John.'

12 Raymond, 'Sunbury County Documents'; Clark, *The Siege of Fort Cumberland*, 83.

13 NBM, Hugh T. Hazen Collection, Hazen and White account book, 1775–9, F82.

14 In addition to the material on Maugerville and Sunbury listed in nn. 8 and 12, see Campbell, 'Simonds, Hazen and White'; Acheson, 'Simonds, James'; Campbell, 'William Hazen'; Raymond , 'Letters Written at Saint John by James Simonds'; Raymond, ed. 'Selections from the Papers and Correspondence of James White'; 'The James White Papers, continued'; Condon, *The Envy of the American States*: 8, 75–7.

15 Spay, 'William Davidson (John Godsman)'; Young, 'Beamsley Perkins Glasier.'

16 Raymond, 'James White Papers,' 52.

17 The history of the Lower St John Acadian settlements is discussed in greater detail in Craig, Dagenais, Ornstein, and Dubay, *The Land in Between.*

18 Hudon, 'Jean Baptiste Grandmaison.'

19 PANS, Minutes of the Executive Council, RG1 vol. 136 and 212; Johnson and Martijn, 'Les Malécites et la traite des fourrures'; Massé, 'La guerre des fourrures'; Hudon, ' Les négociants de Kamouraska.'

20 Laberge, *Histoire de la Côte du Sud*, 89, 92, 165, 116; Hudon, 'Jean-Baptiste Bonenfant'; and 'Jean Baptiste Grandmaison.'
21 ANQQ, Greffes de Me Leveque, obligation du 10 mars 1765.
22 Condon, *The Envy of the American States*, 2, 85; Wright, *The Loyalists of New Brunswick*, 61–92.
23 Condon, *The Envy of the American States*, 99–106; Wright, *Loyalists of New Brunswick*, 124–5; Hannay, 'The Maugerville Settlement,' 84.
24 Hannay, *History of New Brunswick*, 139; Condon, *The Envy of the American States*, 132–3; MacNutt, *New Brunswick*. For a description of the conflict between the Loyalists and the Planters, see Edward Winslow to Ward Chipman, 26 April 1784, in Raymond, *Winslow Papers*: 192
25 But not the Natives who were, in Edward Winslow's words, 'of course compelled to leave the banks of the rivers [particularly the Saint John] and hunt on other grounds.' Raymond, *Winslow Papers*, 510.
26 PANB, land petitions and application books, petition from Augustin Le Blanc and others, 24 November 1784, RS108, F1024. Carleton was appointed in July 1784; Raymond, *Winslow Papers*, 213. He arrived in November, ibid., 251. Leblanc's grant was issued only in Jan. 1786.
27 PANB, land petitions and application books, RS108, F1024–F1039.
28 The Acadians rarely appear in the land petitions book, which recorded all petitions pertaining to landownership sent to the governor and his council, including complaints and challenges. This cannot be attributed to reticence, as the Acadians made extensive use of their right to petition to obtain redress. The small number of protests probably reflects the small number of problems. PANB, Land Petitions Books, RS108, microfilm F1024–F1039. For Acadian behaviour see Griffiths, 'Petition of the Acadian Exiles.'
29 PANB, York County registry office, F 5618, books 1–4, 1785–1815; PANB, land petitions and applications books, F1024–F1038, 1784–1792. These books are indexed.
30 One pound currency = $4. Those who had no title yet to their holdings did not fare any worse, as in January 1785 the governor-in-council had decided that occupants could sell their claim. Applicants for a grant to the property could not get title until it was proven that they had compensated the previous occupant for his improvements, if any. PANB, land petitions and application books, F1024
31 PANB, land petitions and application books, Petition from the Memramcook settlers (1792), F 1038. Brun, 'Histoire socio-démographique du Sud-Est du Nouveau Brunswick,' 63.

32 The small group of families who soon after reconstituted the French Village near Fredericton assimilated to the surrounding English culture within three generations. By 1860, there were no French-speaking people left in the area, although there were still people bearing French surnames.

33 In 1790 Park Holland, surveyor of the Bingham purchase, whose activities led him all the way to the Upper Saint John, described the French as having 'removed themselves in anger.'

34 Brun, 'Histoire socio-démographique du Sud-Est du Nouveau Brunswick,' 63.

35 Marie-Victorin, 'Le portage du Témiscouata,' 73, 76. For a history of the route under the French regime, see Raymond, 'Earliest Route of Travel between Canada and Acadia.'

36 ANQQ, Cours de Justice du Régime anglais, Cours du Banc du Roi, 1784, TL 999; Chipman, *Remarks upon the Disputed Points of Boundary,* 61; Marie-Victorin, 'Le portage du Témiscouata,' 75; Delâge and Gilbert, 'La justice coloniale britannique et les Amérindiens au Québec.'

37 MacNutt, *New Brunswick,* 102; Brymer, *Report on Canadian Archives,* 1895, state papers, New Brunswick, letter from Glenie to Nepean, 24 Mar. 1792: 26.

38 PANB, land petitions and application books, petition 14 Nov. 1789; petition 30 Apr. 1790.

39 Brun, 'Histoire socio-démographique,' 63.

40 Ibid., 60–75; I have covered in greater detail the migrations to Madawaska and the experience of the immigrants in 'Kinship and Migration to the Upper Saint John Valley'; 'Early French Migrations to Northern Maine'; and 'Migrant Integration in a Frontier Society.'

41 French-speaking Madawaska settlers who were not Acadians all came from the St Lawrence Valley. I use the term French Canadians to refer to this group.

42 Laberge, *Histoire de la Côte du Sud,* 74–84.

43 Beauregard, Laberge, 'Famille, parenté et colonisation en Nouvelle France.'

44 Lechasseur et al., *Histoire du Bas St Laurent*; Frenette, et al., *Histoire de la Gaspésie*; Girard and Perron, *Histoire du Saguenay–Lac-St.-Jean.*

45 My study of migrations to Madawaska is based on the reconstitution of all the families mentioned in the parish registers of St Basile, St Bruno, and Ste Luce between 1792 (erection of the first parish) and 1850. This data is supplemented by the 1783 census of the Lower Saint John transcribed by Raymond, Arsenault, *Histoire et généalogie des Acadiens,* and a genealogical dictionary of the Upper Saint John Valley, which traces fami-

lies to their first ancestor in North America: Langlois, *Dictionnaire généalogique du Madawaska*. For a description of family reconstitutions, see appendix 1.

46 Craig, 'Migrant Integration.'

47 PNB, Crown Land Office, survey map of the Mazzerolle grant, 1790.

48 MacNutt, *New Brunswick*, 70–2, 123.

49 PNB, Crown Land Office, survey map of the Soucy grant, 1794.

50 PANB, land petitions and application books, applications of François Violet, 3 Mar. 1824, Celestin Thibodeau, 5 June 1824, and James Cyr alias Crock, 3 Aug. 1827. These petitions are the last that mention a survey at Madawaska.

51 I will use the term 'Charter Family' to refer to all families at Madawaska before 1800.

52 Craig, 'Migrant Integration.'

53 *Bangor Register* (Bangor, ME), 10 October 1827; *Republican Journal* (Belfast, ME), 12 August 1829; PANB, Journal of the House of Assembly, 13 and 20 Feb., 1, 11, and 14 March 1834; 1840: 159–60; Papers of the Legislative Assembly Relating to the Settlement of Madawaska, 1834; Papers of the Legislative Assembly, Report of the Commissioner of Affairs at Madawaska, 1834.

54 PANB, Papers of the Legislative Assembly, Papers Relating to the Settlement of Madawaska; Letter from Mercier, priest, dated 14 Nov. 1833; Certificate of Commissioners Rice and Maclauchlan, 16 Nov. 1833.

55 PANB, Journal of the House of Assembly, 1840, 159–60; MSA, Second annual Report of the secretary of the Maine Board of Agriculture, 12.

56 Since 1838 land suitable for settlement in Maine had been sold for 50 cents an acre. One fourth of the price was to be paid in cash over a four-year period, and the rest in 'settling duties,' work on roads or bridges. The policy was extremely generous and made land accessible to men of limited means. Smith, 'Maine and its Public Domaine.' New Brunswick policies concerning the disposal of crown land were initially less generous. In 1827 London put an end to the granting of free Crown land in British North America. Between 1827 and 1849, land was to be sold. New Brunswick land was disposed of in one of two ways. Two-hundred-acre-settlement lots were available by petition. The Crown land office set the price. Between 1848 and 1856, Crown land at Madawaska sold for 3 shillings an acre. Crown land was also available at public auction at 3 shillings an acre. A would-be farmer purchasing two hundred acres of public land on the British side of the Madawaska Territory would be charged £30 ($120), which had to be paid entirely in cash in four £7 10s.

($28.50) yearly installments. If he purchased the same amount of land from the state of Maine, he would pay $100 (or £25), $25 (£6 5s.) in cash in four installments, and the rest in road labour. Not surprisingly, post-treaty immigrants to the Saint John Valley were initially more likely to settle on the U.S. side. In 1849 the provincial house of assembly passed a labour act, which allowed settlers to pay for their land in labour on local public roads, making New Brunswick land more affordable. After 1872 groups of settlers could obtain a block grant in New Brunswick under the free grant act. Ganong, 'A Monograph of the Origins of Settlements,' 101–2.

57 AAQ, Lettres des prêtres missionnaires, letter dated 16 Sept. 1840.
58 Demographically active couples were not the only people to move in; single people of both sexes came as well. Information about these unmarried immigrants is almost non-existent. The marriage acts of those who married at Madawaska tell us where their parents resided at the time. This helps us locate the origins of migrants who came alone, but does not tell us when they came into the valley, how long they resided there before marriage, how many they were, nor what proportion left still single. The experience of the single migrants escapes us almost entirely.
59 MSL, Second Annual Report, 12.
60 The genealogical data is taken from the usual sources.
61 Deane and Kavanagh, 'Report,' 411, 438.
62 He was the son of Jean Baptiste Cyr and Marguerite Cormier of Beaubassin. He does not appear in the village baptismal records, and thus had to have been born after 1755, when the village was destroyed, and before 1765, when his mother turned 50.
63 The Cyr family was from Beaubassin. LAC, Marriage registers, Lacadie and Napierville; LAC, Census of Lower Canada, 1825, district de Lacadie. The history of the Acadian settlements in the Richelieu can be found in Bergeron, Le Grand Arrangement; DeLery was part of the seigneuries acquired by Gabriel Christie after the Conquest; see Noël, The Christie Seigneuries, esp. ch. 3 and 4. Gabriel Christie also owned the seigneurie of Rivière du Loup at the entrance of the Temiscouata Portage until 1805, when he sold it to M. Fraser, who subsequently acquired the Madawaska seigneurie around Lake Temiscouata.
64 AAQ, Lettres des prêtres missionnaires,16 Jan. 1809.
65 After tracking down the marriages of the father and sisters in the usual genealogical compilations, I obtained a copy of the marriage acts, indicating occupations, from the PRDH (Programme de démographie historique de l'université de Montréal). The Madawaska genealogical sources are

the usual ones. Marie Luce was the daughter of Jean Baptiste, himself the son of Joseph and Marguerite Blanche Thibodeau. Joseph Audibert left a paper trail: his marriage record, a mention in the 1850 U.S. census, his enlistment in the U.S. army, and a small notebook where he consigned his accounts receivable and in which he kept a few letters sent to him. The latter documents are in possession of the family, but a microfilm copy is available at UMFK, Acadian Archives. These letters are the only ones from, or to, a Saint John Valley family for the period before 1870.

66 LAC, Census of the Canadas, Quebec City, 1852.

67 Langellier, 'Tickling the Past.' The Bourbonnais French were farmers, like Langellier's grandparents.

68 Wynn, 'James F.W. Johnston'; Johnston, *Notes on North America*, 70.

69 Craig, 'Before Borderlands.'

70 I considered as 'kin' people who had at least one set of great-grandparents in common, including ancestors of both the husband and wife. Since the Catholic Church did not let people within those degrees of kinship marry without a dispensation, people were likely to know who their third cousins were.

71 This survey was done by James Maclauchlan, warden of the disputed territory, in the winter of 1833 at the demand of the governor. The crops had failed and the settlers had petitioned the provincial government for relief. The survey enumerates all heads of family, gives the size of their households, describes their stock, and their past and present crops. It also distinguishes between labourers, tenants, occupiers of non-granted land and owners of granted land. PANB, Papers of the Legislative Assembly relating to the settlement of Madawaska, 'Return showing the Number of Inhabitants in the settlement of Madawaska with their Stock,' 1833. I could link all of them with my family reconstitution cards, and with the data in Deane and Kavanagh's report.

72 The charter families are people who arrived before 1800 and their direct descendants in the male and female lines.

73 The Catholic Church defined marriages between parties who had at least one set of great-great grand parents in common as consanguineous. Cousins who wished to marry needed a dispensation, and had to pay a fine proportional to their degree of kinship. First cousin marriages however were almost never allowed.

74 Wiggin, *History of Aroostook*, 190–1. This history was written from interviews with prominent county citizens conducted around 1892; the text consists mostly of family histories. See also Paradis, 'John Baker and the Republic of Madawaska' ; SMA, *Message from the President*, 1828, 13–14.

75 Wiggin, *History of Aroostook*, 176; Fort Kent Protestant Cemetery records. Age and nationality are culled from the 1850, 1860, and 1870 U.S. census.

76 Besides Wiggin, see White, *Early History of Caribou Maine*; Mitchell, 'Reminiscence of Early Days'; Collins, *Lumbering then and Now.*

77 PANB, family history files; PANB, land petitions and application books.

78 PANB, family history files, Hammond family; 1850, 1860, 1870 U.S. census.

79 Wiggin, *History of Aroostook*, 177; Fort Kent Protestant Cemetery records.

80 Wiggin, *History of Aroostook*, 196.

81 According to the information reported in the various censuses, almost all American entrepreneurs were married to American women. These men also married late, to considerably younger women.

82 Taylor, *William Cooper's Town*; and *Liberty Men and Great Proprietors*; Longley, 'The Coming of the New England Planters'; Young, 'Planter Settlements in the Saint John Valley'; Wright, 'Cumberland Township'; Campbell, 'A Scots Irish Plantation in Nova Scotia'; Moody, 'Land, Kinship and Inheritance'; Bubar, 'A Planter Family'; Moody, 'Growing up in Granville Township.'

2: Principal Men

1 Raymond, *Winslow Papers*, 162.

2 A similar attitude could be found in British North America; unfortunately, I could not find as revealing a quotation as Dwight's. John Beverley Robinson and John Strachan would have agreed with him for instance. Cook, 'John Beverley Robinson and the Conservative Blueprint.'

3 Taylor, *Liberty Men and Great Proprietors*, 49–59.

4 Taylor, *Liberty Men and Great Proprietors*, 155.

5 Taylor, *William Cooper's Town*, 249–55.

6 Dwight, *Travels in New England and New York*, 2:239.

7 *Message from the President*, Letters from P. Duperré, captain of the militia to the Honorable J. Murray Bliss, 5 September 1818, 29.

8 ANQQ, cour des plaids communs, Anselme et Michel Robichaud vs. Augustin Dubé et Pierre Duperré, 1789, TL15–3527: requête et déclaration des demandeurs, 18 août 1789; certificat d'assignation, août 1789; défense, 17 sept 1789; filé [*sic*] par le demandeur, 14 sept. 1789; réplique, 28 sept. 1789; défense, 26 mars 1790; réplique, 30 mars 1790; motion des demandeurs, 3 juillet 1790; déposition des témoins, 17 sept. 1790; réponse, 19 jan. 1791; arbitrage, 12 jan. 1791; évaluation des dommages, 12 jan. 1791; réponse, 20 Jan. 1791. The history to 1791 is based on these

documents, most of which have been transcribed by Massé in 'La guerre des fourrures au Madawaska-Témiscouata.'

9 Arsenault, *Histoire et généalogie des Acadiens*, vol. 2, 225; vol. 4, 1649; Chipman, *Remarks upon the disputed Points of Boundary*, 68

10 ANQQ, Circuit court and court of King's bench, John Young vs. Michel Robichaud and Uxor, copy of Robichaud's account, filed 1797, TL18-5006. Tulchinsky and Young, 'John Young.' Young was based in Quebec City; he and his partner Simon Fraser were large-scale wholesalers who traded all the way to Rivière du Loup. They also operated a brewery-distillery in Québec city. See Massé, 'La guerre des fourrures au Madawaska.'

11 ANQQ, cour des plaids communs, Anselme et Michel Robichaud vs. Augustin Dubé et Pierre Duperré, 1789, TL15–3527; ANQQ, RG B28, Applications for licences to trade with the Indians (incomplete).

12 ANQQ, Greffes de Me J.C Panet, notaire de Québec, Me Barolet notaire de Québec and Me Joseph Dionne, notaire de Kamouraska. Various acts between 1739 and 1779 refer to Jean Baptiste Lizotte in his various capacities; the sale of the Rivière du Loup seigneurie is in Panet, 20 July 1763. See also Hudon, 'Jean Baptiste Duperré.'

13 ANQQ, Greffes de Me Joseph Dionne, notaire de Kamouraska, 1743–1779. inventaire de Pierre Duperré, 5 oct. 1766, 303–18, 4M01–0477A.

14 MSA, 'Report of John G. Deane and Edward Kavanagh to Samuel E. Smith, Governor of the State of Maine,' 453, 480–1; PNB, Mazzerolle grant, 1790; *Quebec Gazette*, 10 Nov. 1791; Hudon, 'Négociants de Kamouraska'; ANQQ, cour des plaids communs, 1789–91, District de Québec, TL15 #3345, 1788; 3423, 1788; 3026, 1786.

15 ANQQ, Cour des plaids communs, District de Québec, Alexandre McLennan et Pierre Duperré contre Joseph Massigué, 3423, 1788; Hudon, 'Les négociants de Kamouraska.'

16 Raymond, *Winslow Papers*, 395

17 The rest of the story is told by W.O. Raymond, 'State of the Madawaska and Aroostook Settlements in 1831,' 371–2; Chipman, *Remarks*, 62–9; and Massé, 'La guerre des fourrures.'

18 LAC, MG11 « Q » vol. 60, executive council of Lower Canada, C11907.

19 PANB, Journal of the House of Assembly of New Brunswick, 1796, 470; Legislative Assembly, sessional records, RS24–S10, 1796, 18 Feb. 1796; petition of P. Duperré; New Brunswick Catholics were officially enfranchised in 1810, at the initiative of Peter Fraser, Duperré's new patron. MacNutt, *New Brunswick*, 108; Garner, 'The Enfranchisement of Roman Catholics in the Maritime Provinces,' 208–9.

20 PANB, Legislative Assembly, sessional records, RS24–S:16, 1–2, petition of the underwritten inhabitants of the County of York.

21 MacNutt, *New Brunswick*, 102; Brymer, *Report on Canadian Archives*, state papers, New Brunswick, letter from Glenie to Nepean, 24 Mar. 1792, 26.

22 PANB, York County registry office, 17 Nov. 1815, F 5622.

23 Raymond, *Winslow Papers*, 385; PANB, York County registry office, 1 July 1802, F 5618; Land petitions and application books, F 1040.

24 PANB, land petitions and application books, F1041, application from Pierre Duperré, 18 July 1800.

25 PANB, York County registry office 19 Sept. 1789; 30 Aug. 1808, F 5618.

26 Sprague, 'Documentary History of the North Eastern Boundary Controversy,' 294; Young, 'Peter Fraser.' See also Raymond, *Winslow Papers*, 687, editorial note by W.O. Raymond. Peter Fraser was no relation to Simon Fraser of Fraser and Young.

27 John Robinson was perhaps the most well-heeled Loyalist in New Brunswick. His father, Beverley, son of John, administrator of Virginia, had been a childhood friend of George Washington. Robinson was a merchant, a member of the provincial legislature, a provincial treasurer, mayor of Saint John, member of the executive council, and president of the Bank of New Brunswick. He was a cousin to the Robinson mentioned in note 2. T.W. Acheson, 'John Robinson.'

28 Young, 'Peter Fraser.'

29 PANB, land petitions and application books, petition dated 11 Aug. 1814, F1043; York County registry office, F5620.

30 SMA, '*Message from the President,*' Letters from P. Duperré, captain of the militia to the Honorable J. Murray Bliss, 5 Sept. 1818 and 20 Feb. 1819, 30–2.

31 LAC, Winslow papers, M148 vol. 9, 1803–36, Marie Euphrosine Cyr's petition, M148. A surrogate judge was the British equivalent of a judge of probate.

32 AAQ, Lettres des prêtres missionnaires, 14 mai 1812.

33 MSA, Land Office records, Journal of George W. Coffin, Massachusetts land agent. Journey up the Saint John River, Sept. and Oct., 1825.

34 Deane and Kavanagh, 'Report,' 405.

35 Ibid., 408.

36 PANB, Records of the Surveyor General 1784–1912, RS637, 15/b/86 and 87, disputes, cases of land.

37 Genealogical and demographic data from the family reconstitution cards.

38 PANB, York County registry office, 1785–1833.

39 Deane and Kavanagh, 'Report.' Scattered entries.

40 MSA, Maine public documents, Report of the Commissioners appointed under the Resolve of 21 Feb. 1843; PNB, Maps of the Madawaska Survey; PANB, York County registry office, 1785–1833; Carleton County registry office, 1833–50; Victoria County registry office, 1850–80; State of Maine, Fort Kent, ME, Northern registry of the deeds, 1845–1890. The same sources were used to reconstitute the real estate transactions of his brother, as well as Firmin Thibodeau's.

41 NBM, Odell family papers, correspondence 1817–44, letter from Armine S.H. Mountain (Quebec) to William Odell re trip from Fredericton to Quebec city, 31 Jan. 1824, F32–7.

42 University of Maine at Presque Isle, Aroostook room, Melvin collection. Includes copies of the grants and of survey maps from the Crown land office.

43 PANB, Journal of the House of Assembly of New Brunswick, 1844, Appendix C, Northern boundary; Journal of the House of Assembly of New Brunswick, 1849, 209–10; Journal of the House of Assembly of New Brunswick, 1851, 185; Journal of the House of Assembly of New Brunswick, 1854, 330; PANB, Petitions to the House of Assembly, RS24, 849/pe/2/#46; 849/22/3; 849/pe/13/#410; 854/pe/10/#330; 856/pe/6/#241.

44 Andrew, *The Development of Elites in Acadian New Brunswick*, 152

45 PANB, Victoria County registry office, 31 Oct.1872, G/2767/298; LAC, Census of Canada, 1871, New Brunswick, Madawaska parish, C 10385. The town of Edmundston was part of the civil parish of Madawaska.

46 Albert, *Histoire du Madawaska*, 167.

47 MSA, Land Office records, Journal of George W. Coffin, Massachusetts land agent. Journey up the Saint John River, Sept. and Oct. 1825.

48 Sprague, 'Documentary History of the North Eastern Boundary Controversy,' vol. 1, Letter from Peter Fraser, major of the 4th battalion York county militia to the Honorable Lt Col. Geo. Shore, adjutant general York county militia, dated Madawaska 8 Oct. 1825.

49 PANB, York County registry office 10 May 1831, F 5622.

50 *New Brunswick Almanac*, 1840–50; CIHM 38341, 39607–10, 52910, 38427–30.

51 *Parchemin*, Greffes de Me Bacquerisse, 19 and 26 oct. 1754; Pothier, 'Joseph Nicolas Gautier dit Bellair.'

52 PANS, Nova Scotia land papers, RG20, vol. 1, 15685.

53 Andrew, 'Louis Mercure'; Raymond, 'Introduction' to 'State of the Madawaska Settlement,' 377–80; PANB, York County registry office.

54 Raymond, ibid., 379; Andrew, ibid.

55 PANB, York County registry office, 26 June 1809, F 5618.
56 PANB, land petition and application books, 22 April 1797, F1040; Campbell, *Travels in the Interior Inhabited Parts of North America*, 94.
57 At some unspecified date, Mercure sold the lot to a John King of Saint John who received a grant for 500 acres at the mouth of the Salmon River in October 1813 on the strength of this deed of sale. LAC, Lower Canada land papers; exploration and roads; Craig road.
58 Andrew, 'Louis Mercure'; Paradis, 'Louis Mercure, Fondateur du Madawaska,' 49–56; PANB, York County, minutes of the quarter sessions; *New Brunswick Almanac and Register*.
59 Letter from provincial secretary Odell to surveyor general Sproule, 14 July 1787, cited by Raymond in 'First Governor,' 440
60 LAC, St Basile (NB) parish register, 1792–1855.
61 All pre-1800 genealogical information from Charbonneau and Légaré, *Répertoire des actes*. Post 1800 genealogical information from the family reconstitution cards
62 Tremblay, 'Francois Pierre Cherrier'; Morrisseau, 'La famille Cherrier de Saint-Denis sur Richelieu.'
63 Miquelon, 'Marie Anne Barbel'; Plamondon, 'Une femme d'affaire en Nouvelle France'; Miquelon, 'Louis Fornel (Fournel).
64 The CD version of Charbonneau and Légaré, *Répertoire des actes*, which allowed me to follow all those people, ends in 1799.
65 AAQ, Lettres des prêtres missionnaires, 15 août 1807.
66 Genealogical data from the family reconstitution cards, based on the Saint Basile parish register.
67 Deane and Kavanagh, 'Report,' 411–12; PANB, York County, minutes of the quarter sessions.
68 See below, ch. 6 and 7.
69 PANB, Carleton County registry office.
70 PANB, Victoria County registry office, book A, deed dated 25 May 1845 (registered late).
71 New Brunswick Museum, John Emmerson papers, ledger C.
72 AAQ, Lettres des prêtres missionnaires, 27 déc. 1849, et 5 jan. 1850.
73 Greer, *Peasant, Lord and Merchant*, 147.
74 Ibid., 151.

3: A Connective Enterprise: Madawaska Lumbering

1 Wiggin, *History of Aroostook*, 176–7.
2 Lugrin, *State of Agriculture*, vii.

3 Birthplace from the census; birthdate from his gravestone. The 1850 census gives his age as 25; he died in 1895. Samuel Stevens is buried next to him.

4 Laberge, *Histoire de la Côte-du-Sud*, 246.

5 See, for instance, Graeme Wynn's bleak comment: 'While the timber trade advanced the development of the province, it made of New Brunswick's economy a gigantic bandalore, ineluctably tied to the lines of transatlantic commerce to the rise and fall of the market for its staple products.' Wynn, *Timber Colony*, 53.

6 Ibid., 113–14. Taylor, *Liberty Men and Great Proprietors*, 155.

7 Wynn, ibid., 29, 30–3; Lower, *Great Britain Woodyard*, 45–57.

8 Wynn, ibid., 38–40; PANB, Timber records books, 1825–38, RS663/B/2/b.

9 Wood, *A History of Lumbering in Maine, 1820–1861*, 28–30; Taylor, *Liberty Men and Great Proprietors*, 63.

10 Judd, *Aroostook*, 7–8; PANB, provincial secretary correspondence, Madawaska County, RS13 31 to 3, 2/4/1812; 'Report of Charles S. Davis esq., Agent appointed by the executive of the State of Maine, 31/1/1828,' *Correspondence Relating to the Boundary*; Wilmot, *Complete History of Aroostook County*, 42; Raymond, 'Introduction' to 'State of the Madawaska and Aroostook Settlements,' 364; Paradis, 'John Baker and the Republic of Madawaska,' 78–95; SMA, Barrel, 'Report of the special agent appointed by Henry Clay, secretary of state, relative to the alleged agressions of the rights of U.S. citizens by persons claiming authority under the Government of the Province of New Brunswick; 19 Nov. 1827 and 11 Feb. 1828' in *Message from the President*, 13–14.

11 The narrative of the conflict is taken from Jones, *To the Webster Ashburton Treaty*, 3–19, 33–47; Burrage, *Maine in the North Eastern Boundary Controversy*; Sprague, 'The Northeastern Boundary Controversy and the Aroostook War.'

12 PANB, timber correspondence, general correspondence, Baillie to Governor Douglas, 5 Feb. 1829; Baillie to Maclauchlan, 13 Feb. 1829, RS663/E/1/a; Raymond, 'Introduction' to 'State of the Madawaska and Aroostook Settlements.'

13 PANB, timber correspondence, general correspondence, William Odell to Baillie 29 Apr. 1827, RS663/E/1/a.

14 PANB, timber correspondence, general correspondence, Baillie to governor, 5 Aug. 1839; Baillie to Odell, 1 Oct. 1839, RS663/E/1/c.

15 See, for instance, the 1838 petition of Désiré Violette and fifteen other men, all but one local settlers, PANB, timber and sawmill petitions, 1817–65, RS662/A; also PANB, timber correspondence, general corre-

spondence, 21 May 1838, RS663/E/1/b; PANB, timber correspondence, reports on violations and seizures, Rice to Maclauchlan, 18 June 1836, RS663/E/2/a; timber correspondence/ general correspondence 1839–41, John Saunders to lieutenant governor, 29 Mar. 1841, RS663/E/1/c. Saunders stated the settlers 'had permission repeatedly given them in former years to make small quantities of timber in the neighbourhood of their settlement.'

16 George Buckmore to Elijah E. Hamlin, 22 Jan. 1839, *Correspondence Relating to the Boundary*; Raymond, 'Introduction' in 'State of the Madawaska and Aroostook Settlements.'

17 George Buckmore to Elijah E. Hamlin, 22 Jan. 1839, *Correspondence Relating to the Boundary ...*

18 PANB, timber record books, RS663/13/2.

19 Judd, *Aroostook*, 32–7

20 Lowenthal, 'The Maine Press and the Aroostook War.'

21 State of Maine, Northern Aroostook registry of the deeds, 1845–70, Fort Kent ME; PANB, Carleton County registry office, books 1–11, 1832–50, F5024–F5029; Victoria County registry office, 1851–70.

22 LAC, William Maclauchlin to Reade, private secretary to the lieutenant governor, 11 Nov. 1842. MG9A2, vol. 6: 2

23 MSA, Second annual report of the Secretary of the Maine Board of Agriculture, 32.

24 Maine Historical Society Library, Proceedings of the citizens of Aroostook County, 1866.

25 MSA, Report of the joint select committee 1859; Report of the commission appointed to investigate alleged election frauds, 1879.

26 State of Maine, Northern Aroostook registry of the deeds, vol. 3, entry dated 1 Sept. 1853.

27 State of Maine, Northern Aroostook registry of the deeds, vol. 7, 510, entry dated 13 May 1868.

28 Albert, *Histoire du Madawaska*, 327; Ganong, 'A Monograph of the Origins of Settlements,' 103.

29 Lower, *Great Britain Woodyard*, 116.

30 Most timber berths are easy to locate, except for Little River. There were three Little Rivers, and only two of them were tributaries of the Upper Saint John.

31 Smith, *A History of Lumbering in Maine*; Wynn, *Timber Colony*, 52–3.

32 State of Maine, Northern registry of the deeds, 1848–70.

33 Wynn, *Timber Colony*, 137; Judd, *Aroostook*, 45, 49–51.

34 PANB, timber licence book, RS663/B2/2n 1839–48; RS663/B2/16, 1848–60;

RS663/B2/2t 1860–70; RS663/B2/2s, 1859–72.

35 Wiggin, *History of Aroostook*; Judd, *Aroostook*, 49–54, 60–2.

36 Judd, ibid., 54.

37 Wynn, *Timber Colony*, 121–3.

38 PANB, *Political Biographies*, compiled by James C. Graves and Horace C. Graves, biography of James Tibbits; Baird, *Seventy Years of New Brunswick Life*, 54, CIHM 02502.

39 Judd, *Aroostook*, 65–6; UNBA, Lilian M. Maxwell collection, 'Reminiscences of Thomas S. Glasier.' Thomas, born in 1830, was son to Benjamin, and a brother of John, Stephen, and Duncan; Beamsley Glazier from chapter 1 was the uncle of the four men. PANB, York Sunbury Historical Collection, J.S. Glasier papers, RS38/2/1837; Stephen Glasier papers, 1855–60, RS300/MS8–3. Young, 'John Glazier.'

40 Judd, *Aroostook*, 50–2, 60–2; Wiggin, *History of Aroostook*, 11–12.

41 Young, 'John Glazier'; UNBA, 'Reminiscences of Thomas S. Glasier, 1914.'

42 PANB, Journal of the House of Assembly of New Brunswick, 1855, Canada disputed territory fund, clviii–clix.

43 PANB, timber licence books, 1839–71, RS663/B2.

44 Laberge, *Histoire de la Côte-du-Sud*, 245

45 State of Maine, Northern Aroostook registry of the deeds, 10 Feb. 1849 and 16 Nov. 1849.

46 Judd, *Aroostook*, 78.

47 Judd, ibid., 97. Wiggin, *History of Aroostook*, 175; State of Maine, Northern Aroostook registry of the deeds, book of foreclosure.

48 Judd, ibid., 50–3; Wiggin, ibid., 11–12, 174–5.

49 Judd, ibid., 52.

50 Wiggin, *History of Aroostook*, 23.

51 Shepard Cary papers, Houlton, ME, memorandum of Charles Terrio, 26 Sept. 1848. The contract is on a pre-printed form.

52 For a study of the evolution of labour contracts and of the philosophy underpinning them see Steinfeld, *The Invention of Free Labour*.

53 MSA, Shepard Cary correspondence, 1836–1845, William H. Cary to Collin Whitaker, letter dated 17 Sept. 1845.

54 PANB, timber licence books, 1839–70, RS663/B/2.

55 LAC, Provincial census of New Brunswick, 1851, County of Victoria, Parish of Madawaska; Deane and Kavanaugh, 'Report of John G. Deane and Edward Kavanagh to Samuel E. Smith, Governor of the State of Maine,' 386ff; PANB, 'Report of the Commissioners of Affairs at Madawaska, 1834' (hereafter 'Maclauchlan report'); PANB, Victoria

County probate court records, RS73/A, probate record books 1850–1926, F 7308; estate files, 1850–1910, F 7296 (will, petition for letters of administration 29 Jan. 1867, and inventory, 1867); PANB, Timber licence books, 1839–70, RS663/B/2; timber and sawmill petition book, RS633/A, 1817–65; Carleton and Victoria County registries, 1833–50 and 1850–73; NBM, J. Emmerson papers and account books, 1843–1909; See also the biographical notes prefacing the microfilm of his papers made by the PANB, F 12 330–3.

56 He is in the 1833 Maclauchlan report, but not in Deane and Kavanagh's.

57 Albert, *Histoire du Madawaska*, 209–36; Deane and Kavanagh, 'Report'; PANB, *Political Biographies*; Vital records from St Basile parish register.

58 Deane and Kavanagh, 'Report'; 'Maclauchlan report.'

59 PANB, Carleton County registry, 765, 1 July 1836; York County registry, 2722, 24 Oct. 1828.

60 PANB, timber licence book, RS663/B2/2n 1839–48; timber correspondence RS663 E/1/e 1844–9, L. Coomb's letter, 6 May 1846.

61 PANB, Carleton county registry 3148, 8 Nov. 1845; State of Maine, Northern registry of the deeds, 2 Feb. 1848, 1 Sept. 1850, 25 Oct. 1850, 17 Feb. 1851.

62 State of Maine, Northern Aroostook registry of the deeds, 8 Aug. 1848; 18 Mar. 1849.

63 Johnston, *Notes on North America*, 68. Coombs's farms 'contains 1025 acres, of which only 80 were cleared.'

64 UMFK, Acadian Archives, Abraham and Simon Dufour store ledger, 1845–48.

65 Farmer-lumberers can be identified in the ledgers by the nature of their purchases (shanty supplies) and by the fact they settled their accounts in timber. The provincial license lists are another way to identify some of them.

66 State of Maine, Northern Aroostook registry of the deeds, 18 Mar. 1847 and 22 Feb. 1848.

67 U.S. Government, Bureau of the census, 7th census of the United States, State of Maine, County of Aroostook, 1850; 8th census of the United States, State of Maine, County of Aroostook, 1860.

68 There is a Dufour-Levasseur account in the ledger.

69 NBM, Emmerson papers, ledgers C and D; PANB, timber licence book RS663/B2/16, 1848–60; RS663/B2/2t 1860–70; RS663/B2/2s, 1859–72.

70 PANB, MC30, MS1, and MS2, D.D. Glazier and son, account books, timber rafts.

71 State of Maine, Northern Aroostook registry of the deeds, 3 Apr. 1847, 1

and 17 May 1848, 1 May 1860, 27 June 1861; Carleton County registry, 3644, 20 July 1847; Victoria County registry office, book C, 11 Mar. 1852 and 20 Feb. 1858; Victoria County registry, book D 253, 27 Aug. 1863.

72 PANB, Victoria County registry, book C 494, n.d.; book E, 9 May 1866.
73 Andrew, *Development of Acadian Elites*, 150.
74 State of Maine, Northern Aroostook registry of the deeds, 8 Jan. 1848.
75 NBM, Emmerson papers, ledgers C and D.
76 PANB, Victoria County registry office, book A, 20 Aug. 1849 and 20 Aug. 1850.
77 State of Maine, Northern Aroostook registry of the deeds, 18 Oct. 1847.
78 PANB, Victoria County registry office, book A , 20 Aug. 1849 and 20 Aug. 1850.
79 Baird, *Seventy Years of New Brunswick Life*, 54.
80 Little, 'Public Policy and Private Interests,' 37.

4: Millers

1 Baillie, *An Account of the Province of New Brunswick*, 33–4; CIHM 21383.
2 Wynn, *Timber Colony*, 116–17; Judd, *Aroostook*, 84–8, Taylor, *Liberty Men and Great Proprietors*, 156.
3 Judd, *Aroostook*, 86.
4 Wiggin, *History of Aroostook*, 13.
5 Ibid., 82, 94, 112.
6 Wynn, *Timber Colony*, 95; Taylor, *Liberty Men and Great Proprietors*, 156; Judd, *Aroostook*, 84.
7 Wynn has also made this distinction between large, relatively expensive export-oriented mills and smaller custom ones scattered through the province. *Timber Colony*, 95.
8 Deane and Kavanagh, 'Report'; 'Maclauchlan report.'
9 Paradis, 'John Baker and the Republic of Madawaska,' 78–95.
10 PANB, Land petition and application book, 23 Aug. 1824.
11 PANB, York County registry office, 30 Aug. 1829, F 4565
12 PANB, Carleton County registry office, 1733–1850; Victoria County registry office, 1850–73.
13 PANB, Carleton County registry office, 1833–50.
14 PANB, Carleton County registry office, until 1845; after 1845, State of Maine, Northern Aroostook registry of the deeds; Wiggin, *History of Aroostook*, 172–3.
15 Wiggin, *History of Aroostook*, 173–7. The Northern Aroostook registry of the deeds confirms Wiggin's narrative; U.S. Government, Bureau of the

census, 7th census of the United States, State of Maine, County of Aroostook, personal and industrial schedules for Hancock plantation, 1850.

16 Wiggin, *History of Aroostook*, 173–5; State of Maine, Northern Aroostook
registry of the deeds, 1845–80; U.S. Government, Bureau of the Census,
7th census of the United States, State of Maine, County of Aroostook, personal and industrial schedules for Hancock plantation, year 1850; 9th
census of the United States, State of Maine, County of Aroostook, personal and industrial schedules for Fort Kent, 1870; 8th census of the
United States, State of Maine, County of Aroostook, personal schedule
for Fort Kent, 1860. The 1860 industrial schedule for Fort Kent is missing.

17 Wiggin, *History of Aroostook*; State of Maine, Northern Aroostook registry
of the deeds, 1845–80; U.S. Government, Bureau of the Census, 7th
Census, 9th Census, 8th Census.

18 PANB, family history files, Hammond family; Hammond and Coomb
appear as partners for the first time in the Carleton County registry, 8
Nov. 1845, F 3198.

19 State of Maine, Northern Aroostook registry of the deeds, 18 Aug. 1848.

20 Ibid., 28 Sept. 59.

21 U.S. Government, Bureau of the census, 8th census of the United States,
State of Maine, County of Aroostook, personal, agricultural and industrial schedules for Van Buren plantation, 1860.

22 State of Maine, Northern Aroostook registry of the deeds, 25 Oct. 1861, 12
Apr. 1862.

23 U.S. Government, Bureau of the census, 9th census of the United States,
State of Maine, County of Aroostook, industrial schedules for Van Buren
plantation, 1870.

24 PANB, Victoria county registry office; Northern Aroostook registry of the
deeds; Dubay, *The History of Germain Dubé of Hamlin*, 29.

25 MSA, Eighteenth Annual Report of the Bureau of Industrial and Labor
Statistics for the State of Maine, 42.

26 McKinney, 'A. B. Hammond, West Coast Lumberman,' 196–203.

27 U.S. Government, Bureau of the census, 9th census of the United States,
State of Maine, County of Aroostook, industrial schedules for Grand Isle
plantation, 1870.

28 Albert, *Histoire du Madawaska*, 166.

29 And Jean Baptiste Cormier was his father's cousin. Two of Cormier's
sons ran a mill at Grand Isle at the beginning of the century.

30 PANB, Victoria county registry, book E, 28 July 1869. Bijeau paid $250
cash, and the rest was secured by a mortgage. Bijeau was to repay £25 a
year plus interest. Picket sold the mortgage for $500 to a Mary Ward of

Saint John a month later.

31 State of Maine, Northern Aroostook registry of the deeds. The sale was
confirmed by Fraser's executor, 17 Apr. 1845, and registered in October
1859; ibid., 30 Nov. 1864 and 30 Oct. 1867. In 1867 Corriveau is identified
as a miller in Saint Basile. The mill was to be paid off by 1872 at the rate
of $100 a year. However, the mortgage was assigned to a third party,
Patrick Lynch, for $95 in 1877.

32 Deane and Kavanagh, 'Report,' 414.

33 State of Maine, Northern Aroostook registry of the deeds, 16 June 1846,
27 July 1849, 2 Sept. 1862.

34 U.S. Government, Bureau of the census, 9th census of the United States,
1870, Van Buren plantation, industrial schedule; Grand Isle plantation,
population schedule. The residence(s) of large landowner are relatively
easy to identify as they buy and sell real estate frequently, and the deeds
indicate where they live.

35 Militia commissions and civil office appointments are culled from the
various New Brunswick almanacs, as in the previous chapters. The list of
Madawaska state representatives, like the list of members of the house of
legislature of New Brunswick, are taken from Thomas Albert, who lists
them all with the dates of office. Albert, *Histoire du Madawaska*, 416. See
also AAQ, Lettres des prêtres missionnaires, 5 Jan. 1850.

36 Albert, *Histoire du Madawaska*, 245.

37 LAC, Dominion census, 1871, Province of New Brunswick, Victoria
County, Parish of St Basil.

38 *Aroostook Pioneer*, 17 Aug. 1858. Paul Cyr, on the other hand, was a
Democrat. In 1863, Paul's son, Alexis, also a democrat, was elected to the
state house; *Kennebec Journal*, 25 Sept. 1863.

39 PANB, timber licence book, RS663/B2/16, 1848–60; RS663/B2/2t
1860–70; RS663/B2/2s, 1859–72.

40 Albert, *Histoire du Madawaska*, 243.

41 PANB, Victoria County registry, 983, 2 Jan. 1867

42 PANB, probate RG 9 RS 73/A, 24 Aug. 1868. Andrew, 'Levite Thériault,'
PANB, Political Biographies.

43 The information contained in the probate records underscore the shortcomings of the censuses. The census lists neither the fulling mill, not the
smithy.

44 PANB, Victoria County registry, book B, 26 Feb. 56. The purchases
totalled £700 or $2,800.

45 PANB, Victoria county registry, book E, 14 Mar. 1866.

46 LAC, Canadian census, 1871, Province of New Brunswick, County of Victoria, Industrial schedules, Madawaska and Saint Basile.

47 Albert, *Histoire du Madawaska*, 412; Andrew, 'Levite Thériault'; PANB, Political Biographies; Andrew, *Development of Acadian Elites*, 52–6, 153–67.

48 PANB, Journal of the House of Assembly 1854–55, contested elections, 106, and supporting petitions.

49 Watters was a Catholic, a friend of Mgr Langevin, and the executor of his will. He was also a friend of the Ste Luce priest, Rev Dionne. Watters did not get along with Langevin's successor, Hugh McGuirk, and got embroiled in local squabbles between priest and parishioners. ACS/CSA, fonds Collège de Sainte-Anne, fonds Abbé Henri Dionne, F100/34 and 35.

50 Wiggin, *History of Aroostook*, 179.

51 Andrew, *Development of Acadian elites*, 47.

52 Lamoreaux, 'Rethinking the Transition to Capitalism.'

5: General Stores: Capitalism's Beachhead or Local Traffic Controllers?

1 Baird, *Seventy Years of New Brunswick Life*, 91.

2 Rural storekeeping has not attracted much attention from historians, and the existing literature is both recent and limited in number. The pioneer study is Martin, 'Merchants and trade of the Connecticut river valley, 1750–1820.' A well-documented but little-known early study is Wainright, 'A comparative Study in Nova Scotian Rural Economy.' The more recent work includes: Clark, *The Roots of Rural Capitalism*, 156–169; Nobles, 'The Rise of the Merchants in Rural Market Towns'; Sweeney, 'Gentlemen Farmers and Inland Merchants'; Taylor, *Liberty Men and Great Proprietors*, 155; Taylor, *William Cooper's Town*, 107–110; Wermuth, *Rip Van Winkle's Neighbors*, 52–62, 93–103, and 124–33; Bruegel, *Farm, Shop, Landing*; and Newell, *From Dependency to Independence*, 95–101.

In Canada, most of the work on stores has either been done by Douglas McCalla, or focuses on New France. McCalla, 'Rural credit and Rural development in Upper Canada'; 'The Needs of Farm Households'; 'Retailing in the Countryside'; and 'Textile Purchases by Some Ordinary Upper Canadians'; Desrosiers, 'Un aperçu des habitudes de consommation'; Michel, 'Un marchand rural en Nouvelle France'; and 'Endettement et société rurale'; St George, 'Commerce, crédit et transactions foncières'; Pronovost, *La bourgeoisie marchande en milieu rural*; Courville, *Entre ville et campagne*, 138–140, 241–56; Greer, *Peasant*,

Lord, and Merchant, 140–76; Lapointe, 'Les marchands ruraux anglo-phones'; Depatie, 'Commerce et crédit à l'île Jésus.' For a comparison New Brunswick and Lower Canada, see Craig, 'Solder les comptes'; and 'Entrepôt de l'Empire.' Note also work on the function of the stores in the fisheries. In Gaspé and Newfoundland, merchants usually had a monopoly on selling, or on buying fish from fishermen, and took advantage of their position. Ommer, *From Outpost to Outport*; 'The truck system in Gaspé'; and *Merchant Credit*. However, *Merchant Credit* makes plain that the credit system in the fisheries was different from the credit system elsewhere, and that the one can only shed limited light on the other.

3 Taylor, 'A Struggle of Finesse,' 294; Sweeney, 'Gentlemen Farmers and Inland Merchants,' 69; Wynn, *Timber Colony*, 114–15.

4 Sweeney, 'Gentlemen Farmers and Inland Merchants,' 72; Mancke, 'At the Counter of the General Store'; Taylor, *Liberty Men and Great Proprietors*, 155; Clark, *Roots of Capitalism*, 163; Courville, *Entre ville et campagne*, 138; Desrosiers, 'Un aperçu des habitudes de consommation'; Greer, *Peasant, Lord, Merchant*, 169; Nobles, 'The Rise of the Merchants in Rural Market Towns,' 3.

5 Nobles, 'The Rise of the Merchants,' 5.

6 Sweeney, 'Gentlemen Farmers and Inland Merchants'; McCalla, 'Rural Credit and Rural Development in Upper Canada,' 260–1; Newel, *From Dependency to Independence*, 99.

7 McCalla, 'Rural Credit and Rural Development,' 256, 268.

8 For instance, Kendall, *Travels through the Northern Parts of the United States*, 81. He was far from being unique.

9 UMFK, Acadian Archives, Dufour ledger, 1845–8; NBM and PANB, John Emmerson papers and account books F12229–333. Include general journals 1851–67 and 1873–81; memorandum books 1848–87, with gaps; day books 1871–7, with gaps; receiving book 1849–59; delivery book 1845–73; and miscellaneous documents after 1870.

10 Wiggin, *History of Aroostook*, page ?

11 PANB, timber record books, RS663/13/2; timber license books, 1839–71, RS662/B/2.

12 PANB, Victoria County registry office, book A. (like a lot of transactions, this one was registered late, in 1851).

13 UMFK, Acadian Archives, Dufour ledger, 1845–48.

14 Houlton Maine district court, Eastern district, 1847–9. The brothers, listed sometimes as residing in New Brunswick, and sometimes in Maine, sued seven people for a total of $340, Louis Albert for $460.55, and two Freder-

icton merchants, James and Frederick Perley, for $257.20 during the Sept. 1847 and the Feb. 1848 terms. In the Sept. 1849 term, they were sued by François-Xavier St Jean of Rivière Ouelle for $475.75. St Jean alleged that the sum was due him ' for the labour and service of the plaintiff by him before that time done and performed in and about the business of the said defendant (as their clerk) at their request in consideration thereof promised the plaintiff to pay him that sum on demand.' The amount corresponded roughly to one year's salary. The Dufours denied the claim. The case went to trial; the Dufours lost, and had to pay $260 in damages and the court costs, in addition to St Jean's claim.

15 The only information I could find about Vinal comes from the register of the deeds, which identifies him as a lumberer from Bangor.

16 This information is culled from the Victoria County land registry office; the timber licence books, and his commercial books, as well as from the 1851 census, which lists the members of his household and their occupation.

17 PANB, Victoria County probate court records, John Emmerson, 1867, RS73/A.

18 Ommer, *From Outpost to Outport*, 122–36.

19 PANB, Victoria County probate court records, John Emmerson, 1867, RS73/A.

20 I did not analyse all the ledgers and memo books to answer those questions, but sampled them. I analysed one year of the Dufour ledger, 1846, the first year for which the accounts are complete and a good economic year. The timber industry did not crash until the 1847–8 season. I used two years of Emmerson's records: 1853 and 1863 (ledger and memorandum book), as well as his delivery and receiving book. I also followed some customers through the entire series. For ease of calculation, I converted the pound currency used in the books into dollars (£1 = $4). This is the rate of exchange used by Emmerson, besides being the official one at the time.

21 Greer, *Peasant, Lord, and Merchant*, 151.

22 They were in good company: early nineteenth century merchants and manufacturers had a poor understanding of accounting. Lamoreaux, pars. 11–16.

23 The Canadas issued bronze and silver coins in 1858, and paper in 1866. The first 'Canadian' money, in the modern sense of the term, followed Confederation in 1867. See McCullough, *Money and Exchange in Canada to 1900*, 88, 110–12, 172, 179; The Banque de Montréal (founded in 1817), Banque de Québec (1818), Banque du Canada (1819), received a provin-

cial charter in 1821; The Bank of New Brunswick was founded and char-
tered by the province in 1820, and the Bank of Upper Canada in 1821.
The Halifax Banking Company, a private firm, was established in Nova
Scotia in 1825. Additional banks were chartered later; McCullough, ibid.,
85–8, 172, 152; Baskerville, *The Bank of Upper Canada*, xxiv–xxvi; Neufeld,
Money and Banking in Canada, 1–3.

24   Greer, *Peasant, Lord, and Merchant*, 145–51; Mancke, 'At the Counter of the
General Store'; McCalla, 'The Internal Economy of Upper Canada'; 'Rural
Credit and Rural Development in Upper Canada,' 262; and *Planting the
Province*, 146–7; Lapointe, 'Les marchands ruraux anglophones,' 95.

25   McCalla, 'The Internal Economy of Upper Canada'; *Planting the Province*,
66–91, table 5.5, 269; and 'Rural Credit and Rural Development in Upper
Canada.' In the United States, cash appears to have been a more common
form of credit, but never exceeded one third of the credits: Wermuth, *Rip
Van Winkel's Neighbors*, 56, 95, 128; Clark, *The Roots of Rural Capitalism*,
171; Sweeney, 'Gentlemen Farmers and Inland Merchants,' 60–70.

26   At both stores, the dominant form of payment was that used by most
customers, and representing the greater proportion of credit for most customers. At the Dufours, cash was the main source of credit of only 15 per
cent of the customers; country products represented at least half the
credits of one-third of the customers. At Emmerson's, only one customer
in four brought country products to the store at all in 1853; 42 per cent of
the customers never used cash, but 31 per cent used nothing else, and
cash represented at least half the credit of 40 per cent of the customers. In
other words, the averages are not the results of some skewed distribu-
tions of the forms of payments: they are reasonably representative of the
payments of the bulk of the clients.

27   Wainright, 'A Comparative Study in Nova Scotian Rural Economy.'

28   Madawaska Historical Society, Charles Morneault store ledger, 1856–63.
This ledger was made available to me after the completion of this manuscript.

29   AAQ, Lettres des prêtres missionnaires du Madawaska à l'évêque de
Québec, lettres du 15 nov. 1821, 11 sept. 1822, et 27 mars 1824.

30   Shepard Cary papers, Houlton, ME, Memorandum of Charles Terrio, 26
Sept. 1848.

31   AAQ, Lettres des prêtres missionnaires, lettre du 19 fév. 1846.

32   McCullough, *Money and Exchange in Canada to 1900*, 111.

33   This despite the fact the first New Brunswick coins were put in circulation in the early 1860s, the 1-cent bronze in 1861, and the 5-, 10-, and 20-
cent silver coins in 1862. Ibid., 179.

34 According to the *New Brunswick Almanach* for 1864, J. & J. Hegan, 29 Prince William Street, were 'importers of British and foreign dry goods of every description.' The goods listed in their advertising certainly fit this description.

35 For instance, according to the ad in the *New Brunswick Almanac*, Sheffield House, which supplied him with cutlery, accepted only cash; Hasting Brothers, importers of British and foreign dry and fancy goods promised 'low prices for cash.' They also advertised there was no 'second price' in their establishment.

36 NBM, Emmerson receiving book, Methot and Chinic account, 1849. His order was worth £32 3½d.; the discount £1 12s. ½d. Methot and Chinic were major traders in Quebec City. Poulin, ' François Xavier Méthot,'; Filteau and Hamelin, 'Guillaume Eugène Chinic.'

37 PANB, Connors, merchant records, 1875–1923, F 10052.

6: A Tale of Two Markets

1 Gesner, *New Brunswick*, 334; CIHM 35386.

2 Baker and Bacon (for the committee of American Citizens of Madawaska) to Enoch Lincoln, governor of the State of Maine, 9 Jan. 1827, in Sprague, 'Documentary History of the North Eastern Boundary,' 351.

3 MSA, Second Annual Report.

4 Blanchard, *L'Est du Canada français*; Séguin, *La conquête du sol au 19e*; and, 'L'économie agro-forestière'; Hardy et Séguin, *Forêt et société en Mauricie*; Willis, 'Fraserville and Its Temiscouata Hinterland'; Gaffield, 'Boom and Bust'; Little, *Crofters and Habitants*,134–55; and *Nationalism, Capitalism and Colonization*, 100–27.

5 For a survey of the question, see Acheson, 'New Brunswick Agriculture at the End of the Colonial Era'; Lower, *Settlement and the Forest Frontier in Eastern Canada*; MacNutt, *New Brunswick*; Troughton, 'From Nodes to Nodes'; McKinnon and Wynn, 'Nova Scotian Agriculture in the Golden Age,' discuss the same issue for the province of Nova Scotia

6 Baillie, *An Account of the Province of New Brunswick*, 23. CIHM no. 21383; U.S. Department of Agriculture, *Soil Survey, Aroostook County, Maine, North-eastern Part*, series 1959, no. 27; see also *Soil Survey, Aroostook County, Maine, North-eastern Part*, 1964; Canada, Department of Agriculture, *Soils of Madawaska County, New Brunswick*.

7 Baron and Smith, *Growing Season Parameter Reconstruction for New England Using Killing Frost Records*, 24–31.

8 Ward, *An Account of the St John*, 225–8.

9   At present, the frost-free season lasts an average of 198 days, with the last killing frost around 20 May, and the first one around 25 Sept.; killing frosts can occur as late as 28 June and as early as 28 August. U.S. Department of Agriculture, *Soil Survey, Aroostook County, Maine, North-eastern Part,* ser. 1959, no. 27, 75.

10 For a description of early nineteenth-century climatic changes in southern New Brunswick, see Piper, 'Backward Seasons and Remarkably Cold.'

11 [Fisher], *Notitia of New Brunswick for 1836 and Extending into 1837,* 20–1. CIHM no. 10424.

12 Baron and Smith, *Growing Season Parameter Reconstruction,* 24–31

13 Baillie, *Account of the Province of New Brunswick,* 18; [New Brunswick and Nova Scotia Land Company], *Practical Information Respecting New Brunswick,* 9. CIHM no. 21901.

14 Baillie, *Account of the Province,* 18.

15 Ibid., 17.

16 Bidwell and Falconer gave a one- to three-acre a year figure: *History of Agriculture in the Northern United States,* 81.

17 Baillie, *Account of the Province,* 17.

18 [NB and NS Land Company], *Practical Information,* 11.

19 Ibid., 10; Baillie, *Account of the Province,* 17.

20 [NB and NS Land Company], *Practical Information,* 11; Baillie, *Account of the Province,* 19.

21 Bouchette, *A Topographical Description of the Province of Lower Canada,* 147. CIHM no. 44373.

22 MSA, Second Annual Report, 48.

23 [Fisher], *Notitia,* 28.

24 Perley, *A Handbook of Information for Emigrants,* 83; CIHM no. 22479; Baillie, *Account of the Province,* 15; Ward, *An Account of the St John,* 383–4.

25 Baillie, *Account of the Province,* 17.

26 Robb, *Agricultural Progress,* 30. CIHM no. 22568.

27 [Fisher] *Notitia,* 29.

28 MSA,. Second Annual Report, 28, 49. The secretary of the board of agriculture also declared unfounded the rumour that farmers carted off their manure to the nearest brook to get rid of it: 19–20.

29 Robb, *Agricultural Progress,* 15.

30 MSA, Second Annual Report, 19–20.

31 Baillie, *Account of the Province* , 17; Johnston, *Report on Agricultural Capabilities,* 27; [NB and NS Land Company], *Practical Information,* 12.

32 Quoted in Turner, *Rooster: The Story of Aroostook County.*

33 Autobiography of Park Holland, Bangor Historical Society.
34 Campbell, *Travels in the Interior Inhabited Parts*, 99.
35 'Journal des visites pastorales de Mgr Plessis,' 124–9.
36 Grave, *The 1812 Journal of Lieut. John Le Couteur*, 99.
37 Bouchette, *The British Dominions in North America*, 321–2. CIHM no. 42806. The dates of Bouchette's trips are taken from his biography in the Dictionary of Canadian Biography. Bouchette had visited the settlement for the first time in 1807, but his comments at the time had been particularly laconic: 'les chaumières sont pour la plupart proprement bâties et les champs et les jardins biens cultivés.' Bouchette, *A Topographical Description*, 561.
38 [Fisher], *History of New Brunswick*, 53.
39 Baker and Bacon to Enoch Lincoln, governor of the State of Maine, 1 Sept. 1827 in Sprague, 'Documentary History of the North Eastern Boundary,' 351.
40 'Report of John G. Deane and Edward Kavanagh,' in W.O. Raymond, ed., 'State of the Madawaska and Aroostook settlements in 1831,' 455–6.
41 Johnston, *Report on the Agricultural Capabilities*, 65, CIHM no. 22199.
42 Johnston, *Notes on North America*, 74, CIHM no. 35748.
43 Bidwell and Falconer, *History of Agriculture*, 229–30.
44 LAC, Winslow papers, M150, vol. 14, Thomas Costin, 'Instructions to Travel by Canoe up to the Temicouata Lake,' n.d.
45 Lewis and McInnis, 'Agricultural Output and Efficiency,' 74.
46 Ibid., 72.
47 Deane and Kavanagh, 'Report,' 454.
48 Ibid., 455. See also Deane and Kavanagh, 'Wilderness Journey,' 15.
49 Deane and Kavanagh, 'Report,' 455.
50 Stephenson, *Recollection of a Long Life*, 29.
51 [Fisher], *Notitia*, 98.
52 Baird, *Seventy Years of New Brunswick Life*, 90. CIHM no. 02502. Johnston also described the local dark bread made from a mixture of buckwheat, barley, and rye.
53 Johnston, *Notes on North America*, 68, 79.
54 Day, *Aroostook: The First Sixty Years*, ch. 12.
55 MSA, *Second Annual Report*, 17.
56 Wiggin, *History of Aroostook*, 295.
57 Ward, *An Account of the St John*, 86.
58 Johnston, *Report on the Agricultural Capabilities*, 51.
59 Presque Isle *Loyal Sunrise*, 12 October 1866.
60 MSA, Second Annual Report, 23.

296 Notes to pages 148–51

61 PANB, Journal of the House of Assembly of New Brunswick, 1872, Appendix: 'Description of Victoria County,' by Charles Lugrin, XI. See also Lugrin, *Facts concerning the Fertile Belt*, CIHM no. 09213.
62 The Aroostook County board of agriculture seems to have been the only group not only not to have condemned extensive farming, but to actually have advocated it as the most cost effective in a region where land is cheap, labour dear, and markets limited. MSA, Second Annual Report, 24.
63 MSA, Twenty First Annual Report , XV and XVIII.
64 The nature of the sources and the methodology are described in detail in appendix 1.
65 Productive farms are here defined as those with at least five acres of improved land, and growing grain crops. Household reporting 150 or 200 bushels of potatoes could have grown that amount on half an acre using only a spade and a hoe. This was not farming, but gardening. U.S. agricultural censuses exclude low-end farms from their tally, so it was necessary to make the data from the different sources as consistent as possible. The field production of the 'non-farms' is also excluded from the total farm production figures.
66 Not all sources allow the researcher to determine both the number of farms and the number of households. This explains why the two tables do not include the same years.
67 This is the amount put forward by Hobbs-Pruitt, 'Self Sufficiency and the Agricultural Economy.' Pruitt's calculations are based on the production of eighteenth-century Massachusetts farms, which did not grow potatoes. Thirty-four bushels is therefore an overestimate of the grain needs of a nineteenth century farm family.
68 U.S. Department of Agriculture, *Soil Survey, Aroostook County, Maine, North East Part*, 75. For historical crop failures, see AAQ, Lettres des prêtres missionnaires, 18 Oct. 1814, 3 Oct. 1816, 25 May 1817; PANB, Petition de Duperré au Gouverneur du N.B., 1 mai 1797, *Bangor Register*, 10 Oct. 1827; *Republican Journal*, 12 Aug. 1829; *Gleaner and Northumberland Schediasma*, 28 July 1829; diary section of the *Journal of the House of Assembly of New Brunswick* for 13 and 20 Feb. 1834 and 1, 11, and 14 Mar. 1834; *Royal Gazette of New Brunswick*, 28 June 1837; PANB, Journal of the House of Assembly, 1840, 159–60; Journal of the House of Assembly, 1854–55, 106–7; Papers of the Legislative Assembly relating to the settlement of Madawaska, 1834; and Report of the Commissioner of Affairs at Madawaska, 1834; LAC, New Brunswick Executive Council, vol. 32, 78–136.
69 AAQ, Lettres des prêtres missionnaires, 1792.

70 Officials at the time blamed the weather for the plight of the farmers. See PANB, Papers of the Legislative Assembly, assistance to Madawaska settlers.
71 MSA, Twenty First Annual Report.
72 MSA, 'Report of the Board of Agriculture, Aroostook County Society,' 178.
73 Johnston, *Report on the Agricultural Capabilities of New Brunswick*, 59
74 MSA, 'Report of the Board of Agriculture, Aroostook County Society,' 183.
75 MSA, Second Annual Report, 19.
76 Ibid. The Long Reach farmers studied by Liza Piper did not act differently. Piper, 'Backward Seasons and Remarkably Cold.'
77 PANB, 'Maclauchlan report.'
78 U.S. Bureau of the Census, 8th and 9th censuses of the United States; LAC, 1861 census of N.B; 1871 census of Canada.
79 Deeds of maintenance are found at the registrar of the deeds.
80 ACS/CSA, fonds Collège de Sainte-Anne, fond Abbé Henri Dionne, livre de comptes, entrées et reçus, 1835–43.
81 At the beginning of the century, a typical Upper Canadian mill would produce one barrel of flour from five or six bushels of wheat. Six bushels (360 lb) worth $7.20 produced 210 lb of flour worth $6.42, if flour sold for $6 a barrel (196 lb), 40 lb of middling, and 65 lb of bran. The miller kept 30 lbs of wheat for himself. Dunning and Porter, *Bellamy Mill Cookbook*. Millers could offer up to $1.20 a bushel for wheat and sell the flour for $6 a barrel.

7: A Hierarchy of Farmers

1 Robb, *Agricultural Progress*, 18.
2 Catholics were expected to tithe 1/26 of their grain, potatoes, and peas. There were no tithes on hay or animal products
3 Clark, *Roots of Rural Capitalism*, 293, 327–9; Kulikoff, 'The Transition to Capitalism,' 136.
4 Wermuth, *Rip Van Winkle's Neighbors*, 107–8, 112, 124; Bruegel, *Farm, Shop and Landing*: ch. 4 , 90–125; McInnis 'Marketable Surpluses'; McCalla, *Planting the Province*.
5 McInnis, 'Marketable Surpluses'; Atack and Bateman, *To Their Own Soil*.
6 Danhof, *Changes in Agriculture*, 120.
7 I have treated the shanties as non-regional markets because they were completely dependent on overseas demand for timber and lumber for

their existence. The remark from the *Presque Isle Loyal Sunrise* quoted in the previous chapter shows that northern Aroostookians thought along the same lines. The shanties were a place where agricultural commodities were converted into a commodity for export.

8 AAQ, Lettres des prêtres missionnaires du Madawaska à l'évêque de Québec, 3 Mar. 1799; 22 July 1799; 15 Aug. 1807.

9 ACS/CSA, Fonds Collège de Sainte-Anne, fond Abbé Henri Dionne, 1835–1836–1837, cahier de dîmes de l'abbé Henri Dionne.

10 PANB, Papers of the Legislative Assembly, Schedule of Persons entitled to the bounty for raising grain on New Land, 1818–1831.

11 Farmers claiming the bonus on extremely high quantities of grain provide us with indirect evidence of local lumbering activities. The bonus grain had to be grown on land cleared in the past two years. In the best case, an individual cannot clear more than two acres a year. Even assuming the clearing team was a man and four strapping sons, they would have cleared twenty acres over two years. The best yields reported on new land by contemporary sources are 20 bushels an acre, or 400 bushels on twenty acres. In short, a pioneering family could not grow 500 bushels of bonus-eligible grain. But a farmer who had put together a lumbering team and clear-cut part of his claim could. The next spring after the logs were hauled off to the river and the underbrush and branches burned, he could broadcast wheat on the clearing, wait for the harvest, and expect a tidy sum from the government. The loggers may even have helped with the harvest and were possibly paid in wheat.

12 Biographical data are taken from the family reconstitution cards, the county registry office records, and from Maclauchlan and Deane and Kavanagh's reports.

13 ACS/CSA, cahier de dîmes de l'abbé Henri Dionne.

14 See appendix 1 for details of calculations.

15 [Fisher], *Notitia*, 28; MSA, Second Annual Report,194.

16 Lewis and McInnis, 'Agricultural Output,' 75–6; Bittermann, 'Middle River,' Bittermann, MacKinnon, and Wynn. 'Of Inequality and Interdependence.'

17 Danhof, *Changes in Agriculture*, 50.

18 The land registry records contain only records of sales of granted land. Deane and Kavanagh provided the prices of a few farms on ungranted as well as granted land.

19 AAQ, Lettres de prêtres missionnaires, 22 sept. 1843. This is the only lease I could find.

20 Wages are from UMFK, Acadian Archives, Dufour ledger; NBM, Emmerson account books; and Cary papers, Houlton, ME.

21 This assumes that farm values did not increase during the period, and that the type of farms valued at $500 in 1850 would still be valued at $500 in 1870.

22 Ganong, 'A Monograph of the Origins of Settlement,' 103. In Maine, the new commercial commodities were potatoes and potato starch. In New Brunswick farmers continued producing fodder, but for more distant markets.

23 And they were outproducing Nova Scotian farms. See Bittermann, MacKinnon, and Wynn, 'Of Inequality and Interdependence.'

24 Eschelbach-Gregson, 'Specialization in Late-Nineteenth Century Midwestern Agriculture'; and 'Rural Response to Increased Demand'

25 The situation was similar in Nova Scotia. See Bittermann, MacKinnon, and Wynn, 'Of Inequality and Interdependence.'

26 Ranking based on the 1835 tithes for the entire valley. ACS/CSA, fonds Collège de Sainte-Anne, fond Abbé Henri Dionne, 1835–1836–1837, cahier de dîmes de l'abbé Henri Dionne.

27 Craig and Weiss, 'Agricultural Productivity Growth.'

28 The labour shortage estimates are based on the number of improved acres reported in the census, on the number of males age sixteen and over listed in the household, servants included, but excluding men listed as invalid or 'non-productive,' as well as the odd physician or lawyer. The estimates also assume an adult male could take care of a maximum of twenty improved acres

29 According to my father-in-law (b. 1926), who spent his entire life in northern Aroostook, farm labourers still earned 50 cents a day for twelve hours of work in the 1930s.

30 UMFK, Audibert papers, 1844–54.

31 The workforce in the woods is even more elusive: the censuses do not enumerate the shanties and the only company records I had found were useless on that count.

32 Robb, *Agricultural Progress*, 18.

33 Rutman, 'Assessing the Little Communities of Early America.' For an earlier, Canadian perspective see Harris, 'The Simplification of Europe Overseas.'

34 Cohen, *Women's Work, Markets and Economic Development*, 75–82.

35 McMurry, *Transforming Rural Life*.

36 Craig and Weiss, 'Agricultural Productivity Growth,' 527–48.

8: The Homespun Paradox: Domestic Cloth Production and the Farm Economy

1 Hallock, 'Aroostook and the Madawaska.' Despite his mawkishness and his obsession with Evangeline, Hallock was an unusually accurate observer. His descriptions fit in very well with the picture we can derive from the other sources.

2 Murton, 'La Normandie du Nouveau Monde.'

3 Pullen, *In Fair Aroostook.*

4 Murton, 'La Normandie du Nouveau Monde,' 30–1. Tourists were not told the women had learned their 'traditional' skills in school, where they were encouraged to use patterns made by professional designers.

5 Atack and Bateman, *To Their Own Soil*, 205. Other authors make the same link between farm commercialization and the demise of textile production. See Cohen, *Women's Work*, 75–82; Jensen, *Loosening the Bonds*, 87; Craig and Weiss, 'Agricultural Productivity Growth'; Weiss, 'Long Term Changes in US Agricultural Output,' 337; McMurry, *Transforming Rural Life*, 70–8.

6 The data in this chapter are taken from the New Brunswick and Canadian censuses, unless otherwise noted. There is no data on textile production in the American censuses. See appendix 1 for description of sources.

7 McCallum, *Unequal Beginnings*, 88. Other historians have attributed the continuation of domestic cloth production in Quebec to poverty and the need to avoid expenses. See Ruddel, 'Domestic Textile Production in Colonial Quebec'; and 'The Domestic Textile Industry'; Little, *Crofter and Habitants*, 145–6; Lamontagne and Harvey, *La production textile domestique au Québec.*

8 Atack and Bateman, 'Marketable Farm Surpluses'; McInnis, 'Marketable Surpluses in Ontario Farming.'

9 Craig, Rygiel and Turcotte, 'The Homespun Paradox'; and 'Survival or adaptation?'; Craig and Rygiel, 'Femmes, marchés et production textile.'

10 Courville, Robert, and Séguin, *Atlas historique du Quebec*, 59–60; Boisvert, 'La production textile au Bas Canada'; Inwood and Wagg, 'Domestic Cloth Production.' This 1993 article departs from Inwood's earlier perception of weaving as part of a strategy of self-sufficiency, itself a 'rational economic decision not to participate in market exchanges.' Inwood and Grant, 'Gender and Organization in the Canadian Cloth Industry,' 17. By 1993 Inwood argued that 'limited demand for female labour in rural areas made home manufacturing one of the ways that

farm women ... could reduce the need for factory purchases or generate income.' Inwood and Wagg, 'Domestic Cloth Production,' 347.

11 Inwood and Wagg, 'Domestic Cloth Production.'
12 Hood, 'Industrial Opportunities.'
13 The 1851 Canadian census estimated the weight of fleeces at 2 14/16 lb in Upper Canada, 2 4/16 in Lower Canada, and 2 7/16 to 2 43/100 in the United States; Adrienne Hood reckoned 1 lb of raw wool (2/3 lb of clean wool) produced one yard of fabric. In our articles, Judith Rygiel and I have estimated that the homespun typically woven in New Brunswick, a wool weft/cotton warp fabric, required .38 lb to .65 lb of raw material per linear yard of 30 to 32-inch-wide fabric. The heaviest material contained .16 lb of cotton and .62 lb of wool per yard. The smaller figures are based on cloth samples available at the Museum Village of King's Landing, north of Fredericton; the higher figures are derived from schedule 6 for Charlotte County. Craig et Rygiel, 'Femmes, marchés et production textile.'
14 The New Brunswick mills are listed in schedule 6; the U.S. ones in the industrial schedule.
15 NBM, Emmerson papers, ledger D.
16 PANB, probate RG 9 RS 73/A, 24 Aug. 1868.
17 Wallace-Casey, 'Providential Openings,' 29–44.
18 *McAlpine Saint John Directory.*
19 This is based on the amount of raw material calculated in Craig and Rygiel, 'Femmes, marchés et production textile.'
20 PANB, Connors merchant records, 1875–1923.
21 But enough to cover two-thirds of the needs of his clients.
22 Based on the occupations reported in the personal schedule of the 1871 census, and on the same information in the U.S. census for 1870.
23 Afterwards cash annuities and credit lines at the store became increasingly common instead of support in kind.
24 The deeds of maintenance involved a transfer of landed property, and thus were entered in the registry of the deeds. PANB, York County registry office, 1785–1833; Carleton County registry office 1833–50; Victoria County registry office, 1850–73; Madawaska County registry office, 1873–1890; State of Maine, Northern Aroostook registry of the deeds, 1845–90. I went through the records until 1890 because deeds were not always registered in a timely fashion.
25 A suit took seven to eight yards of material; a short gown or blouse, two to three, an apron or a cap, one yard.
26 McGregor, *Historical and Descriptive Sketches,*195–6; and *British America,* 299, 247; see also Cozzens, *Acadia or a Month with the Blue Noses.*

27 PANB, York County registry office, deed dated 10 Apr. 1831, F 5622.

28 McGregor, *Historical and Descriptive Sketches*, 195–6; McGregor, *British America*, 247, 299.

29 PANB, York County registry office, deed dated 7 Aug. 1803, F5618.

30 Wallace-Casey, 'Providential Openings,' 29–44; Mancke. 'At the Counter of the General Store.'

31 Stephenson, *Recollection of a Long Life*, 28.

32 *NB Reporter and Fredericton Advertiser*, 8 June 1880.

33 Ibid., 8 Sept. 1880.

34 Ibid., 11 November 1880.

35 Ibid., 23 November 1881.

36 Mcgrath, ed., *The County: Land of Promise*, 111; Simard, 'Le lin au Madawaska au 19e siècle,' 9–25; 'Concours agricole au Madawaska, 1879,' *Le moniteur acadien*, 1 Jan. 1879, collection of excerpts published in Michaud, *Brève histoire du Madawaska*, 92, 96. 'Il y a cent ans,' 17; 'Memoirs of Alice Michaud Cyr'; Bélanger-Violette, 'Le fait français au Madawaska Américain,' 241.

37 *Saint John Evening Globe*, 25 Sept. 1866.

38 Craig and Rygiel, 'Femmes, marchés et production textile.' The industrial schedule for Charlotte County itemized the inputs and their value.

39 The wages were culled from Dufour, Emmerson and Connor's ledgers and daybooks; for teachers' compensation see MSA, *Twenty-first annual report of the superintendent of common schools*.

40 This rate of payment is higher than the one found in the Doaks papers, a merchant family in Doaktown on the Miramichi (central New Brunswick) in the 1880s: 10 cents a yard for weaving and 15 cents a pound for spinning; PANB, Doak family papers.

41 Here are Mrs Martin's rates: adult male waistcoat: 50 cents; adult male pants: 50 to 60 cents; adult male vest: 50 cents; adult male coat: $1.50; boy's vest: 35 cents; boy's coat 80 cents to $1.20; boy's *capote* (an unstructured Canadian hooded coat): 80 cents to $1.00. Without knowing what the garments exactly looked like, it is difficult to estimate how long it took to make them. Based on my own experience, an unlined, collarless waistcoat or vest would take an afternoon to sew by hand. A pair of pants may take longer, depending on the type of opening and waistband. A well-made, unlined coat with lapels, cuffs, and patch pockets would take the better part of two days. Seamstressing and weaving, then, appear to have been paid at comparative rates.

42 The only 'Mrs. Joseph Martin' in the vicinity of the store was Judith Martin, who was 57 years of age in 1871. Benoni Michaud and his wife

were listed as lodgers in the area in 1861; they had disappeared by 1871. Apparently, female weavers were entitled to their own store accounts, even when under the authority of a husband. Mrs Michaud was not paid as well as Mrs Martin: a shirt can take a whole day to make by hand, unless the pattern is greatly simplified.

43 Cohen, *Women's Work, Markets and Economic Development.*
44 Craig and Weiss, 'Agricultural Productivity Growth,' 544.
45 Craig. 'La transmission des patrimoines fonciers'; 'Land Transmission Practices'; 'La femme face à la transmission des patrimoines'; 'Farm Transmission and the Commercialization of Agriculture'; and 'Marchés et transmission des patrimoines fonciers.'

9: Consumption and the World of Goods

1 Hallock, 'Aroostook and the Madawaska,' 697.
2 Hoops sold for between 6s.3d. and 7s.6d.
3 McKendrick, Brewer and Plumb, *The Birth of a Consumer Society.*
4 Brewer and Porter, ed., *Consumption and the World of Goods*; Schurman and Walsh, *Material Culture*; Shammas, 'The Domestic Environment'; 'Consumer Behaviour in Colonial America'; and *The Pre-Industrial Consumer*; Weatherill, 'A Possession of One's Own'; and *Consumer Behaviour and Material Culture*; Thirsk, 'Popular Consumption'; and *Economic Policy and Projects*; Nenadic, 'Middle Rank Consumers'; Lemire, 'Consumerism In Pre-Industrial and Early Industrial England'; and *Fashion's Favorite*; Coyner, 'Class Consciousness and Consumption'; Schama, *The Embarassment of Riches*; Roche, *Histoire des choses banales*; Cailly, 'Structure sociale et consommation'; and 'Structure sociale et patrimoine'; Jouhaud, 'Des besoins et des goûts'; Baulant et Vari, ' Du fil à l'armoire'; Ruddel, 'Clothing, Society, and Consumer Trends.' Generally speaking, French-Canadian historians are more interested in material culture than in consumption. See Wallot, et al., *Civilisation matérielle au Bas Canada*; Hardy, 'Quelques aspects du niveau de richesse'; and *La vie quotidienne.*
5 Brewer and Porter, *Consumption and the World of Goods*; Schurman and Walsh, *Material Culture*; Breckman, 'Disciplining Consumption'; Walton, 'To Triumph before Feminine Tastes'; Tiesten, 'Redefining Consumer Culture'; De Grazia and Furlough, *The Sex of Things.*
6 Atack and Bateman, *To Their Own Soil*, 205; Weiss, 'Long Term Changes in U.S. Agricultural Output,' 337.
7 Craig and Weiss, 'Agricultural Productivity Growth: Osterud, *Bonds of Community*, 211.

8   Jensen, *Loosening the Bonds*, 87; Mancke, 'At the Counter of the General Store.'
9   Breen, 'An Empire of Goods'; and 'Baubles of Britain.'
10 Shammas, 'How Self-sufficient Was Early America?' 267; Hood, 'The Gender Division of Labor'; and 'The Material World of Cloth Production'; Ulrich, 'Wheels, Looms, and the Gender Division of Labor'; Ruddel, 'Domestic Textile Production'; and 'The Domestic Textile Industry'; Dessureault and Dickinson, 'Farm Implements and Husbandry.'
11 Taylor, 'A Struggle of Finesse,' 299–302, 296.
12 PANB, Victoria County probate court records, John Costello, 1865, John Emmerson, 1867.
13 Unless otherwise specified, the sources used here are the same as in chapter 7: UMFK, Acadian Archives, Dufour ledger, 1845–48; NBM , John Emmerson papers and account books, PANB, F12229 to F 12333 (general journals, 1851–67; memorandum books, 1848–87, with gaps; receiving book, 1849–59; delivery book, 1845–73).
14 *The New Brunswick Almanac and Register, 1864*, CIHM 38435; NBM, *McAlpines Saint John Directory*.
15 *Merchants' and Farmers' Almanach, 1855*. CIHM 36660.
16 Advertising can be found in the *New Brunswick Almanac and Register* (1831–69), the *Merchants' and Farmers' Almanac* (1855–64), and *Barnes's New Brunswick Almanach* (1869–79).
17 Oil lights were a recent invention. Abraham Gesner, who invented kerosene, gave the first demonstration of the product in 1846, and began marketing it in 1850. *Merchants' and Farmers' Almanac*, 1858. CIHM 36663
18 This is also obvious from the Audibert account book. Between 1848 and 1855, Audibert purchased goods in ten different stores: West and Niles, Bodfish, Gagnon, Hunt, Pages (lumber only), Joseph Nadeau, Hartt, Moses Jackson, J. Heald, and G. Seeley. As far as can be told, these were all located in Fort Kent or vicinity. UMFK, Acadian Archives, Joseph Audibert papers, account book 1848–54.
19 McCalla, 'The Needs of Farm Households.'
20 This distribution of goods is also similar to that in other parts of British North America. In St Hyacinthe in the late eighteenth century, fabric and food were already the two leading categories (27 per cent and 18 per cent). Food and textiles also lead at the stores studied by McCalla and distributed through Upper Canada. Food represented between 20 and 40 per cent of the purchases, and textiles between 12 and 26 per cent. Groceries, textiles, iron and hardware (together, including nails), clothing

and footwear, produce, and miscellaneous goods were the leading categories in the five 1861 stores investigated, see Desrosiers, 'Un aperçu des
habitudes de consommation; McCalla, 'The Needs of Farm Households';
and 'Retailing in the Countryside.'
21 Mancke, 'At the Counter of the General Store.'
22 Bought in bulk, meal cost 0.025 cents a pound, and flour 0.037, assuming
selling prices of 12s.6d. per cwt of meal and 35s. for a barrel of flour.
23 The owners of a store near Montreal I have investigated elsewhere made
the distinction between several types of tea: Argenteuil Museum, Caril-
lon, QC, Dewar and Hopkins daybooks, Sept. 1834–Aug. 1836; Jan.
1837–Dec. 1842; June 1851–Dec. 1852, and 1856–7; the Boulé account is
found in the receiving book. Craig, 'Entrepôt de l'Empire.'
24 'Grey' cotton is a corruption of the French *grège* and refers to unbleached
cotton. It is not really grey in colour.
25 Houlton, ME, Houlton Probate Court, inventory of J.B. Cyr, 26 Dec. 1845.
26 Houlton, ME, Houlton Probate Court, inventory of Benjamin Madore dit
Laplante, 25 Nov. 1860.
27 Emmerson sold the oil for 6s. ($1.20) a gallon or 1s.6d. ($0.30) a bottle;
The NB Oil Co sold the oil for 5s.6d. ($1.10) a gallon, and as low as 4s. a
gallon ($0.80) in large quantities (5bbl or more). The lamps fetched 6s3d
($1.85) at the store, and 3s.6d. to 30s. ($0.65 to $12.00) in Saint John in
1858. The Saint John prices are the ones listed in the NB Oil Co advertisement in the *Merchants' and Farmers' Almanac* for 1858.
28 Vital Thibodeau, however, purchased a cricket ball in 1863.
29 UMFK, Acadian Archives, Audibert papers, Joseph Audibert account
book.
30 PANB, York County registry office, deed dated 7 Aug. 1803.
31 See chapter 1.
32 See chapter 2.
33 PANB, York County registry office, deed dated 10 April 1831.

Conclusion

1 Carter, 'An Economy of Words.'
2 MacNutt, 'Thomas Baillie,' 229–41.
3 Lamoreaux, 'Rethinking the Transition to Capitalism.'

Appendix 1: Sources and Methods

1 See Craig, 'Migrant Integration in a Frontier Society,' for this.

2 Langlois, *Dictionnaire généalogique*; Arsenault, *Histoire et généalogie des Acadiens*; Charbonneau et Légaré, *Répertoire des actes*.

3 The family reconstitution cards cover the period from 1792 to 1855, and I supplemented their data with death records up to 1890.

4 PANB, Journal of the Legislative Assembly of New Brunswick, 1852, appendix 1, population returns and other statistics, Victoria County, 228–30.

5 AAQ, Lettres des prêtres missionnaires du Madawaska à l'évêque de Québec, 3 Mar. 1799; 22 July 1799; 15 Aug. 1807.

6 ACS/CSA, fonds Collège de Sainte-Anne, fonds Abbé Henri Dionne, 1835–37, cahier de dîmes de l'abbé Henri Dionne, F100/34/v.

7 AAQ, Lettres des prêtres missionnaires, 16 July 1831 and 16 Sept. 1840; ACS, cahier de dîmes de l'abbé Henri Dionne.

8 PANB, Papers of the Legislative Assembly, schedule of Persons entitled to the Bounty.'

9 Raymond, 'Introduction' to 'State of the Madawaska and Aroostook Settlements in 1831.' Raymond provided an extensive introduction and occasional footnotes. The document is transcribed in extenso, with the exception of the census section, which I found in the original held by the Maine State Archives.

10 University of Maine, Orono, Fogler library, special collections, 'Report of the Commissioners appointed under resolve of February 21, 1843.'

11 1850: MSA, US census, Agricultural schedule for Hancock, Madawaska, and Van Buren plantations, Aroostook County; 185 : PANB, Journal of the Legislative Assembly of New Brunswick, 1852, appendix 1, population returns and other statistics, Victoria County, 228–30; 1860: US census, agricultural schedule for St Francis plantation, St John plantation, Glazier Lake (T17R10), Eagle Lake plantation, Wallagrass (T17R7), Fort Kent plantation, Allagash (T16R10), Frenchville plantation, New Canada (T14R11, T12R16), Madawaska plantation, Grand Isle plantation, Van Buren plantation, letter GR1, letter LR2, letter FR1; 1861: LAC, New Brunswick census, parishes of St Francis, Madawaska, St Basile and St Leonard, M558–9; 1870: US census, agricultural census for St Francis plantation, St John plantation, Eagle Lake plantation, Unincorporated territory above St Francis, Wallagrass (T17R7), Fort Kent, Allagash (T16R10), Dickeyville, New Canada, Madawaska, Grand Isle, Van Buren, Connor plantation, Hamlin plantation, Cyr plantation (TRR1, T18R10, T17R6); 1871 census of Canada, New Brunswick, parishes of St Francis, Madawaska, St Basile and St Leonard, schedules 4–6, C 10385, C 10386.

12 Lewis and McInnis, 'Agricultural Output and Efficiency in Lower Canada'; McInnis, 'Marketable Surplus in Ontario Farms.'

13 Bittermann, 'Middle River'; Bittermann, MacKinnon, and Wynn, 'Of Inequality and Interdependence.'
14 Johnston, *Report on the Agricultural Capabilities of the Province of New Brunswick.*
15 Atack and Bateman, *To Their own Soil.*
16 Deeds of maintenance are found at the Northern registry of the deeds (opened in 1845) in Fort Kent for the Maine side, at the York County registry office (1784–1831), the Carleton County registry office (1831–50), and the Victoria County registry Office (1850–73) for New Brunswick.
17 Manual containing 'The Census Act' and Instructions to Officers Employed in the Taking of the First Census of Canada, 1871. Sessional papers (No 56) 34 Victoria, 1871.
18 Craig, Rygiel, and Turcotte, 'The Homespun Paradox'; and 'Survival or Adaptation?' Craig and Rygiel, 'Femmes, marchés et production textile.'

Bibliography

Archival Sources

Archives de l'archidiocèse de Québec

Lettres des prêtres missionnaires du Madawaska à l'Evêque de Québec, 1785–1850

Archives de la Côte-du-Sud et du Collège de Sainte Anne

Fonds Collège de Sainte-Anne, Fonds Abbé Henri Dionne, 1835–7; Cahier de dîmes de labbé Henri Dionne, F100/34/V; Livre de comptes – entrées et reçus, 1835–43, F100/34/37; Autres, F100/34/63, 74, 81, 84, 87, 88; F100/35/18, 78.

Archives Nationales du Québec á Québec

Circuit Court and Court of King 's Bench, *John Young vs. Michel Robichaud and Uxor*, copy of Robichaud's account, filed 1797, TL18–5006
Cour des Plaids Communs, 1789–91, TL15–3345, 3423, 3527, 3943
Cours de Justice du Régime anglais, Cour du Banc du Roi, 1784, TL999
Greffes de Me Joseph Dionne, notaire de Kamouraska, 1743–79. Inventaire de Pierre Duperré, 5 Oct. 1766, 303–18, MIC 4M01–0477A
Greffes de Me. N.C. Levesque, Notaire de Québec, 1768, MIC 4M01–6177

Bangor Historical Society

Park Holland, 'Life and Diary' (unpublished typescript), 1790

County Documents

State of Maine, Eastern District, Houlton District Court, Houlton, ME,
   1847–61
State of Maine, Houlton Probate Court, Houlton, ME, 1845–1900
State of Maine, Northern Aroostook Registry of the Deeds, Fort Kent,
   1845–90

Harvard University

Harvard University Graduate School of Business Administration, Baker
   Library, R.G. Dun & Co. Collection, Canada, Vol. 328 III 106

Library and Archives Canada

Dominion census of Canada, 1871. County of Victoria, Parishes of St Francis,
   Madawaska, St Basile, and St Leonard
Executive Council of Lower Canada. MG11 'Q,' vol. 60, microfilm C11907
Journaux de l'assemblée législative de la province du Canada, Appendices,
   vol. 11, session 1852–3
Lower Canada Land Papers: Exploration and Roads, Craig Road, Road to
   New Brunswick 1810–19, RG1L3, vol. 27
Prudent L. Mercure papers, MG30 C5
New Brunswick Executive Council, MG9 A1, vol. 32, pp. 78–136. Agricultural
   crop failures, 1817–55
New Brunswick Lieutenant Governor [Colebrook]. Correspondence, letter-
   book, 1841–2, MG9A2
New Brunswick Lieutenant Governor [Harvey]. Correspondence, letterbook,
   MG24A17
Parchemin (searchable database of Quebec notarial records to 1779, including
   a brief description of the content of the acts)
Provincial Census of New Brunswick, 1851: County of Victoria, Parishes of St
   Francis, Madawaska, St Basile, and St Leonard
Provincial census of New Brunswick, 1861: County of Victoria, Parishes of St
   Francis, Madawaska, St Basile, and St Leonard
Edward Winslow Papers, MG23 D2

Madawaska Historical Society

Charles Morneault, store ledger, 1858–63

Maine Historical Society Library

Proceedings of the Citizens of Aroostook County at a Mass Meeting Held at the Court House, Houlton, 1 March 1866, to Consider the Agricultural and Lumbering Interests of the County. Houlton, ME: Times Office, 1866 (pamphlet 1114)

Shepard Cary, Correspondence with Collin Whitaker, 1836–45, Coll. 411 Box1/1 Ms. 86–44

Maine State Archives

Commission on the Settlement of the Public Land, Report, Augusta, ME, 1870

Land Office Records, Journal of George W. Coffin, Massachusetts land agent, Journey up the St John River, Sept.-Oct. 1825.

Maine Public Documents. Eighteenth Annual Report of the Bureau of Industrial and Labor Statistics for the State of Maine, 1904. Augusta, ME: Kennebec Journal Print, 1905

– Maine Legislature, *Report of the Commission Appointed to Investigate Alleged Election Frauds in Certain Towns and Plantations in Aroostook County.* Augusta, ME: E.F Pillsbury and Co, 1879

– Report of the Commissioners on Claims of Settlers on Proprietors' Land in the County of Aroostook, made in pursuance of resolve of February 27, 1873. Augusta, ME: Noah Baker Printer, 1874.

– Report of the Commissioners Appointed under the Resolve of February 21, 1843, to Locate Grants and Determine the Extent of Possessory Claims under the Late Treaty with Great Britain

– Second Annual Report of the Secretary of the Maine Board of Agriculture, 1857. Augusta, ME: Stevens and Sayward, 1858

– Twenty-First Annual Report of the Secretary of the Maine Board of Agriculture for the Year 1876. Augusta, ME: Sprague, Owen and Nash, 1876

– Twenty-First Annual Report of the Superintendent of Common Schools, 1874. Augusta, ME: Sprague, Owen and Nash, 1876

Maine State Papers, Documentary History of the North-Eastern Boundary Controversy, 2nd session, 20th congress, 1828–9

'Report of the Board of Agriculture, Aroostook County Society,' *Transactions of the Agricultural Societies of Maine* (1859): 177–78.

'Report of John G. Deane and Edward Kavanagh to Samuel E. Smith, Governor of the State of Maine, with appendix containing a census of the population' (published, with the exception of the census, in the New Brunswick Historical Society *Collection*, ed. W.O. Raymond)

Survey maps accompanying the report of the land agents sent by Maine and
  Massachusetts to settle the claims arising from under article 4 of the treaty
  of Washington (1845)

Maine State Library

Maine Public Documents. Maine Legislature. Report of the Joint Select Com-
  mittee to Investigate the Frauds in the Late Elections among the French
  Population in the County of Aroostook. Augusta, ME: Stevens and
  Sayward, 1859

New Brunswick Museum, Saint John

J. Emmerson Papers and Account Books, 1843–1909 (also on microfilms at
  PANB)
Hugh T. Hazen Collection, Hazen and White account book, 1775–9, F82
McAlpine Saint John Directory. Saint John: 1863 and 1864
Odell family papers, Correspondence 1817–44, F32–7

Parish Registers (original accessible at the parishes)

St. Basile, NB, Registres paroissiaux, 1792–1857 (microfilm available from
  LAC)
St Bruno, ME, Registres paroissiaux 1838–50
Ste Luce, ME, Registres paroissiaux, 1842–58

Private Archives

Shepard Cary papers, in possession of Mr Frank Peltier, Houlton, ME

Province of New Brunswick Crown Land Office, Fredericton

Survey map of the Mazzerolle grant, 1790
Survey map of the Soucy Grant, 1794
Maps of the Madawaska Survey conducted by Land Commissioners J.A.
  Maclauchlan and John C. Allen to settle the claims arising under the treaty
  of Washington, 1844–8

Provincial Archives of New Brunswick, Fredericton, New Brunswick

Connors, Robert, Merchant Records, 1875–1923, F 1052

County Registry Offices: York County Registry Office, 1785–1833; Carleton County Registry Office, 1833–50; Victoria County Registry Office, 1850–73; Madawaska County Registry Office, 1873–90

Crown Land Office, Surveyor General George Sproule Papers, 1774–1817

Department of Natural Resources and Crown Land: Rules, Regulations and Order in Council, 1837–56, RS107; Timber correspondence 1809–36, RS663 E/1; Timber Records Books, 1825–38; RS663/13/2; Timber sales and account books, 1839–71, RS663/B; Timberland and sawmill correspondence, RS 663/D/25; Timberland and sawmill records, 1843–64, RS663/D/6; Timber and sawmill petitions, 1817–65, RS633A

Doak family papers, MC 1055 MS 8F1

D.D. Glazier and Son, Account Books: timber rafts, MC30, MS1, and NS2.

Journal of the House of Assembly, Charles S. Lugrin, State of Agriculture in Victoria County, Appendix, 1872

Journal of the House of Assembly of New Brunswick, 1786–1867

Journal of the House of Legislature of New Brunswick, 1867–80

Journals of the Executive Council, 1783–1850

Journals of the Legislative Council of the province of New Brunswick from the first session, 1786 to the 4th session of the 9th general assembly, 1830, Fredericton, 1831

Land Petitions and Application Book, 1784–1825, RS108, microfilm F1024–F1039

Legislative Assembly, sessional records, RS24

Minutes of York County Sessions, 1821–3 and 1831–2

Papers of the Legislative Assembly: papers relating to the settlement of Madawaska, Assistance to Madawaska settlers, RS24/1834/RE.l; Schedule of Persons Entitled to the Bounty for Raising Grain on New Land, 1818–31

Papers of the Legislative Assembly Relating to the Settlement of Madawaska, 1834: Report of the Commissioner of Affairs at Madawaska, 1834 (contains Maclauchlan report, 'Return Showing the Number of Inhabitants in the Settlement of Madawaska with Their Stock,' 1833)

Political Biographies. Comp. by James C. Graves and Horace C. Graves

Provincial Secretary, correspondence, RS13

Public Accounts/Blue Books, 1845–59, RS536/A and 1859–7, RS845

Records of the Surveyor General, 1784–1912, RS637, Disputes, cases of land

Report of the Commissioners to Settle the Claims of Land under the 4th Article of the Treaty of Washington, 1848

Report on Violations, Disputes and Seizures, RS663/E/2

Vertical files, Family history files, Hammond family.

Victoria County Probate Court Records, RS73A, Probate Record Books
    1850–1926, Mic. F 7308; Estate files 1850–1910, F 7296
York Sunbury Historical Collection, J.S. Glasier papers, RS38/2/1837;
    Stephen Glasier papers, 1855–60, RS300/MS8–3

Provincial Archives of Nova Scotia, Halifax

Minutes of the Executive Council, RG1 vol. 136 and 212
Nova Scotia Land Papers, RG20 vol. 1, microfilm 15685

State of Massachusetts Archives

Twentieth Congress of the United States, 1st session. *Message from the Presi-
    dent of the United States with Documents relating to Alleged Aggressions on the
    Rights of Citizens of the United States by the Authorities of New Brunswick on
    the Territory in Dispute between the United States and Great Britain, March 4,
    1828.* Washington, DC: Duff Green, 1828

United States Bureau of the Census

Fourth Census of the United States, 1820 (photographic reproduction in
    Prudent L. Mercure papers, LAC)
Seventh Census of the United States, State of Maine, County of Aroostook,
    year 1850, personal and agricultural schedules for Hancock, Madawaska,
    and Van Buren plantations; industrial schedule for Hancock plantation
Eighth Census of the United States, State of Maine, County of Aroostook,
    personal, agricultural and industrial schedules for 1860 (personal sched-
    ules are available on microfilms from the U.S. National Archives; the agri-
    cultural and industrial schedules from the Maine State Archives)
Ninth Census of the United States, State of Maine, County of Aroostook, per-
    sonal, agricultural and industrial schedules for 1870 (personal schedules
    are available on microfilms from the U.S. National Archives; the agricul-
    tural and industrial schedules from the Maine State Archives)

University of Maine at Fort Kent

Acadian Archives, Abraham and Simon Dufour, store ledger, 1845–8
– Audibert papers, 1844–54

University of Maine, Orono, Fogler Library, Special Collections

Report of the Commissioners Appointed under Resolve of February 21, 1843,
   to Locate Grants and Determine the Extent of Possessory Claims under the
   Late Treaty with Great Britain
Report of the Commissioners Appointed under Resolve of April 12, 1854 to
   Locate Grants and Determine the Extent of Possessory Claims under the
   Late Treaty with Great Britain

University of Maine at Presque Isle

Library, Aroostook room, Melvin collection

University of New Brunswick Archives, Fredericton

Governor Harvey's letterbook
Lillian M. Maxwell Collection. 'Reminiscence of Thomas S. Glasier, 1914'

Primary and Secondary Sources

Acheson, T.W. 'John Robinson.' *Dictionary of Canadian Biography* 6: 654–5.
– 'James Simonds.' *Dictionary of Canadian Biography* 6: 717–20.
– 'New Brunswick Agriculture at the End of the Colonial Era: A Reassess-
   ment.' In *Farm, Factory and Fortune: New Studies in the Economic History of
   the Maritime Provinces,* ed. Kris Inwood, 37–60. Fredericton: Acadiensis
   Press, 1993.
Albert, Abbé Thomas. *Histoire du Madawaska.* Quebec: Imprimerie francis-
   caine missionnaire, 1920.
Allen, Robert C. *Enclosure and the Yeoman.* Oxford: Clarendon Press, 1992.
An Almanac for the year of our Lord 1830. St John: H. Chubb, 1831. CIHM
   38414.
Andrew, Sheila M. *The Development of Elites in Acadian New Brunswick,
   1861–1881.* Montreal and Kingston: McGill-Queen's University Press, 1997.
Andrew, Sheila. 'Levite Thériault.' *Dictionary of Canadian Biography* 12:
   1034–6.
– 'Louis Mercure.' *Dictionary of Canadian Biography* 5: 589–90.
Appleby, Joyce Oldham. *Capitalism and a New Social Order: The Republican
   Vision of the 1790s.* New York: New York University Press, 1984.
– *Economic Thought and Ideology in Seventeenth Century England.* Princeton,
   NJ: Princeton University Press, 1978.
– 'The Vexed Story of Capitalism Told By American Historians.' *Journal of the
   Early Republic* 21(2001): 1–18.

Arsenault, Bona. *Histoire et généalogie des Acadiens.* 7 vol. Ottawa: Lemeac, 1978.

Atack, Jeremy, and Fred Bateman. 'Marketable Farm Surpluses: North Eastern and Midwestern United States, 1859 and 1860.' *Social Science History* 8 (1984): 371–94.

– *To Their Own Soil: Agriculture in the Antebellum North.* Ames: University of Iowa Press, 1987.

Baillie, Thomas. *An Account of the Province of New Brunswick, including a Description of the Settlement, Institutions, Soil and Climate of that Important Province, with Advice to Emigrants.* London: Printed for J. G. & F. Rivington, 1832.

Baird, William Thomas. *Seventy Years of New Brunswick Life: Autobiographical Sketches.* Saint John: G.E. Day, 1890.

Barnes's New Brunswick Almanach for the Year of our Lord [...]. .Saint John: Barnes, 1869–76. CIHM 39264–66, 27934–35, 27675, 27799, 32010, 27800 (1872 and 1874 missing).

Baron, William R., and David C. Smith. *Growing Season Parameter Reconstruction for New England Using Killing Frost Records, 1697–1947.* Oronto, ME: Maine Agricultural and Forest Experiment Station, bulletin 846, Nov. 1996.

Barron, Hal. *Those Who Stayed Behind: Rural Society in Nineteenth Century New England.* Cambridge: Cambridge University Press, 1984.

Baskerville, Peter. *The Bank of Upper Canada.* Toronto: Champlain Society, 1987.

Baulant, Micheline and Stéphane Vari. 'Du fil à l'armoire: Production et consommation de linge à Meaux et dans ses campagnes, XVII–XVIII siècles.' *Ethnologie française* 16 (1986): 273–80.

Beauregard, Yves, Alain Laberge, et al. ' Famille, parenté et colonisation en Nouvelle France. ' *Revue d'histoire de l'Amérique française* 39 (winter 1986): 396–400.

Beckett, J.V. *The Agricultural Revolution.* Oxford: Blackwell, 1990.

Bélanger-Violette, Marcella. 'Le fait français au Madawaska Américain.' PhD thesis. Université St Louis, Edmundston, NB, 1953.

Bergeron, Adrien. *Le Grand Arrangement des Acadiens au Québec.* 7 vol. Montreal: Elysée presse, 1981.

Bernard, Antoine. *Histoire de la survivance Acadienne.* Montreal: Clercs de St Viateurs, 1935.

Bidwell, Percy, and John Falconer. *History of Agriculture in the Northern United States, 1620–1860.* New York: Peter Smith, 1941.

Bittermann, Rusty. 'Farm Households and Wage Labour in the Northeastern

Maritimes in the Early 19th Century.' In *Contested Countryside: Rural Workers and Modern Society in Atlantic Canada, 1800–1950*, ed. Daniel Samson, 34–69. Fredericton: Acadiensis Press, 1994.

– 'The Hierarchy of the Soil: Land and Labour in a 19th Century Cape Breton community.' *Acadiensis* 18 (autumn 1988): 33–55.

– 'Middle River: The Social Structure of Agriculture in a Nineteenth Century Cape Breton Community,' MA thesis, University of New Brunswick, 1987.

Bittermann, Rusty, Robert MacKinnon, and Graeme Wynn. 'Of Inequality and Interdependence in the Nova Scotian Countryside, 1850–70.' *Canadian Historical Review* 74, no. 1 (March, 1993): 1–43.

Blais, Christian. 'Pérégrinations et conquête du sol (1755–1836) : L'implantation acadienne sur la rive nord de la Baie-des-Chaleurs.' *Acadiensis* 35, no. 1 (autumn 2005): 3–23.

Blanchard, Raoul. *L'Est du Canada français*. Montreal: Beauchemin, 1935.

Bogue, Allan G. *From Prairie to Corn Belt: Farming on the Illinois and Iowa Prairies in the Nineteenth Century*. Chicago: University of Chicago Press, 1963.

Boisvert, Michel. 'La production textile au Bas Canada: L'exemple Laurentien.' *Cahiers de Géographie du Québec* 40 (Dec. 1996): 421–37.

Bouchard, Gérard. 'Family Structures and Geographic Mobility at Laterrière, 1851–1935.' *Journal of Family History* 2 (Dec. 1977): 350–69.

– *Quelques arpents d'Amérique: Population, économie, famille au Saguenay, 1838–1971*. Quebec: Boréal Express, 1996.

– 'Les systèmes de transmission des avoirs familiaux et le cycle de la société rurale au Québec du XVIIᵉ au XXᵉ.' *Histoire sociale/Social History* 31 (May 1983): 35–60.

Bouchard, Gérard, Jeannette Larouche, and Lise Bergeron. 'Donation entre vifs et inégalités sociales au Saguenay: Sur la reproduction familiale en contexte de saturation de l'espace agraire.' *Revue d'histoire de l'Amérique française* 46 (1993): 443–62.

Bouchard, Gérard, et Régis Thibeault. 'L'économie agraire et la reproduction sociale dans les campagnes saguenayennes (1852–1871).' *Histoire sociale/Social History* 36 (Nov. 1985): 237–58.

Bouchette, Joseph. *The British Dominions in North America, or, A Topographical and Statistical Description of the Provinces of Lower and Upper Canada, New Brunswick, Nova Scotia, the Islands of Newfoundland, Prince Edward, and Cape Breton: including Considerations on Land-Granting and Emigration : to which are Annexed, Statistical Tables and Tables of Distances, &c*. London: H. Colburn and R. Bentley, 1831.

- *A Topographical Description of the Province of Lower Canada with Remarks upon Upper Canada, and on the Relative Connexion of both Provinces with the United States of America*. London: W. Faden, 1815.
Boydston, Jeanne. 'The Woman Who Wasn't There: Women's Market Labor and the Transition to Capitalism in the United States.' *Journal of the Early Republic* 16 (1996): 183–206.
Braudel, Fernand. *Afterthoughts on Material Civilization and Capitalism*. Baltimore: Johns Hopkins University Press, 1979.
- *Civilisation matérielle, économie et capitalisme, 15e-18e siècle*. Vol. 2. *Les jeux de l'échange*. Paris: Colin, 1967.
Breckman, Warren. 'Disciplining Consumption: The Debate about Luxury in Whilhelmine Germany.' *Journal of Social History* 24 (1991): 485–505.
Breen, T.H. '"Baubles of Britain": The American and Consumer Revolutions of the Eighteenth Century.' *Past and Present* 119 (May 1988): 73–103.
- 'An Empire of Goods: The Anglicization of Colonial America, 1690–1776.' *Journal of British Studies* 25 (Oct. 1986): 467–99.
- 'The Meaning of Things; Interpreting the Consumer Economy in the Eighteenth Century.' In *Consumption and the World of Goods*, ed. John Brewer and Roy Porter, 249–60. London: Routledge, 1993.
Brewer, John, and Roy Porter, eds. *Consumption and the World of Goods*. London: Routledge, 1993.
Bruce, Elliott. *Irish Migrants in the Canada: A New Approach*. Montreal and Kingston: McGill-Queens University Press, 1988.
Bruegel, Martin. *Farm, Shop, Landing: The Rise of a Market Society in the Hudson Valley, 1780–1860*. Durham, NC: Duke University Press, 2002.
Brun, Régis Sigefrois. 'Histoire socio-demographique du Sud-Est du Nouveau Brunswick: Migrations acadiennes et seigneuries anglaises, 1760–1810. ' Société historique Acadienne, *Cahiers* 3 (Jan.–March 1969): 58–88.
Brymer, Douglas. *Report on Canadian Archives*. Ottawa, 1895.
Bubar, John 'A Planter Family: The Bubars of New England and New Brunswick.' In *Making Adjustment: Change and Continuity in Planter Nova Scotia, 1759–1800*, ed. Margaret Conrad, 198–201. Fredericton: Acadiensis Press, 1990.
Buckley, Kenneth 'The Role of Staple Industries in Canada's Economic Development.' *Journal of Economic History* 18 (1958): 434–50.
Burrage, Henry F. *Maine in the North Eastern Boundary Controversy*. Portland, ME: Marks, 1919.
Bushman, Richard Lyman. 'Markets and Composite Farms in Early America.' *William and Mary Quarterly* 3d. ser. 55 (July 1998): 351–74.

– *Puritan to Yankee*. New York: Norton, 1970.

Cailly, Claude. 'Structure sociale et consommation dans le monde proto-industriel rural textile: Le cas du Perche ornais au XVIIIe siècle.' *Revue d'histoire moderne et contemporaine* 45 (1998): 746–74.

– 'Structure sociale et patrimoine du monde proto-industriel rural textile au XVIIIe siècle.' *Revue historique* 290 (1993): 443–77.

Campbell, Carol. 'A Scots Irish Plantation in Nova Scotia, Truro 1760–1775. ' In *Making Adjustment: Change and Continuity in Planter Nova Scotia, 1759–1800*, ed. Margaret Conrad. 153–64. Fredericton: Acadiensis Press, 1990.

Campbell, Patrick. *Travels in the Interior Inhabited Parts of North America in the Years 1791 and 1792*. Edinburgh, 1793.

Campbell, Rod C. 'Simonds, Hazen and White: A Study of a New Brunswick Firm in the Commercial World of the Eighteenth Century.' MA thesis, University of New Brunswick, 1970.

– 'William Hazen.' *Dictionary of Canadian Biography* 5 : 415–17.

Campbell, W.E. *The Road to Canada: The Grand Communication Route from Saint John to Quebec*. New Brunswick Military Heritage Series, vol. 5. Fredericton: Goose Lane Editions, 2005.

Carter, Kathryn. 'An Economy of Words: Emma Chadwick Stretch's Account Book Diary, 1859–1860.' *Acadiensis* 29, 1 (autumn 1999): 43–57.

Charbonneau, Hubert, and Jacques Légaré. *Répertoire des actes de baptême, mariage, sépulture et recensements du Québec ancien*. 47 vols. Montréal: Presses de l'université de Montréal, 1988.

Chipman, Ward. *Remarks upon the Disputed Points of Boundary: Under the Fifth Article of the Treaty of Ghent*. Saint John, NB, 1838.

Clark, Christopher. 'Household Economy, Market Exchange, and the Rise of Capitalism in the Connecticut Valley, 1800–1860.' *Journal of Social History* 13 (winter 1979): 169–89.

– *The Roots of Rural Capitalism: Western Massachusetts, 1780–1860*. Ithaca, NY: Cornell University Press, 1990.

Clark, Ernest. *The Siege of Fort Cumberland, 1776: An Episode in the American Revolution*. Montreal and Kingston: McGill-Queen's University Press, 1995.

Cohen, Marjorie. *Women's Work, Markets and Economic Development in Nineteenth Century Ontario*. Toronto: University of Toronto Press, 1988.

Collins, S.W. *Lumbering Then and Now*. [Caribou, ME]: The Company, [1954].

Condon, Ann Gorman. *The Envy of the American States: The Loyalist Dream for New Brunswick*. Fredericton: New Ireland Press, 1984.

Conrad, Margaret, ed. *Intimate Relations, Family and Community in Planter Nova Scotia, 1759–1800*. Fredericton: Acadiensis Press, 1994.

– *Making Adjustment: Change and Continuity in Planter Nova Scotia, 1759–1800.* Fredericton: Acadiensis Press, 1990.
– *They Planted Well: New England Planters in Maritime Canada.* Fredericton: Acadiensis Press, 1988.
Cook, Terry. 'John Beverley Robinson and the Conservative Blueprint for the Upper Canadian Community.' *Ontario History* 64 2 (June 1972): 79–94.
Cooper, J.P. 'In Search of Agrarian Capitalism.' *Past and Present* 80 (Aug. 1978): 20–65.
Correspondence Relating to the Boundary between the British Possessions in North America and the United States under the Treaty of 1783. London, 1840. CIHM, 21252.
Côté, Martine. 'L'exploitation des forêts publiques sur la Côte-du-Sud, 1830–1900; un exemple de la perméabilité de la frontière Canado-américaine.' Paper presented at the Congrès de l'institut d'histoire de l'Amérique française, Oct. 1991.
Courville, Serge. 'La crise agricole du Bas Canada: Éléments d'une réflexion géographique.' *Cahier de géographie du Québec* 24 (1980): 193–229, 383–428.
– 'Croissance villageoise et industrie rurale dans les seigneuries du Québec, 1815–1851.' In *Sociétés villageoises et rapports villes-campagnes au Québec et dans la France de l'ouest, XVII–XXe siècles,* ed. F. Lebrun et N. Séguin, 205–20. Trois Rivières: Université du Québec à Trois Rivières / Presses Universitaires de Rennes, 1987.
– *Entre ville et campagne: L'essor du village dans les seigneuries du Bas Canada.* Quebec: Presses de l'Université Laval, 1990.
– 'Un monde rural en mutation: Le Bas Canada dans la première moitié du XIXe siècle.' *Histoire sociale/Social History* 40 (1987): 237–58.
– 'Villagers and Agriculture in the Seigneuries of Lower Canada: Conditions of a Comprehensive Study of Rural Quebec in the First Half of the Nineteenth Century.' *Canadian Papers in Rural History* (1986): 121–49.
Courville, Serge, J.-C. Robert, and Normand Séguin. *Atlas historique du Québec.* Quebec: Presses de l'université Laval, 1995.
– 'The Spread of Rural Industry in Lower Canada, 1831–1851.' *Journal of the Canadian Historical Association* (1991): 41–70.
Coyner, Sandra. 'Class Consciousness and Consumption: The New Middle Class during the Weimar Republic.' *Journal of Social History* 10 (1977): 310–31.
Cozzens, Frederic S. *Acadia or a Month with the Blue Noses.* New York, 1859.
Craig, Béatrice. 'Agriculture and the Lumberman's Frontier: The Madawaska Settlement, 1800–1870.' *Journal of Forest History* 12 (July 1988): 125–37, reprinted under the title 'Occupational Pluralism in British North America'

in *Interpreting Canada's Past*. Vol. 1. *Pre-confederation*, ed. J.M. Bumsted, 366–394. Toronto: Oxford University Press, 1993.

– 'Agriculture et marché au Madawaska, 1799–1850.' *River Review/Revue rivière* 1 (1995): 13–38.

– 'Agriculture in a Pioneer Region: The Upper St John Valley in the First Half of the Nineteenth Century.' In *Farm, Factory and Fortune: New Studies in the Economic History of the Maritime Provinces*, ed. Kris Inwood, 17–36. Fredericton: Acadiensis Press, 1993.

– 'Before Borderlands: Yankees, British, and the St John Valley French.' In *New England and the Maritime Provinces: Connections and Comparisons*, ed. Stephen J. Hornsby and John G. Reid, 74–93. Montreal and Kingston: McGill-Queen's University Press, 2005.

– 'Le développement agricole dans la haute vallée du St Jean en 1860.' *Revue de la Société historique du Canada* 3 (1993): 13–26.

– 'Early French Migrations to Northern Maine, 1785–1850.' *Maine Historical Society Quarterly* 25 (spring 1986): 230–47.

– 'Entrepôt de l'Empire: Le magasin général rural au milieu du XIXe siècle.' In *Familles, rapports à la terre et aux marchés, logiques économiques, France et Suisse, Canada et Québec, 18e-20e siècles*, ed. Gerard Beaur, Christian Dessureault, and Joseph Goy, 33–46. Rennes: Presses Universitaires de Rennes, 2005.

– 'Farm Transmission and the Commercialization of Agriculture in Northern Maine in the Second Half of the Nineteenth Century.' *History of the Family* 10 (2005): 327–44.

– 'La femme face à la transmission des patrimoines au XIXe siècle: Droit, coutume et pratiques.' In *Transmettre, hériter, succéder: La reproduction familiale en milieu rural, France–Québec, XVIII-XX siècles*, ed. R. Bonnain, G. Bouchard, and J. Goy, 231–42. Lyons, Paris, andVilleurbane: Presses Universitaires de Lyons, L'école des hautes études en sciences sociales, Programme pluriannuel en sciences humaines Rhones-Alpes, 1992.

– 'Kinship and Migration to the Upper St John Valley, 1785–1842.' *Quebec Studies* 1 (spring 1983): 151–64.

– 'Land Transmission Practices among Northern Maine French Canadians in the Nineteenth Century.' In *New England–New France, 1600–1850*, P. Benes, 69–81. Boston: Boston University Press, 1992.

– 'Marchés et transmission des patrimoines fonciers au XIXe siècle.' In *Nécessités économiques et pratiques juridiques: Problèmes de la transmission des exploitations agricoles (XVIIIe–XIXe siècles*. ed. G. Bouchard, L. Goy, and A.L. Head-König, *Mélanges de l'Ecole Française de Rome. Italie et Méditerranée* 110, no. 1 (1998): 405–8.

– 'Migrant Integration in a Frontier Society: The Madawaska Settlement, 1800–1850.' *Histoire sociale/Social History* 38 (Nov. 1986): 277–98.
– 'Solder les comptes: Les sources de crédits dans les magasins généraux ruraux de l'est canadien au milieu du XIXe siècle.' *Journal of the Canadian Historical Association* 13 (2003): 23–48.
– 'La transmission des patrimoines fonciers dans le Haut St-Jean au XIXe siècle.' *Revue d'histoire de l'Amérique française* 45 (Dec., 1991): 207–28.
– 'Y-eut-il une "révolution industrieuse" en Amérique du Nord?' In *Famille, terre et marchés: Logiques économiques et stratégies dans les milieux ruraux (XVIIe–XXe)*, ed. Christian Dessureault, John A.Dickinson, and Joseph Goy, 33–48. Montreal: Septentrion, 2003.
Craig, Béatrice, Maxime Dapenais, Lisa Ornstein, and Guy Dubay. *The Land in between: Madawaska 13000 BP to World War One*. Gardiner, ME: Tilbury House, forthcoming.
Craig, Béatrice, and Judith Rygiel. 'Femmes, marchés et production textile au Nouveau Brunswick au XIXe siècle.' *Histoire et mesure* 15, no.1 (2000) : 83–112.
Craig, Béatrice, Judith Rygiel, and Elizabeth Turcotte. 'The Homespun Paradox: Market-Oriented Production of Cloth in Eastern Canada in the Nineteenth Century.' *Agricultural History* 76 (winter 2002): 28–57.
– 'Survival or Adaptation? Domestic Rural Textile Production in Eastern Canada in the latter Part of the Nineteenth Century.' *Agricultural History Review* 49 (2001): 140–71.
Craig, Béatrice, and M.H. Sorg. 'Patterns of Infant Mortality in the Upper St John Valley French Population, 1791–1838,' *Human Biology* 55 (Feb. 1983): 100–13.
Craig, Lee A., and Thomas Weiss. 'Agricultural Productivity Growth during the Decade of the Civil War.' *Journal of Economic History* (1993): 527–48.
Danhof, Clarence. *Changes in Agriculture, The Northern United States*. Cambridge, MA: Harvard University Press, 1969.
Day, Clarence. *Aroostook: The First Sixty Years*. First published as a serial in the Fort Fairfield Review, 1951–7.
Deane, John G., and Kavanagh, E. 'Report of John G. Deane and Edward Kavanagh to Samuel E. Smith, Governor of the State of Maine.' In *State of the Madawaska and Aroostook Settlements in 1831*, ed. W.O. Raymond. New Brunswick Historical Society *Collections*, 3, 1907.
– 'Wilderness Journey: A Nineteenth Century Journal.' *Maine History Newsletter* 16 (Apr. 1980): 3–4, 15; (July 1980): 5–7, 15–16; (Oct. 1980):8–11, 16.
De Grazia, Victoria, and E. Furlough. *The Sex of Things: Gender and Consump-*

tion in Historical Perspectives. Berkeley and Los Angeles: University of California Press, 1996.

Delâge, Denys, and Gilbert, Etienne. 'La justice coloniale britannique et les Amérindiens au Québec, 1760–1820. II – En territoire colonial.' *Recherches amérindiennes au Québec* 32, 2 (2002) : 107–17.

Dépatie, Sylvie. 'Commerce et crédit à l'île Jésus, 1734–1775: Le rôle des marchands ruraux dans l'économie des campagnes montréalaises.' *Canadian Historical Review* 84 (June 2003): 147–76.

– 'La transmission du patrimoine au Canada (XVIIe–XVIIIe siècle): Qui sont les défavorisés?' *Revue d'histoire de l'Amérique française* 54 (2004): 557–70.

– 'La transmission du patrimoine dans les terroirs en expansion: un exemple canadien au XVIIIe siècle.' *Revue d'histoire de l'Amérique française* 44 (1990): 171–98.

Desrosiers, Claude. 'Un aperçu des habitudes de consommation de la clientèle de Joseph Cartier, marchand général à St Hyacinthe à la fin du XVIII.' *Communications historiques / Historical Papers* (1984): 91–110.

Dessureault, Christian, and John A. Dickinson. 'Farm Implements and Husbandry in Colonial Quebec, 1740–1840. ' In *New England–New France, 1600–1850*, ed. Peter Benes, 110–21. Boston: Boston University Press, 1992.

De Vries, Jan. 'Between Purchasing Power and the World of Goods: Understanding the Household Economy in Early Modern Europe.' In *Consumption and the World of Goods*, ed. J. Brewer and R. Porter, 85–132. London: Routledge, 1993.

– 'The Industrial Revolution and the Industrious Revolution.' *Journal of Economic History* 54 (1994): 340–61.

DiMatteo, Livio, and Peter George. 'Patterns and Determinants of Wealth among Probated Decedents in Wentworth County, Ontario, 1872–1902.' *Histoire sociale/Social History* 31 (1998): 1–33.

Ditz, Toby. *Property and Kinship, Inheritance in Early Connecticut, 1750–1820*. Princeton, NJ: Princeton University Press, 1986.

Dubay, Guy. *The History of Germain Dubé of Hamlin, and Some of His Descendants, as Told by Them*. Privately published, 1989.

Dunning, Phil, and Christopher Porter. *Bellamy Mill Cookbook*. Morrisburg, ON: St Lawrence Parks Commission, n.d.

Dwight, Timothy. *Travels in New England and New York*. 1821. Reprint, 4 vols. Cambridge, MA, 1969.

Ellis, Richard E., et al. 'A Symposium on Charles Sellers' *The Market Revolution: Jacksonian America, 1815–1846*.' *Journal of the Early Republic* 12 (1992): 445–76.

Eschelbach-Gregson, Mary. 'Long-Term Trends in Agricultural Specialization in the United States: Some Preliminary Results.' *Agricultural History* 70 (1996): 90–101.

– 'Rural Response to Increased Demand: Crop Choice in the Midwest, 1860–1880.' *Journal of Economic History* 53 (June 1993): 332–45.

– 'Specialization in Late-Nineteenth Century Midwestern Agriculture.' *Agricultural History* 67 (1993): 16–35.

Feller, Daniel. 'The Market Revolution Ate My Homework.' *Reviews in American History* 25 (1997): 408–15.

Filteau, Huguette and Jean Hamelin. 'Guillaume Eugène Chinic.' *Dictionary of Canadian Biography* 10: 189–91.

Fisher, Peter. *History of New Brunswick. As originally published in 1825, with a few explanatory notes by W.O. Raymond.* Saint John: New Brunswick Historical Society, 1921.

– *Notitia of New Brunswick for 1836 and Extending into 1837, Comprising Historical, Geographical, Statistical and Commercial Notices of the Province, by an Inhabitant.* Saint John: H. Chubb, 1838.

Frenette, Yves, Jules Bélanger, and Marc Desjardins. *Histoire de la Gaspésie.* Québec: IQRC, 1981.

Gaffield, Chad. 'Boom and Bust: The Demography and Economy of the Lower Ottawa Valley in the Nineteenth Century.' *Communications historiques / Historical Papers* (1982): 172–95.

– 'Children, Schooling, and Family Reproduction in Nineteenth-Century Ontario.' *Canadian Historical Review* 72 (1991): 157–91.

Gagan, David. *Hopeful Travellers, Families, Land and Social Change in Mid-Victorian Peel County, Canada West.* Toronto: University of Toronto Press, 1981.

– 'Land, Population and Social Change: The Critical Years in Canada West.' *Canadian Historical Review* 59 (1978): 299–306.

Ganong, William F. 'Additions and Corrections to Monographs in the Place Nomenclature, Cartography, Historic Sites, Boundaries, and Settlement: Origins of the Province of New Brunswick.' Royal Society of Canada, *Proceedings and Transactions*, 2nd. ser., 12 (1906): 146–7.

– 'Monograph of the Evolution of the Boundaries of the Province of New Brunswick.' Royal Society of Canada, *Proceedings and Transactions*, 2nd series, 7 (1901): 137–49.

– 'A Monograph of Historic Sites in the Province of New Brunswick.' Royal Society of Canada, *Proceedings and Transactions*, 2nd. ser., 5 (1899): 213–353.

– 'A Monograph of the Origins of Settlement in the Province of New Brunswick.' Royal Society of Canada, *Proceedings and Transactions*, 2nd. ser., 10 (1904): 3–186.

Garigue, Philippe. 'St Justin: Une réevaluation de l'organisation com-
munautaire.' In *Léon Gérin et l'habitant de St Justin*, ed. L.C. Falardeau et
Philippe Garigue, 131–46. Montreal: Presses de l'université de Montréal,
1968.

Garner, John. 'The Enfranchisement of Roman Catholics in the Maritime
Provinces.' *Canadian Historical Review* 34 (Sept. 1953): 208–9.

Gates, Paul W. *The Farmer's Age: Agriculture, 1815–1860*. New York: Holt,
Rinehart and Winston, 1960.

Gérin, Léon. 'L'habitant de St Justin: Contribution à la géographie sociale du
Canada.' In *Léon Gérin et l'habitant de St Justin*, ed. L.C. Falardeau and
Philippe Garigue, 49–130. Montreal: Presses de l'Université de Montréal,
1968.

Gerriets, Marilyn. 'Agricultural Resources, Agricultural Production and Settlement at Confederation.' *Acadiensis* 31 (Spring 2002): 129–56.

– 'Economics and History: Old Texts and New Approaches.' *Acadiensis* 29,
no. 1 (autumn 1999): 146–56.

Gervais, Diane. 'Succession et cycle familial dans le comté de Verchères,
1870–1950.' *Revue d'histoire de l'Amérique française* 50 (1996): 69–94.

Gesner, Abraham. *New Brunswick: with Notes for Emigrants: Comprehending the
Early History, an Account of the Indians, Settlement, Topography, Statistics,
Commerce, Timber, Manufactures, Agriculture, Fisheries, Geology, Natural
History, Social and Political State, Immigrants, and contemplated Railways of
that Province*. London: Simmonds & Ward, 1847.

Gilje, Paul, ed. 'Special Issue on Capitalism in the Early Republic.' *Journal of
the Early Republic* 16 (summer 1996): 159–308.

Girard, Camil, and Normand Perron. *Histoire du Saguenay–Lac-St.-Jean*.
Quebec: IQRC, 1989.

Grant, Charles. *Democracy in the Connecticut Frontier Town of Kent*. New York:
AMS Press, 1961.

Grave, Donald E. *The 1812 Journal of Lieut. John Le Couteur, 104th Foot: 'Merry
Hearts Make Light Days.'* Ottawa: Carleton University Press, 1993.

Green, Jack P., and J.R. Pole. *Colonial British America; Essays in the New
History of the Early Modern Era*. Baltimore: Johns Hopkins University Press,
1984.

Greer, Allan. *Peasant, Lord, and Merchant: Rural Society in Three Quebec
Parishes, 1740–1840*. Toronto: University of Toronto Press, 1985.

Greven, Philip. *Four Generations: Population, Land and Family in Colonial
Andover, Mass*. Ithaca, NY: Cornell University Press, 1972.

Griffiths, Naomi E.S. 'Petition of the Acadian Exiles, 1755–1785: A Neglected
Source.' *Histoire sociale/Social History* 11 (May 1978): 215–23.

Gruenwald, Kim. *River of Enterprise: The Commercial Origins of Regional Identity in the Ohio Valley, 1780–1850*. Bloomington: Indiana University Press, 2002.

Hallock, Charles. 'Aroostook and the Madawaska.' *Harper's Monthly Magazine* 27 (1866): 688–98.

Hannay, James. *History of New Brunswick*. Saint John: A.J. Bowes, 1909.

– ed. 'The Maugerville Settlement, 1763–1824.' New Brunswick Historical Society *Collections* 1 (1893–4): 63–88.

– ed. 'Sunbury County Documents.' New Brunswick Historical Society *Collections* 1 (1893–4): 89–152.

Hardy, Jean Pierre. 'Quelques aspects du niveau de richesse et de vie matérielle des artisans de Québec et de Montréal, 1740–1755.' *Revue d'histoire de l'Amérique française* 40 (winter 1987): 339–72.

– *La vie quotidienne dans la vallée du Saint Laurent, 1790–1835*. Montreal: Septentrion, 2001.

Hardy, René, and Norman Séguin. *Forêt et société en Mauricie, 1830–1930: La formation de la région de Trois Rivières*. Montreal: Boréal, 1984.

Harris, R. Cole. 'The Simplification of Europe Overseas.' *Annals of the Association of American Geographers* 67, no. 4 (1977): 469–83.

Head, George, esq. *Forest Scenes and Incidents in the Wilds of North America, being a diary of a winter's route from Halifax to the Canadas*. London, 1829.

Henretta, James. 'Families and Farms: *Mentalité* in Pre-Industrial America.' *William and Mary Quarterly* 3d ser., 35 (1978): 3–33.

– *The Origins of American Capitalism*. Boston: Northeastern University Press, 1991.

Hobbs-Pruitt, Bettye. 'Self-Sufficiency and the Agricultural Economy of Eighteenth-Century Massachusetts.' *William and Mary Quarterly* 3d ser., 41, (July 1984): 333–64.

Hoffman R., J.J. McKusker, R.R. Menard, and P.J. Albert, eds. *The Economy of Early America: The Revolutionary Period, 1763–1790*. Charlottesville: University Press of Virginia, 1988.

Hood, Adrienne. 'The Gender Division of Labour in the Production of Textiles in Eighteenth-Century Rural Pennsylvania (Rethinking the New England Model).' *Journal of Social History* 27 (spring 1994): 537–61.

– 'Industrial Opportunities: From Hand Weaving to Mill Production, 1700–1830.' In *Textile in Early New England: Design, Production and Consumption*, ed. Peter Benes, 135–51. Boston: Boston University Press, 1999.

– 'The Material World of Cloth Production and Use in Eighteenth Century Rural Pennsylvania.' *William and Mary Quarterly*, 3d ser., 53 (Jan. 1996): 43–66.

Hudon, Paul-Henri. 'Jean-Baptiste Bonenfant, marchand de Rivière Ouelle.' Société de généalogie de Québec, *L'ancêtre* 21, no. 9 (May 1995): 323–34.
- 'Jean-Baptiste Dupéré, marchand à Rivière-Ouelle.' Société de généalogie de Québec, *L'ancêtre* 22, no. 7 (Mar. 1996): 243–54.
- 'Jean-Baptiste Grandmaison (1716–93): Un ancêtre fort actif.' Société de généalogie de Québec, *L'ancêtre*, 25, nos. 1–2 (Oct.–Nov. 1998): 19–27.
- 'Les négociants de Kamouraska, le Madawaska et les anglophones.' Société de généalogie de Québec, *L'ancêtre*, 25 nos. 3–4 (Dec.–Jan. 1998–9): 77–92.
Ibister, John. 'Agriculture, Balanced Growth and Social Changes in Central Canada since 1850: an Interpretation.' *Economic Development and Cultural Changes* 25 (1976–1977), 673–97.
'Il y a cent ans.' *Le Brayon* 4 (Apr. 1976): 17.
Innis, Harold A. *Essays in Canadian Economic History.* Toronto: University of Toronto Press, 1956.
- *The Fur Trade in Canada: An Introduction to Canadian Economic History.* Toronto: University of Toronto Press, 1956.
- *Problems of Staple Production in Canada.* Toronto: University of Toronto Press, 1933.
Innis, Stephen. *Creating the Commonwealth: The Economic Culture of Puritan New England.* New York: Norton, 1995.
Inwood, Kris, and Janine Grant. 'Gender and Organization in the Canadian Cloth Industry, 1870.' *Canadian Papers in Business History* 1 (1989): 17–31.
Inwood, Kris, and Janine Roelens. 'Labouring at the Loom: A Case Study of Rural Manufacturing in Leeds County, Ontario, 1870.' *Canadian Papers in Rural History* 6 (1990): 215–35.
Inwood, Kris, and Jim Irwin. 'Land, Income and Regional Inequality: New Estimates of Provincial Income and Growth in Canada, 1871–1891.' *Acadiensis* 31, no. 2 (Spring 2002): 157–84.
Inwood, Kris, and Phillis Wagg. 'Domestic Cloth Production in Rural Canada circa 1870.' *Journal of Economic History* 53 (June 1993): 346–58.
- 'Wealth and Prosperity in Nova Scotia Agriculture, 1851–1871.' *Canadian Historical Review* 75 (June 1994): 239–64.
Jackson, Charles T. *First Report on the Geology of the Public Lands in the State of Maine.* Boston: Dutton and Wentworth, 1837.
Jedrey, Christopher. *The World of John Cleaveland: Family and Community in Eighteenth Century New England.* New York: Norton, 1979.
Jensen, Joan. *Loosening the Bonds: Mid-Atlantic Farm Women, 1750–1850.* New Haven, CT: Yale University Press, 1986.

Johnson, Laurence, and Charles A. Martijn. 'Les Malécites et la traite des fourrures.' *Recherches amérindiennes au Québec* 24, no. 3 (1994): 25–44.

Johnson, Paul E. 'The Market Revolution.' In *Encyclopedia of American Social History*, eds. Mary Kupiec Caylor, Elliott. J. Gorn, and Peter W. William. 1: 545. New York: Scribner, 1993.

Johnston, J.F. *Notes on North America: Agricultural, Economical and Social*. Edinburgh and London: W. Blackwood, 1851.

– *Report on the Agricultural Capabilities of the Province of New Brunswick*. Fredericton: J. Simpson, 1850.

Jones, Howard. *To the Webster Ashburton Treaty: A Study in Anglo-American Relations, 1783–1843*. Chapel Hill: University of North Carolina Press, 1977.

Jones, Leslie. *History of Agriculture in Ontario, 1613–1880*. Toronto: University of Toronto Press, 1946.

Jouhaud, Christian. 'Des besoins et des goûts: La consommation d'une famille de notables bordelais dans la première moitié du XVIIe siècle.' *Revue d'histoire moderne et contemporaine* 27 (Oct.–Dec. 1980): 631–46.

'Journal des visites pastorales de Mgr Plessis, évêque du Québec en Acadia, 1811, 1812, 1815.' Société historique Acadienne, *Cahiers* 11 (Mar.–Sept. 1980).

Judd, Richard. *Aroostook: A Century of Logging in Northern Maine*. Orono: University of Maine Press, 1989.

Kendall, Thomas Augustus. *Travels through the Northern Parts of the United States in the Years 1807 and 1808*. Vol. 3. New York: J. Riley, 1809.

Keyssar, Alexander. 'Widowhood in Eighteenth Century Mass.: A Problem in the History of the Family.' *Perspectives in American History* 8 (1974): 83–119.

Kulikoff, Allan. *The Agrarian Origins of American Capitalism*. Charlotteville: University Press of Virginia, 1992.

– 'The Transition to Capitalism in Rural America.' *William and Mary Quarterly*, 3d ser. 46 (Jan. 1989): 120–42.

Laberge, Alain, ed. *Histoire de la Côte du Sud*. Quebec: 1QRC, 1993.

Lamontagne, Sophie-Laurence, and Fernand Harvey. *La production textile domestique au Québec, 1827–1941: Une approche quantitative et régionale*. Ottawa: Musée des sciences et technologies, 1998.

Lamoreaux, Naomi R. 'Rethinking the Transition to Capitalism in the Early American Northeast.' *Journal of American History* (Sept. 2003): 437–61. http://www.historycooperative.org/journals/jah/90.2/lamoreaux.html (accessed 10 Mar. 2004).

Langellier, Kristin M. 'Tickling the Past: Straining to Catch the Sound of My Own Voice.' *Echoes: The Northern Maine Journal* 45 (July–Sept. 1999): 33–7.

Langlois, Mgr. Henri. *Dictionnaire généalogique du Madawaska. Répertoire des mariages du diocèse d'Edmunston, N.B. et du comté d'Aroostook, recherches et compilations par Henri Langlois.* 8 vols. St Basile, NB: privately published, 1971.

Langmaid, K.K., J.G. Losier, and J.K. McMillan. *Soils of Madawaska County, New Brunswick: New Brunswick Soil Survey Report No. 8.* Canada, Department of Agriculture, research branch, n.d.

Lapointe, Claire. 'Les marchands ruraux anglophones de la région de Montréal entre 1765 et 1840, Niveau de vie et activités commerciales.' Master's thesis, Université de Montréal, 1991.

Lavallée, Louis. 'La transmission du patrimoine dans la seigneurie de Laprairie, 1667–1760.' In *Évolution et éclatement du monde rural : structures, fonctionnement et évolution différentielle des sociétés rurales françaises et québécoises, XVIIe-XXe siècles.* Travaux publiés sous la direction de Joseph Goy et Jean-Pierre Wallot et rassemblés par Rolande Bonnain. 341–52. Paris: Éditions de l'École des hautes études en sciences sociales, 1986.

Le Goff, T.J.A. 'The Agricultural Crisis in Lower Canada, 1802–12: A Review of a Controversy.' *Canadian Historical Review* 55 (March 1974): 1–31; 'Response,' by G. Paquet and J.P. Wallot, and 'Reply,' by Le Goff, *Canadian Historical Review* 56 (June 1975): 134–72.

Lechasseur, Antonio *et al. Histoire du Bas St Laurent.* Quebec: IQRC, 1986.

Lemire, Beverly. 'Consumerism in Pre-Industrial and Early Industrial England: The Trade in Second Hand Clothes.' *Journal of British Studies* 27 (1988): 1–24.

– *Fashion's Favorite: The Cotton Trade and the Consumer In Britain 1660–1800.* New York: Oxford University Press, 1992.

Lemon, James. *The Best Poor Man's Country: A Geographical Study of Early Southeastern Pennsylvania.* Baltimore: Johns Hopkins University Press, 1972.

– 'Comments on James Henretta's 'Family and Farm.'' *William and Mary Quarterly* 3d ser., 37 (1980): 688–700.

Lewis, Frank D., and Marvin McInnis. 'Agricultural Output and Efficiency in Lower Canada, 1851.' *Research in Economic History* 9 (1984): 45–87.

Lewis, Frank D., and M.C. Urquhart. 'Growth and the Standard of Living in a Pioneer Economy: Upper Canada, 1826 to 1851.' *William and Mary Quarterly,* 3d ser., 56 (Jan. 1999): 151–81.

Lewis, Timothy D. 'Rooted in the Soil: Farm Family Persistence in Burton Parish, Sunbury County, New Brunswick, 1851–1901.' *Acadiensis* 31, no. 1 (autumn 2001): 35–54.

Lindstrom, Diane. *Economic Development in the Philadelphia Region, 1810–1850.* New York: Columbia University Press, 1978.

Little, J.I. *Crofters and Habitants: Settler Society, Economy, and Culture in a Quebec Township, 1848–1881.* Montreal and Kingston: McGill-Queen's University Press, 1991.

– *Nationalism, Capitalism and Colonization in Nineteenth-Century Québec: The Upper St Francis District*. Montreal and Kingston: McGill-Queen's University Press, 1989.

– 'Public Policy and Private Interest in the Lumber Industry of the Eastern Townships: The Case of C.S.Clark and Company, 1854–1881.' *Histoire sociale/Social History* 19, no. 37 (May 1986): 9–38.

Longley, R.S. 'The Coming of the New England Planters to the Annapolis Valley.' In *They Planted Well: New England Planters in Maritime Canada*, ed. Margaret Conrad, 14–29. Fredericton: Acadiensis Press, 1988.

Lowenthal, David. 'The Maine Press and the Aroostook War.' *Canadian Historical Review* 32 (Dec. 1951): 315–36.

Lower, A.R.M. *Great Britain Woodyard*. Montreal: McGill-Queen's University Press, 1936.

– *Settlement and the Forest Frontier in Eastern Canada*. Toronto: University of Toronto Press, 1936.

Lugrin, Charles. *Facts Concerning the Fertile Belt of the New Brunswick Land and Lumber Company (Limited) New Brunswick (Canada)*. Saint John: J. & A. McMillan, 1884.

MacBeath, George B. 'New England Settlements in Pre-loyalist New Brunswick.' New Brunswick Historical Society *Collections* 18 (1962), 27–33.

MacKinnon, Robert. 'Roads, Cart Tracks, and Bridle Paths: Land Transportation and the Domestic Economy of Mid-Nineteenth Century Eastern British North America.' *Canadian Historical Review* 84 (June 2003): 177–216.

MacKinnon, Robert and Graeme Wynn. 'Nova Scotian Agriculture in the Golden Age: A New Look.' In *Geographical Perspectives on the Maritime Provinces*, ed. Douglas Day, 47–59. Halifax: Saint Mary's University, 1988.

Mackintosh, W.A. 'Economic Factors in Canadian History.' *Canadian Historical Review* 4 (March 1923): 12–25.

MacNutt, W.S. *New Brunswick: A History, 1784–1867*. Toronto: University of Toronto Press, 1963.

– 'Thomas Baillie.' *Dictionary of Canadian Biography* 9: 21–9.

Main, Gloria. 'The Red Queen in New England.' *William and Mary Quarterly* 3d ser. 56 (Jan. 1999): 121–50.

Maisonneuve, Daniel. 'Solidarité familiale et exode rural: Le cas de Saint Damase, 1852–1861.' *Cahier Québécois de démographie* 14 (Oct. 1985): 231–40.

Mancke, Elizabeth. 'At the Counter of the General Store: Women and the Economy in Eighteenth Century Nova Scotia.' In *Intimate Relations: Family and Community in Planter Nova Scotia, 1759–1800*, ed. Margaret Conrad, 167–81. Fredericton: Acadiensis Press, 1995.

Mann, John. *Travels in North America, particularly in the Provinces of Upper and Lower Canada and New Brunswick and in the States of Maine, Massachusetts and New York.* Glasgow, 1824. Reprinted, Fredericton, NB: Saint Anne Point Press, 1978.

Marie-Victorin, Frère. 'Le portage du Témiscouata: Notes critiques pour servir à l'histoire d'une vieille route coloniale.' Société Royale du Canada, *Proceedings and Transactions,* sec. 1 (1918): 55–93.

Martin, John F. *Profits in the Wilderness: Entrepreneurship and the Founding of New England Towns in the Seventeenth Century.* Chapel Hill: University of North Carolina Press, 1991.

Martin, Margaret E. 'Merchants and Trade of the Connecticut River Valley, 1750–1820.' *Smith College Studies in History* 24 (1938–9).

Martin, Paul Louis. 'Review of Janet Cook, *Coalescence of Style: An Ethnic Heritage of the St John River Valley.*' *Revue d'histoire de l'Amérique française* 55 (spring 2002): 609.

Massé, Jean-Claude. 'La guerre des fourrures au Madawaska-Témiscouata.' Société de généalogie de Québec, *L'ancêtre* 26, 3–4 (Nov.–De. 1999): 89–97.

Matson, Cathy. *Merchants and Empire: Trading in Colonial New York.* Baltimore and London: Johns Hopkins University Press, 1998.

May, Herbert. 'A Place to Stand: Families, Land and Permanence in Toronto Gore Township, 1820–1890.' *Canadian Historical Association, Historical Papers* (1980): 185–211.

McCalla, Douglas. 'Consumption Stories: Some Evidence on Consumer Buying in Rural Upper Canada.' Paper presented to the Canadian Economic History conference, Kananaskis, Alberta, 1999.

– 'The Internal Economy of Upper Canada: New Evidence on Agricultural Marketing before 1850.' *Agricultural History* 59 (1985): 397–416.

– 'The Needs of Farm Households: Farm Family and Purchases from Two Upper Canadian Stores in 1861.' *Espace et culture / Space and Culture,* ed. Serge Courville and Normand Séguin. Quebec: Presses de l'Université Laval, 1995.

– 'The Ontario Economy in the Long Run.' *Ontario History* 90 (1998): 97–115.

– *Planting the Province: The Economic History of Upper Canada.* Toronto: University of Toronto Press, 1993.

– 'Retailing in the Countryside: Upper Canadian General Stores in the Mid-Nineteenth Century.' *Business and economic history* 26 (winter 1997): 393–403.

– 'Rural Credit and Rural Development in Upper Canada, 1790–1850.' In *Merchant Credit and Labour Strategies in Historical Perspective,* ed. Rosemary Ommer, 265–72. Fredericton: Acadiensis press, 1990.

– 'Textile Purchases by Some Ordinary Upper Canadians, 1808–1861.' Paper presented at Canadian Historical Association annual meeting, Edmonton, 2000.

McCallum, John. *Unequal Beginnings: Agriculture and Economic Development in Quebec and Ontario until 1870*. Toronto: University of Toronto Press, 1980.

McCullough, A.B. *Money and Exchange in Canada to 1900*. Toronto: Dundurn Press, 1984.

McCusker, John. 'Measuring Colonial Gross Domestic Product: An Introduction.' *William and Mary Quarterly* 3d ser., 56 (Jan. 1999): 3–9.

McCusker, John J., and Russell R. Menard. *The Economy of British America, 1607–1789*. Chapel Hill: University of North Carolina, 1985.

Mcgrath, Anna Fields, ed. *The County: Land of Promise: A Pictorial History of Aroostook County, Maine*. Norfolk, VA: Donning Company, 1989.

McGregor, John, esq. *British America*. Vol. 2. Edinburgh: William Blackwood; London: T. Cadell, 1832. .

– *Historical and Descriptive Sketches of the Maritimes Colonies of British America*. London: Longman, 1828.

McInnis, Marvin. 'Marketable Surpluses in Ontario Farming, 1860.' *Social Science History* 8 (1984): 395–424.

– 'Ontario Agriculture at Mid-Century.' In *Perspectives on Canadian Economic History*, ed. Douglas McCalla, 49–83. Toronto: Copp Clark Pitman, 1987.

– 'Perspectives on Ontario Agriculture, 1815–1930.' *Canadian Papers in Rural History* 8 (1992): 17–128.

– 'A Reconsideration of the State of Agriculture in Lower Canada in the First Half of the Nineteenth Century.' *Papers in Canadian Rural History* 3 (1982): 9–49.

McKendrick, Neil, John Brewer, and J.H. Plumb, eds. *The Birth of a Consumer Society: The Commercialization of Eighteenth Century England*. Bloomington: Indiana University Press, 1982.

McKinney, Gage. 'A.B. Hammond, West Coast Lumberman.' *Journal of Forest history* 28 (1984): 196–203.

McMillan's New Brunswick Almanac and Register for the Year of our Lord [...]. St John: J. & A. McMillan, 1866–9. CIHM 29831–29660.

McMurry, Sally 'American Rural Women and the Transformation of Dairy Processing, 1820–1880.' *Rural History* 5 (1994): 143–53.

– *Transforming Rural Life: Dairying Families and Agricultural Changes, 1820–1885*. Baltimore: Johns Hopkins University Press, 1996.

McNabb, Debra A. 'Land and Settlement in Horton Township, N.S. 1760–1830.' MA thesis. University of British Columbia, 1986.

McNeil, Alan. 'Early American Communities on the Fundy: A Case Study of Annapolis and Amherst Townships, 1767–1824.' *Agricultural History* 62 (1989): 101–19.

– 'Society and Economy in Rural Nova Scotia, 1761–1861.' PhD thesis, Queen's University, 1990.

'Memoirs of Alice Michaud Cyr, written ten years ago at the age of 91.' *Cyr Plantation Centennial, 1870–1970*. n.p., 1970.

The Merchants' and Farmers' Almanac for the Year of our Lord [...]. Saint John: S.L. Avery, 1840–46 and 1850–63. *CIHM* 36842–43, 36873, 42087, 36874–76, 36659–68.

Merril, Michael. 'Cash Is Good to Eat: Self-sufficiency and Exchange in the Rural Economy of the United States.' *Radical History Review* 3 (winter 1977): 42–71.

– 'Putting Capitalism in Its Place.' *William and Mary Quarterly* 3d ser. 52 (April 1995): 315–26.

Michaud, Guy R. *Brève histoire du Madawaska: Débuts à 1900*. Edmundston, NB: les éditions GRM, 1984.

Michel, Louis. 'Endettement et société rurale dans la région de Montréal au dix-huitième siècle.' In *Sociétés villageoises et rapports villes-campagnes au Québec et dans la France de l'ouest, XVII-XXe siècles*, ed. F. Lebrun and N. Séguin, 171–82. Trois Rivières: Université du Québec à Trois Rivières and Presses Universitaires de Rennes 2, 1987.

– 'Un marchand rural en Nouvelle France: François-Augustin Bailly de Messein, 1709–1771.' *Revue d'histoire de l'Amérique française* 33 (1979): 215–62.

– 'Varennes et Verchère, des origines au milieu du XIXe siècle: État d'une enquête.' In *Évolution et éclatement du monde rural: Structures, fonctionnement et évolution différentielle des sociétés rurales françaises et québécoises, XVIIe-XXe siècles*. Travaux publiés sous la direction de Joseph Goy et Jean-Pierre Wallot et rassemblés par Rolande Bonnain. 325–40. Paris: Éditions de l'école des hautes études en sciences sociales, 1986.

Miquelon, Dale. 'Louis Fornel (Fournel).' *Dictionary of Canadian Biography* 4: 44–5.

– 'Marie Anne Barbel.' *Dictionary of Canadian Biography* 3: 224–5.

Mitchell, Bailey. 'Reminiscence of Early Days.' *Gleanings: The Journal of the Caribou Historical Society* 2 (1982).

Moody, Barry. 'Growing up in Granville Township.' In *Intimate Relations: Family and Community in Planter Nova Scotia*, ed. Margaret Conrad, 78–97. Fredericton: Acadiensis Press, 1996.

– 'Land, Kinship and Inheritance in Granville Township, 1760–1800.' In *Making Adjustments: Changes and Continuity in Planter Nova Scotia, 1759–1800*, ed. Margaret Conrad, 165–79. Fredericton: Acadiensis Press, 1991.

Moogk, Peter N. 'John Young.' *Dictionary of Canadian Biography* 5: 877–83.

Moore, W.D. 'Sunbury County 1760–1830.' MA thesis, University of New Brunswick, 1977.

Morrisseau, Henri. 'La famille Cherrier de Saint-Denis sur Richelieu: Un salon aristocratique à la fin du dix huitième siècle. ' *Revue de l'université d'Ottawa* 16 (1946): 301–38.

Morrison, F.B. *Feeds and Feeding: A Handbook for the Student and Stockman.* 1898 20th ed. Ithaca, NY: Morrison Publishing, 1936.

Murton, James. 'La Normandie du Nouveau Monde: La société Canada Steamship Lines, l'antimodernisme et la promotion du Québec ancien.' *Revue d'histoire de l'Amérique française* 55 (summer 2001): 3–44.

Mutch, Robert. 'Yeoman and Merchant in Pre-industrial America: Eighteenth-Century Massachusetts as a Case Study.' *Societas* 7 (autumn 1977): 279–302.

Nenadic, Stana. 'Middle Rank Consumers and Domestic Culture in England and Scotland, 1720–1840.' *Past and Present* 145 (Nov. 1994): 122–56.

Neufeld, E.P. *Money and Banking in Canada.* Toronto: McClelland and Stewart, 1964.

The New Brunswick Almanac and Register for the Year of our Lord [...]. St. John: H. Chubb, 1831–54. CIHM 38415–23, 32341, 39607–09, 38425, 3839610, 52910, 38427–34.

The New Brunswick Almanac and Register for the Year of our Lord [...]. St. John: J & A McMillan, 1864–5. CIHM 38435–6.

[New Brunswick and Nova Scotia Land Company.] *Practical Information Respecting New Brunswick , Including Details Relatives to Its Soil, Climate, Production and Agriculture.* London: P. Richardson, 1843.

Newell, Margaret Ellen. *From Dependency to Independence: Economic Revolution in Colonial New England.* Ithaca, NY: Cornell University Press, 1998.

Nobles, Gregory. 'The Rise of the Merchants in Rural Market Towns: A Case Study of Eighteenth Century Northampton, Mass.' *Journal of Social History* 43 (1990): 5–23.

Noël, Françoise. *The Christie Seigneuries: Estate Management and Settlement in the Upper Richelieu Valley, 1760–1854.* Montreal and Kingston: McGill-Queen's University Press, 1992.

North, Douglas Cecil. *The Economic Growth of the United States, 1790–1860.* Englewood Cliffs, NJ: Prentice Hall, 1961.
- 'Location Theory and Economic Growth.' *Journal of Political Economy* 62 (June 1955): 243–58.
Ommer, Rosemary E. *From Outpost to Outport: A Structural Analysis of the Jersey-Gaspé Cod Fishery, 1767–1886.* Montreal and Kingston: McGill-Queen's University Press, 1992.
- ed. *Merchant Credit and Labour Strategies in Historical Perspective.* Fredericton: Acadiensis Press, 1990.
- 'The Truck System in Gaspé, 1822–77.' *Acadiensis* 19, no. 1 (1989): 91–114.
Osterud, Nancy Grey. *Bonds of Community: The Lives of Farm Women in Nineteenth Century New York.* Ithaca, NY: Cornell University Press, 1991.
Ouellet, Fernand. *Histoire économique et sociale du Québec, 1760–1850: Structures et conjonctures.* Montreal: Fidès, 1966.
- 'Le mythe de l'habitant sensible au marché.' *Recherches sociographiques* 17 (1976): 115–32.
Paquet, Gilles, and Jean Pierre Wallot. 'Crise agricole et tensions socio-ethniques dans le Bas Canada, 1802–1821.' *Revue d'histoire de l'Amérique française* 26 (Sept. 1972): 185–237.
Paradis, Roger. 'John Baker and the Republic of Madawaska: An Episode in the Northeastern Controversy.' *Dalhousie Review* 52 (1972): 78–95.
- 'Louis Mercure, Fondateur du Madawaska. ' Société historique acadienne, *Cahiers* 28 (1989): 49–56.
Perkins, Edwin J. *The Economy of Colonial America.* New York: Columbia University Press, 1980.
Perley, Moses Henry. *A Handbook of Information for Emigrants to New Brunswick.* Saint John: H.Chubb, 1854.
Piper, Liza. 'Backward Seasons and Remarkably Cold: The Weather over Long Reach, New Brunswick, 1812–1821.' *Acadiensis* 34, no. 1 (autumn 2004): 31–55.
Plamondon, Lilianne. 'Une femme d'affaire en Nouvelle France: Marie Anne Barbel.' *Revue d'histoire de l'Amérique française* (1977): 165–85.
Plessis, Mrg. 'Le journal des visites pastorales de Mgr Joseph Octave Plessis, Evêque de Québec en Acadie 1811–1812–1813. ' Société historique acadiennes, *Cahiers,* 1–3 (Mar.–Sept. 1980) : 124–9.
Poulin, Pierre. 'François Xavier Méthot.' *Dictionary of Canadian Biography* 8: 628–30.
Price, Jacob. M. 'The Transatlantic Economy.' In *Colonial British America: Essays in the New History of the Early Modern Era,* ed. Jack P. Greene and J.R. Pole. Baltimore: Johns Hopkins University Press, 1984.

Pronovost, Claude. *La bourgeoisie marchande en milieu rural (1720–1840)*.
   Québec: Presses de l'Université Laval, 1998.
Public Archives of Canada. *Report on Canadian Archives: Being an Appendix to
   Report of the Minister of Agriculture*. Ottawa: Edmond Cloutier, 1895.
Pullen, Clarence. *In Fair Aroostook: Where Acadia and Scandinavia's Subtle Touch
   Turned a Wilderness into a Land of Plenty*. Bangor, ME: Bangor and Aroost-
   ook Railway Company, 1902.
Raymond, W.O. 'Earliest Route of Travel between Canada and Acadia.
   Olden-time Celebrities Who Used It. ' Royal Society of Canada *Proceedings
   and Transactions* 2 (1921): 33–46.
– 'The First Governor of New Brunswick and the Acadians of the River of St
   John.' Royal Society of Canada, *Transactions*, ser. 3, vol. 8 (1914): 415–52.
– 'Introduction' to 'State of the Madawaska and Aroostook settlement in
   1831. Report of John G. Deane and Edward Kavanagh to Samuel E. Smith,
   Governor of the State of Maine, and other documents,' New Brunswick
   Historical Society *Collections* 3 (1907): 344–86.
– ed. 'James White Papers.' New Brunswick Historical Society *Collections*
   (1894–8).
– ed. 'The James White Papers, Continued, A.D. 1781–88,' New Brunswick
   Historical Society *Collections* 2 (1899–1905): 30–72.
– ed. 'Letters Written at Saint John by James Simonds, A.D. 1764–1785.' New
   Brunswick Historical Society *Collections* 1 (1894–7): 160–86.
– ed. 'Papers Relating to Townships on the St John.' New Brunswick Historical Society *Collections* 2 (1904–5): 287–357.
– *The River St John*. 1910, reprint, Sackville, NB, 1943.
– ed. 'Selections from the Papers and Correspondence of James White, esq.,
   A.D. 1762–1783.' New Brunswick Historical Society *Collections* 1 (1894–7):
   306–40.
– ed., *Winslow papers, AD 1776–1826*. Boston: Gregg Press, 1972.
Robb, James. *Agricultural Progress: An Outline of the Course of Improvement in
   Agriculture, considered as a Business, an Art and a Science, with Special Refer-
   ence to New Brunswick*. Fredericton: J. Simpson, 1856.
Roche, Daniel. *Histoire des choses banales: Naissance de la consommation XVIIe-
   XIXe siècle*. Paris: Fayard, 1997.
Rothenberg, Winnifred. *From Market Place to a Market Economy: The Transfor-
   mation of Rural Massachusetts, 1750–1850*. Chicago: University of Chicago
   Press, 1992.
– 'The Market and the Massachusetts Farmers, 1750–1855.' *Journal of Eco-
   nomic History* 41 (June 1981): 283–314.
Ruddel, David-Thiery. 'Clothing, Society, and Consumer Trends in the Mon-

tréal Area, 1792–1835.' In *New England–New France*, ed. Peter Benes, 122–34. Boston: Boston University Press, 1992.

– 'Consumer Trends, Clothing, Textile and Equipment in the Montreal Area 1792–1835.' *Material History Bulletin/Bulletin d'histoire de la culture matérielle* 32 (fall 1990): 45–64.

– 'Domestic Textile Production in Colonial Quebec, 1608–1840.' *Material History Bulletin / Bulletin d'histoire de la culture matérielle* 31 (1990): 39–49.

– 'The Domestic Textile Industry in the Region of and City of Quebec, 1792–1835.' *Material History Bulletin / Bulletin d'histoire de la culture matérielle* 17 (1983): 95–126.

Russel, Howard S. *A Long Deep Furrow: Three Centuries of Changes in New England.* Hanover, NH: University Press of New England, 1976.

Rutman, Darett B. 'Assessing the Little Communities of Early America.' *William and Mary Quarterly*, 3d ser., 43 (April 1986): 163–78.

– 'Community Study.' *Historical Methods* 13, no. 1 (winter 1980): 29–41.

– 'People in Process. The New Hampshire Towns of the Eighteenth Century.' *Journal of Urban History* 1, no. 3 (May 1975): 268–92.

Rygiel, Judith. 'The Homespun Economy: Persistence of Handweaving in New Brunswick in the Nineteenth Century.' PhD diss., Carleton University, 2004.

Sandwell, Ruth W. 'Rural Reconstruction; Towards a New Synthesis in Canadian History.' *Histoire sociale/Social History*, 27, no. 53 (May 1994): 1–32.

Santerre, Renaud. 'Donations de fermes et sécurité des agriculteurs âgés, 1850–1990.' In *Famille, économie et société rurales en contexte d'urbanisation, XVIIe-XXe siècles*, ed. Gérard Bouchard et Joseph Goy, 35–48. Paris: EHESS, 1990.

Schama, Simon. *The Embarassment of Riches: An Interpretation of Dutch Culture in the Golden Age.* New York: Knopf, 1987.

Schurman, Anton J., and Lorena S. Walsh. *Material Culture: Consumption, Life Style, Standard of Living, 1500–1900.* Proceedings of the 11th International Economic History Congress, Milan, September 1994.

Séguin, Norman. *La conquête du sol au 19e.* Quebec: Boréal Express, 1977.

– 'L'économie agro-forestière: Genèse du développement au Saguenay au 19e siècle.' In *Agriculture et colonisation au Québec*, ed. N. Séguin. Montreal: Boréal, 1980.

Sellers, Charles. *The Market Revolution: Jacksonian America, 1815–1846.* New York: Oxford University Press, 1991.

Shammas, Carol. 'Consumer Behaviour in Colonial America.' *Social Science History* 6 (1982): 67–86.

- 'The Domestic Environment in Early Modern England and America.' *Journal of Social History* 14 (1980): 1–24.
- 'How Self-sufficient Was Early America?' *Journal of Interdisciplinary History* 13 (autumn 1982): 247–72.
- *The Pre-industrial Consumer in England and America*. Oxford: Oxford University Press, 1990.

Shannon, Fred. *The Farmer's Last Frontier, Agriculture, 1860–1897*. New York: Holt, Rinehart and Winston, 1966.

Sheridan, Richard B. 'The Domestic Economy.' In *Colonial British America; Essays in the New History of the Early Modern Era*, ed. Jack P. Greene and J.R. Pole, 43–85. Baltimore: Johns Hopkins University Press, 1984.

Simard, Cyril. 'Le lin au Madawaska au 19e siècle: Les "Brayons" n'étaient pas les seuls à filer ce 'mauvais coton."' *Revue de la Societé historique du Madawaska* 15 (Oct.–Dec. 1987): 9–24.

Smith, David C. *A History of Lumbering in Maine, 1861–1960*. Orono: University of Maine Press, 1972.

- 'Maine and Its Public Domaine: Land Disposal in the Northeastern Frontier.' In *The Frontier in American Economic Development: Essays in Honour of Paul Wallace Gates*, ed. David M. Ellis, 113–40. Ithaca, NY: Cornell University Press, 1969.

Snell, James G. 'Maintenance Agreements for the Elderly: Canada, 1900–1951.' *Journal of the Canadian Historical Association* 3 (1992): 197–216.

Snydacker, Daniel. 'Kinship and Community in Rural Pennsylvania, 1749–1820.' *Journal of Interdisciplinary History* 8 (summer 1982): 41–61.

Spay, W.A. 'William Davidson (John Godsman).' *Dictionary of Canadian Biography* 4: 197–9.

Sprague, J.F. 'Documentary History of the North Eastern Boundary Controversy.' *Collection of the Piscataquis County Historical Society*. Vol. 1. Dover, ME: Observer Press, 1910.

Steinfeld, Robert J. *Coercion, Contract and Free Labor in the Nineteenth Century*. Cambridge: Cambridge University Press, 2002.

- *The Invention of Free Labor: The Employment Relation in English and American Law and Culture, 1350–1870*. Chapel Hill: University of North Carolina, 1991.

St. George, Lisa. 'Commerce, crédit et transactions foncières: Pratiques de la communauté marchande du bourg de l'Assomption, 1748–1791.' *Revue d'histoire de l'Amérique française* 39 (1986): 323–43.

Stephenson, Isaac. *Recollection of a Long Life*. Privately published. Chicago, 1915.

Stiles, Deborah. 'The Gender and Class Dimension of a Rural Childhood: Martin Butler in New Brunswick, 1857–1871.' *Acadiensis* 33, no. 1 (fall 2003): 73–86.

Stokes, Melvyn, and Stephen Conway, eds. *The Market Revolution in America: Social, Political and Religious Expressions, 1800–1880.* Charlottesville: University Press of Virginia, 1996.

Sweeney, Kevin, M. 'Gentlemen Farmers and Inland Merchants: The Williams Family and Commercial Agriculture in Pre-revolutionary Western Massachusetts.' In *The Farm*, ed. Peter Benes, 60–73. Boston: Boston University Press, 1988.

Sylvester, Ken, M. ' "En part égale": Family, Inheritance, and Market Change in a Francophone Community on the Prairies, 1880–1940.' *Journal of the Canadian Historical Association* 9 (1998): 39–62.

Tanguay, Mgr. *Dictionnaire Généalogique des familles canadiennes.* 7 vols. Montreal : Eusèbe Sénécal, 1871–90.

Taylor, Alan. *Liberty Men and Great Proprietors: The Revolutionary Settlement on the Maine Frontier, 1760–1820.* Chapel Hill: University of North Carolina, 1990.

– ' "A Struggle of Finesse": Creditors and Debtors on the North Eastern Frontier, 1780–1820.' In *Merchant Credit and Labour Strategies in Historical Perspectives*, ed. Rosemary Ommer, 290–302. Fredericton: Acadiensis Press, 1990.

– *William Cooper's Town: Power and Persuasion on the Frontier of the Early American Republic.* New York: Knopf, 1995.

Thirsk, Joan. 'Popular Consumption and the Mass Market in Sixteenth to Eighteenth Centuries.' *Material History Bulletin* 31 (1990): 51–8.

– *Economic Policy and Projects: The Development of a Consumer Society in Early Modern England.* Oxford: Oxford University Press, 1978.

Tiesten, Lisa. 'Redefining Consumer Culture: Recent Literature on Consumption and the Bourgeoisie in Western Europe.' *Radical History Review* 57 (1993): 116–59.

Tremblay, Yves-Jean. 'Francois Pierre Cherrier.' *Dictionary of Canadian Biography* 5: 147–9.

Troughton, Michael J. 'From Nodes to Nodes: The Rise and Fall of Agricultural Activity in the Maritime Provinces.' In *Geographical Perspectives on the Maritime Provinces*, ed. Douglas Day, 25–46. Halifax: Saint Mary's University, 1988.

Turner, Philip B. *Rooster: The Story of Aroostook County.* Bar Harbor, ME: Acadia Publishing, 1988.

U.S. Department of Agriculture. 'Soil Conservation Service in Cooperation with the University of Maine Agricultural Extension Station.' *Soil Survey, Aroostook County, Maine, North-eastern Part* (1964).
− 'Soil Conservation Service in Cooperation with the University of Maine Agricultural Experiment Station.' *Soil Survey, Aroostook County, Maine, North-eastern Part* 25, no. 3 (1958).
− 'Soil Conservation Service in Cooperation with the University of Maine Agricultural Extension Station.' *Soil Survey, Aroostook County, Maine, North-eastern part* 27 (1959).
Ulrich, Laurel Thatcher. 'Wheels, Looms, and the Gender Division of Labor in Eighteenth-Century New England.' *William and Mary Quarterly* 3d ser. 54 (Jan. 1998): 3–36.
Vickers, Daniel. 'Competency and Competition: Economic Culture in Early America,' *William and Mary Quarterly* 3d ser. 47 (1990): 3–29.
Waciega, Lisa Wilson. 'A "Man of Business": The Widow of Means in Southeastern Pennsylvania, 1750–1850.' *William and Mary Quarterly* 3d ser. 44 (1987): 39–60.
Wagg, Phyllis. 'The Bias of Probate: Using Deeds to Transfer Estates in Nineteenth-Century Nova Scotia.' *Nova Scotia Historical Review* 10, no. 1 (1990): 74–87.
Wainwright, Kennedy. 'A Comparative Study in Nova Scotian Rural Economy, 1788–1872, Based on Recently Discovered Books of Account of Old Firms in Kings County.' *Collections of the Nova Scotia Historical Society* 30 (1954): 78–119.
Wallace-Casey, Cynthia. 'Providential Openings: The Women Weavers of Nineteenth Century Queens County, New Brusnwick.' *Material History Review* 46 (fall 1997): 29–44.
Wallot, J.P., et al. 'Civilisation matérielle au Bas Canada.' *Bulletin d'Histoire de la culture matérielle* 17 (1983).
Walton, Whitney. 'To Triumph before Feminine Tastes: Bourgeois Women's Consumption and Hand Methods of Production in Mid-Nineteenth Century Paris.' *Business History Review* 60 (1986): 541–63.
Ward, Edmund. *An Account of the St John and Its Tributary Rivers and Lakes.* Fredericton: Sentinel Office, 1841.
Waters, John J. 'Family, Inheritance and Migration in Colonial New England: The Evidence from Guildford, Connecticut.' *William and Mary Quarterly*, 3d ser. 49 (Jan. 1982): 64–86.
− 'Patrimony, Succession and Social Stability: Guilford, Connecticut in the Eighteenth Century.' *Perspectives in American History* 10 (1976): 131–60.
− 'The Traditional World of the New England Peasants: A View from Seven-

teenth Century Barnstable.' *New England Historical and Genealogical Register* 30 (Jan. 1976): 3–21.

Weatherill, Lorna. *Consumer Behaviour and Material Culture in Britain, 1660–1760*. London: Routledge, 1988.

– 'Consumer Behaviour and Social Status in England, 1660–1750.' *Continuity and Change* 1 (1986): 191–216.

– 'A Possession of One's Own: Women and Consumer Behaviour in England, 1660–1749.' *Journal of British Studies* 25 (1986): 131–56.

Weiss, Thomas. 'Long Term Changes in U.S. Agricultural Output per Worker, 1800–1900.' *Economic History Review* (1993): 324–41.

Wermuth, Thomas. 'New York Farmers and the Market Revolution: Economic Behaviour in the Mid-Hudson Valley.' *Journal of Social History* 32 (1998): 179–96.

Wermuth, Thomas. *Rip Van Winkle's Neighbors: The Transformation of Rural Society in the Hudson River Valley, 1720–1850*. Albany: SUNY Press, 2001.

Whalen, Hugh. *The Development of Local Government in New Brunswick*. Fredericton: Department of Municipal Affairs, 1964.

White, Stella King. *Early History of Caribou Maine, 1843–1895*. (n.p., 1943).

Wiggin, Edward. *History of Aroostook*. Presque Isle, ME: Star Herald Press, 1922.

Willis, John. 'Fraserville and Its Temiscouata Hinterland, 1874–1914, Colonization and Urbanization in a Peripheral Region of the Province of Québec.' MA thesis, Université du Québec à Trois Rivières, 1981.

Wilmot, Thomas Ashby. *Complete History of Aroostook County, and Its Early and Late Settlers*. (n.p., 1978). Originally published as a series of articles in the *Mars Hill View*, Blaine, ME, 23 Dec. 1909 to 12 Jan. 1911.

Wilson, Catharine. 'Tenure as a Family Strategy over the Life Cycle.' Paper presented at the Canadian Conference on Economic History, Niagara-on-the-Lake, May 1997.

Wilson, Lisa. *Life after Death: Widows in Pennsylvania, 1750–1850*. Philadelphia: Temple University Press, 1992.

Wolf, Stephanie Grauman. *Urban Village: Population, Community and Family Structure in Germantown, Pennsylvania, 1683–1800*. Princeton, NJ: Princeton University Press, 1976.

Wood, Richard. *A History of Lumbering in Maine, 1820–1861*. 1935. Orono: University of Maine Press, 1961.

Wright, Esther Clark. 'Cumberland Township: a Focal Point of Early Settlement on the Bay of Fundy.' In *They Planted Well: New England Planters in Maritime Canada*, ed. Margaret Conrad, 36–41. Fredericton: Acadiensis Press, 1988.

- *The Loyalists of New Brunswick*. Fredericton: n.p., 1955.
Wynn, Graeme. 'James F.W. Johnston.' *Dictionary of Canadian Biography* 8: 435–6.
- 'New Brunswick Parish Boundaries in the Pre-1861 Census years.' *Acadiensis* 6 (spring 1977): 95–105.
- *Timber Colony: A Historical Geography of Early Nineteenth Century New Brunswick*. Toronto: University of Toronto Press, 1981.
Young, D. Murray. 'Beamsley Perkins Glasier, Glasior, Glazier. *Dictionary of Canadian Biography* 4: 299–301.
- 'Peter Fraser.' *Dictionary of Canadian Biography* 6: 330–2.
- 'Planter Settlements in the St John Valley.' In *They Planted Well: New England Planters in Maritime Canada*, ed. Margaret Conrad, 29–35. Fredericton: Acadiensis Press, 1988.
Zoltvany, Yves F. 'Aubert de la Chesnay.' *Dictionary of Canadian Biography* 2: 26–34.

Index

www.ingramcontent.com/pod-product-compliance
Lightning Source LLC
Chambersburg PA
CBHW022133020426
42334CB00015B/873